TABLE OF CONTENTS

Summary i

Introduction ix

Acknowledgements xiii

Chapter ONE   TODAY'S FORGOTTEN HALF: 1
STILL LOSING GROUND
Samuel Halperin

The Forgotten Half in 1988 • Who Are the Forgotten Half Today? The Changing Profile of America's Youth and Young Adults • The Coming Youth Population Boom • A More Painful Transition to the Labor Market • Jobs for Out-of-School Youth • Labor Market Problems of Out-of-School Youth • Earnings: The Dismal Decline Continues — "It's *(Still)* the Economy, Stupid!" • How Young Families Managed — or Didn't • The Household Living Arrangements of Young Americans — or "Why Don't They Ever Leave Home?" • Out-of-Wedlock Births: New Norm for Teens? • Home Ownership: The Young Family's American Dream • Health Insurance • Young Americans Behind Bars • Is There Still A Safety Net? If So, Does It Work? • The Rising Tide of College Enrollment

Chapter TWO   PUBLIC OPINION 27
AND THE YOUTH OF AMERICA
Daniel Yankelovich

Overview • Looking at the Survey Data • The Role of Government • Moral Values • Attitudes Toward Youth • Toward a New Youth Strategy • The Community College Component • From Entitlement to Reciprocity: The Micro-Lending Concept • Wooing Public Support

Chapter THREE   THE CHANGING 41
AMERICAN FAMILY
Carol Emig

Backdrop to Change • American Children: A Changing Population • Family Life: Still Harried After All These Years • Evolving Family Structure: Daddy Doesn't Live Here Anymore • Family Income: The Advantages of Two Parents • Children's Health and Safety • Dilemmas of Education • Risk-Taking by Adolescents: What's the Matter With Kids Today? • Recent Major Policy Changes • What's Ahead for Families and Children?

Chapter FOUR   COMMUNITIES: POWERFUL 59
RESOURCES FOR AMERICA'S YOUTH
Martin Blank and Carol Steinbach

A New Breed of Youth-Focused Initiatives • The Policy and Political Environment • Youth and Communities in the 1990s: Six Driving Trends • Sampling Youth and Community Initiatives • Do Youth and Community Initiatives Improve Outcomes for Children, Youth and Young Families? • Recommendations

Chapter FIVE   YOUTH AND SCHOOL REFORM: 83
FROM THE FORGOTTEN HALF
TO THE FORGOTTEN THIRD
Jack Jennings and Diane Stark Rentner

Comprehensive Reforms • School-Based Reforms • Other Approaches to Reform • How Reform is Affecting Students • Conclusions and Recommendations

Chapter SIX	**POSTSECONDARY EDUCATION: ....101 STUDENT *SUCCESS* NOT JUST ACCESS** *Lawrence E. Gladieux and Watson Scott Swail*	Chapter NINE	**REFLECTIONS ON A DECADE OF ....159 PROMOTING YOUTH DEVELOPMENT** *Karen Pittman and Merita Irby*

Chapter SIX — **POSTSECONDARY EDUCATION: STUDENT *SUCCESS* NOT JUST ACCESS** 101
Lawrence E. Gladieux and Watson Scott Swail

Who Goes to College? • Who Goes Where? • Who Completes? • Why Haven't We Done Better? • Whither Public Policy? • Higher Education's Responsibility

Chapter SEVEN — **PREPARING YOUTH FOR EMPLOYMENT** 115
Thomas Bailey and Vanessa Smith Morest

Improving the Workforce Development System • Proposed Workforce Development Strategies • Policy Changes of the 1990s • Carl D. Perkins Vocational and Applied Technology Education Act (1990) • School-to-Work Opportunities Act (1994) • Goals 2000: Educate America and the National Skill Standards Board (1994) • Workforce Investment Act (1998) • Community Colleges • Assessment of Progress and Implementation • Looking Ahead

Chapter EIGHT — **TEN YEARS OF YOUTH IN SERVICE TO AMERICA** 137
Shirley Sagawa

Support for Service Grows • Development of AmeriCorps • Presidents' Summit of 1997 • School-Based Service-Learning • Community-Based Service • College Campus-Based Service • Full-Time Service • Youth Corps and YouthBuild • The Future: A National Commitment • Funding Sources • Strengthening Quality

Chapter NINE — **REFLECTIONS ON A DECADE OF PROMOTING YOUTH DEVELOPMENT** 159
Karen Pittman and Merita Irby

The Call for a Cohesive Strategy for Preparing Young People for Adulthood • The Paradigm Shift: Six Assertions • The Priorities Drift • An Emerging Agenda • A Success Story

Chapter TEN — **ON THE HORIZON: AMERICA'S YOUTH FACE THE NEW CENTURY** 171
Harold Howe II

Reaching Upstream to Prevent Damaged Lives • Academic Excellence Vs. Decent Lives for Children and Youth • Race, Ethnicity and Schooling • Conclusion

About the Authors 179

Members, William T. Grant Foundation Commission on Work, Family and Citizenship (1986-88) 182

THE FORGOTTEN HALF REVISITED

SUMMARY

This 200-page report reviews what our nation has accomplished for late-adolescents and young adults (especially ages 18-24) in the decade since the publication of the predecessor reports of the William T. Grant Foundation Commission on Work, Family and Citizenship, *The Forgotten Half: Non-College Youth in America* and *The Forgotten Half: Pathways to Success for American Youth and Young Families* (both 1988).

The individually shaded consensus from the 15 authors represented here, while not quite a "viewing with alarm," is that many developments have not been encouraging. To be sure, in some areas, progress has been made, particularly in rising educational attainment and one or two other downward-trending indices. Overall, however, the record of advances in the last decade in the arenas of the authors' professional expertise – whether family life, schools, communities, employment, national service, or youth development – provides but a slim reed of hope for a better deal for much of the nation's youth and young families.

Statistical Overview. Samuel Halperin's review of demographic and economic data in Chapter One paints a generally discouraging picture of non-college youth "losing ground" on a host of indices, although he notes substantial gains on the single most important predictor of success in America, namely rising educational aspirations and increased attainment. Sounding a note that echoes throughout this report, Halperin points to the educational factor as the currently most reliable proxy for both the nation's social and economic health and the success of the young. The numbers, he says, are mildly encouraging. Overall educational attainment rose for adults age 16 and over between 1990-1997, and the highest level of education achieved rose for all age cohorts. Still, the widely held notion that "almost every American goes to college" turns out to be a myth. In fact, in 1996 almost half of all adults (48.2 percent) either did not complete high school or terminated their formal education after graduation.

On the all-important correlation between educational attainment and family income, only one student in three (34 percent) from a low-income family went to college, while more than four of five students from upper-income families did so (83.4 percent). Clearly, Halperin concludes, "the nation's challenges for the next decade are to remove this family income bias, to further raise educational attainment, and to increase the academic achievement of all students."

An especially significant demographic fact, Halperin points out, is that the previously declining numbers of American youth began to reverse direction in 1996. Between then and the year 2005, the number of 18-24 year-olds is projected to rise from 24.7 million to 29.1 million (an 18 percent increase), a reversal that can be expected to create "painful transitions in the labor market." Adding weight to the demographics is the increasing job instability of the 1980s and 1990s, i.e., youth working with more employers for shorter job tenures, punctuated by periods of unemployment, and taking longer to find permanent employment.

In terms of jobs for out-of-school youth, recently declining national unemployment rates (about 4.5 percent at publication) have not helped much. Some 11.0 percent of males and 9.0 percent of females ages 16-24 were out of work in May, 1998. Predictably, as in 1989, members of minority groups today experience substantially higher unemployment rates than whites – over 30 percent. Thus, despite a strongly growing economy, and with the support of rising levels of educational attainment, young people in the job market were actually worse off in 1997 than in 1989.

Even when they do work, youth still don't earn as much as their counterparts of ten years ago. Significantly, earning rates are bifurcating. As median family income has stagnated since 1973, the richest five percent of workers have seen their share of earnings increase, while the poorest 40 percent have seen their share decline. In 1997, for example, only 26 percent of all young workers who had earned a high school diploma (or GED) were working full-time and earning at the four-person poverty wage level ($309 per week or more). Indeed, inflation-adjusted earnings for the young and less well-educated were one-third less in June of 1998 than what their counterparts were earning 24 years ago.

Nor are young families managing as well. Among three basic indicators (median real income, poverty rates of young families, and poverty rates of children in young families), the poverty rates are higher at all levels of educational attainment, except among college graduates. Moreover, fewer young adults are leaving home than did ten years ago; more than 40 percent among all males and 50 percent among minorities still live under their parents' roofs because of economic reasons.

In terms of out-of-wedlock births, the correlations among teen motherhood, infant health risks, and poverty remain high. Unfortunately, out-of-wedlock births have almost become a national norm; one of three births is to an unmarried mother, and among unmarried teens, the rate has now quintupled since 1960, from 15 percent to 76 percent in 1994. But there is some good news on this front. The birth rate among unmarried women ages 15-24 has fallen slightly, from 88 per 1,000 in 1989 to 83 per 1,000 in 1995. Nearly all of the decline, however is among young women ages 20-25, not among teens.

Home ownership rates among the young, also highly correlated with educational attainment, have fallen in the past decade, as has coverage by health insurance. The number of young Americans behind bars is increasing; between 1985 and 1996 the national incarceration rate went up 119 percent. Estimates are that among men under age 25 the rate more than doubled in the period. Importantly, these rates substantially undercount the number of young men under the aegis or control of the justice system. On any given day in America, one in ten males ages 20-29 were in jail or prison, on parole, or on probation.

Halperin concludes with a telling question: Is there still a safety net, and does it still work? Without the safety net provided by AFDC, TANF, SSI, the Earned Income Tax Credit, and other federal programs, 21.6 percent of all Americans would have fallen below the poverty line in 1996; as it was, the figure was still substantial – 11.5 percent. Discouragingly, the percentage of young males requiring the assistance of these programs rose 38 percent from 1989 to 1996. Here again, educational attainment makes the crucial difference. Dropouts were nearly twice as likely to need government support as high school graduates and 12 times more likely to do so than college graduates. In Halperin's concluding words: "In the decade since *The Forgotten Half* was published, many of America's young people continued to experience deep social and economic traumas [while] social pathologies rose."

The Impact of Trends and Forces. Reporting in Chapter Two on shifting attitudes about the key forces that have affected the lives of members of The Forgotten Half in the last decade, **Daniel Yankelovich** sees the balance among important trends shifting toward the negative in education, governmental responses, moral values, and public attitudes toward youth.

As the nation has become more conscious of the importance of education and skills, the translation of public concern about schools into public action has been difficult and erratic. The society's demand for high skills has rushed ahead of the capabilities of schools and work institutions to meet the new requirements of a global economy. "Schools," Yankelovich says, "have been massively resistant to change."

Across a mass of survey data reflecting attitudes about educational accomplishments, preparation for the workforce, the demand for higher educational standards, the importance of teaching values, the importance of public safety and order, rising educational aspirations, the dropout problem, and job skills and training, the overall trend is in a negative direction for The Forgotten Half. Among the most telling findings: (1) Almost half of all Americans, almost two-thirds of all employers, and more than three-fourths of all professors do not believe that a high school diploma is a guarantee that a student has learned the basics; (2) six out of ten Americans say academic standards are too low in their children's schools; and (3) almost three-fourths of all Americans say that "drugs and violence" are serious problems in their local schools.

Reviewing public attitudes about the role of government, Yankelovich reports a widespread public perception that government has failed in dealing with such key problems as poverty, crime, and drug abuse, and that Americans reject programs that "do not respect the fundamental value[s] of self-reliance" and "self-determination." Eighty percent of Americans say that "giving people the resources to be self-sufficient instead of encouraging dependence would enhance public confidence in government." Survey data on moral values show a perceived decline in the ability of families to successfully transmit to their children the values of respect, responsibility, and civility. Some 79 percent of Americans believe that children growing up today are not taught good moral values. Parents, as the principal teachers of values, are blamed for not doing an adequate job, and over half of parents express misgivings about their own capabilities in this area.

American attitudes toward youth are "surprisingly negative," reports Yankelovich. More than two-thirds, for example, consider youngsters to be "rude," "irresponsible," and "wild," and only 12 percent of Americans say it is common for teens to be helpful and friendly. Nonetheless, an adult willingness to help young people is still present. More than half of Americans think "helping kids get a good start" is more important than creating more jobs, protecting citizens from crime, or helping the poor and homeless. Two problems – teen pregnancy and youth crime – stand out as sources of negative attitudes toward youth.

A new youth strategy, Yankelovich concludes, must avoid the chief mistake of the past, which has been to adopt either a "magic bullet" or "cure-everything-at-once" approach. Such policies never win broad public support. Priorities must be set, he says, and must include more effective school-to-work policies and practices; taking primary action at local and regional, not national, levels; intensified development of "second-chance" institutions; improved assessment of job capabilities; programs to teach and reinforce positive values; and nongovernmental public financing mechanisms for youth programs.

Among the institutions best positioned and most able to serve as launching platforms for a renewed effort for The Forgotten Half, Yankelovich says, are America's community colleges, which: (1) have a track record of success, (2) are locally based, (3) do not serve only the "cream" of young people, (4) have close ties with local employers, and (5) are well positioned to learn from each others' mistakes. Yankelovich also suggests adopting micro-lending as a tested strategy for developing community resources to support efforts aimed at assisting young people.

Changes for the Family. In Chapter Three, **Carol Emig** examines how conditions and circumstances have changed for the American family in the past ten years; she also suggests some policy changes that can serve to strengthen young families.

Among the most important demographic changes Emig cites are the past and anticipated growth of the under-18 population (from 62 million in 1990 to 77.6 million by 2020), and that population segment's growing racial and ethnic diversity (white, non-Hispanic children are expected to make up only 55 percent of the youth population by 2020).

Among the most significant developments affecting families has been the "march of mothers," especially single mothers, into the workforce – from 53 percent of mothers in 1980 to 66 percent in 1996. As these mothers worked, 60 percent of their children under age 6 were in some kind of day-care in 1995. At the same time, both the number of children living with two parents (down to 68 percent in 1997) and the number of births outside marriage (stabilized at one-third in 1994) reflect significant changes in recent years. Median family income for female-headed households with children was lower in 1993 than in 1975, and was only a third of median family income for married couples with children.

At 20 percent, the number of children living in poverty has not changed for the past 11 years (1985-1996), and a greater percentage of children live in poverty today than in 1970, when the child-poverty rate was 15 percent.

Happily, the trend line is declining with respect to the infant death rate, however; in 1960 it was 26 per 1,000 live births, while it stood at 7.6 per 1,000 in 1996. The homicide rate for 15-19 year-old black males "is perhaps the most single horrifying statistic in the child and family field," Emig asserts. It increased threefold between 1985 and 1996, and now stands at 100.4 per 100,000, more than eight times the homicide rate for white males the same age.

Emig reports education data much in line with her fellow authors: notable increases in the number of young adults attending college, modest improvement in achievement test scores in the public schools, a steady school completion rate over the decade (85 percent), but substantial differences in completion rates across racial groups, with most minorities still lagging behind whites.

Risk-taking behavior fluctuated over the decade. Between 1985 and the early 1990s, smoking, drinking, and drug abuse by adolescents declined, but has increased through 1997. The number of both male and female sexually active teens–and thus the risk of out-of-wedlock childbirth–seems to be waning. Births to teens increased between 1986 and 1991, but have since declined; however, the 1996 rate (54.4 births per 1,000) remains slightly higher than the 1986 rate (50.2 births per 1,000).

Among the major policy changes affecting the quality of life for youth have been the Personal Responsibility and Work Reconciliation Opportunity Act (PRWORA) of 1996, which reversed 60 years of welfare policy in several respects: the bloc grant structure of funding, time limits on cash payments to families, new work requirements for eligibility, requirements for unmarried teen parents, and the setting of specific employment goals for states.

Among the future directions for policy advocated by Emig are: (1) putting more attention and resources into investment in early childhood health and education ("the single smartest investment the nation could make in its children"); (2) enhanced income for poor families with children via a system of tax credits; and (3) better child care for low-income families, including an expanded Head Start program (still reaching only a third of eligible children in 1996). Also needed are family-supportive arrangements with employers, private health insurers and HMOs, efforts from religious and social service organizations, more family support centers, state welfare-to-work programs, welfare reform efforts, family planning services, and media campaigns on family issues.

How Communities Have Responded. Addressing the changes in how communities have approached issues facing The Forgotten Half in the past decade, **Martin J. Blank** and **Carol Steinbach** are heartened by "a new breed of youth-focused initiatives." They sense a new determination to achieve results; a commitment to community-level creativity and ingenuity ("top down solutions don't work"); contributions from multiple community sectors; the growing realization that efforts for young people must be complemented by support for families in their neighborhoods; and the growth of a spirit of entrepreneurialism in the efforts to help youth. Communities across the country, say Blank and Steinbach, are focusing more intently on their roles as keepers of values, problem solvers, and as human "ecosystems." They see six trends driving the relationship between youth and communities: (1) a focus on results and performance, (2) a new stress on building community assets, (3) a focus on broader stakeholder participation, (4) a focus on involving neighborhood residents across the age spectrum, (5) a recognition of the importance of race and culture, and (6) a renewed sense of the importance of building public will.

Blank and Steinbach describe in some detail a series of service reform efforts, youth development initiatives, community development efforts, and school reform initiatives drawn from communities across the country to illustrate their contention that much is happening on the community level that is of positive consequence for improving the lives of The Forgotten Half.

School Reform. In Chapter Five, **Jack Jennings** and **Diane Stark Rentner** focus attention on school reform efforts. Overall, they report, many students in The Forgotten Half of the late 1980s were helped to seek and get more education and training. In consequence, with respect to *starting* postsecondary education at least, what was once The Forgotten Half has become more nearly a Forgotten Third. The bad news, however, is that those left behind, and those who do not complete a college degree often face a bleaker economic future than that of The Forgotten Half a decade ago.

Among the comprehensive reforms that have taken hold in public schools during the past decade are increasing course work, higher graduation requirements, and standards and assessment-based reform. Strictly school-based reforms include the creation of reform "networks" among schools and districts, e.g., the Coalition of Essential Schools and High Schools That Work; the school choice movement (magnets, charter schools); and increasing attention to professional development. Other reforms include more interventions in troubled schools, improved teacher quality, more equitable school funding, and the institution of service-learning.

American students' performance compared to students from other countries remains troublingly low. "The curriculum may have to be altered to expose Americans to more difficult subjects earlier and to teach them in more depth," say Jennings and Rentner. Other difficulties persist: "Frequently, discrete reforms are too new, too isolated, or too hard to quantify to show a direct effect on students."

Among the authors' recommendations for those not fully benefiting from America's education system is closer attention to "in-betweens" – those who begin postsecondary education and leave before obtaining a degree. To help these youth, more remedies are needed for the three causes of incompletion: lack of funds, lack of preparation, and lack of interest in what college has to offer. The High Schools That Work program, the authors suggest, models what should be available to students across the country – the chance to master rigorous college-preparatory material.

Postsecondary Education. Taking up the theme of postsecondary educational attainment as the key to success for many in The Forgotten Half, **Lawrence E. Gladieux** and **Watson Scott Swail** argue in Chapter Six that the evidence of the last ten years is unambiguous: the least educated still get the smallest piece of the economic pie. Among those who go to college, factors such as quality of preparation, colleges chosen, and courses of study are powerful determinants to entrée into good jobs and successful careers. The key to success, more and more, is *completion* of postsecondary studies, not just getting in the college door. The salient fact in postsecondary education over the past quarter-century has been that in the face of rising enrollments, the rates of degree completion have remained flat. In other words, the equation is broken: access ≠ success.

The most clear-cut advance in postsecondary opportunity in recent years has been the achievement in gender parity; in fact, women today make up more than 55 percent of the postsecondary population. The downside of that fact is that The Forgotten Half today is disproportionately male.

At the same time, because institutional choice (e.g., public vs. private, two-year vs. four-year) is linked to family income and background, opportunities are immediately constrained from another quarter: those from lower income backgrounds tend to select two-year institutions. As they leave college, they are less likely to receive the same rewards as those who earned a bachelor's degree or higher. And, even though more students are increasingly able to receive postsecondary instruction without setting foot on a campus (through distance learning and virtual instruction), these advances by no means address the needs of all students, least of all those without access to the technology.

Among the reasons we have not done as well at getting students out of college as we have in getting them into college are: the rising costs of higher education, the quality of prior schooling, family and cultural attitudes toward higher education, and lack of awareness of opportunities. The cost of an already expensive college education during the 1980s rose sharply, at three times the rate of inflation; average inflation-adjusted tuition doubled from 1981 to 1996. Student financial aid has not closed the gap, and among those most at risk, borrowing remains the only way to get a college education. Unfortunately, say Gladieux and Swail, the entire college-aid system is "moving away from need-based principles and becoming less responsive to The Forgotten Half, and reducing opportunities for students with the least resources."

But while financial means and student aid continue as significant variables for college completion, they are not the most important; that distinction goes to academic preparation. Research has repeatedly shown that students who take progressively more challenging coursework through high school are more likely not only to plan for and enroll in college, but to finish. "For many students," say Gladieux and Swail, "the die is cast by the eighth grade."

Public policy responses to improve higher education completion rates can take several directions. An obvious one is to lift student performance and academic preparation, and to raise standards. In the short-term, we also need more strategies to reach out directly to disadvantaged students; this is "retail, not wholesale work." But improving performance and preparation alone will not meet the needs of low-income students. Critical differences can often be made by interested individuals and mentors, as well as by "I Have a Dream"-type programs. But in the larger scheme, the reality is that public policy has too long focused on access while paying too little attention to helping young people successfully negotiate the postsecondary system.

Here, higher education, too, has a responsibility and, if demography is destiny, postsecondary institutions have their work cut out for them. For example, in 1995, only one-third of American institutions sponsored a pre-collegiate outreach program for disadvantaged students. Outstanding models of pre-collegiate intervention cited by the authors include those of the University of North Carolina, Xavier University, the University of California, as well as programs run by the states of California and Wisconsin.

Getting Ready for the World of Work. After completing high school, American young people basically have three options: work, community college, or a four-year college. These three choices also constitute paths to three different levels of the occupational hierarchy, according to **Thomas Bailey** and **Vanessa Smith Morest** in Chapter Seven.

The authors rehearse the perspectives, recommendations, and provisions of five national reports[1] and cite the provisions of four pieces of legislation[2] in the 1990s that have addressed the problems of workforce preparation. Unfortunately, the system for developing the workforce in the United States has long been "characterized by extreme flexibility and wide variations in quality," the authors say. They point to eight basic strategies that cut across the reports and legislation and assess the progress made in each area. The eight strategies include: improvement in academic skills; strengthened SCANS skills; a greater emphasis on standards; innovative pedagogies, including the integration of academic work and vocational instruction; participation of employers in education; making pathways to particular occupations more transparent; facilitating the transition of The Forgotten Half to postsecondary education; and continued emphasis on "second chance" efforts.

In sum, the authors conclude that none of the strategies or policy changes has penetrated to the core of schooling and pedagogy; "it is still difficult," they say, "to discern a broad, consistent national movement." Among the reasons for this lack of success, Bailey and Morest advance the following: political opposition to both a more structured educational system and to a more regulated labor market; the absence of a tradition of employer participation in the nation's education system; a perceived restriction of employment opportunities imposed by early career decisions; and elusive evidence about the success of specific strategies. "Finally," they conclude, "one central implication of the last decade is that, certainly at the secondary school level, we should dispense with the distinction between educational policy and workforce development policy."

Youth Service. In Chapter Eight, **Shirley Sagawa** lays out the last decade's history of the development of service opportunities for students and young people in (a) school-based programs like Learn and Serve America, (b) community-based programs like 4-H and Scouting, (c) college-based service like Campus Compact and Work Study, (d) full-time youth service with programs like AmeriCorps, and the (e) Youth Service and Conservation Corps and YouthBuild. She discusses the objectives and targeted audiences for each and points out successes, shortcomings, and what has been learned.

Evaluations of service programs reveal that youth respond positively to them and that they have strong positive impacts on academic performance, character building, and values formation. Sagawa notes that it is possible "to make service the common experience of every child growing up in America, and an abiding ethic valued by our most important public and private institutions." In contrast to the opportunities that existed for youth service a decade ago, a national youth service infrastructure has now been developed, and public interest in service as a responsive strategy to the challenges faced by many youth has grown. Service can now begin in the earliest grades and be integrated into learning at every level of the curriculum.

But if the benefits of service are to be consolidated and expanded, and if we are to make service a reality for every youngster, several commitments are required. Chief among them is that funders of all sorts must look comprehensively at their approaches to youth development, civic engagement, and service delivery, in order to discover how youth service advances these goals. Second, organizations and institutions that use volunteers to serve youth need to learn how to involve young people in those very service activities. Third, educational institutions at all levels should work to connect service to learning

---

[1] *A Nation at Risk* (1983), *Workforce 2000* (1987), *The Forgotten Half* (1988), *America's Choice: High Skills or Low Wages!* (1990), and *Report of the Secretary's Commission on Achieving Necessary Skills (SCANS)* (1991).

[2] *Perkins Vocational and Applied Technology and Education Act* (1990), *School-to-Work Opportunities Act* 1994), *Goals 2000: Educate America Act* (1994), *Workforce Investment Act* (1998).

in the earliest grades. Finally, communities across the country should create a new service opportunity for youth, a "Summer of Service," targeted at middle-school youth. For a relatively modest investment of $1 billion annually, Sagawa argues, half of the eighth graders in the country could add service to their developmental experience. Connecting service to earning money for college could also pay rich dividends.

In terms of funding, Sagawa says, moving to multi-year rather than annual grants will help attract supplementary funding. In addition, school districts should consider supporting youth service corps as alternative schools for youth having difficulty in the regular classroom. Existing youth service programs should consider pursuing fee-for-service funding, and youth corps should be eligible for job-training and other dollars, whether the source of funds is federal, state, or local government.

To strengthen the quality of service programs for youth, Sagawa argues, high-quality research and evaluation efforts are called for, especially to assess the impact of service programs on at-risk youth. Greater professionalism within the youth service field is also needed, but should not come at the expense of opportunities for young people themselves to assume leadership roles.

Youth Development. Ten years ago, *The Forgotten Half* was in the forefront of a call to shift the energy of the nation's concern for its youth from deterrence to development. That call has generated "a surprising energy and enthusiasm," according to **Karen Pittman** and **Merita Irby,** writing in Chapter Ten. But, they assert, "the most significant change over the past decade has not been in the quality or quantity of programs or policies that promote youth development, although there have been improvements in both. It is in the increased acceptance of youth development as a broad goal requiring intentional monitoring and intervention."

Pittman and Irby outline six dimensions of this "paradigm shift": (1) moving beyond the prevention of problems for youth to full preparation for productive lives; (2) moving beyond "quick fixes" to continuing and real engagement and relationships between adults and youth, (3) moving beyond basic services to continuing support, (4) moving the youth development effort beyond schools and into communities, (5) moving service delivery beyond simple coordination among service providers to a new vision of both early and sustained efforts, and (6) moving beyond labeling youth by their problems to a deeper understanding of their total situations: "Targeting is fine, labeling isn't."

Although the authors encourage this "paradigm shift," they acknowledge that it has muddied the waters. Problems arise when youth service providers try to work on the six paradigmatic elements one by one instead of as a package. Youth development requires all of them working in tandem.

In counterpoint, Pittman and Irby offer six broad suggestions to strengthen the insights and thrust of the youth development movement. First, the primary focus has to be placed on the young people themselves, not on the programs targeting them. It may be that more effort on monitoring and coordinating will yield better results for youth than "big-ticket claims on implementing." Second, practitioners need to engage public systems and connect to popular issues. The message about and need for youth development appears in a variety of contexts, e.g., school reform, juvenile justice, youth employment, and health – all fertile soil. Third, link youth development to larger community development and change efforts. Increasingly, community development experts are seeing young people not just as service recipients but also as community residents, resources, and potential investments. Fourth, promote continuing efforts to define youth indicators, i.e., indices for tracking youth problems and progress. We do not so much need more information, the authors say, as we need to better organize the cornucopia of information we already have. Fifth, we need to reinforce the importance and wisdom of parents. They are the best source of knowledge and are their children's best role models. Sixth, we should shift "from lists to lenses." Current language about youth development is both too broad and too narrow. What are required are multiple inputs over a sustained period in order to build "formulas" for the right mixes of the right resources to apply to problems.

In a brief, concluding case study, Pittman and Irby discuss how the 78 Beacon Schools in New York City moved through the "paradigm shift" they recommend.

Youth Facing the New Century. In a final essay, education statesman **Harold "Doc" Howe II,** the former chair of the William T. Grant Foundation Commission, looks toward what we can expect for youth in the years ahead.

For Howe, what *The Forgotten Half* revealed about the power of prevention remains salient; it is the least expensive strategy for meeting the problems of youth, "offering new and powerful possibilities" for the future. But now, he says, if we intend to keep alive the concept of *The Forgotten Half* as a "call to both conscience and action, we must broaden its scope to include the entire river of experience that lies before maturity."

The great effort necessary to complete the youth agenda that *The Forgotten Half* laid before the nation comprises two main tasks. First, we must complete the shift in our focus from the narrower field of school reform to the broader concerns of improving children's lives as a whole. Within the arena of school reform itself, two main projects stand out: (1) to escape the narrow emphasis on standards and tougher curricula, in order to (2) continue moving in the direction of building comprehensive change in schools from the bottom up. Overall, he says, school reform efforts should be about maintaining our focus on raising achievement. But equally fruitful, if not more so, will be efforts to increase opportunities for youth, based on well-developed talents, purposeful and trusting relationships with adults, and connections to the broader community. School reform efforts alone, he writes, often fail without such broader and deeper supports.

The second major re-focusing Howe calls for concerns race, ethnicity, and schooling. The dangerous and debilitating gap between haves and have-nots continues to grow in America, and poor and minority children are the most forgotten. Two questions should frame our response to this fundamental fact, Howe argues: (1) What should our policy be toward language learning in America schools by students who don't speak English? Here, Howe places his wager firmly on bilingual education as offering the best chance of success; and (2) What school-based activities are needed to help students understand our country's diverse population and their own rights and obligations in it? Here, Howe sees our nation's greatest challenge, no less than building what Henry Louis Gates calls "a truly common public culture." Because the public schools are inevitably the first testing ground for the future, we must redouble our efforts to teach our children about each other.

"Perhaps what America needs in order to move forward," Howe concludes, "is to see more clearly the enormous possibility for young people's success that lies within our reach – a new moral vision to give us strength against the often disheartening realities of daily life…Our country needs to be reminded that young people do grow up…and their success in life is the best investment we could make."

THE FORGOTTEN HALF REVISITED

INTRODUCTION

In 1986, the William T. Grant Foundation established a 19-member Commission on Work, Family and Citizenship, also known as the Commission on Youth and America's Future.* Its charge was to "evaluate current knowledge, stimulate new ideas, increase communication among researchers, practitioners and policymakers and, thus, help our nation chart a better future for youth."

At the time, public policy in the human services was focused on a so-called "rising tide of mediocrity" in our public schools and, to a lesser extent, on the pathologies of youth and the "casualties of adolescence." The Grant Foundation Commission rejected this problem-oriented view and determined "to speak in a different voice." Under the leadership of Harold Howe II, U.S. Commissioner of Education in the Lyndon Johnson Administration, a set of principles soon evolved that shifted the Commission's focus away from the narrowly defined academic issues of the school reform debate toward broader considerations of society's role in helping young people meet their full potential. Only by creating a new set of attitudes and a new social compact with young people, the Commission argued, could America begin to create better futures for individual youth and, in turn, for the country.

Five principles emerged to guide the Commission's inquiry and to shape its published recommendations in 1988:

1. Schools are only one of the institutions responsible for assisting youth to become all that they can be. While underscoring the importance of schools as a central institution in young people's lives, the Commission rejected "school bashing" and the widely held premise that inadequate schools are to blame for most of the difficulties that young people face. Instead, it contended that parents, families, employers, public and private human service providers, community-based institutions and every level of government all have important roles to play in helping young people succeed — in life, not just in school. Taking a broad view beyond schooling, the Commission advocated the need for lifelong learning and the value of work — both paid and unpaid — not only as an economic necessity but as major avenues to self-sufficiency, personal fulfillment and civic participation.

2. Understanding how young people succeed requires interdisciplinary inquiry. Their accomplishments are a function of the opportunities and support they experience at home, in school, at work and in the broader community — as well as the obstacles they must overcome in each of these domains. In recent decades, research on youth issues had been growing but the results were fragmented and disparate. The Commission knew that studying school failure, youth unemployment, substance abuse or premature pregnancy in isolation — research on "small pieces of large problems" — too often missed the vital *connections* among the conditions of young people's lives that in combination can increase or diminish their chances of success.

The Commission's composition reflected its interdisciplinary approach. It comprised business and union leaders, academics in the social and behavioral sciences, state policymakers and advocates — all of whom brought a special lens to bear on the needs of youth. To enrich their study, established scholars were asked to consider key issues and research findings that would shed light on what young people need to succeed and the obstacles that stand in their way. Over two dozen working papers in a broad range of youth-related fields and disciplines added to the variety of perspectives and breadth of research and knowledge about practice that the Commission was created to synthesize.

3. Attention to the strengths of young people and their interdependence with adults is needed to balance the frequent overemphasis on why young people fail. By looking, in the Commission's words, "with renewed respect at youth, where they stride as well as where they stumble," it hoped to discover how best to strengthen connections and shared values among young people and adults. Adolescents are not only preparing for the future — and

---
* The membership of the Commission is listed on page 182.

facing formidable challenges in the process — they are *already* playing important roles in our families, communities and workforce. They need our help — and we need theirs. Mutual interdependence — a give-and-take relationship based on rights and responsibilities — is central to a productive relationship between young people and adults. It is also the foundation of a strong citizenry in a participatory democracy.

4. It is never too late to make a difference. The Commission approached youth issues from a life-span, intergenerational perspective. It vigorously supported early and timely prevention and intervention whenever possible, in the belief that the multiplier effect of years of positive development is the best insurance against the many risks of adolescence. The panel rejected the sometimes assumed corollary that the human capacity to change and to tap one's full potential is largely spent by age five or six. There are many points of intervention, the Commission reasoned, when support and help can make the difference in a young person's ability to succeed. Academic transition periods are especially stressful because they frequently coincide with other physical, emotional and social developmental changes. Moving from middle school to high school, deciding on postsecondary education, and making the crossover between school and work are some of the critical turning points at which many young people need a helping hand. Young people of all ages, along with parents and other adults on whom they rely to meet their basic needs, respond well to positive support when it is flexible, appropriate and available when needed. The Commission was concerned, however, that too little constructive attention is focused on older adolescents — until they show unmistakable signs of "problem behavior." In response, it decided to concentrate its work on young people, particularly those between the ages of 16 and 24 and young families under age 30.

5. Adolescents are, first and foremost, individuals with unique talents, temperaments and learning styles. While acknowledging its responsibility to define a core set of opportunities and supports likely to be of universal value to all youth, the Commission underscored the importance of identifying differences among individuals and groups, the necessity of responding to them flexibly and creatively, and the potential of an individual's personal qualities as strengths to be encouraged and celebrated.

The Commission's two major 1988 reports — *The Forgotten Half: Non-College Youth in America* and *The Forgotten Half: Pathways to Success for America's Youth and Young Families* — and three dozen background papers and follow-up documents published between 1987 and 1993, drew a picture not of "a nation at risk" but of a nation's promise — its young people who need only a fair chance to succeed. One of the Commission's conclusions was that *in every state across the country, communities are looking for, and finding, innovative ways to better prepare young people to meet the demands of tomorrow.* If these creative efforts are to make a difference in the lives of many, not just some, youth, they must be examined, evaluated, refined and brought to scale. Because America's future depends on the successful contributions of all our young people and society's willingness to help them make the transition to adult roles and responsibilities, efforts must be made to adapt, extend and coordinate what research and evaluation tells us works.

A more sobering finding, and *perhaps the Commission's most lasting contribution, disclosed the extent to which so many of our young people must make the transition to adulthood with only minimal or no assistance and preparation.* This group, the approximately half of America's 16-24 year-old youth who are not likely to go on to postsecondary education, the Commission termed "The Forgotten Half." For this large group, economic and social prospects appeared increasingly grim in 1988.

During the course of its study, the Commission directed its attention, first, to how young people make the transition from school to the world of work and, second, to the roles young people play in their families, in their communities and, eventually, as parents themselves. In both cases, it asked two sets of questions: 1) What are the opportunities that help young people become productive workers, responsible parents and participatory citizens, as well as the obstacles that deter them? and 2) What can be done to lower or eliminate those hurdles and enable more young people to meet their potential?

As data were accumulated and analyzed, it became increasingly clear that young people have been rocked by seismic shifts in how three of society's most fundamental institutions — work, family and community — function.

Today's youth, far more than their parents and grandparents, have had their opportunities and expectations brought up short by: 1) declining real income caused by a shift from a manufacturing to a service-based economy, the loss of unionized wages and full-time jobs, and slowed productivity; 2) sea changes in the structure of families that have rapidly increased the number of single-parent families even as economic factors increasingly required a second paycheck in order to maintain their standard of living; and 3) a growing absence in neighborhoods and communities of "the ties that bind" — relationships with caring adults that open doors to young people and provide them with sources of information and values that can help them find their way in the larger world.

Particularly disturbing was the Commission's presentation of data about declining real income. It documented clearly the uncertainties and insecurities that have become an accepted part of too many young people's lives. Particularly hard hit were young parents. Of course, every young family expects to "pay its dues," to experience some financial struggle as its skills develop and its earning power slowly grows. But the gap in income between young families in the late 1980s and the rest of America, as reported by the Commission, widened by nearly a third over the prior two decades. In 1967, the median income of young families was equal to about 77 percent of all American families. By 1986, that proportion had fallen to only 52 percent.

In its final report in November 1988, the Commission reported that many young families were on the brink of economic disaster. Instead of confidence in greater opportunities and a progressively better standard of living than their parents enjoyed, the future promised many young families a sharply abridged version of the American Dream. Young men and women entering adulthood in the mid- to late 1980s could expect to earn 25 percent less throughout their lifetimes than the generation that preceded them. The earnings patterns were particularly bleak for youth lacking postsecondary education. Regardless of race or ethnicity, workplace earnings and years of schooling are highly correlated. So, while young college graduates lost six percent of their earnings from 1973 and 1986, young males between the ages of 20 and 24 with only a high school education took a 28 percent cut. Those with no high school diploma or GED certificate reeled under a 42 percent decline in purchasing power.

Of course, good jobs with substantial earning potential did and do exist. But then, as now, they were increasingly lodged at the high end of the wage/skill continuum, and were far fewer in number than those clustered at the low skill, low-wage end. Without postsecondary training to acquire specialized skills, the Commission concluded, young men and women simply would not be able to compete for positions that offer a decent family-supporting wage, health and other insurance protections, and the promise of someday owning a home.

In exploring the adequacy of existing opportunities for youth who need further training, the Commission found a profoundly troubling disparity in the extent to which society assists young people who are college bound and those who are not. Its 1988 analysis showed that young people who go on to college routinely benefit from combined public and private subsidies that easily total more than $20,000 over four years. Yet young people whose talents and interests require other forms of education and skills training besides an academic degree — or those who simply have never been encouraged or enabled to aspire to college — receive very little help.

Why should this disparity exist?, the Commission asked. America depends on the success of this half of our youth as much as on the achievements of its college-educated youth. But the Commission found that only about five percent of the students eligible for job training under federal employment programs actually received it and then only for about four months. All told, members of The Forgotten Half received about one-tenth the financial support available to their college-going peers.

If young people are truly America's future, the Commission reasoned, then common sense, equity and fair play argue for the creation of many more pathways to success for *all* our young people. The Forgotten Half, who have been at the back of the queue and whose ability to move forward has been steadily eroded, need this attention most of all. This conclusion rings today at least as true as it did a decade ago.

The Commission's recommendations for helping young people find purpose, direction and opportunities for success were based on a strong conviction: business and government leadership must simultaneously launch spirited and determined efforts to create many more career-ladder opportunities for well-prepared, entry-level workers to earn a family wage. If not, the Commission warned, efforts to create better futures for individual youth and, in the process, to reverse what seemed then a sharp decline in international economic competitiveness and domestic tranquility, will falter. But these commitments must go hand-in-hand with comprehensive efforts to build on young people's talents and capacities and to prepare them to prosper as workers, parents and citizens. The Commission advocated a multiple strategy including 1) creating closer relationships among young people and adults; 2) expanding access to coordinated and community-based services, supports and service-learning experiences; and 3) extending and improving educational and employment training opportunities and policies.

What did the Commission achieve? Just before the Commission began its work in 1986, an article in *The Brookings Review* served as a cogent reminder of the limitations inherent in blue ribbon panels. In describing what it called "Commissionitis," the article pointed out that national commissions, despite their numerous virtues, are simply not strong enough to overcome the fragmented way public policy is developed in the United States. They usually have limited power, little authority and less accountability. As a result, commissions often overstate problems to capture attention and propose lofty ideals and "pie-in-the-sky" remedies far removed from real world possibilities. The Commission determined to avoid these pitfalls.

A decade after its publication, there is scant evidence that the Commission overstated the plight of many American youth and young families. Recent data presented in Chapter One, below, show that young people are still in a free-fall of declining earnings and dimmed expectations. At the same time, their need for a more effective transition from school to employment and the growth of a variety of youth employment and training policy measures, including national and community service, reflect a new national awareness of what young people need to succeed as workers, family members and citizens. This is all to the good.

In its recommendations, the Commission avoided "silver bullet" solutions or sweeping — and unfundable — legislative answers. The Commission knew that no single initiative in a country as diverse in geography, resources, values and interests as the United States would be able to reverse the trends identified in *The Forgotten Half* reports. Instead, it defined and, in many cases, rediscovered multiple pathways to help give young people direction and to take them where their talents and best efforts would lead. In pointing to these pathways, the Commission called on all sectors to help build and shape them — with government, the private sector, schools, churches, families and young people each playing a vital part.

Given what the Commission knew needed to be accomplished for all of America's young people, especially its Forgotten Half, it is not surprising that the progress achieved in the intervening decade has been far less than the Commission would have hoped. But the increased dialogue about young people's role in society that has subsequently occurred should not be underestimated. At least in part this renewed attention is attributable to the Commission's persistent and pragmatic efforts to create an environment — particularly at the national and state levels — in which thought and action on the key elements of its reports could take root and grow.

Realizing the short-term impact and limited shelf life of even the best reports, the William T. Grant Foundation directed the Commission staff to build on the momentum generated by *The Forgotten Half* reports in an extended, but clearly time-limited, period following their publication. This follow-up activity used the Commission's visibility, neutrality and well-respected standing in many youth-serving sectors and its access to a small, flexible pool of resources to share information among policymakers and practitioners on the central issues affecting young people. Equally as important, it sought to increase collaboration and partnership among key policy, research and membership organizations. The Commission follow-up helped to ensure a continuing focus on the multidimensional aspects of the school-to-employment transition and the full range of supports and opportunities that young people and their families need. A firm belief of the Commission — and a central idea of collaboration — was that no single partner can take sole credit for what must be achieved together. In effective partnerships there is always enough credit to share.

As a result of the Commission's work, the term "The Forgotten Half" has entered the policy, research and media vernacular. This addition to

America's collective vocabulary has enriched our ability to understand and value all young people and to consider new directions that will benefit not just youth but society in general. The acid test of our country's future will be whether or not we choose to attend to the issues of equity, fairness and mutual responsibility to a shared future. It is a commitment that the young men and women of The Forgotten Half remind us of and one which we forget at our own peril.

In this spirit of *remembering and acting,* and animated by requests from several youth-serving community-based organizations, I, as former Study Director of the Grant Foundation Commission, asked former members of the Commission and scholars who had assisted its earlier deliberations two questions: How had The Forgotten Half fared in the past decade and what has transpired in the various areas studied in the 1988 reports, that is, families, communities, schooling, preparation for employment, postsecondary education, service, youth development and such?

With the generous support of the **Walter S. Johnson, Ewing Marion Kauffman, Annie E. Casey** and **William T. Grant Foundations**, we have compiled a cross-section of perspectives, new data and recommendations in answer to these questions.

Unlike the Commission's work from 1986-88, no effort was made in this report to reach consensus. Each author was asked to present his/her own data and views about what has happened in the decade since the publication of *The Forgotten Half* and, then, to set forth what, in their individual judgments, the American people should commit themselves to in the decade ahead, 1998-2008. While differing in details, the authors of the chapters that follow all share the Commission's belief in young people's strength and promise and its conviction that we must, as a nation, take firm and continuing steps to ensure that they are "forgotten no more." This ten-year review — a reality check on where we are and where we are going — is offered with humility befitting the magnitude of the task still ahead.

Samuel Halperin,
editor

ACKNOWLEDGEMENTS

This report is the product of many hands: foundation officers who wished to bring renewed attention to the needs and conditions of America's youth and young families; the 15 chapter authors who brought their professional expertise to bear, looking back a decade and peering into the future to suggest a fairer deal for The Forgotten Half; practitioners in community-based organizations who urged this reprise as a useful tool to strengthen their daily interventions on behalf of youth.

The staff of the Center for Labor Market Studies at Northeastern University, notably Andy Sum, Neil and Neeta Fogg, provided voluminous labor market and demographic data. Larry Mishel gave the first chapter the benefit of his keen intellect, while Vinny Spera rendered invaluable assistance with the added perspective of a young policy analyst. Bruce Boston helped to distill the essence of the report for those without the time or interest to explore its varied pathways.

Susan Kim was both creative and tireless in turning disparate manuscripts into the text and graphic figures you see before you. George Kaplan, a fine writer in his own right, edited and pruned the chapters while preserving the various authors' essential messages. Atelia Melaville, who served with the original Grant Foundation Commission, also helped to sharpen this report's focus.

To all these contributors: my admiration and my thanks.

Samuel Halperin

CHAPTER ONE

TODAY'S FORGOTTEN HALF: STILL LOSING GROUND

Samuel Halperin

As this report nears completion in late 1998, the American people seemingly enjoy an almost unprecedented "boom time." Unemployment and inflation are at near-record lows of the past quarter-century. Stock market averages had reached once-unimaginable heights. Consumer confidence and housing sales are strong. Most new college graduates are being courted with multiple job offers. And a transfer of family wealth — as much as one trillion dollars — to the children of the World War II generation is well underway. National exuberance about the state of the economy — "millennial giddiness," Joel Kotkin and David Friedman call it — carried deep into 1998 as reflected in politics and much of the media.

Against this national backdrop, however, America's underlying social and economic problems are seldom mentioned. Poverty and what to do about it are among the large questions rarely considered. Simultaneously, emerging federal and state budget surpluses fuel politicians' calls in an election year for further tax cuts and still smaller roles for the public sector to deal with persistent social problems.

America's economic gains in the late 1990s are, thus, being recorded in a world apart from, and increasingly unrelated to, the particular world inhabited by The Forgotten Half. Nearly across the board — whether one is looking at the data for education, earnings, social well-being, home ownership, family formations, health insurance, employment, incarceration or almost any other determinant of personal and social progress — those with only a high school education or less than a bachelor's degree have lost considerable ground versus their counterparts only a decade earlier.

THE FORGOTTEN HALF IN 1988

In 1988, The Forgotten Half faced increasingly bleak earnings prospects and serious doubt as to their ability to create and sustain healthy and economically viable families. As the data and analysis that follow reveal, few gains were registered in the last decade and, in many vitally important sectors, we are witnessing stagnation or, worse yet, substantial social and economic regression.

When it issued its two reports on The Forgotten Half in 1988, the William T. Grant Foundation Commission told the nation that, even in a comparatively prosperous time, a huge portion of its young people — specifically those with 12 or fewer years of schooling and high school graduates who did not go on to pursue postsecondary studies — had fallen far behind in the struggle for social stability and economic well-being, and that prospects for improvement were at best uncertain. Heavy media coverage of the Commission's two major reports focused the public's attention on such disturbing facts of the mid- and late-1980s as these:

- *Unemployment among out-of-school teenagers was 15.8 percent but more than double that for black teens at 32.4 percent.*
- *Inflation-adjusted annual earnings in 1986 for 20-24 year-old male workers had fallen 25 percent during the previous 13 years, from $12,166 to $9,027.*
- *Median incomes of families headed by 20-24 year-olds had dropped 27 percent over the same 13-year span.*
- *The proportion of 20-24 year-old males who were married and living with their spouses had plummeted by almost one half, from 39.1 to 21.3 percent between 1974 and 1986.*
- *In 1986, almost one-third of the families headed by a person under age 25 were poor, triple the rate for all American families and more than double the overall poverty rate a generation earlier in 1967.*

In revisiting this scene of the late 1980s, and comparing it with that of the late 1990s, a detailed statistical examination is called for,* and that is the aim of this first chapter of *The Forgotten Half Revisited*.

---

* Data cited do not necessarily contrast the period 1988-89 with that of 1998-99, but are the most comparable data available at the time of publication. Also, since the transition of many youth into the labor force and family responsibilities is taking longer than formerly, we include data on young adults as well as on teenagers. Much of the data for this chapter, based on official U.S. government statistical sources, were assembled for this volume largely by the professional staff of the Center for Labor Market Studies at Northeastern University (CLMS), including director Professor Andrew M. Sum and senior research associates Drs. Neal and Neeta Fogg.

BAD NEWS

Educational attainment continues to be heavily influenced by family income. High school graduation rates for those in the lowest family income quartile are 25 percent lower than for those in the top quartile, while those in the top income quartile may be as much as ten times more likely to earn a college degree than those in the bottom quartile. (Barton, 1997)

Despite a strong economy and generally rising educational attainment, the full- and part-time employment rates of 16-24 year-olds in 1997 were one to three percentage points lower than in 1989. Minority youth had full-time employment rates 20 to 30 percentage points below their white counterparts.

In March 1997, more than one-quarter of out-of-school youth, although working full-time, were earning less than the poverty line income standard for a four-person family. Young men under age 25 were earning about one-third less (inflation-adjusted) than their counterparts were earning a generation earlier; young women 16.5 percent less.

Except for children living in families headed by four-year college graduates, poverty rates for children were higher in 1997 than in 1989.

Home ownership among young families fell from 49 percent in 1980 to 38 percent in the 1990s.

The number of incarcerated young men under age 25 doubled between 1986 and 1995. Ten percent of all 20-29 year-old males were either in jail, in prison, on probation or on parole.

Of the four million births annually, one in eight is to a teenager; one in four to an unmarried mother; one in four to a mother with less than a high school education; one in three to a mother living in poverty. (Zill, 1992)

Among teenage mothers ages 15-17, those who are unmarried tripled from 23 percent in 1950 to 84 percent in 1996. Older unmarried teen births (ages 18-19) increased eightfold, from nine percent in 1950 to 71 percent in 1996.

The rate of teen (15-19 years) deaths by accident, homicide and suicide rose between 1985 and 1995 from 63 to 65 per 100,000. (Kids Count, 1998)

The juvenile violent crime arrest rate (ages 10-17) rose from 305 to 507 per 100,000 between 1985 and 1995. (Kids Count, 1998)

The teen birth rate (per 1,000 females ages 15-17) rose from 31 to 36 between 1985 and 1995. (Kids Count, 1998)

The percentage of families with children headed by a single parent rose from 22 to 26 between 1985 and 1995. (Kids Count, 1998) Black children are three times as likely as whites to live in a single-parent family.

BETTER (AND MIXED) NEWS*

The percentage of Americans age 16 or over who completed a high school diploma or GED rose from 28.3 percent in 1990 to 31.4 percent in 1997, while those earning a bachelor's degree or higher rose from 17.4 to 20.7 percent.

The nation's annual dropout rate for youth age 16 or over fell from 9.5 percent in 1985 to six percent in 1991, then rose again to 7.3 percent in 1996. The Forgotten Half (those adults with 12 grades of schooling or less) fell from 51.2 percent in 1990 to 48.2 percent in 1997. The "dropout pool" — 18-24 year-olds who did not graduate from high school and who are not currently enrolled in school — still exceeds 3.1 million, or one of every eight persons in this age group.

Among 16-24 year-olds, those beginning a postsecondary education program leading to a degree rose from 35.5 percent in 1983 to 47.4 percent in 1996, a one-third increase in only 13 years. The high school graduating class of 1996 enrolled in two- and four-year colleges at a record 67 percent.

However, among 25-29 year-olds, graduation rates varied widely: half of all Asians had earned a bachelor's degree, one in three whites, one in seven blacks, and only one in ten Latinos. Overall, only 32 percent of this age group had earned a bachelor's or higher degree.

Parents' educational levels rose sharply from 1970 to 1990: The percentage of fathers with less than a high school education declined from 43 to 19; mothers with less than a 12th grade education fell from 38 to 17 percent. Fathers with a bachelor's degree or higher rose from 13 to 23 percent. (Condition of Education 1997)

African American students today are almost as likely to earn a high school diploma as are white students. The percentage of blacks ages 25-29 who completed high school rose from 58.8 percent in 1971 to 86 percent in 1996. But only 42.5 percent of graduates earned an educational credential beyond high school within ten years of their graduation, compared with 52.7 percent of whites. (Nettles, 1997)

Annual earnings for African Americans who earned associate's, bachelor's and advanced degrees were comparable to whites, but those with only a high school diploma earned less than their white counterparts.

* Unless otherwise indicated, these data derive from tabulations of the Center for Labor Market Studies, Northeastern University. See Sources at the end of Chapter One.

The Forgotten Half *Revisited*   Chapter One

WHO ARE THE FORGOTTEN HALF TODAY? THE CHANGING PROFILE OF AMERICA'S YOUTH AND YOUNG ADULTS

This chapter reviews a variety of statistical sources describing the condition of young Americans, age 16 and older. Although many youth experience difficulties in the labor market well into their late twenties, we focus first on 18-24 year-olds and, more particularly, on *The Forgotten Half, those approximately ten million young people who neither complete high school nor continue their formal education beyond high school graduation.*

Upon reflection, the reader of this re-analysis and update will note that *those young people who have earned only a high school diploma, and even those who have completed some college but have no degree past high school — 20 percent of the workforce — are experiencing serious difficulties in the labor market and in providing a decent quality of life for themselves and their families.*

Between 1988 and 1997, the number of 18-24 year-old civilians fell 3.8 percent, from 25.8 to 24.8 million. As Americans generally increased their rate and longevity of school attendance, the number who could be termed part of The Forgotten Half fell even more sharply: from 12.4 million in 1988 to 9.7 million in 1997, a decline of 22 percent. Thus, today's Forgotten Half is comprised of about 40 percent of the nation's young, noninstitutionalized civilian population. Adding members of the armed forces and inmates of jails and prisons would probably raise the total proportion to 42 percent of all 18-24 year-olds.

As Figure 1-22 (at the end of this chapter) shows, the sharp decline in the size of The Forgotten Half over the past decade is due entirely to declines in the number of whites and non-Hispanic/Latino blacks. By contrast, Hispanics, Asians and American Indians in The Forgotten Half rose sharply to the point that Hispanics now outnumber African Americans.

Statistics on educational attainment — i.e., years of formal schooling completed — are a universally-accepted proxy for the economic and

---

Still Losing Ground

American Educational Attainment Continues to Climb

Figure 1-1: Highest Level of Educational Attainment of the Adult Population (Age 16 and Over), March/April 1990 and March 1997

(numbers in percent)

	1990	1997	Change
Total	100	100	
Still a Student	9.0	8.8	-0.2
8th Grade or Less	9.1	6.9	-2.2
9th-12th Grade, No Diploma	13.8	9.9	-3.9
High School Diploma or GED	28.3	31.4	3.2
Some College, No Degree	16.9	15.7	-1.2
Associate's Degree	5.5	6.4	1.0
Bachelor's Degree	11.4	14.1	2.7
Master's Degree	3.9	4.5	0.6
Professional Degree	1.5	1.2	-0.2
Doctoral Degree	0.6	0.9	0.2

SOURCE: 1990 Census Public Use Microdata Files and March 1997 Current Population Survey; tabulations by Center for Labor Market Studies at Northeastern University (hereafter CLMS).

---

* About ten percent of 18-24 year-olds earn the GED, up five percentage points from 1993. However, youth earning regular high school diplomas declined by an almost identical five percentage points.

social health of a nation. Looking in Figure 1-1 at the educational breakdown of Americans age 16 or over from 1990 to 1997, we note significant increases in the percentage of the population earning a high school diploma or GED (General Educational Development certificate) and of those earning bachelor's, master's and doctor's degrees, accompanied by a substantial decline in "dropouts," that is, those without a high school credential of any type. That is certainly good news.

Adjusting the educational data for age subgroups, Figure 1-2 also shows definite if slow progress in raising overall educational attainment. Rising participation rates in postsecondary education are particularly striking (as discussed in Chapter Six, below.) Young Americans and their parents are far better educated (some would rather say "credentialed") than earlier generations.

Improvement in American educational attainment is a long-term and rather remarkable trend. From 1971 to 1997, the percentage of 25-29 year-olds who had completed high school rose from 77.7 to 87.4 percent; those who had attended "some college" rose from 43.6 to 57.1 percent; and those who had completed four or more years of college rose from 22 to 32 percent.

During the years emphasized in this report, 1989 to 1996, high school graduation rates rose 1.8 percentage points; the one-or-more-years-of-college rate rose 13.4 percentage points; and the four-year college completion rate rose 3.8 percentage points. The high school graduation rates of blacks rose from 82.8 percent in 1989 to over 86 percent in 1997; their "some college" rate rose from 42.1 to 55.9 percent; and their college graduation rates rose from 15.4 to 17 percent. Latinos or Hispanics, on the other hand, made scant progress: their high school graduation rate rose from 61 to only 61.1 percent; the "some college" rate rose from 44.3 to 50.9 percent; while their college graduation rate actually fell slightly, from 16.5 to 16.4 percent.

Equally striking, however, is the revelation that our population as a whole is not as educationally well credentialed as many Americans assume. Excluding young adults under age 25 who are still in school, *almost half of all adults (48.2 percent) either did not complete high school or terminated their formal education after graduation.* Fewer than 15 percent earned only a bachelor's degree, while 6.6 percent received a degree beyond it. Obviously, then, the widely-encountered stereotype

Figure 1-2: Highest Level of Educational Attainment of the Adult Population (Ages 16 to 44), by Age Subgroup, March 1997

(numbers in percent)

	All Ages	16-24	25-34	35-44
Total	100	100	100	100
Still a Student	8.8	54.9	—	—
8th Grade or Less	6.9	2.5	3.7	4.0
9th-12th Grade, No Diploma	9.9	9.2	8.9	8.0
High School Diploma or GED	31.4	19.6	31.6	34.5
Some College, No Degree	15.7	8.0	19.8	18.9
Associate's Degree	6.4	1.8	8.8	8.9
Bachelor's Degree	14.1	3.8	21.2	17.9
Master's Degree	4.5	0.1	4.1	5.5
Professional Degree	1.2	0.0	1.2	1.6
Doctoral Degree	0.9	0.0	0.7	0.8

SOURCE: CLMS from March 1997 Current Population Survey.

Figure 1-3: Highest Level of Educational Attainment of 25-34 Year-Olds, March/April 1990 and March 1997

(numbers in percent)

Category	1990	1997
8th Grade or Less	3.9	3.7
9th-12th, no diploma	12.0	8.9
High School Diploma or GED	30.7	31.6
Some College, no degree	22.4	19.8
Associate's	8.4	8.8
Bachelor's	17.2	21.2
Master's	3.5	4.1
Professional	1.6	1.2
Doctorate	0.3	0.7

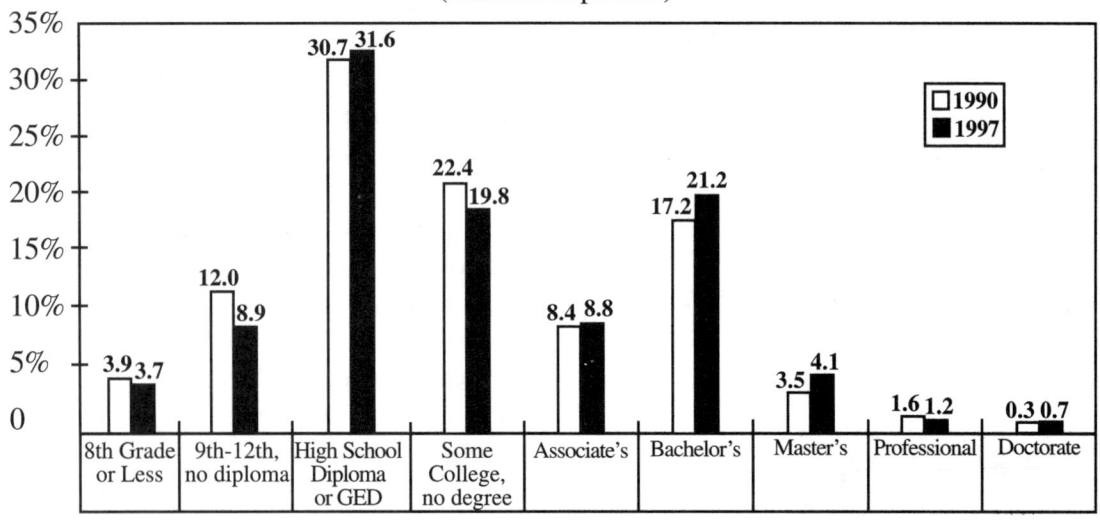

SOURCE: CLMS from 1990 Census of Population and Housing and March 1997 Current Population Survey.

Figure 1-4: Comparisons of Selected Aspects of the Educational Attainment of 25-34 Year-Olds in 1990 and 1997

(numbers in percent)

Educational Attainment	1990	1997	Change
No High School Diploma or GED	15.9	12.6	- 3.3
"Forgotten Half" (12 or fewer years)	46.6	44.2	- 2.4
One or More Years Postsecondary Education	53.4	55.8	+2.4
Bachelor's Degree or Higher	22.6	27.2	+4.6

SOURCE: CLMS from 1990 Census of Population and Housing Public Use Microdata Files and March 1997 Current Population Survey.

---

that "everybody in America goes to college" is hardly accurate. While more Americans than ever — and a rising proportion of new high school graduates — do pursue some postsecondary education, less than 24 percent of adults age 25 or older (and 32 percent of high school graduates ages 25-29) have earned a bachelor's or higher degree.

Educational attainment varies by gender, race and ethnicity. Among the population ages 25-29 in 1997, women completed high school at 3.1 percentage points greater than men (88.9 versus 85.8 percent). They also earned bachelor's degrees at three percentage points higher than men (29.3 versus 26.3 percent). In the same age group, black and white high school graduation rates have about equalized (86.2 versus 87.6 percent, respectively). The Hispanic high school graduation rate lagged further behind, at 61.8 percent.

With regard to bachelor's or higher degrees, however, wide gaps in attainment remain for those age 25 and over: whites 24.6 percent, blacks 13.3 percent, and most notably, Asians and Pacific Islanders 42.2. One-half of 25-29 year-old Asians had earned a bachelor's degree compared with one in three whites, about one in seven blacks and only one in ten Latinos.

Despite scattered gains, educational attainment in the United States continues to be heavily influenced by family income. As Paul Barton of the Educational Testing Service has documented, high school graduation rates of students in the lowest income quartile (67 percent) are more than 25 percent lower than the graduation rates of students in the highest quartile (94 percent). Thirty-four percent of high school graduates from low-income families went directly to college in the next school year versus 83.4 percent of those from high-income families. Similarly, despite the availability of many federal, state, local and private higher education financial assistance programs, a student from the top family income quartile is far more likely to earn a postsecondary education degree than a student from the bottom income quartile. (See discussion in Chapter Six.)

The nation's challenges for the next decade are to remove this family income bias, to further raise educational attainment, and to increase the academic achievement of all students, especially in literacy and numeracy. No less a challenge is converting that enhanced achievement into higher productivity for the economy and substantially higher earnings for American workers who possess the requisite skills and personal attributes.

These several challenges are the focus of Chapters Five to Seven. Sadly, as we shall document, young people's collective increase in years of formal educational study has not been universally rewarded with higher earnings. In fact, according to the research of Larry Mishel of the Economic Policy Institute, *even young men and women with a baccalaureate degree and one to five years of work experience earned, in real terms, seven percent less in 1997 than in 1989.*

THE COMING YOUTH POPULATION BOOM

Between 1981 and 1995, the number of young American adults, ages 18-24, declined sharply, from 30.2 to 24.9 million, a fall of almost 18 percent. However, beginning in 1996 that trend of declining numbers began to reverse. The Center for Labor Market Studies foresees the number of 18-24 year-olds rising from 24.7 million in 1996 to 27.1 million in 2000 and 29.1 million in 2005. (To add perspective, in November 1998, 18-24 year-olds will constitute one-eighth of the United States' voting-age population.) According to the U.S. Census Bureau's "middle level projection series," this age cohort should increase by 21 percent from 1995 to 2010. (In fact, given higher-than-projected immigration, both legal and illegal, that projection may well be understated. About six percent of the nation's 18-24 year-olds have entered the U.S. since 1990 and perhaps one-quarter of these new immigrants have serious educational deficits.)

Given the vexing interrelated problems of the nation's many dysfunctional high schools and juvenile and adolescent crime, the increase in numbers of high school students (ages 16+), reflecting the aging of the mini-baby boom generation (those born between 1975 and 1989), is also worthy of attention. In 1990, there were 6.38 million high school students age 16 and older. By 1997, there were 7.94 million, an increase of over 20 percent. (Perhaps 200,000 of this increase can be attributed to the Census Bureau's recognition in 1994 that it had underestimated foreign immigration in the 1990 Census.)

This substantial impending growth of young adults has many implications, some of which this report will explore. With a growth rate of 21 percent, compared with a non-elderly population expansion of only 15 percent, inescapable questions arise: Will the American labor market be able to absorb the young adults entering the pipeline? Will they have the skills to function effectively in the new economy? Will they earn enough to support a decent standard of living for themselves, their families and their children?

Also, as has become increasingly clear, the growing young adult population will be substantially different from its predecessors in a number of key respects. People of color will comprise a much larger fraction of the workforce. The "white majority," which in 1995 comprised 68 percent of all young adults, will decline in 2010 to 62.6 percent or less. Over this same 15-year period, the number of African American young adults is projected to increase 23 percent, Asians and American Indians 56 percent, Hispanics 57 percent and white, non-Hispanics only 11 percent.

America's pronounced racial, linguistic and ethnic diversity will only increase. The implications of this fact for the workforce, for social harmony and for national cohesion will challenge the best minds and talents of our times, as they already are doing on issues of immigration, affirmative action and bilingual education.

A MORE PAINFUL TRANSITION TO THE LABOR MARKET

In 1997, about nine percent of 16-19 year-olds were neither enrolled in school nor working, down from 11 percent in 1985. Fourteen percent of all these so-called "detached youth" were black or Hispanic and eight percent were white. Black "detached youth" had declined from 18 percent in 1985 to 14 percent in 1997.

Annette Bernhardt and her colleagues studied two cohorts of young *white* men, the first from 1966-1981, the more recent from 1979-1994. According to their principal findings, based on National Longitudinal Surveys:
(1) the transition to permanent employment is taking longer; (2) young workers who do not go on to college, especially high school dropouts, are more likely to experience periods of unemployment and to rely on part-time jobs for a greater number of years; (3) those attending college are more likely to work while enrolled and to draw out their studies. Further, 30 year-olds who were employed for two or more years in a full-time, year-round job constituted 63 percent of the earlier cohort versus only 56 percent of the more recent cohort. Young male workers were less likely to make a single transition to the labor market than to move back and forth between work, unemployment and formal enrollment in education. Job instability increased markedly during the 1980s and 1990s; youth worked for more employers and had shorter tenures with one employer.* Compared to the past, young workers in recent years also experienced significantly lower permanent wage growth. "It is not so much that more educated workers are doing better, but that less educated workers are doing worse." Bernhardt et al conclude:

A new generation is entering a transformed labor market, and especially for those without a college degree, the prospects for a living wage, stable employment, and upward mobility are not at all guaranteed. Our evidence suggests that entry into the workforce and career development have become more volatile processes, and in particular, job instability has increased. Partly as a consequence, long-term wage growth during these key years has been hit on two fronts — it has stagnated and become more unequal. To the extent that wage growth represents upward mobility, it is clear that the prospects for such mobility have deteriorated in recent years. Those without a four-year college degree have clearly gotten hit the hardest, and this represents the majority of workers. But workers higher up the skill and education ladder have also experienced growing inequality and job instability within their ranks...Absent a dramatic shift in the American economy, the net result is that the recent cohort can expect lower and more unequal lifetime wage growth than their predecessors.

As we shall see, what Bernhardt and her colleagues found for white young adults applies with far greater force for young workers of color.

More Education = More Employment

Figure 1-5: Employment and Unemployment Rates of 16-24 Year-Old Youth by Highest Level of Educational Attainment, 1997
(numbers in percent)

Education Level	Unemployed	Employed part-time	Employed full-time
High School Dropout	50.5	14.6	34.9
High School Graduate	25.7	14.3	60.0
1s Postsecondary Education	17.1	15.7	67.2
4 or More Years of College	9.2	8.5	82.3

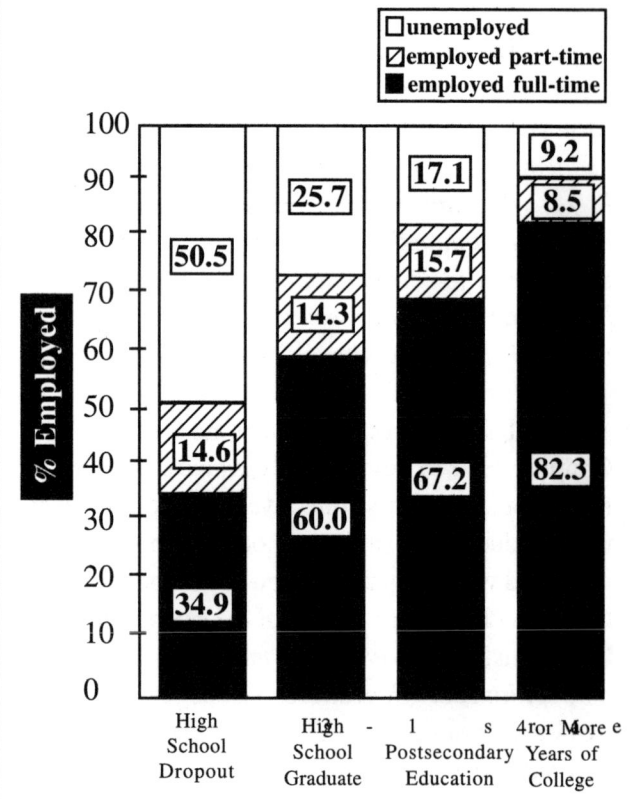

SOURCE: CLMS based on monthly Current Population Surveys, 1997.

---

* A 1998 Bureau of Labor Statistics survey of almost ten thousand persons found that a typical worker holds 8.6 different jobs between ages 18 and 32.

JOBS FOR OUT-OF-SCHOOL YOUTH

Among the most persistent problems in the American economy for many years have been the high youth unemployment rates and relatively low rates of full-time work by America's out-of-school 16-24 year-olds. In 1996, for example, the official national unemployment rate was 5.4 percent. In 1997, it had fallen to 4.9 percent and in August 1998 to 4.5 percent. In sharp contrast, the 1997 unemployment rate for males ages 16-24 was 11.8 percent and 10.7 percent for females. In May 1998, their unemployment rates were, respectively, 11.0 and 9.0 percent.

Age is a significant variable, of course. While the overall unemployment rate in 1997 for 16-24 year-olds was 11.8 percent, 16-17 year-old males were unemployed at a rate of 19.1 percent; 20-24 year-old males at less than half that rate, 8.9 percent. Females' unemployment rates, 10.7 overall, ranged from 17.2 percent for 16-17 year-olds to 8.1 percent for 20-24 year-olds.

In 1989, a year after publication of *TFH*, 72.1 percent of 16-24 year-olds, on average, were employed full- or part-time. In 1997, in the midst of a strong and growing economy, the employment rate was actually lower: 71.1 percent. In the eight intervening years, this rate, as measured by the monthly Current Population Surveys, had dipped as low as 68 percent. Of those fortunate enough to find *full-time* work (35 or more hours a week), 59.4 percent of all out-of-school youth were employed full-time in 1989, but only 56.3 percent in 1997 — three percentage points below the 1989 rate.

Once again, full-time employment rates were highly correlated with educational attainment. High school dropouts were employed full-time over this period at rates as low as 30 percent and never higher than 36 percent. High school graduates, on the other hand, had full-time jobs at rates almost twice as high: from 58 to 64 percent. Including both full- *and* part-time work, the correlation between reported legal employment and educational attainment is starkly depicted in Figure 1-5.

The 1997 full-time employment rates were also highly correlated with educational attainment, with rates of 34.9, 60.0, 67.2 and 82.3 percent for high school dropouts, high school graduates, those with 1-3 years of college, and four-year college graduates, respectively. These may be compared with the 1989 rates of 36.5, 64, 71.4 and 82.9 percent. The key point, once again, is that not only was there no improvement in full-time employment rates of out-of-school youth between 1989 and 1997 but, *despite generally rising educational attainment and a very strong economy, the full-time employment record for young people was actually somewhat worse in 1997 than in 1989.* For The Forgotten Half, those with only a high school diploma or less, there has been no progress in their employment fortunes.

Two fundamental facts are most striking: (1) even *in an economy so often characterized by "boom," only 60 percent of young persons with only high school equivalency held full-time work in 1997, and (2) even that number was lower than the 64 percent of 1989 and 1990.*

Predictably, these labor force surveys demonstrate that it is most minorities who consistently experience substantially lower employment than whites. In 1997, the employment rate of young white youth (full- and part-time) averaged 74.7 percent, 59.3 percent for those employed full-time. Rates for Hispanic youth were 64.6 percent overall and 53.4 percent full-time. Black youth, by contrast, had an overall employment rate of 54.8 percent and a full-time employment rate of only 42.1 percent.

But these correlations between employment rates, race and ethnicity are powerfully ameliorated by educational progress. Figure 1-6 displays the dramatic effects that additional years of schooling have on the employment experiences of black, white and Hispanic young people.

At the same time, Figure 1-6 demonstrates that race, and not just education, still matters in the workplace. The difference in employment rates between white high school graduates and white four-year college graduates, for example, is roughly 14 percentage points, while the difference between black and white high school graduates is larger: 17 percent. And blacks with 1-3 years of postsecondary education are employed at a lower rate than white high school graduates and 11.4 percentage points lower than their white educational counterparts.

LABOR MARKET PROBLEMS OF OUT-OF-SCHOOL YOUTH

Professor Andrew Sum and his colleagues at Northeastern University's Center for Labor

Education and Race Both Matter

Figure 1-6: Employment Rates of 16-24 Year-Old Out-of-School Youth in Selected Race and Schooling Categories, 1996

(numbers in percent)

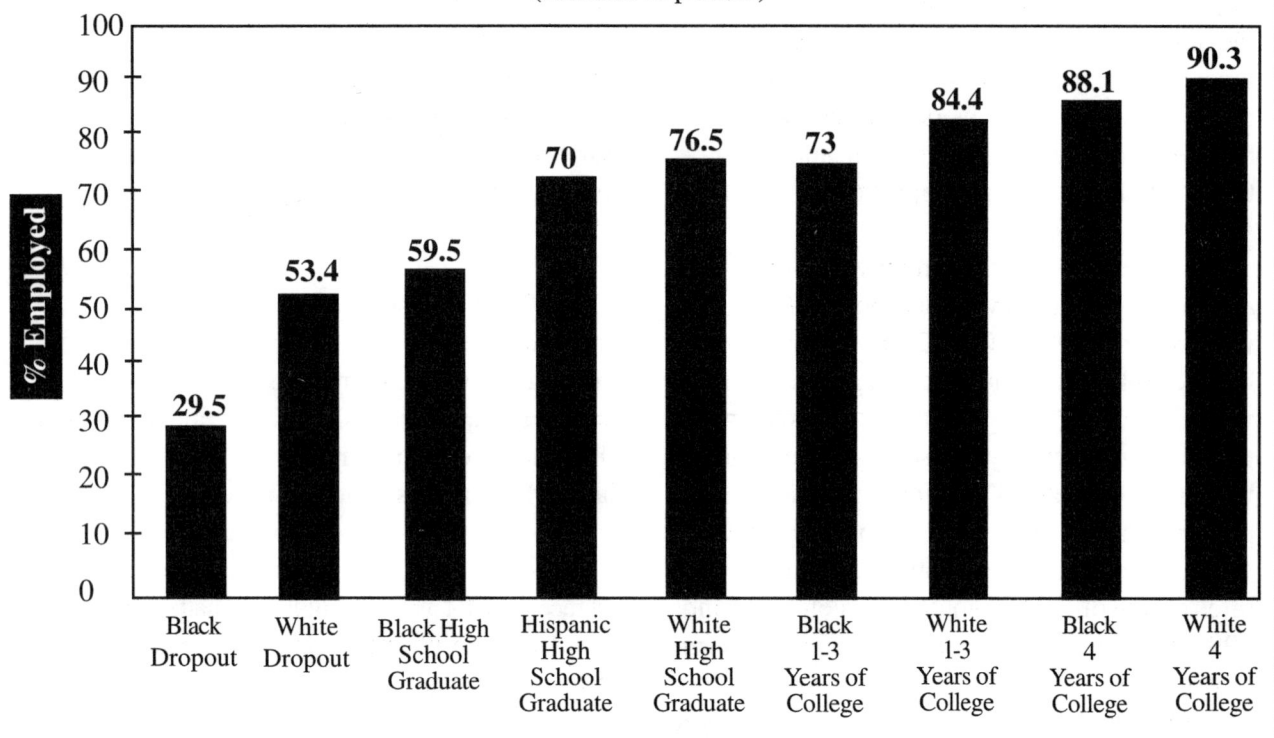

Category	% Employed
Black Dropout	29.5
White Dropout	53.4
Black High School Graduate	59.5
Hispanic High School Graduate	70
White High School Graduate	76.5
Black 1-3 Years of College	73
White 1-3 Years of College	84.4
Black 4 Years of College	88.1
White 4 Years of College	90.3

SOURCE: CLMS based on monthly Current Population Surveys, 1996.

Market Studies (CLMS) have spotlighted the labor market problems of the nation's 17-24 year-olds who are not currently enrolled in a formal educational program. Their research tells much about three salient issues: (1) how these young people are faring in the labor market today compared with similar age cohorts in 1989, (2) how the widely-heralded economic boom of the mid-to-late 1990s affected them and (3) the educational characteristics that seem to influence young people's labor market problems.

CLMS analyses depict four types of mutually exclusive labor market problems:

(1) unemployment. (This follows the official Bureau of Labor Statistics' definition, i.e., persons not working but actively looking for a job or awaiting recall from a temporary layoff.)

(2) employed part-time (less than 35 hours a week) for economic reasons, such as inability to find a full-time job. Typical part-time work is 20-21 hours a week.

(3) not working and not actively looking for work but reportedly wanting to be employed now.

(4) working full-time but unable to earn an annual income above the four-person family poverty line. In March 1997, this meant earnings of about $7.72 per hour, $309 per week, or $16,068 annually.

As Figures 1-7 through 1-9 show, despite some recent modest improvements, probably traceable to the relatively strong economy, the stark reality is that, in March 1997, 21 of every 100 out-of-school youth, ages 17-24, were either unemployed, underemployed or not actively seeking work even though they wanted a job (Figure 1-7). More striking yet, *26 of every 100 out-of-school youth, although working full-time, were earning less than the poverty line income standard for a four-person family.*

As we have come to understand in the latter decades of this century, earning and learning are highly correlated. Thus, it is no surprise that those with the least formal education suffer the most in the labor market. In March 1997, 58 of every 100 school dropouts experienced one of the four labor market problems cited above, as did 46 percent of high school graduates but only 19 percent of four-year college graduates. Surprisingly, however, young people with 13-15 years of schooling, but no bachelor's degree, actually fared worse in the labor market than those completing 12 years of study (Figure 1-8).

Summarizing the three figures, CLMS researchers concluded that, as a consequence of their low rates of full-time employment and weekly earnings, only 11 percent of young high school dropouts in March 1997 were employed full-time and earning $309 or more per week, contrasted with 26 percent of high school graduates and 57 percent of four-year college graduates (Figure 1-9).

Thus, between 1989 and 1997, the least educated members of The Forgotten Half not only failed more frequently to find jobs that would support families above the poverty line but, in fact, were less likely to be employed in such jobs in 1997 than they were at the end of the 1980s.

As Boesel, Alsalam and Smith conclude from their careful study of the labor market and GED recipients:

> *Neither the high school diploma nor "some college" have been sufficient to enable young adults to maintain earnings over the years since the 1970s. It seems unlikely that, in the absence of other macroeconomic changes, education policy alone can reverse this trend.*

Boom or No Boom, It's Still a Tough Job Market for Young People

Figure 1-7: Incidence of Various Labor Market Problems Among Out-of-School 16-24 Year-Olds, March 1989 to March 1997

(Numbers in Percent. N=14.55 million youth)

Labor Market Problem	March 1989	March 1991	March 1995	March 1997
Unemployed	9.0	11.1	10.0	10.1
Employed Part-Time for Economic Reasons	6.1	8.2	7.2	6.3
Not in Labor Force But Want a Job Now	5.2	5.2	4.9	4.8
Worked Full-Time at a Weekly Wage Below the Four-Person Poverty Line	23.6	27.0	26.6	26.2
Any of the Above Problems	43.9	51.5	48.7	47.4

SOURCE: CLMS tabulations from March Current Population Surveys, 1989, 1991, 1997.

Figure 1-8: Percentage of 17-24 Year-Old, Out-of-School Youth Experiencing Various Labor Market Problems, by Years of Schooling Completed, March 1997

(N=14.55 million youth)

Labor Market Problem	Less Than 12 Years[1]	12 Years[2]	13-15 Years	16 or More Years
Unemployed	15.3	9.6	7.8	3.2
Employed Part-Time for Economic Reasons	6.9	6.5	6.1	4.5
Not in Labor Force But Want a Job Now	8.2	4.1	3.6	1.0
Worked Full-Time at a Weekly Wage Below the Four-Person Poverty Line	27.9	25.7	31.7	10.3
Any of the Above Problems	58.3	45.9	49.2[3]	19.0

SOURCE: CLMS from March 1997 Current Population Survey.
NOTES:
[1] This group includes persons with 12 years of schooling completed but no high school diploma or GED.
[2] This group includes GED recipients and persons with a regular high school diploma.
[3] Note that persons with 1-3 years of college experienced more labor market problems than high school graduates.

Figure 1-9: Percentage of Out-of-School 17-24 Year-Old Civilians Working Full-Time and Earning Weekly Wages Above the Four-Person Poverty Line, by Educational Attainment, March 1997

(numbers in percent)

Educational Attainment	Employed Full-Time in a Wage and Salary Job	% of Full-Time Earning $309+ Per Week	Employed Full-Time and Earning $309+ Per Week
All	**54.4**	**51.8**	**28.2**
Less Than 12 Years or 12 Years But No Diploma	38.9	28.1	10.9
12 Years With High School Diploma or GED	52.0	50.5	26.3
13-15 Years	71.7	55.7	39.9
16 or More Years	67.4	84.7	57.1

SOURCE: CLMS from March 1997 Current Population Survey.

EARNINGS: THE DISMAL DECLINE CONTINUES — "IT'S *(STILL)* THE ECONOMY, STUPID!"

It is now widely understood — if nonetheless ignored in most contemporary political discourse — that median family income in the United States has stagnated since 1973. While the top 40 percent of families enjoyed rising incomes, and the top five percent reaped immense and unprecedented rewards, the bottom 40 percent experienced declining, sometimes sharply declining, real income.

According to the U.S. Census Bureau, in 1973 the top 20 percent of the nation's households received 43.6 percent of total household income. By 1993, their share had increased to 48.2 percent. The richest five percent saw their income rise from 16.6 percent in 1973 to 20 percent in 1993. The middle three-fifths of America's families received 48.2 percent of total household income, squeezed down from 52.2 percent two decades earlier. And the poorest quintile saw their small share fall even further, from 4.2 to 3.6 percent.

Commenting on this changing distribution of income, John Cassidy questioned the validity of the notion that we Americans are, in fact, a predominantly "middle class" nation:

> ...the country has now split into four groups. At the top, there is an immensely wealthy elite, which has never had it so good. At the bottom, there is an underclass, which is increasingly divorced from the rest of society. And between these extremes

there are, instead of a unified middle class, two distinct groups: an upper echelon of highly skilled, highly educated professionals, who are doing pretty well; and a vast swath of unskilled and semiskilled workers, who are experiencing falling wages, stagnant or declining living standards, and increased economic uncertainty. To label this group "middle class" doesn't make sense. The phrase implies two things — rising living standards and a high degree of economic security — that no longer apply.

In this bifurcating economic environment, with increasing disparities of income, how have America's youth and young families fared?

- In 1989, a year after publication of *TFH,* the median real weekly earnings of young men under age 25 and employed full-time were $351 a week. This represented a drop of fully 24 percent from the 1973 level of $463. However, by the second quarter of 1998, real weekly wages of young male workers had declined even further, to $335. To be sure, the strong U.S. labor market in the first half of 1998 did push up real weekly wages to the highest levels of the 1990s. The Bureau of Labor Statistics reported that the median full-time weekly wages of young men rose nearly six percent in the first half of 1998. Subtracting 1.7 percent inflation from June 1997 to June 1998, young male workers had real weekly wage gains of four percent — the best performance in over 20 years. These are impressive results, but *the bottom line is that inflation-adjusted earnings were still almost one-third below what their counterparts were earning 24 years — a full generation — earlier.*
- The picture for young women was only slightly less gloomy. Their weekly earnings fell from $350 in 1973 to $305 in 1998.
- Although the wage gap between young men and young women has narrowed in the past quarter century, *both* genders suffered sharp wage losses. In 1973, young women employed full-time earned only 75 percent as much as young men. By 1997, that ratio had risen to 92 percent, but progress in closing the gender wage gap was illusory, mostly because of the persistent and sharp decline in the wages of young men, less due to improvement in women's wages.

Marital status is closely correlated with the incidence of poverty. Some scholars believe that falling real wages lead to falling marriage rates, as well as increased crime and the reduced ability of young unwed fathers to pay child support. Other scholars recognize the correlation but differ on the issue of causation.

Robert Lerman of American University and The Urban Institute, for example, argues that declines in marriage rates between 1971 and 1989 *preceded* reductions in earnings: the "trend away from marriage accounted for nearly half the increase in income inequality and more than the entire rise in child poverty rates." He continues:

> *...between 1971 and 1989, the proportion of children living in the husband-wife families fell from 91 percent to 83 percent among whites and from about 61 percent to 40 percent among blacks. Had the marriage rates of mothers remained at the 1971 levels, poverty rates among black children would have declined from 41 percent in 1971 to about 30 percent in 1989, instead of rising to 43 percent. Nearly one-third of poor black children would have escaped poverty. For white children, poverty would have fallen from the observed twelve percent to ten percent. Thus, changes in marriage rates prevented the racial gap from narrowing sharply.*

Regardless of which came first, declining earnings and marriage rates, coupled with increasing child poverty and one-parent families, all accelerated sharply in the past quarter century. Between 1970 and 1996, the proportion of children under age 18 who were living with two parents declined from 85 to 68 percent. The percentage of children in one-parent families jumped from 12 to 28 percent, while the married proportion of 25-29 year-old men fell from 81 to 53 percent. Also, in the same time period, the proportion of 18-24 year-olds maintaining a family household fell by almost half, from 38 to 20 percent. Overall, in 1970, 10.5 percent of women and 19.1 percent of men ages 25-29 had never been married; by 1996 those percentages had soared to 37.6 and 52 percent, respectively. The dramatic decline of real earnings for both genders is illustrated in Figure 1-10.

The Gender Gap Narrows As Both Men and Women Lose Earnings

Figure 1-10: Median Real Weekly Earnings of Full-Time Employed Young Adults Under Age 25 by Gender, 1973-97

(in inflation-adjusted 1997 dollars)

Year	Men	Women	Ratio of Women to Men
1973	$463	$350	75.6%
1979	$424	$334	78.8%
1989	$351	$318	90.6%
1991	$336	$314	93.4%
1995	$319	$290	90.9%
1996	$314	$290	92.3%
1997	$317	$292	92.1%
% Change 1973-89	-24.2%	-9.2%	
% Change 1989-97	-9.7%	-8.2%	
% Change 1973-97	-31.5%	-16.5%	

SOURCE: CLMS from U.S. Bureau of Labor Statistics weekly earnings data from CPS household surveys.

- Another way to describe the declining economic fortunes of young men is to compare the median weekly earnings of full-time workers under age 25 with those of men over age 25. In 1967, the under-25s earned 74 percent as much as older men. That ratio dropped to 67 percent in 1973, 54 percent in the 1982-91 period, and only 51.5 percent in 1997.
- Young employed women also experienced the same relative deterioration in comparison to older full-time female workers. In 1967, their earnings ratio was 93.7 percent; in 1973, 85.1 percent; in 1989, 72 percent; in 1996, 64 percent, and to a low in 1997 of 63.2 percent — less than two-thirds of what older women workers earned.
- *For both genders, then, both the absolute and relative earnings of full-time employed young adults are at 25-year lows. Despite the vaunted American "economic miracle" of the late 1990s, things have only gotten worse, not better, for many of the young people chronicled in TFH in 1988.*

HOW YOUNG FAMILIES MANAGED — OR DIDN'T

TFH reports of 1988 provided important facts about older adolescents as well as young families and their children. Young families were defined as "primary" families headed by a person under the age of 30, that is, families consisting of two or more persons related by blood, marriage or adoption living in an independent household (but not the households of others).

Three basic indicators of the well-being of such young primary families are examined here, although this brief treatment cannot do justice to the many varieties of families that exist in the United States today and their varying economic conditions:

(1) Median real (inflation-adjusted) annual incomes of young families
(2) Poverty rates of young families
(3) Poverty rates of children in young families

Median Annual Incomes (in 1996 dollars)

In 1989, the real median annual income of young families with a household head under age 30 was $30,435. Over the next three years, however, these families lost 12 percent of their incomes during the recessionary environment of the early 1990s. By 1996, that median income had recouped somewhat, to $28,500, but still remained 6.4 percent lower than seven years earlier. Leaving aside technical questions about the adequacy of the Consumer Price Index for All Urban Consumers (the CPI-U) which is used to adjust nominal incomes for inflation, the conclusion is that, *from 1973 to 1996, the average young family household suffered an inflation-adjusted income loss of over 14 percent.*

The 14 percent loss greatly understates the economic pain experienced by certain categories of America's young families. Over this same 24-year period, young families headed by a non-Hispanic black lost 33.2 percent of their income; those headed by Hispanics lost 18.2 percent; and those headed by high school dropouts lost 33.6 percent. *Even those young families headed by high school graduates experienced a real loss in purchasing power of 22 percent.*

As *TFH* reported in 1988, only four-year college graduates and their families did well over the years. Their real income gain from 1973 to 1996 was 17.3 percent. In 1996, young families headed by a high school dropout earned about $15,000 annually, compared with $26,000 for those headed by a high school graduate and over $53,000 by a four-year college graduate. *In the 1990s, the wide income gaps correlated with formal educational attainment continued to widen, not narrow. Yet, young families of all educational levels, even four-year college graduates, earned less in real terms in 1996 than in 1989 (Figure 1-11).*

Poverty Rates of Young Families

- The percentage of Americans of all ages living in poverty rose from 12.8 to 13.7 percent between 1989 and 1996.
- By the end of the 1980s, the poverty rate among America's *young* families was 21 percent. During the recessionary and low growth years of 1990-92, that rate rose sharply, to 26 percent. In 1996, the young family poverty rate was 24 percent, still three percentage points higher than in 1989. *Despite the economic boom of the late 1990s, about one-quarter of America's*

Regardless of Education, Real Incomes of Young Families are Down

Figure 1-11: Median Real Income of Young Families by Highest Level of Educational Attainment, 1989 and 1996
(in constant 1996 dollars)

Education Level	1989	1996
Dropout	$16,449	$15,000
High School Graduate	$29,237	$25,940
Some College	$37,960	$32,054
College Graduate	$55,843	$53,200

SOURCE: CLMS tabulations from March 1990 and March 1997 CPS surveys. Note that those with 1-3 years of college suffered proportionately larger declines in real income than high school graduates.)

young families still live below the poverty line.

- As in the data on median annual incomes, poverty rates among young families vary greatly by family type and the presence of children. While the 1996 poverty rate among young, married couple families was only ten percent, among female-headed young families (including single women without children) it was 56 percent, and among single-parent families headed by women it was 62 percent.
- Poverty rates also vary enormously by the educational level of the family head. *In 1996, one-half of all young families headed by a high school dropout were poor, as were one-fourth of those headed by a high school graduate versus only one out of 40 families headed by a college graduate.*

Poverty Rates Among Children in Young Families

- Children under age 18 comprise about a quarter of the population but almost 40 percent of the total poor. The percentage of children in poverty has remained around 20 percent since 1981.
- In 1989, 35 percent of all children in young families were poor, nearly double the rate of 1973. Between 1989 and 1992, the poverty rate among these children rose sharply, from 35 to 42 percent. Since then, poverty rates have declined somewhat, but they still remained at 38 percent in 1996, three percentage points higher than in 1989.

Poverty: The Flip Side of Education

Figure 1-12: Poverty Rates of Young Families by Highest Level of Educational Attainment of Household Head, 1989 and 1996
(numbers in percent)

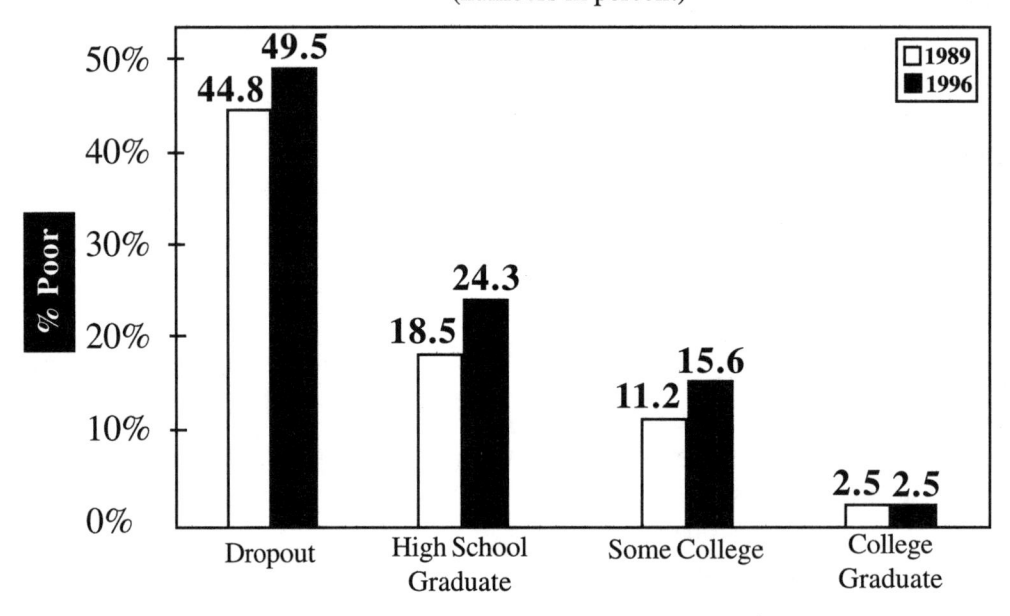

Education	1989	1996
Dropout	44.8	49.5
High School Graduate	18.5	24.3
Some College	11.2	15.6
College Graduate	2.5	2.5

SOURCE: CLMS tabulations from March 1990 and March 1997 CPS surveys.

- Children living in single-mother families are the most likely to be poor. During the period 1989-96, 70 percent or more of such children were poor. Marginal improvements in the poverty data for children in single-mother families have occurred since 1992 as more single mothers became employed and earned higher wages. Still, 59 percent of children under age six lived in below-poverty-level families in 1996.
- Poverty rates of children in young families are quite high among all racial and ethnic groups, but they are much higher among minority children. In 1996, according to the Federal Interagency Forum on Child and Family Statistics, ten percent of white children lived in poverty-level families, compared with 40 percent of black and Hispanic children.
- Poverty among children in 1996 varied widely by the educational attainment of the family head. Among families headed by a young adult lacking a high school diploma, 64 percent of the children were poor versus 34 percent for high school graduates and only

seven percent for four-year college graduates. *Except for children living in families headed by four-year college graduates, all poverty rates for children were higher in 1996 than they were in 1989.*

THE HOUSEHOLD LIVING ARRANGEMENTS OF YOUNG AMERICANS — or "WHY DON'T THEY EVER LEAVE HOME?"

As we have seen, young adults continue to experience substantial declines in their median real (inflation-adjusted) annual earnings. Compared with 1989, fewer young adults were able to support a family of four above the poverty line in 1996. Based on the U.S. Census Bureau's Current Population Survey, 32 percent of young adult men (ages 20-29) were living at home in 1974. By 1990, that percentage had risen to 40 percent and by 1997 to 41.5 percent. Among young African American and Hispanic men, the percentage of those still at home with parents or other relatives had risen to 50 percent or more.

As Carol Emig discusses at length in Chapter Three, changes in the composition of the American family in recent decades have been profound. The proportion of married adults over age 18 fell from 71.7 percent in 1970 to 60.3 percent in 1996. In 1996, 63 percent of white adults were married contrasted with only 42 percent of black adults, a sharp decrease from the 64 percent marriage rate of blacks in 1970. Divorced persons constituted the fastest growing segment of the population, quadrupling from 4.3 million in 1970 to 18.3 million in 1996 — ten percent of all adults. In the

More Young People Are Still Living At Home

Figure 1-13: Percent of 20-29 Year-Olds Living in the Homes of Parents or Other Relatives, by Race/Ethnic Origin and Highest Level of Educational Attainment, 1974, 1990 and 1997

(numbers in percent)

		MALES 1974	MALES 1990	MALES 1997	FEMALES 1974	FEMALES 1990	FEMALES 1997
	All	32.2	39.8	41.5	21.5	28.5	30.1
	White, non-Hispanic	30.9	37.0	37.3	20.0	26.3	28.1
	Black, non-Hispanic	44.2	53.4	51.6	31.5	35.3	34.8
	Hispanic	30.6	43.2	48.7	20.2	33.0	32.7
Years of Schooling	Student	69.4	73.6	73.5	73.4	67.0	63.2
Years of Schooling	Less than 12 Years	32.0	42.0	44.1	16.0	26.7	24.7
Years of Schooling	12 Years	28.6	38.7	41.1	17.2	24.5	26.5
Years of Schooling	13 to 15 Years	29.0	31.2	33.8	21.1	21.4	24.9
Years of Schooling	16 Years	19.1	22.5	22.3	14.6	18.2	18.2
Years of Schooling	17 or More Years	11.0	18.5	11.0	10.5	14.8	6.8

SOURCE: CLMS tabulations from March Current Population Surveys, 1974, 1990, 1997.

wake of these facts, the proportion of children under age 18 living with two parents fell from 85 to 68 percent between 1970 and 1996.

Once again, educational attainment, so strongly correlated with earning power, was directly related to young males' ability to leave home and form independent households. While 44 percent of those lacking a high school diploma lived at home in March 1997, only 22 percent of those holding a bachelor's degree and 11 percent of those with a master's or higher degree did so.

The patterns for young women are quite similar, although the percentages of women who live with their spouses or head their own households as single parents is greater than for men. In 1997, 30 percent of 20-29 year-old females still lived with parents or other relatives, an increase of almost nine percentage points since 1974. As with males, race, ethnicity and educational attainment were significant variables in determining young women's ability to form independent households.

OUT-OF-WEDLOCK BIRTHS: NEW NORM FOR TEENS?

Teen births and out-of-wedlock childbearing have a profound effect on the futures of America's young people. Babies born to teenagers are at greater risk of low birth weight, serious and long-term disability and infant death in the first year of life. Also, as reported by the Robin Hood Foundation and Child Trends,

Compared with children whose mothers were 20-21 when they were born, children whose mothers were 17 or younger when they were born tend to have lower cognitive scores and more difficulty in school; have poorer health yet receive less health care; have less stimulating and supportive home environments; have higher rates of incarceration; and have higher rates of adolescent childbearing.

Young women who give birth out-of-wedlock are most apt to remain single parents and to raise their children in poverty. Without a second breadwinner in the family, and because of their generally low educational attainment and limited paid work experience, these young women and their children are at high risk of continued poverty and dependency.

In 1988, when *TFH* was published, the overall birth rate of 15-24 year-old women, married and unmarried, was 88 births per 1,000 women. By 1995, that rate had fallen to 83 per 1,000. Nearly all of the decline occurred among 20-24 year-olds, while 18 and 19 year-olds experienced a three-point increase in their birth rate. From 1986 to 1991, the birthrate of 15-19 year-old women rose 24 percent, but from 1991 that rate declined 12 percentage points, from 62.1 births per 1,000 women to 54.7 in 1996. (This latest rate represents a remarkable decline from the historic high of 96.3 per 1,000 in 1957.) While the overall decline in childbearing was 4.4 births per 1,000 women, the declines among African American women and those of "other races" were particularly sharp at 17.7 and 15.8 births per 1,000, respectively. Only among Hispanic women was there an increase: 3.5 births per 1,000.

According to the National Center for Health Statistics' 1995 National Survey of Family Growth, the proportion of teenagers who are sexually experienced has stabilized, reversing the steady increases of the past two decades. Condom and other contraceptive use is up among both teen men and women.

Between 1989 and 1995, total U.S. births among young women declined by 7.5 percent, by 6.2 percent among white women and by 13.4 percent among black women. Black teenagers' birth rate fell 21 percent between 1991 and 1996 to the lowest rate ever recorded, 91.7 per 1,000. However, total births among Hispanic women soared by 27.4 percent so that, in 1995, nearly half of all births — 48 percent — occurred among minority women whose birth rates were more than double that of non-Hispanic whites. Overall, childbearing within marriage continued to decline sharply, from four million in 1960 to 2.7 million in 1996. The birth rate for all married women declined by almost half, from 157 to 84 per thousand.

Prior to 1980, most teenagers giving birth were married. Today, out-of-wedlock births are virtually the norm, with one of every three births in 1996 to an unmarried mother. Among teenage mothers under age 20, those who were unmarried quintupled, from 15 percent in 1960 to 76 percent in 1994. In the same time period, births to unmarried mothers ages 20-24 increased ninefold, from five to 45 percent. Overall, while the total number

Figure 1-14: Proportion of All Births Among Young Women, Ages 15-24, That Were Out-of-Wedlock, by Race and Ethnic Group, 1989 and 1995

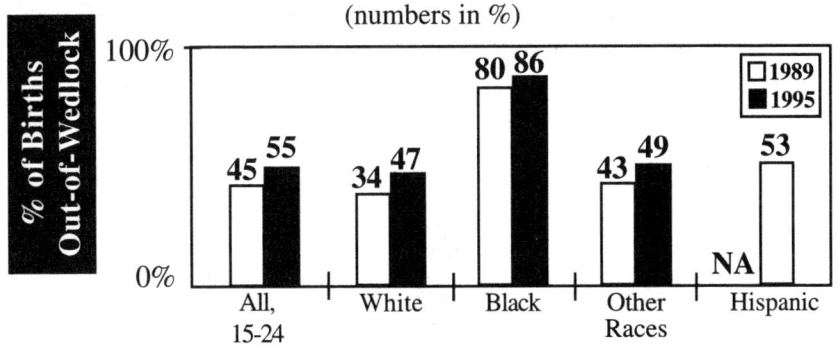

(numbers in %)

Group	1989	1995
All, 15-24	45	55
White	34	47
Black	80	86
Other Races	43	49
Hispanic	NA	53

SOURCE: National Center for Health Statistics. September, 1991. "Advanced Report of Final Natality Statistics, 1989." Monthly Vital Statistics Report, vol. 40, no. 8, Supplement; ____. 1997 ____, 1995. vol. 45, no. 11, Supplement. Tabulations by CLMS.

Figure 1-15: Percentage of Births to Unmarried Mothers by Age, 1950-96

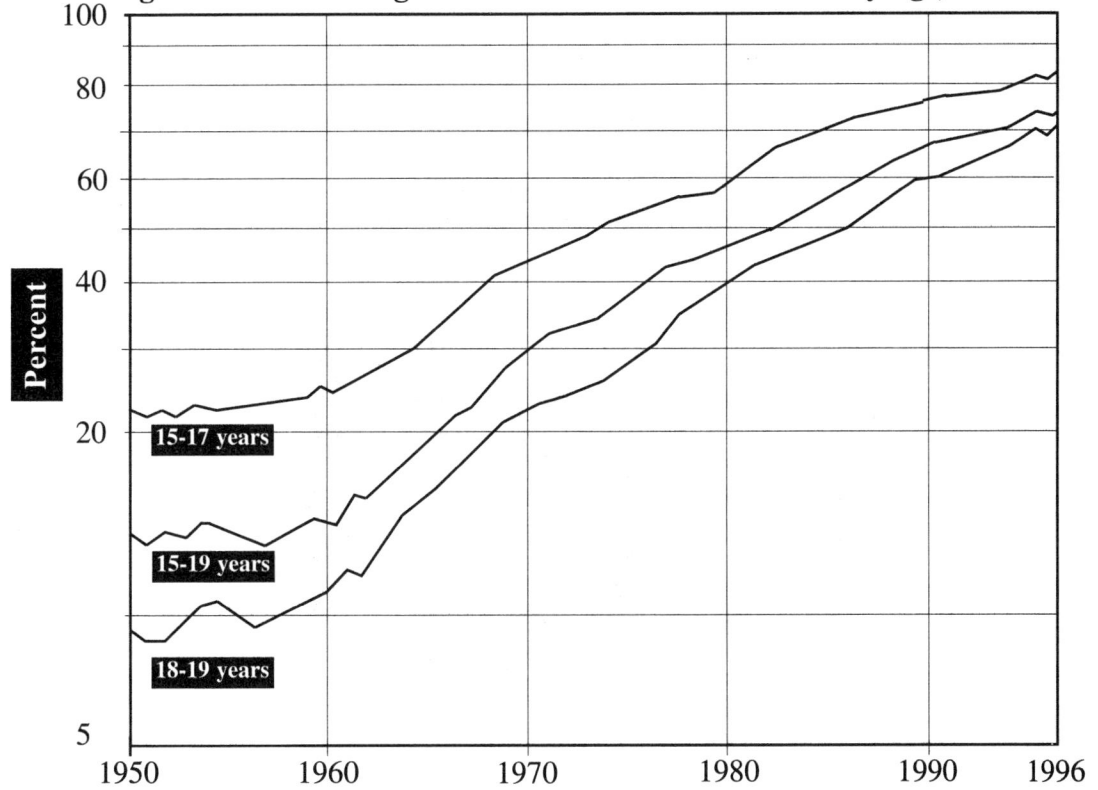

SOURCE: National Center for Health Statistics. "Teenage Births in the United States: National and State Trends, 1990-96." April 1998.

---

of U.S. births among young women declined, the share of births out-of-wedlock rose from 45 percent in 1989 to 55 percent in 1995. Among white women, 47 percent of 1995 births were out-of-wedlock; among Hispanics and women of "other races" the ratio was one out of two births and among black women 86 percent.

HOME OWNERSHIP: THE YOUNG FAMILY'S AMERICAN DREAM

In 1995, 36 percent of all U.S. households with children (including both renters and owners) faced severe housing problems, defined as physically inadequate, crowded or costing more than 30 percent of household income.

Owning one's own home, even a heavily mortgaged one, has long been considered a central feature of the American Dream. Here, too, the reality is grim for families headed by an individual aged 20-29 and living independently of other households. Based on the annual Current Population Surveys, such families' home ownership rate fell from 49 percent in 1980 to 38 percent in 1990, where this rate has remained substantially unchanged through 1997.

As we have noted, the falling or, at best, stagnating real incomes of the majority of wage-earners is certainly part of the explanation for this decline in home ownership. Rising home prices are another. According to the Fannie Mae/Freddie Mac home-price index, the average price of homes nationwide increased by nearly 330 percent between 1975 and mid-1995, compared with a rise in the Consumer Price Index of about 220 percent. Thus, on average, home prices have more than doubled in the past two decades. First-time buyers who can't "trade up" are obviously hardest hit by such inflation.

Non-Hispanic white families are almost three times as likely as blacks and twice as likely as Hispanics to own their homes. Despite recent gains in overall minority home ownership, only 17 percent of young black families owned in 1997 versus 47 percent of whites, thus constituting a major source of widening wealth inequality in the nation today.

Given the widening earnings differentials, it is not surprising that home ownership rates also correlate highly with the educational level of the family head, ranging in 1997 from 22 percent for high school dropouts to 55 percent for four-year college graduates. What is especially noteworthy is the widening gap in home ownership rates based on educational attainment. In 1980, young college graduates' ownership rate exceeded that of high school graduates by only seven percentage points (59 vs. 51 percent). By 1997, however, that gap had widened to 18 points (55 vs. 37 percent).

HEALTH INSURANCE

Young people are usually considered to be among our healthiest citizens. Yet, given the low educational attainment and depressed earnings levels of much of this population, when disease and accidents strike, the victims are largely uninsured. Given the persistence of poverty, it is not surprising that 15 percent of all children — 10.7 million children — had no health insurance in 1997. Young adults ages 18-24 were the least insured age group in the nation, only 30 percent having coverage.

The Fading Dream of Home Ownership

Figure 1-16: Home Ownership Rates Among Families Headed by 20-29 Year-Olds, by Presence of Children, 1980, 1990 and 1997

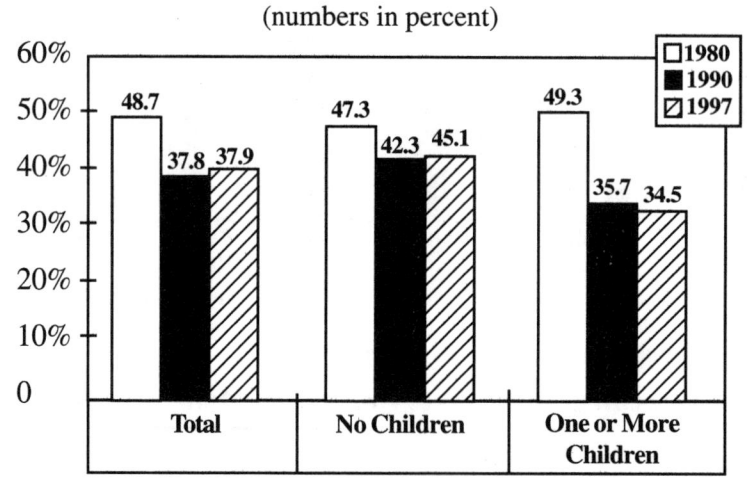

(numbers in percent)

	1980	1990	1997
Total	48.7	37.8	37.9
No Children	47.3	42.3	45.1
One or More Children	49.3	35.7	34.5

SOURCE: CLMS from March 1980, 1990, 1997 Current Population Surveys.

Figure 1-17: Home Ownership Rates Among Families Headed by 20-29 Year-Olds, by Highest Level of Educational Attainment of Family Head, 1997

(numbers in percent)

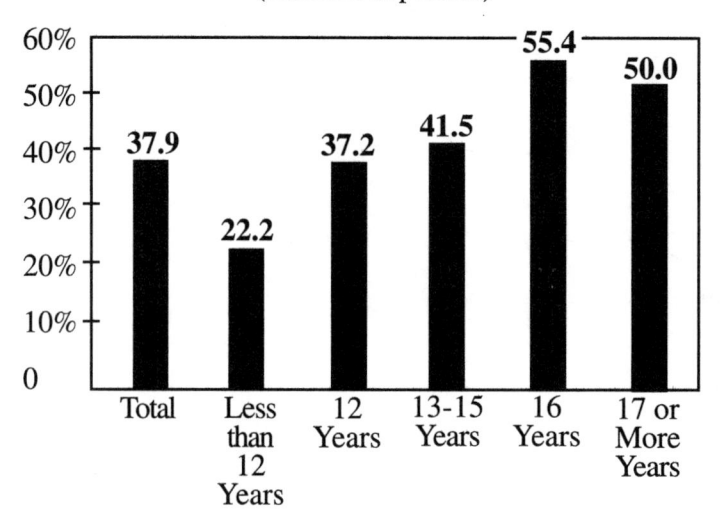

Total	Less than 12 Years	12 Years	13-15 Years	16 Years	17 or More Years
37.9	22.2	37.2	41.5	55.4	50.0

SOURCE: CLMS tabulations from March 1997 Current Population Survey.

Between 1976 and 1979, the number of 20-29 year-old males with any type of health insurance coverage fell from 79 percent to 66 percent. Among young women, the decline was from 84 to less than 77 percent. While young adult men are the least insured age/gender group in the nation, young women of childbearing age are also especially vulnerable.

Using March 1997 Current Population Survey data, Kenneth Thorpe and Curtis Florence found that 5.1 million out of 11.3 million uninsured children under age 19 were eligible in 1996 for Medicaid but were not participating. Four out of five parents of uninsured children were themselves uninsured.

Employer-provided health insurance used to cover more than half of all employed young men (60 percent in 1979). In recent years, employee "downsizing" in large firms and employee wage and benefit "give-backs" have greatly eroded even this partial coverage. In 1996, according to the Current Population Survey, only 43 percent of young men and 41 percent of young women enjoyed employer-financed health insurance. And, as we have seen elsewhere in this chapter, insurance coverage is highest among our best educated young people and highest among white non-Hispanics. Minority group members and those with the fewest years of schooling are the least likely to have health insurance of any type.

YOUNG AMERICANS BEHIND BARS

As we are painfully aware, Americans, especially young ones, are increasingly becoming inmates in federal and state prisons and local jails. Between 1985 and 1996, the total number of inmates rose from 744,000 to 1,631,000. Overall, the incarceration rate in this 11-year period nearly doubled from 313 to 615 inmates per 100,000 residents.

Because the Bureau of Justice Statistics has not released data since 1991 on the age distribution of inmates in state prisons and local jails (it does publish the age distribution of federal inmates), it is not possible to identify precisely what fraction of the total incarcerated population is under age 25 or 30. However, CLMS estimates (as seen in Figure 1-20) that the number of incarcerated young men under age 25 likely doubled between 1986 and 1995, from 178,000 to 359,000. Moreover, because the total number of young men under age 25 declined in this period, the true incarceration rate of young men more than doubled, from 1.3 to 2.8 percent.

These estimated incarceration rates substantially undercount the number of young men under the control of the criminal justice system. Due to prison overcrowding and the high costs of

A Great American Growth Industry

Figure 1-18: Total Number of Inmates in Federal and State Prisons and Local Jails, 1985 to 1996
(in thousands)

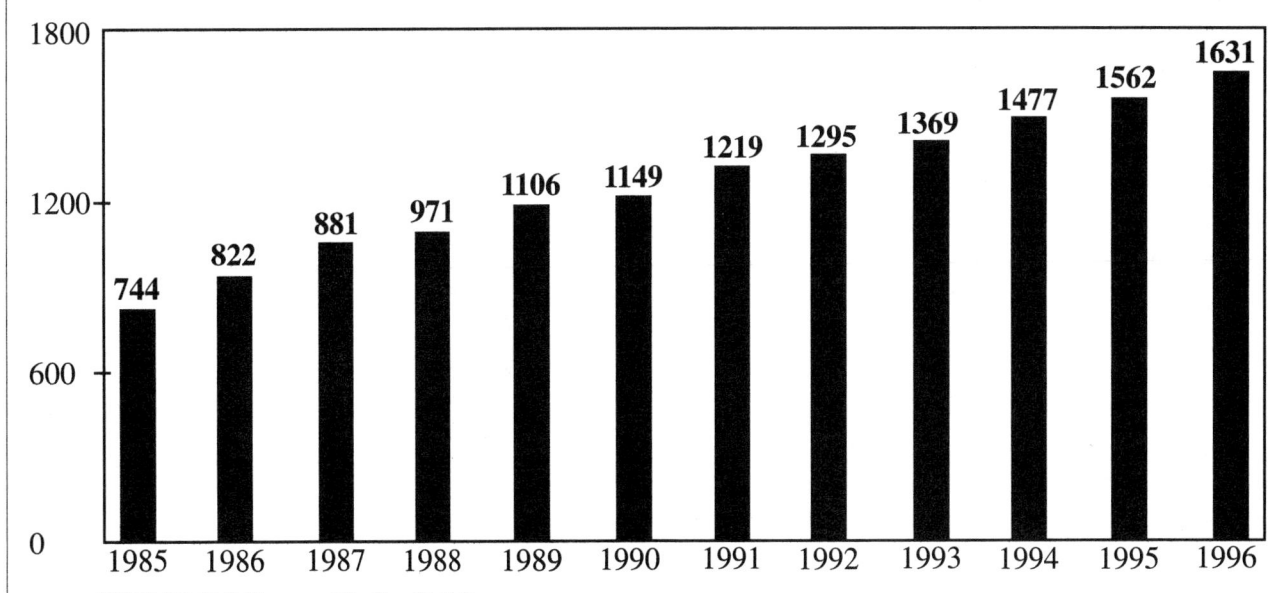

Year	Inmates
1985	744
1986	822
1987	881
1988	971
1989	1106
1990	1149
1991	1219
1992	1295
1993	1369
1994	1477
1995	1562
1996	1631

SOURCE: U.S. Bureau of Justice Statistics.

incarceration, many young men, rather than undergoing lengthy incarcerations, are placed on probation or flow in and out of jails, prisons and parole.

In 1994, according to the National Sentencing Project (NSP), on any given day, ten percent of all 20-29 year-old males were in jail, in prison, on probation or on parole. That rate varies considerably by race/ethnic group. Seven percent of young white males were under the control of the criminal justice system compared with 12 percent of Hispanic males and 30 percent of young black males. In the nation's inner cities, this criminal justice involvement ratio may reach close to 33 percent, according to NSP. (In 1995, over five million persons of all ages were under some form of correctional supervision.)

Naturally, criminal conviction and incarceration have long-term adverse effects on the employability and earnings of these young men. Incarceration reduces work experience and the acquisition of skills, two major determinants of future earnings potential. Young men convicted of crimes earn significantly less as young adults than their non-convicted counterparts with similar demographic characteristics. And such low earnings are linked in turn with the social problems and pathologies cited earlier.

Lest these grim data on crime and incarceration contribute further to the rampant perception of youth as predators and criminals — a perception reported by Daniel Yankelovich in the next chapter — a balanced presentation is in order. According to Independent Sector, six out of ten youth currently volunteer in various forms of

Figure 1-19: Estimated Numbers of Young Male Inmates in Federal and State Prisons and Local Jails, 1986 and 1995

Year	(A) Total Number of Men (18-24) in the Population	(B) Number in Prisons and Jails	(C) Percent in Prisons and Jails
1986	13,502,061	177,952	1.3
1995	12,904,674	359,419	2.8
Absolute Change, 1986-1995	-597,387	181,467	1.5
Relative Change, 1986-1995	-4.4	102	115.4

SOURCES: (i) Population data for young men in column (A) are derived from the Current Population Surveys (March 1996 and March 1995) for the civilian non-institutional population adjusted to include the incarcerated population; (ii) Estimates of the total incarcerated male population are derived from the U.S. Department of Justice, Bureau of Justice Statistics.

Figure 1-20: Criminal Justice Control Rates of 20-29 Year-Old Men
(numbers in percent)

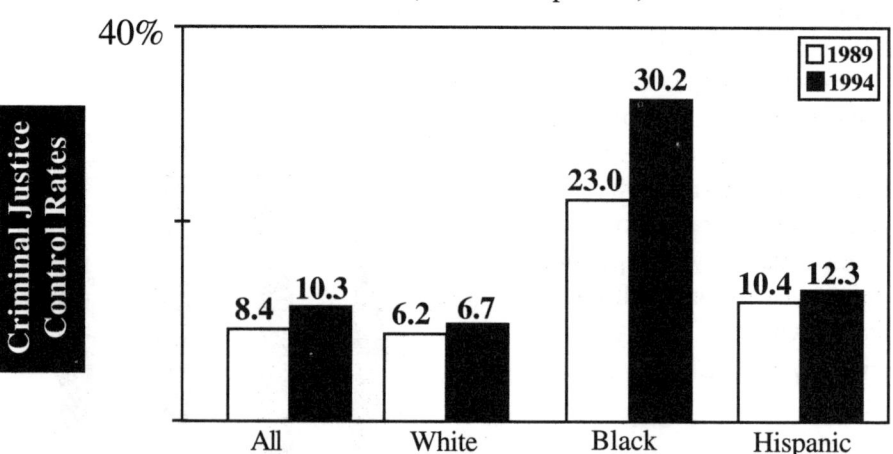

	1989	1994
All	8.4	10.3
White	6.2	6.7
Black	23.0	30.2
Hispanic	10.4	12.3

SOURCE: Mauer Marc and Tracy Huling, "Young Black Americans and the Criminal Justice System: Five Years Later." The Sentencing Project, Washington, DC, October 1995.

community service, and a 1996 Harris poll found almost 90 percent of youth willing to participate in programs to reduce drug use and crime in their communities. More to the point, according to the federal Office of Juvenile Justice and Delinquency Prevention, 99.5 percent of youth never get into trouble with the law or have only a single brush with it. Finally, juvenile crime is at its lowest rate in nearly a decade, with both property and violent crime down significantly since 1992 — all despite spectacular media coverage to the contrary. (See Coalition for Juvenile Justice, *False Images? The News Media and Juvenile Crime*.)

VOTING BEHAVIOR

Although 18-21 year-olds became eligible to vote in 1972, their use of the franchise has been even more dismal than that of older Americans. In the 1996 presidential election, 65.9 percent of the entire voting age population was registered to vote and 54.2 percent actually voted. Among 18-24 year-olds, 48.2 percent were registered, while only 32.4 percent cast ballots. (In 1972, 58.2 percent were registered and 49.6 percent voted.)

Unlike older people, homeowners, married couples, those with more schooling, high incomes and good jobs, most young adults today are disconnected from the political process — and apparently pay the price for that choice.

IS THERE STILL A SAFETY NET? IF SO, DOES IT WORK?

To what extent, if any, do government transfer programs ameliorate the rather dire economic conditions faced by the least educated and least healthy Americans at the end of the 20th Century? According to the Center on Budget and Policy Priorities in its 1998 study, *Strengths of the Safety Net,* one should consider not merely earned income but federal government transfer programs (both cash and in-kind benefits) as well if we are to understand the true state of America's least educated, least healthy and least independent citizens. Such programs include Aid to Families with Dependent Children (AFDC, now called Temporary and Necessary Assistance for Families — TANF), Supplemental Security Income (for those with mental and physical disabilities), food stamps, school lunches, public housing, rental housing subsidies, the Earned Income Tax Credit (EITC) for low-income working families and Medicaid.

The Center concluded that, without these various safety nets, 57.5 million people — 21.6 percent of all Americans — would have been classified in 1996 as below the poverty line. Counting the benefits as income, however, reduced the number of those below the poverty line by nearly half, to 30.5 million persons, or 11.5 percent of the total U.S. population. Stated affirmatively, "government benefit programs lifted 27 million people out of poverty in 1996," including 31.9 percent of all otherwise poor children. AFDC aided half the nation's poor children, and food stamps assisted about 80 percent of all poor children. However, the government safety net program that helped the most was EITC, lifting 2.4 million children — 37.3 percent of all poor children — out of poverty in 1996.

Using data in the March 1996 Current Population Surveys, the Center for Labor Market Studies found that the percent of 18-29 year-old males who were aided by one of these five programs (AFDC, SSI, Housing Assistance, Food Stamps or Medicaid) rose from 9.1 percent in 1989 to 12.6 percent in 1996. About one of every four young African American men, one of every five young Hispanic males and one in 12 young white males were helped by one or more of these benefit programs. Among young women, 21 percent received one or more of these safety net benefits, compared with 12.5 percent of young males. The percentage of young women receiving benefits rose from 15 percent in 1989 to almost 21 percent in 1996. Here, too, minority women — usually single mothers — received benefits disproportionate to their share of the total population: 41 percent of all young blacks and 31 percent of Hispanics versus only 14 percent of young white women.

Once again, educational attainment makes a crucial difference. Dropouts were nearly twice as likely to receive government supports as high school graduates (49 versus 27 percent) and 12 times more likely to do so than college graduates (49 versus four percent).

In sum, many members of The Forgotten Half continue to levy a heavy burden on society — in high incidence of poverty, dependence on public benefits and in raising children unable to contribute positively and fully to our economy and polity.

THE RISING TIDE OF COLLEGE ENROLLMENT

While harsh — and at times unfair —

Figure 1-21: Percent of Eligible 16-24 Year-Olds Enrolled in College, 1983-1996
(numbers in percent)

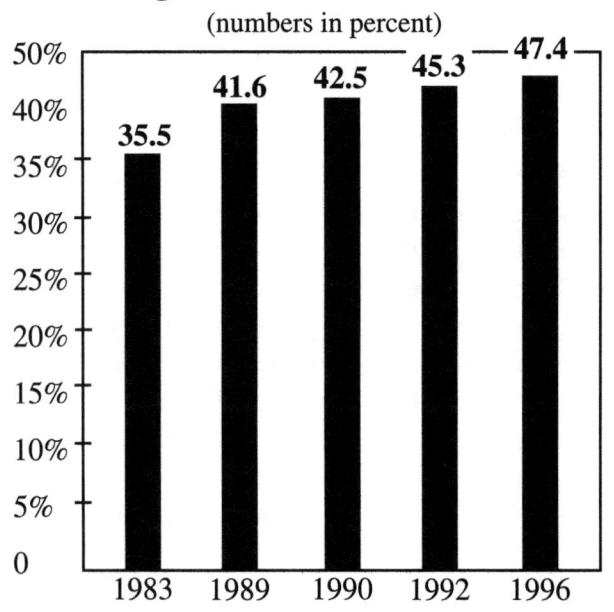

Year	Percent
1983	35.5
1989	41.6
1990	42.5
1992	45.3
1996	47.4

SOURCE: CLMS tabulations of CPS surveys, selected years.

NOTE: "Eligible" designates 16-24 year-olds who have completed high school but not college.

criticism of the *quality* of American public education has become a leading characteristic of our times, there have been some noteworthy developments on the quantitative side — in terms of young Americans' aspirations for and actual completion of more years of formal education.

In 1985, 9.5 percent of the nation's high school students age 16 or over left school each year prior to graduation. By 1991, that annual dropout percentage had fallen by more than one-third, to six percent. From 1994 to 1996, however, this dropout measure rose again to an average of 7.3 percent, possibly reflecting a somewhat improved job market for teenagers which encourages some of them to leave school and accept full-time employment, and the increasing percentage of poor and especially immigrant youth in our schools who experience high dropout rates.

Despite this historically improving trend, the "dropout pool" remains quite substantial; young adults ages 18-24 who did not graduate from high school and who were not enrolled in school in 1996 totaled 3.1 million persons, fully one of every eight persons in this age group. To be sure, many dropouts do return eventually to formal schooling and/or earn the alternative GED certificate. The majority, however, will lack the skills essential to employment success in today's economy.

In postsecondary education, the record of the last decade is remarkable. Using a measure of the "college-eligible" population (16-24 year-olds who have graduated from high school but not yet obtained a bachelor's degree and left college), the ratio of those actually *beginning* a program leading to an A.A., B.A., B.S. or advanced degree to the eligible population was 35.5 percent in 1983, 41.6 percent in 1989 and 47.4 percent in October 1996. *This 12 percentage point rise — a one-third increase in only 13 years — represents a major trend in American youth's postsecondary education behavior and a continuation of the nation's post-World War II "democratization" of educational opportunity.*

Unfortunately, youth attending non-degree-granting postsecondary education and training programs are not included in these enrollment totals. However, according to the National Center for Education Statistics, enrollments of all ages in noncollegiate postsecondary institutions in the fall of 1995 totaled 850,000, including 279,000 in public and 571,000 in private institutions. The latter category includes about 390,000 students in proprietary schools. Of these, 263,000 were enrolled in less than two-year programs of study.

When *TFH* was published in 1988, 59 percent of each year's high school graduating class was enrolling in two- or four-year colleges in the following October. (In itself, this was an increase from only 49 percent in 1980.) The Class of 1996 continued this major social trend, reaching a record 67 percent in 1997. (Thus, as Chapters Five and Six contend, in one sense, we now have a "Forgotten

Third" in place of the former Forgotten Half.)

Disaggregating these historical high enrollment rates by gender and race, we find that, in 1997, women enrolled in colleges at a ratio of 70 to every 63 men. White college enrollment rates were up 3.1 percentage points from the late 1980s while African American enrollments rose more, by 4.5 percentage points. Enrollment rates among Latinos, on the other hand, fell by two percentage points.

Overall, a majority of high school graduates in each racial or ethnic group who graduate from high school now *begin* college immediately after graduation: 64 percent of white youth, 53 percent of African Americans and 51 percent of Hispanics. Of those attending college, about 64 percent enroll in a four-year college or university immediately following high school graduation.

When the entire national pool of 16-24 year-olds is analyzed (excluding those still in high school and those who had already earned a baccalaureate degree and left college), a record proportion of over 47 percent of this young age group were attending college in 1996. This contrasts with only 35.5 percent 13 years earlier, in 1983.

These enrollment increases, however, mask serious underlying problems in American postsecondary education. For one, five years after enrolling, over half (52 percent) of freshmen entering four-year colleges or universities have not yet graduated. In fact, this graduation rate has been declining steadily at both public and private institutions since 1983, when it stood at 58 percent. As Gladieux and Swail well document in Chapter Six, *beginning postsecondary studies is far from completing them.* America's love affair with postsecondary education has much unfinished business to address.

* * *

With the notable exception of the increasing formal educational attainment of young adults, the picture which emerges from this brief summary of the current state of America's youth and young families is scarcely encouraging. In the decade since *TFH* was published, many of America's young people continued to experience deep social and economic traumas. As workers' real earnings declined further, family incomes, independent living arrangements, health insurance and sound, two-parent families also declined, while incarceration, out-of-wedlock births, dependency and other indicators of social pathologies rose.

Yet, the past decade has not been an unalloyed disaster for The Forgotten Half or for all young people. In the chapters that follow, we shall encounter many large and small victories on behalf of our young people and the blossoming of many hopeful initiatives that hold promise that many of our younger citizens, through hard work, responsible action, favorable labor market conditions and increased public and private supports, *can* escape the dire circumstances that cause so many older adults to "forget" the young and avert lending them a helping hand up out of poverty and neglect.

In particular, our chapter authors will survey what has happened over the past decade in American public opinion, families, communities, schooling, preparation for employment, postsecondary education, national service and youth development. They will conclude their individual chapters with personal visions of a nation in which youth and young families will no longer be "forgotten" but, rather, make their positive contributions to our national well-being.

> "The arena of national politics is dispiriting. Pit bull partisanship. The sleight-of-hand of the image manipulators. Politicians walking the tightrope over an angry electorate... The problems are frightening but in themselves are not as perplexing as the questions they raise concerning our capacity to gather our forces and act. The prevailing mood is cynicism. To mobilize the required resources and bear the necessary sacrifices calls for a high level of motivation. Is it possible that our shared values have disintegrated to the point that we can no longer lend ourselves to any worthy common purpose?"
> — *John W. Gardner. National Renewal. Washington, DC: Independent Sector/National Civic League, 1995.*

Figure 1-22: Number of 18-24 Year-Old Civilians, by Highest Level of Educational Attainment and Race/Ethnic Origin, March 1988 and March 1997

(in thousands)

	1988	1997	Absolute Change	Percent Change
TOTAL	**25,811.4**	**24,833.8**	**-977.6**	**-3.8**
High School Student	1,993.5	2,493.0	499.5	25.1
Postsecondary Student	7,167.8	8,171.5	1,003.7	14.0
Less than 12 Years Completed	3,674.6	3,332.1	-342.5	-9.3
12 Years Completed	8,728.4	6,333.2	-2,395.2	-27.4
13 or More Years	4,247.1	4,504.0	256.9	6.0
White, non-Hispanic	18,796.3	16,451.6	-2,344.7	-12.5
Black, non-Hispanic	3,508.5	3,550.6	42.1	1.2
Hispanic	2,642.1	3,605.5	963.4	36.5
Other, non-Hispanic	864.5	1,226.1	361.6	41.8
FORGOTTEN HALF, TOTAL	**12,403.0**	**9,665.3**	**-2,737.7**	**-22.1**
White, non-Hispanic	8,386.8	5,612.2	-2,774.6	-33.1
Black, non-Hispanic	1,947.5	1,641.5	-306.0	-15.7
Hispanic	1,794.0	2,075.6	281.6	15.7
Other, non-Hispanic	274.7	336.0	61.3	22.3

SOURCE: March 1998 and March 1997 Current Population Survey, tabulations by CLMS.

SOURCES

Barton, Paul E. *Toward Inequality: Disturbing Trends in Higher Education.* Princeton, NJ: Policy Information Center, Educational Testing Service, 1997.

Bennefield, Robert L. *Health Insurance Coverage: 1997.* Washington, DC: U.S. Census Bureau, Current Population Reports, P60-202, September 1998.

Bernhardt, Annette et al. "Summary of Findings: Work and Opportunity in the Post-Industrial Labor Market." New York, NY: Institute on Education and the Economy, Teachers College, Columbia University, February 1995 (manuscript) and "Work and Opportunity in the Post-Industrial Labor Market," *IEE Brief,* No. 19, February 1998.

Boesel, David, Nabeel Alsalam and Thomas M. Smith. *Educational and Labor Market Performance of GED Recipients.* Washington, DC: National Library of Education, Office of Educational Research and Improvement, U.S. Department of Education, NLE 98-2033, 1998.

Bryson, Ken and Lynne M. Casper. *Household and Family Characteristics: March 1997.* Washington, DC: U.S. Census Bureau, March and June 1997, P20-509 and 509ER.

Casper, Lynne M. and Loretta E. Bass. *Voting and Registration in the Election of November 1996.* Washington, DC: U.S. Department of Commerce, Census Bureau, P20-504, July 1998.

Cassidy, John. "Who Killed the Middle Class? The economy is fine, but most Americans are not..." *The New Yorker,* October 16, 1995, pp. 113ff.

Coalition for Juvenile Justice. *False Images? The News Media and Juvenile Crime.* Washington, DC: 1997.

Curtis, Lynn A. *The State of Families; Family, Employment and Reconstruction.* Milwaukee, WI: Families International, 1995.

Day, Jennifer C. *Projections of the Voting-Age Population for States: November 1998.* Washington, DC: U.S. Department of Commerce, Census Bureau, P25-1132, April 1998.

Day, Jennifer and Andrea Curry. *Educational Attainment in the United States: March 1997.* Washington, DC: U.S. Department of Commerce, Census Bureau, P20-505, May 1998.

Day, Jennifer C. and Andrea E. Curry. *School Enrollment — Social and Economic Characteristics of Students: October 1996* (update). Washington, DC: U.S. Census Bureau, P20-500, June 1998.

Facts at a Glance. Washington, DC: Child Trends, October 1997.

Federal Interagency Forum on Child and Family Statistics. *America's Children: Key National Indications of Well-Being, 1998.* Washington, DC: U.S. Government Printing Office, 1998.

Kids Count Data Book, 1998. Baltimore, MD: Annie E. Casey Foundation, 1998.

Kotkin, Joel and David Friedman. "As Wall Street Pats Itself on the Back, Trouble Lurks Behind the Boom." *The Washington Post,* May 24, 1998, pp. C1, 4.

Lerman, Robert I. "The Impact of the Changing U.S. Family Structure on Child Poverty and Income Inequality," *Economica* (London School of Economics and Political Science), vol. 63, 1996, pp. S119-S130. See also his letter in *The New Republic,* June 22, 1998, pp. 4-5.

May, Richard. *1993 Poverty and Income Trends.* Washington, DC: Center on Budget and Policy Priorities, March 1995.

Mishel, Lawrence, Jared Bernstein and John Schmitt. *The State of Working America 1998-99.* Washington, DC: Economic Policy Institute/Cornell University Press, 1998.

Mortenson, Thomas G. "Institutional Graduation Rates by Control, Academic Selectivity and Degree Level 1983 to 1998." *Postsecondary Education Opportunity,* July 1998.

National Center for Education Statistics, U.S. Department of Education. *The Condition of Education 1997* and *1998.* Washington, DC, 1998.

National Center for Education Statistics, U.S. Department of Education. *Subsequent Educational Attainment of High School Dropouts.* Washington, DC: U.S. Government Printing Office, June 1998.

National Vital Statistics System. *Teenage Births in the United States: National and State Trends, 1990-96.* Hyattsville, MD: National Center for Health Statistics, U.S. Department of Health & Human Services, April 1998.

Nettles, Michael T. and Laura W. Perna. *The African American Education Data Book. Volume III: The Transition from School to College and School to Work.* Fairfax, VA: Frederick D. Patterson Research Institute of The College Fund/UNCF, 1997.

Saluter, Arlene F. and Terry A. Lugaila. *Marital Status and Living Arrangements: March 1996.* Washington, DC: U.S. Department of Commerce, Economic and Statistics Administration, Census Bureau, P20-496, March 1998.

Thorpe, Kenneth E. and Curtis S. Florence. *Covering Uninsured Children and Their Parents.* New York, NY: The Commonwealth Fund, May 1998.

U.S. Census Bureau, Current Population Reports. *Marital Status and Living Arrangements: March 1996.* (1998)

U.S. Department of Education, National Center for Education Statistics. *The Condition of Education 1997.* Washington, DC, 1998.

U.S. Department of Education, National Center for Education Statistics. *Education and the Economy: An Indicators Report.* NCES 97-269, Washington, DC, 1997.

U.S. Department of Justice Statistics. *Correctional Populations in the United States, 1995.* Washington, DC, 1995.

U.S. Department of Labor, Bureau of Statistics. *Monthly Labor Review,* March 1998.

Ventura, Stephanie J., Sally C. Curtin, T.J. Mathews. *Teenage Births in the United States: National and State Trends, 1990-96.* Washington, DC: U.S. Department of Health and Human Services, Centers for Disease Control and Prevention, National Center for Health Statistics, 1998.

Zill, Nicholas. "Trends in Family Life and School Performance," Paper presented August 22, 1992 to American Sociological Association.

The Center for Labor Market Studies at Northeastern University is the nation's most consistent and continuing source of labor market data on young people and their social and economic status. Data cited in this chapter were often updated from earlier publications of the Sar Levitan Center for Social Policy Studies, Institute for Policy Studies, The Johns Hopkins University:

Mangum, Garth, Stephen Mangum and Andrew Sum. *A Fourth Chance for Second Chance Programs.* January 1998.

Sum, Andrew and others. *A Generation of Challenge; Pathways to Success for Urban Youth.* June 1997.

Sum, Andrew, Neeta Fogg and Neal Fogg. *Out-of-School, Out of Luck? Demographic and Structural Change and the Labor Market Prospects of At Risk Youth.* May 1997.

Sum, Andrew, W. Neal Fogg and Robert Taggart. *From Dreams to Dust: The Deteriorating Labor Market Fortunes of Young Adults.* August 1996.

"Yet, the past decade has not been an unalloyed disaster for The Forgotten Half or for all young people. In the chapters that follow, we shall encounter many large and small victories on behalf of our young people and the blossoming of many hopeful initiatives that hold promise that many of our younger citizens, through hard work, responsible action, favorable labor market conditions and increased public and private supports, can escape the dire circumstances that cause so many older adults to 'forget' the young and avert lending them a helping hand up out of poverty and neglect."

CHAPTER TWO

PUBLIC OPINION AND THE YOUTH OF AMERICA

Daniel Yankelovich

The William T. Grant Foundation Commission's reports of 1998 on the "The Forgotten Half" painted a grim picture of the prospects for a huge proportion of our nation's youth. They showed that half of the nation's young people, the half with the least education and technical skills, faced an economy with fewer good jobs for the unskilled, a society largely unaware of their plight and unaware of the guidance and support services they needed to cope with the challenges of the future.

How has this situation changed over the past decade? Has it improved or worsened, and in what ways? Has the size of the at-risk group grown larger or smaller? Is it still appropriate to speak of a Forgotten Half? If not, how should this group of young people be characterized? What new approaches and strategies for assisting young Americans make sense in today's world?

OVERVIEW

Over the past decade both positive and negative forces have affected the prospects for The Forgotten Half. Unfortunately, the balance is weighed toward the negative.

The positive forces grow out of the recent dynamism of the American economy, and also out of the public's growing awareness that to cope in the new global economy young people must acquire greater skills and higher levels of education than in the past. The public is increasingly aware that these skills are indispensable to making a decent living and to avoiding downward social mobility.

In the early 1990s, most Americans were gloomy and depressed about the economy and convinced that the nation was on the wrong track. (More than any other factor, this outlook cost George Bush his reelection.) By the middle of the decade, however, the economy began to improve.

The pickup in the economy cheered most Americans because all but the bottom fifth of families benefited from it. To be sure, the haves gained proportionately more than the have-nots, reinforcing recent income trends moving us in the direction of a widely separated two-tier society. But after years of stagnation and decline, income rose sharply for the top fifth and moderately for the middle 60 percent. The devastating trend of loss of income for the bottom fifth has, however, continued unabated, leaving this large group of Americans stranded despite the rising tide of the economy. In the job market, the combination of spreading automation along with industry's ability to outsource a wide variety of jobs has driven salaries down for unskilled and semiskilled labor. Today, prospects for young Americans without skills are as grim as prospects are glowing for those with the right skills. As a consequence of this new reality, over the past decade the nation has grown more education- and skill-conscious. In earlier years, most Americans were complacent about their schools and the education their children received. The typical response was, "many schools are awful, but my kid's school is just fine. My kids are getting as good as education as I did, even better in some ways."

Until the late 1980s, most parents did not realize that the kind of education they themselves had received was no longer adequate for the world in which their children would have to compete. Therefore, they judged the schools by the standards of their own education. As the realization grew that their children require higher levels of skills and education to keep from falling behind, they began to pay more attention to the need to improve the schools, to raise their standards, and to connect the skills they taught more directly to the requirements of the workplace.

Today, the majority of Americans support school reform and higher standards, but it has proved difficult to translate public concern into effective action of the sort that would equip today's young people with the skills, knowledge and outlook they need to cope successfully with the economy of the future. Schools and workplaces, especially schools, have shown themselves to be massively resistant to change. Though they may eventually adapt to the new requirements of the economy, the majority of our children are not doing so in a timely fashion.

No one deliberately raised the bar on the skills and education Americans require to adapt to the new high-tech economy. And, unfortunately, no policies were put in place to accommodate this new life circumstance. We are living through a phase of our national existence where the majority of Americans have grown disillusioned with, and mistrustful of, big government and its costly bureaucratic policies. Whereas a generation ago the plight of The Forgotten Half would have inspired a host of government policies designed to assist young Americans to make the transition to a different kind of economy, in today's political climate there is little temptation to insist that the federal government come to their aid. The majority of Americans assume that the involvement of big government might well make the situation worse, not better: they assume that government will fail to do the job efficiently, fairly, economically and effectively. Thirty years ago, more than three quarters of all Americans (76 percent) trusted the federal government to "do the right thing most of the time." Now, the situation is totally reversed: three quarters of all Americans (76 percent) *mistrust* the government to do the right thing most of the time.

In addition to the swift and massive growth of mistrust in governments to solve social problems, there has been a profound attitude change in attributing blame and responsibility for individual success in life. A trend toward Social Darwinism shows up clearly in my firm's annual tracking studies of social change. Our Scan data* reveal a shift away from the kind of egalitarianism dominant in the 1960s and 1970s which assumed that everyone was entitled to share in the bounty of available resources, even if this required large-scale redistribution. The assumption then was that unequal results were society's fault, and that it was society's obligation to address and correct them. We are now moving back toward the traditional American value that people are responsible for their own lives, and that the reality of life is that there inevitably will be both winners and losers. This conception limits the society's moral and legal obligations. Unequal results are no longer deemed to be society's fault, but are attributed to the failure of individuals to survive and prosper.

Thus, a number of circumstances have combined to produce a "sink or swim" social environment for Americans at the bottom of the economy. The skill/education bar has been raised beyond the ability of our school and work institutions to meet the new requirements of the global economy, the federal government lacks the support and credibility it needs to take remedial action on the scale required, and the larger society has adopted a moral attitude that leaves it to the resources of the individual to find his or her own way in an often brutal world.

Under these circumstances, it is hardly surprising that some young Americans who are having a rough time coping with this environment have turned to various forms of antisocial, self-defeating behavior — crime, drugs, violence, teenage pregnancy. Arrest rates for young adults, unwed teen age pregnancy and victimization rates have grown steadily over the past few decades.

The turn to antisocial forms of acting out their frustration has proved to be self-defeating. Older Americans regard such behavior with fear, disgust, bewilderment — and a bad conscience. Public Agenda research, summarized in the next section, shows that the majority of Americans take a disapproving and somewhat punitive attitude toward this outburst of antisocial behavior. To some extent, they blame themselves. They fear that the current crop of American parents are failing in their most serious moral responsibility: to bring up the next generation of young Americans as caring, responsible, loving, effective, morally mature adults. This fear, however, has not led either to a realistic assessment of the problem or to imaginative and effective proposals for actions to deal with it.

The net result is a largely negative appraisal of the next generation on the part of average Americans, especially of those on the nation's lowest economic and social rungs.

LOOKING AT THE SURVEY DATA**

This section summarizes relevant survey data to document and amplify the assertions made above. After this summary, I have added a third and final section in response to the invitation of the American Youth Policy Forum to "give us your strongest, most passionate and well reasoned advocacy of what *you* would like

---

*Daniel Yankelovich Group SCAN – A Trend Identification Program.
**This section on Survey Data was researched and written by Barbara Lee.

see happen in public thinking and public policy in the next decade or so, 1998-2008." I therefore end with some ideas suggested by the research for ways to improve the life chances of those young Americans who are willing to help themselves, if the resources they need to do so are made available to them.

Education

The condition of education is one of the major concerns of the public today. Education is seen as a powerful tool for the future and an absolute requirement for long-term success. But there is a widespread concern among the general public, parents, teachers, students and employers that schools may not be providing young people with an adequate education.

- Education is considered one of the most important problems facing local communities. (CBS News/New York Times, 1996)
- A Gallup survey found that when the American public is asked to grade the public schools of the nation, only 22 percent give them an "A" or "B." (Phi Delta Kappa/Gallup Survey of the Public's Attitudes Toward the Public Schools, 1997)
- While more positive about their local public schools, even here fewer than half (46 percent) felt they deserved an "A" or "B" grade. (Phi Delta Kappa/Gallup) A central aspect of this concern is the belief that schools are not adequately preparing students for the world of work.
- Almost one-half (47 percent) of Americans surveyed in 1995 said they do not believe a high school diploma is a guarantee that a student has learned the basics. ("Assignment Incomplete: The Unfinished Business of Education Reforms," a Public Agenda Report, 1995)
- One-third of teachers and school administrators share this assessment. (Ditto)

Skepticism About Preparation for Work Force

Employers and college professors who encounter recent high school graduates are even more dubious than teachers and students about how well high schools are preparing students for work force entry or college education.

- Nearly two-thirds (63 percent) of employers and 76 percent of professors of college freshmen express the view that a high school diploma is no guarantee of a knowledge of basic skills. (Public Agenda Report for *Education Week*, 1998)
- Employers complain particularly that the graduates they see lack basic math, writing, grammar and spelling skills. (Ditto)
- 52 percent of the college professors say the students they observe lack the skills necessary to succeed in college. (Ditto)

Need for Higher Standards

By overwhelming margins, parents and teachers, as well as employers and college professors believe that setting clear guidelines for what students are expected to learn and know would improve academic performance.

- Two-thirds (67 percent) of the American public believe that using standardized national tests to measure the academic achievement of students would improve student achievement. (Phi Delta Kappa/Gallup Survey of the Public's Attitudes Toward the Public Schools, 1997)
- An even larger majority (88 percent) agree that it would improve academic achievement if high school graduation were made contingent on the ability to write and speak English well. (Public Agenda Report "First Things First: What Americans Expect From the Public Schools," 1994)
- Six out of ten Americans (61 percent) say academic standards are too low in their own local schools, rising to seven in 10 African-American parents with children currently in public schools (70 percent). (Ditto)
- When people are asked to compare private to public schools, over half (53 percent) attribute higher academic standards to private schools. (Public Agenda Report "Assignment Incomplete: The Unfinished Business of Education Reform," 1995)
- High school students as well as adults feel the need for higher standards. Three out of four students endorse the requirement that they show they can write and speak English well before being allowed to graduate. (Public

Agenda Report "Getting By: What American Teenagers Really Think About Their Schools," 1997)

Effect of Higher Standards

Will students faced with higher standards be more likely to drop out of school? The majority of adults believe that higher standards will have the opposite effect.

- Six out of 10 Americans believe that higher standards will "encourage students from low-income backgrounds to do better in school," compared to 29 percent who think higher standards will lead more disadvantaged students to become discouraged or drop out. (Phi Delta Kappa /Gallup 1994)
- About one-third of the general public (32 percent) and only one in four parents (26 percent) want to ease standards by "making some allowances because inner-city kids come from disadvantaged backgrounds." (Ditto)

The Importance of Teaching Values

While parents are seen as having the ultimate responsibility for imparting values to their children, schools are seen as having an important supportive role. All segments of the community agree that it is a part of public education to impart the values that the next generation needs.

- Large majorities, over 70 percent, of parents, teachers and economic leaders agree that values such as responsibility, honesty, tolerance of others and good work habits are "absolutely essential" for schools to teach. (Public Agenda Report "Assignment Incomplete: The Unfinished Business of Education Reform," 1995)
- Students rate values like hard work, good work habits and honesty and tolerance of others among the most important things for high schools to teach. (Public Agenda Report "Getting By: What American Teenagers Really Think About Their Schools," 1997)
- Approximately half of America's teachers say that values are more important to teach than academics, with another nine percent finding values equally important. (Public Agenda Report "Given the Circumstances: Teachers Talk About Public Education Today," 1996)

Safety and Order

Americans are concerned that too many public schools are so disorderly and undisciplined that learning cannot take place. This is joined with a rising concern about school safety.

- Lack of discipline, the use of drugs, fighting and violence are seen as major problems facing local public schools. (Phi Delta Kappa /Gallup 1994)
- More than half of the public (54 percent) say teachers are doing only a "fair" or "poor" job dealing with discipline. (Public Agenda Report "First Things First: What Americans Expect From the Public Schools," 1994)
- Almost three-fourths of Americans (72 percent) say "drugs and violence" are serious problems in their local schools. (Ditto)
- The large majority of high school students (71 percent) also feel that "too many disruptive students" are a serious problem, though fewer (48 percent) regard drugs and violence in schools as a serious problem. (Public Agenda Report "Getting By: What American Teenagers Really Think About Their Schools," 1997)

Rising Educational Aspirations

The educational aspirations of high school students are high and on the rise. Over the decade from 1982, a college education came to be seen as a necessity.

- In 1992, nearly seven out of 10 high school seniors said they hoped to graduate from college, compared with 39 percent in 1982. (*Youth Indicators,* 1996)
- The desire for postsecondary education cuts across gender, ethnic and socioeconomic lines. In every subgroup, the vast majority aspire to more than a high school education. Even among high school seniors in the lowest performance quintile, 87 percent felt a high school diploma was not enough

and wanted to obtain at least some further education. (Ditto)

There is a realistic basis for this level of aspiration. The earnings gap between high school graduates and college graduates has increased substantially. In 1980, males with four or more years of college earned 19 percent more than high school graduates. By 1993, this gap had widened to 57 percent, and the trend continues to climb. (*Youth Indicators,* 1996)

Are These Aspirations for Higher Education Being Achieved?
Despite these high aspirations, the traditional college path does not often work out: many 18 year-olds end up with just a year or two of attendance, no certification and no saleable skill. An analysis by the Educational Testing Service indicates that attrition rates are high and are getting worse, not better.

- Of those students who graduated from high school in 1992, only 56 percent were enrolled in postsecondary education two years later. (*Youth Indicators,* 1996)
- Of students who started at community colleges in 1989, just 37 percent had attained any degree five years later and only six percent had earned a bachelor's degree. (Educational Testing Service, "Toward Inequality," 1997)
- Of students who entered college in 1989 seeking a bachelor's degree (whether or not they attended a two- or four-year college) 46 percent had a four-year degree five years later, five percent had an associate's degree and three percent a certificate. (Ditto)
- The chances of completing college are considerably worse for those from the bottom fourth in socioeconomic status ranking. Whether they enter a community college or seek a four-year degree, only about three out of seven will make it. The gap is continuing to widen between youth from high and low income families. (Ditto)

An intensive analysis of students leaving college concludes that attrition rates are not just the reflection of financial constraints. The research shows that many factors associated with leaving school relate to institutional practices and culture.

The Educational Testing Service concludes that "Financial aid that ignores the established college completion pattern will fall far short of increasing the intended achievements of degrees. More students starting college will mean high proportions who are not finishing. They will often end up with neither an academic or an occupational credential and owe money on college loans as well. The spotlight should be focused on institutions with noncompletion rates higher than expected, based on the makeup of their student bodies." (See also Chapter Six, below.)

The Dropout Problem
Young adults have completed more years of education over the past decade but increases since 1975 have been small. After rising steadily until 1976, the percent of 25-29 year-olds who completed four years of high school has risen only slightly since then, hovering at about 86-87 percent (*Youth Indicators,* 1996).

One encouraging change is the steady climb in the number of blacks completing high school, now almost equal to whites. However, Hispanics, projected to become the nation's largest ethnic minority by the early 21st century, are dropping out of high school at a rate almost triple the U.S. average, with no sign of improvement. While the dropout rate for other populations has declined over the last 20 years, the overall Hispanic dropout rate started higher and has shown little improvement. Only 57 percent of young adult Hispanics (25-29) have a high school diploma. (*Youth Indicators,* 1996) Dropout rates also relate to family income. Young people with family incomes in the bottom fifth are five times as likely to drop out as are their peers in the top quintile. (National Center for Education Statistics, *Dropout Rates in the United States,* 1996)

Follow-up studies of 1992 high school dropouts reveal that they are at an extreme disadvantage in employment and earnings. In the first full year following their expected graduation, 33 percent of the dropouts had no earnings; over a two-year period 19 percent did not obtain any job. In 1970, a high school dropout could earn about 84 percent of what a high school graduate earned; by 1993, the ratio had dropped to two-thirds. (*Youth Indicators,* 1996)

Job Skills and Job Training
Americans recognize that a significant problem for youth is a lack of job training and job skills and see a need to increase services to youth that would better prepare them for employment.

- Two out of three Americans see a lack of job skills as a serious problem for young adults aged 17-21 in their communities. (Yankelovich Partners, "Young Adults At Risk Survey," 1995)
- Fewer than one out of four (23 percent) consider the quality of education and job training of young people to be excellent or good. (Peter Hart, Council on Competitiveness, 1991)
- Many more see a need for more job training (67 percent) and job placement (62 percent) services. (Yankelovich Partners, "Young Adults At Risk" Survey, 1995)
- An analysis of the United States as compared to six other industrial democracies found it at or near the bottom in the effectiveness of its employment services and school-to-work programs. ("Why People Don't Trust Government," Nye, Zelikow & King, Harvard, 1997, p.72)
- When asked who should take the lead in providing job training for youth, 43 percent named individuals and businesses, 35 percent put the emphasis on government programs and funding and 20 percent volunteered that both should be involved. (CNN/USA Today/Gallup survey, 1995)

The Role of the Government

Confidence in government has declined steadily over the past few decades. Even while the federal government is perceived as successful in some areas, such as providing for the national defense or maintaining a growing economy, it is seen as a failure in dealing with key social problems such as poverty, crime and drug abuse.

- A plurality of Americans (47 percent) think that government programs and policies do more to hinder than to help families. (Hart-Teeter, 1997)
- A bare majority (49 percent) rates the federal government as successful in supporting quality education. On other noneconomic issues, the large majority rate the federal government as unsuccessful in solving the problems of reducing drug abuse (76 percent), reducing crime (69 percent), improving moral values (65 percent) and reducing poverty (63 percent). (Ditto)

Why Government Programs are Faulted

While the public does see the government as having a responsibility in such areas as reducing poverty, the effect of its efforts to date is regarded as more harmful than helpful. Most importantly, Americans reject any program that does not respect the fundamental value of self-reliance. Welfare is a prime example of a program that aroused public disfavor since it was seen as undermining the work ethic and the family.

- Almost three-fourths of Americans feel that government would inspire substantially greater confidence if it focused on "respecting the moral values of the public." Eighty percent say that "giving people the skills and resources to be self-sufficient instead of... encouraging dependence" would enhance public confidence in government. (Ditto)
- Before the 1996 changes in the welfare system, 69 percent of the American public supported the view that the welfare system did more harm than good because it encouraged the breakup of the family and discouraged the work ethic. (NBC News/Wall Street Journal, 1995)
- In contrast, aiding working poor families is seen as a way to strengthen families and family values. Seventy-nine percent believe that guaranteeing that families in which the parents work will not fall below the poverty line would be an effective government policy. (Wirthlin Quorum Poll, 1995)

Increasingly, people are moving away from the point of view that government needs to provide for everybody and toward the conviction that more emphasis be put on individual self-determination. There is more of a focus on individual responsibility for outcomes, good or bad.

- Only 16 percent of Americans feel that government is responsible for the well-being of all its citizens, while four times as many say that individuals are responsible for their own well-being. (Hart-Teeter, 1997)
- Poverty is more likely to be attributed to

people not doing enough to help themselves (60 percent) than to circumstances beyond their control (30 percent). (NBC News/Wall Street Journal, 1995)
- There is a strong belief in the American Dream. The overwhelming majority (85 percent) still see America as a place where "people who work hard to better themselves can get ahead." (CNN/USA Today/ Gallup survey, 1995)

Moral Values

One of the most serious concerns in society today is a decline in moral values. The public see declining values as a key component in major social and political issues. Attitudes toward young people are framed within the perception of a decline in the family's ability to transmit successfully the values of respect, responsibility and civility to their children.

- When asked the source of the most serious problems in our society, 51 percent attribute them mainly to a decline in moral values; only 37 percent said they stem from economic and financial pressures on the family. (NBC News/Wall Street Journal, 1996)
- A 1996 DYG study found that 87 percent of Americans (up from 76 percent in 1994) shared the conviction that our nation's social morality has eroded. This belief is seen across gender, age and race differences.
- The proportion who see a decline in family values increased from 62 percent in 1989 to 76 percent in 1995.

("American Family Values," Michaels Opinion Research, 1995)

Parents' Responsibility

As the principal teacher of values, parents are blamed for not doing an adequate job in transmitting the right values to the next generation. There is a pervasive feeling that parents are neglecting this prime responsibility.

- 79 percent of Americans believe that children growing up today are not taught good moral values as much as when they were growing up. (Yankelovich Partners Inc. "The State of the American Family," 1993)
- 74 percent agree that parents today are not taking enough responsibility for teaching their children moral values. (Los Angeles Times Poll, 1996)
- More than six in 10 (63 percent) say it's very common for parents to have children before they are ready to take responsibility for them. (Public Agenda, "Kids These Days: What Americans Really Think About the Next Generation," 1996)

Parents' Concern About Values

When pressed, American parents admit to some concern about how adequately they teach values to their children.

- The large majority of parents rate themselves as doing an excellent (37 percent) or good (59 percent) job of teaching their children about morals and values (Los Angeles Times Poll, 1996). This finding is consistent with other polls in which parents are asked about their own performance.
- However, over half (52 percent) of parents with teenagers and 46 percent of those with children under the age of 13 admit that they are sometimes worried about doing a good job teaching values to their children. ("American Family Values," Michaels Opinion Research, 1995)

Difficult Time to Raise Children

In general, the public recognizes that these times are harder for both parents and children than when they were growing up.

- Eight of 10 Americans think it's much harder for parents to do their job these days. (Public Agenda, "Kids These Days: What Americans Really Think About the Next Generation," 1996)
- Equal numbers (79 percent) think children have a harder time growing up today than their parents did. (ABC News/Washington Post, 1990)
- There is widespread recognition that teenagers live in a more difficult world, in which they must face social problems like drugs, gangs or crime (62 percent). (Public Agenda, "Kids These Days: What Americans Really Think About the Next Generation," 1996)

Attitudes Toward Youth

While there may be sympathy for the difficulties of parents and children in the current social climate, the overall attitude toward young people is surprisingly negative. A recent survey of attitudes toward young people, (Public Agenda, "Kids These Days: What Americans Really Think About the Next Generation," 1996) concluded that "Most Americans look at today's teenagers with misgiving and trepidation, viewing them as undisciplined, disrespectful and unfriendly." There is a widespread feeling that kids are in trouble because they are not developing the ethical and moral values needed to become responsible adults in society. This conclusion was based on such findings as:

- 67 percent of Americans choose negative adjectives such as "rude," "irresponsible" and "wild," when they are asked what comes to their minds when they think about American teenagers.
- 41 percent say it is common to find teenagers who have poor work habits and lack self-discipline.
- Only 12 percent say it is common for teens to be helpful and friendly and treat other people with respect.
- Only one in five (19 percent) say it's very common for parents to be good role models and teach their kids right from wrong.

This judgment is not simply based on casual impressions from the media. Those who have a lot of direct contact with teenagers are as critical of them as everyone else.

But Willingness to Assist Youth Exists

Notwithstanding their extensive criticisms of young people, Americans have not given up on kids and feel that helping young people is of paramount importance to our society. And they believe that reclaiming the lives of even the most troubled teens is possible.

- More than half (52 percent) say that helping kids get a good start is more important than creating more jobs, protecting citizens from crime, or helping the poor or homeless.
- Almost three-fourths (74 percent) say that given enough help and attention, just about all youngsters can learn and succeed in school.
- 85 percent believe that given enough attention and the right kind of guidance even teenagers who are always getting into trouble at school and in their neighborhoods can be helped.

What Are Seen as Appropriate Solutions?

Since Americans define the problem with youth as predominantly moral in nature and the crux of the problem as parents' lack of responsibility, they are not attuned to governmental solutions. Rather they look to schools, community center programs and volunteer organizations like the Boy Scouts as a more effective way of helping kids.

- From a list of possible ways to help young people, two out of three (67 percent) identified improving the quality of public schools as a "very effective" way. Large numbers also believe that increasing after-school activities in community centers (60 percent) or involvement with volunteer organizations dedicated to kids like the Boy Scouts (53 percent) would also be effective resources.
- Only 10 percent felt that increasing government funding for such welfare programs as AFDC and food stamps would be a very effective way to help young people.

Why is the Public So Upset About Young People?

The public's perception of youth is strongly affected by such social problems as teenage pregnancy, youth crime and drug abuse. Although three out of four adolescents engage in little or no risky behavior, there is much more awareness of the one in four who are in significant trouble, ranging from teenage pregnancy and drug abuse to juvenile delinquency and more serious crimes. (Estimates from J. G. Dryfoos, *Adolescents at Risk,* 1990)

Teen Pregnancy

When President Clinton identified teen pregnancy as the nation's most serious social problem in his 1995 State of the Union Address, his words resonated with the public. Teen pregnancy is seen as a symptom of the erosion of family cohesiveness and is closely associated with out-of-wedlock births. One of the strongest arguments of opponents of the welfare system was that it encouraged teenagers to have kids out of wedlock, a belief shared by six out of 10 Americans. (Public Agenda, "The Values We Live By: What Americans Want from Welfare Reform," 1996)

- 72 percent of adults believe that the growth in teen pregnancies is a very important problem. (Gordon S. Black Corporation for *USA Today,* 1997)
- In the current climate of tolerance of diverse life styles, fewer than half of the public (46 percent) condemn out-of-wedlock births on moral grounds (Roper Center Family Values Survey, 1997). But there is a realistic perception on the part of the public that teen pregnancy is detrimental. By wide margins, the public believes that all teen mothers face economic hardships: that they are more likely to receive welfare, less likely to complete high school and more likely to experience poverty and a lifetime of low earnings. (Henry J. Kaiser Family Foundation, "Why Have Births to Unmarried Teens Increased?" 1997)

While teen child bearing is not a new phenomena, what has changed is the proportion of births that are to unmarried teens: in 1960, only 15 percent of teen mothers were unmarried, compared to 48 percent in 1980 and 75 percent in 1994. (Henry J. Kaiser Family Foundation, "Why Have Births to Unmarried Teens Increased?" 1997). Since the 1970s there has been both a dramatic rise in the proportion who have had sexual intercourse as teens and also the severing of the link between sex and marriage.

Having an unplanned baby as a teen can hurt a young woman's economic and educational prospects:

- Many young mothers end up on welfare. Almost half of all teenage mothers and over three-fourths of unmarried teen mothers go on welfare within five years of the birth of their first child. Fifty-two percent of all mothers on welfare had their first child as a teenager. (National Campaign To Prevent Teen Pregnancy, "Whatever Happened to Childhood? The Problem of Teen Pregnancy in the United States," 1997)
- Fewer than one-third of teens who begin their families before age 18 ever complete high school. (Ditto)
- The children of teen mothers are faced with a host of disadvantages — more health problems, poorer academic performance, higher rates of behavior problems, a higher frequency of parental abuse and neglect.
- Teen parenting leads to repetitive negative consequences. The teen daughters of teen mothers are 22 percent more likely to become teen mothers themselves. The sons are 13 percent more likely to end up in prison.

The teen birth rate has declined from 1991, its highest point in the past two decades. The recent decrease reflects a leveling off of teen sexual activity as well as the increased number of teens using contraception effectively. But the U. S. rate of teen births remains higher than in other industrialized democracies.

Youth Crime

What adults think about young people is influenced by their concern about crime and their perception that young people have a heavy share in the increase in crime over the past few decades.

- Despite the fact that crime rates have shown a recent decrease, a 1996 survey found that crime still topped the list of important problems facing the country today, more of a concern than jobs and unemployment. (CBS News/ New York Times, 1996)
- The public is concerned that youth crime is on the rise. Eighty-six percent believe that crimes committed by teenagers in this country had increased from last year; only two percent saw a decrease. (Ditto)
- 81 percent see teenage violence as a big problem in most of the country, though not as bad in their own community. (Ditto)

The "get tough" attitude to crime in general carries over to youth, with widespread support for more stringent policies for juvenile criminals.

- The large majority of Americans (83 percent) would mete out the same punishment to juveniles convicted of their second or third crimes as to adults with comparable conviction records. (Gallup for CNN/USA Today, 1994)

- In a 1994 Gallup survey, 61 percent favored the death penalty for a teenager who is convicted of murder, up from 24 percent in 1957.

At the same time, the public also supports early intervention programs for high-risk youth and spending federal funds to provide positive social programs for poor youth.

- 65 percent of respondents to a 1994 Gallup crime survey favored the use of federal funds for social programs such as midnight basketball and other activities for poor children.
- Given a choice of methods for reducing crime in this country, 64 percent favored putting money and effort into preventive methods, such as better education and job training, over improving law enforcement (27 percent). (Wirthlin Group, 1994)

TOWARD A NEW YOUTH STRATEGY

Our society does not have an impressive track record on creating effective social policies. We are not nearly as proficient in this arena of our public life as we are in fields like business entrepreneurship, science, technology, pop culture, sports and finance. Therefore, the best starting point for a new youth strategy is to avoid the most common mistakes made in the past so as not to repeat them. At the present stage in the history of social policy, we know a great deal more about what doesn't work than what does.

Perhaps the most familiar of all social policy mistakes is the "magic bullet" approach: the advocacy of a single simple solution to a complex problem (e.g., "jobs," "education," "housing," "affirmative action," "just say no," "lock them up and throw away the key").

An equally familiar mistake is the "everything-at-once" policy. It goes to the opposite extreme of the magic bullet fantasy. Recognizing the complexity of problems, like those of the inner city, it warns us that to make a dent in them, we must do everything at the same time: offer better education *and* job training *and* economic development *and* mentoring *and* child care *and* drug rehabilitation *and* improved transportation *and* stronger civil rights enforcement *and* outreach services, etc. The result is virtually the same as doing nothing.

The public has grown weary of these and other ineffectual social engineering strategies, especially those that require large tax expenditures and government bureaucracies. It is certainly futile to search for a single answer, a magic bullet, to solve the problems of the poor and those at greatest risk in our society. The plight of the poor and less educated is too serious and deep-rooted to lend itself to any one simple solution. Consider job training. More effective job training is surely an indispensable part of any overall strategy, but by itself it will not improve the odds for the majority of our nation's poorest and least well educated for a variety of reasons: most young people at risk don't know what they should be trained for; the jobs for which they are trained may not exist or may become obsolete; they may lack the incentive or knowledge to translate the training into the kind of job that would give them the benefits they seek, etc.

The unavailability of a single solution does not mean, however, that we must swing toward the everything-at-once strategy. These sorts of strategies are particularly appealing to those most deeply committed to solving the problems of the inner city. So complex and interdependent are these that it is easy to fall into the everything-at-once trap. And it is a trap, because experience has shown that such strategies never win either the public support or the practical implementation they need to be successful.

The dilemma of what to do about the inner city should not be identified totally with the problems of The Forgotten Half, that is, those unlikely to go on to postsecondary education. Inner city youth constitute only one part of this population. It is an important part but still a minority. The strategy I am proposing should prove effective for the majority of this population, including the majority of inner city young people who are capable of self-help. Unfortunately, there exists a minority of inner city youth who cannot be reached through self-help programs, including this one. That grim reality should be confronted from the outset.

For the majority of The Forgotten Half population, there is no need to do everything that ought to be done all at the same time, however desirable that might be in principle. Priorities can be set, and public support won gradually in response to hard evidence of success for programs with limited objectives.

Over the long run, a number of disparate elements must fit together as in a jigsaw puzzle. In addition to job training, some of these elements are:

- More effective school-to-work transition policies and practices.
- Primary action at the local and regional, as distinct from the national level.
- The development of large numbers of badly needed second-chance institutions.
- Vast improvements in tools for assessing peoples' job capabilities and for matching people to jobs.
- Programs to teach and to reinforce the moral virtues of responsibility, perseverance, cooperation, self-discipline and hope.
- Financial mechanisms other than government programs for supporting young people who are willing and able to make the effort to help themselves.
- Large-scale efforts to win public support for programs that will inevitably require patience and suffer setbacks, even though they can promise to deliver extraordinary long term results.

Lest this inventory of requirements seem too daunting for practical solutions, I would emphasize that our society is fortunate in having in place an institution ideally equipped to manage the majority of these tasks: the nation's sprawling network of two-year community colleges. Typically, these are overworked, under-funded, low status institutions that are taken for granted and are almost never given the resources and opportunities they need to fulfill their potential promise. With the right kind of support they can create massive improvements in the life chance prospects of at-risk youth.

My proposed strategy has three major elements:

1. A core institution. A vastly expanded community college capability.

2. A financing mechanism. A new mechanism for financing young people's self-help efforts based on the principles of micro-lending.

3. A base in public support. A massive effort by both the political structure and the civil society to win and maintain public support through a strategy that faithfully reflects the moral convictions of the American public.

In a short paper reporting on public opinion survey data I can do no more than hint at how this three-part youth strategy might develop if it were to receive the attention it needs to convert it from one observer's personal statement to a practical public policy.

The Community College Component

The advantages of building on the strengths of the nation's community colleges are obvious and compelling:

- They have a track record of success in helping people develop the skills they need to make the school-to-work transition.
- They are local institutions (in contrast, for example, to our nation's network of research universities which are national and international in their orientation). They have close ties with state legislatures and other regional institutions.
- They do not seek to "cream" the youth population, recruiting the young people with high SAT scores. They are popular institutions with virtually open admissions.
- They have close ties with local employers who can assist in training and job placement.
- They are well positioned to learn from each other's mistakes and successes.

However promising their potential may be, the nation's community colleges need a great deal of support and added resources if they are to compensate for a deeply flawed K-12 system of public education and also to assume the task of easing the school-to-work transition for the most needy part of our youth population in the context of the new global economy.

As noted earlier, fewer than two out of five young people (37 percent) who enter community colleges had attained a degree of any sort five years later. Also, the incompletion rate varies enormously from one community college to another. The reason, I believe, is traceable to the difficulty of the task these institutions have assumed. On the one hand, the population being served is burdened with all manner of economic, practical and cultural handicaps. And on the other, the community colleges must navigate their way through a rapidly changing and highly technical job market whose skill requirements are often difficult to define and to impart. Also, many community colleges are still mired in the single-path approach to education, where education at one level is assumed to be nothing but a preparatory step for more education at higher levels.

The wide variability in success rates suggests that some community colleges know how to educate and train this population appropriately, and others do not.

The discovery of wide variability in best practice is potentially a very promising development. As a society, we know a lot about how to spread best practice to a wider base of institutions. What we need to add is the political will to do so.

The first step in developing a new youth strategy is to consult with leading community colleges in every state in the nation, individually and collectively, to develop models of best practice so as to improve the completion rate significantly. Policies should be adapted to the idiosyncrasies of individual states and regions. This consultation should go beyond the staffing and resource needs of community colleges as they now exist. They should explore what resources the community colleges need in order to add several new capabilities to their existing ones.

One would be a new and powerful individual assessment and guidance capability. Most young people do not know what opportunities are open to them, what requirements these demand, and what their own potential undeveloped gifts are. One of the most striking characteristics of less well-educated populations is their lack of information. The nation has access to many resources to fill this need: computer-driven data bases, new methods of individual assessment and new concepts of "multiple intelligences" that do not try to fit everyone into the same mold. The trick is to match these new resources to the individual. Community colleges are well positioned to offer this added service, if given the resources to do the job.

Community colleges are also well positioned to become second-chance institutions. Indeed, they already serve that function. I suspect that the majority of young people in the least affluent half of the population lack the maturity and the incentive when they are growing up to take full advantage of their educational opportunities, even when these are adequate. Later on, in their 20s or 30s or even later in life, they develop the requisite maturity and incentive, but have no practical means of taking a shot at a second chance. Community colleges already serve one part of this population. It would not take a great stretch for them to expand and publicize these capabilities so that millions more could take advantage of them.

From Entitlement to Reciprocity: The Micro-Lending Concept

Acquiring the skills one needs to win in the new global economy requires a capital expenditure as much as, say, a start-up bio-tech venture does. Individuals need to invest now to develop assets and skills that will pay off in later years. This is not the traditional way to think about skill development because capital expenditures are usually associated with building plant and equipment rather than human capital, and linked to business enterprise rather than individual skills. But the structure of the financing requirements are strikingly similar. Also, one of the defining characteristics of the new economy is the premium paid to human capital. Those who are fortunate enough to develop the education and skill credentials the market needs can virtually write their own ticket.

Until recently, access to capital has been the exclusive privilege of the haves. The lack of access to capital is the plight of the poor all over the world. Some years ago, a Bangladesh banker, Mohammad Yunis, innovated a system called micro-lending which made small amounts of capital available to women in the villages of Bangladesh though the Grameen Bank. Contrary to expectations, the default rate on the repayment of the loans was lower than for the business elites of Bangladesh.

This creative and successful example of social entrepreneurship caught the imagination of people all over the world. At present, micro-lending to make capital available to people who would not qualify for conventional financing has proven itself in a number of countries such as Poland and in a variety of applications in the United States. Virtually the only application that has suffered relative failure is in the inner city where default rates on loans have proven unsatisfactory from a self-sustaining enterprise point of view (though not necessarily from a public policy perspective).

As experience with micro-lending increases, it has become clear that careful implementation is the key to success. As bankers know all too well, you can't simply loan money to people who want and need it, and expect to be repaid. You need to observe specific guidelines and policies. But — and this is the encouraging note — if you follow these guidelines, micro-lending is showing itself to be a practical, self-sustaining way to finance projects of people with no other access to capital. Why, then, shouldn't individuals have access to the capital they need to invest in themselves and their own future?

Doing so creates a dual benefit. For the individual, it creates and reinforces independence, self-confidence, hope and optimism. For our society, it offers a strategy that is consonant with public values rather than in conflict with them. My trend studies show a steady increase in support for the moral principle of reciprocity and against the principle of entitlements. Public sentiment here is unambiguous. "No one should feel entitled to get something for nothing," is what people say emphatically. "Unless you are a child, an old person or too sick to help yourself, you should give something back for what you get." An important part of a viable strategy, therefore, is that assistance for at-risk youth be financed by methods such as micro-lending, work-study programs and education awards granted in exchange for national service in programs like AmeriCorps. These are programs that are based on the moral principle of reciprocity, not on the idea that people have a moral and legal right to expect the taxpayers to finance their skill development beyond the level of public education available to all.

Wooing Public Support

This consideration brings us to the third prong of my proposed youth strategy: the effort to win public support by making the moral principles underpinning the strategy match those of the American public. To launch and maintain a strategy of this sort, strong public support is a must.

To people unfamiliar with the subculture of the world of social policy, this aspect of the strategy might appear to be its least controversial element. At first glance, aligning the strategy with the moral values of the American public seems innocuous and desirable on principle. Unfortunately, however, the values of the public at large are at many points in direct conflict with the values of the social policy subculture. What seems like ordinary common sense to the majority of the public may seem insensitive, even cruel, to the social policy professional. For example, the public is far more discipline-minded and less tolerant of those who refuse to help themselves than most policy professionals are. The doctrine of need-based entitlements on which most of our public policies are based reflects the values of the social policy subculture. A great deal of public resistance to government social policy, especially welfare policy before its 1996 reform, reflected the public's views that the government was acting in an immoral fashion in helping to perpetuate a dependency life style that deeply offended the moral sensibilities of the majority. The principles that best reflect the public's own social morality are these:

- Reciprocity rather than entitlement.
- Compassion rather than legal obligation.
- Self-reliance and responsibility on the part of the individual.
- Evidence of strong motivation and effort. A willingness to make sacrifices in order to take advantage of opportunities.
- Evidence of strong family values.
- Refusal of further assistance to those who flout the rules (e.g., drug abuse, alcoholism, chronic failure to show up).
- Showing courtesy to and respect for others.
- Not rewarding people for antisocial, dependent behavior.

The issue can be stated in simple, fundamental terms. There is a traditional American ethos embodied in the idea of the "American Dream:" if you work hard, live by the rules and make the effort to better yourself through education, you can succeed in our society better than in any other nation on earth. I have been tracking this ethos for more than 40 years. Despite all of the transformations in social values in recent years, this faith persists. For some in The Forgotten Half it may be a bit battered and bruised, but beneath the surface it continues to have an astonishing vitality and potential. In my view, it is indispensable that a strategy for The Forgotten Half be grounded in this traditional faith.

The problems of the economically and educationally least favored Americans are not simple or tractable. They will not vanish overnight, even if the economy continues to thrive. A steady, patient, efficient long term strategy that will endure over decades is needed. The public will support such a strategy, but only if it reflects their values.

CHAPTER THREE

THE CHANGING AMERICAN FAMILY

Carol Emig

Chapter One described changes in the economic, educational and social landscape of one group of American adolescents and young adults — those of ages 16 to 24 who are neither in college nor college-bound. This chapter provides additional context for understanding the world of The Forgotten Half by examining how conditions and circumstances have changed in the last ten years, as well as the major policy changes in those years that affect children and families. The chapter also describes conditions and circumstances facing those teenagers and young adults among The Forgotten Half who are already raising children of their own.

BACKDROP TO CHANGE

When *The Forgotten Half* was released in 1988, unsettling social, economic and demographic trends affecting American families and their children were already well underway. The child poverty rate seemed permanently stalled at around 20 percent, thereby erasing much of the progress of the previous two decades in lessening childhood privation. In 1983, a blue ribbon commission had warned that, educationally, we were "a nation at risk."[1] Though not the first, it was by far the most publicized of a series of alarms on the state of elementary and secondary education in America. On virtually every measure of child well-being, racial and ethnic disparities persisted, with minority children and youth generally faring worse than their white peers. The 1980s also saw the continuation of a number of fundamental changes in family life that had begun years earlier, including increasing rates of separation, divorce and nonmarital childbearing, of mothers working outside the home and of children in a variety of child care arrangements.

Several of these changes were a departure from those of the 1960s and 1970s, decades in which many of the indicators of child and family well-being had improved dramatically. The child poverty rate, for example, declined throughout 1960s and was relatively stable for much of the 1970s. Medical advances had contributed to a rapid decline in the infant mortality rate and to the availability of vaccines for diseases that had disabled and even killed children in earlier decades. More young people were completing high school and going on to at least some college. The development of safe and effective contraceptives contributed to smaller families, which research indicates generally benefits children.

The downturns and upheavals of the late 1970s and early 1980s came against this backdrop of earlier progress. Two developments, in particular, provoked considerable debate and reflection over their causes, consequences and possible remedies. First, continuing racial disparities in education, child poverty and child health suggested that earlier civil rights triumphs, while essential, were not sufficient to address fundamental social inequalities. Second, increases in nonmarital childbearing, divorce and separation led many experts and policymakers to wonder whether America's children were unintentional victims of changing adult social norms. In both cases, some sought policy remedies, while others argued that the underlying causes, and thus the solutions, lay in cultural and individual choices.

In this context, *TFH* and other reports were necessary reminders to the nation that we needed to examine the social, economic and policy contexts in which American families were living and raising their children. Strengthening families and improving the daily lives and future prospects of children have since become familiar rallying cries for proposed policy and cultural changes emanating from every part of the political spectrum.

But how have the subjects of this rhetorical barrage fared in the subsequent years? Are children healthier and better educated? Are families stronger and more economically secure?

Have public policies and social norms changed to address the existing and emerging needs of children and families? This chapter attempts to answer these and related questions through an analysis of the leading indicators of child and family well-being and of the major policy changes of the last decade or so. It concludes with recommended areas for future action.

The last ten years have been neither the best nor the worst of times for American children and families. Taken as a whole, the vast array of reliable statistics on children and families paints a mixed picture of their status, as illustrated in this section. In some areas, such as infant and child mortality and immunizations, there have been noteworthy improvements. In others, such as substance abuse and violence, there have been troubling setbacks. In still other areas, such as achievement scores and the overall child poverty rate, there has been little change despite the prominence of educational and economic issues in the policy discussions of the last decade.

The data, when disaggregated, also reveal persistent differences in well-being by race and ethnicity, although in areas such as achievement scores, the gaps are narrowing. The large growth in single-parent families has also become an increasingly important variable, exerting considerable influence over families' economic and social well-being. (See discussion in Chapter One, above.)

AMERICAN CHILDREN: A CHANGING POPULATION

The population of children is simultaneously growing in number, diminishing as a proportion of the total population and increasing in racial and ethnic diversity. These multiple changes will challenge communities in their decisions about resource allocations and schools in their efforts to educate an increasingly diverse student population. The experiences and attitudes of this next generation of adult citizens will also influence our ability to maintain a pluralistic and democratic society.

The Size of the Child Population. Between 1990 and 1997, the number of children rose by more than five million, reaching 69.5 million in 1997. The Census Bureau projects that the population of children under age 18 will continue to increase for several decades to come and will grow to 77.6 million by 2020.

Children as a Proportion of the Total Population. While the number of children in the country has been growing for several years, children have been declining as a proportion of the population over a much longer period of time. In 1960, children were 36 percent of the total U.S. population. By 1980, they were 28 percent and, by 1997, they were 26 percent. The Census Bureau projects a continued decline to 24 percent by 2010, remaining there through 2020.

The Diversity of the Child Population. America's child population has become increasingly diverse since at least the 1960s, a trend that demographers predict will continue far into the future. The percentage of white, non-Hispanic children declined from 74 percent in 1980 to 66 percent in 1997, and will continue to decrease, to about 55 percent by 2020.

Historically, African American children have been the largest group of minority children in the country. Since at least 1980, 15 percent of U.S. children have been African American, while the proportion of children who are Hispanic has grown. (For the reader's ease, I generally use the terms white and African American throughout this chapter to mean *non-Hispanic* whites and *non-Hispanic* African Americans. When this is not the case, I note it in an endnote.) In 1997, Hispanics and African Americans each comprised about 15 percent of the child population. In numbers, there were slightly more Hispanic children than black children. By 2020, the child population is projected to be 22 percent Hispanic and 16 percent African American.

FAMILY LIFE: STILL HARRIED AFTER ALL THESE YEARS

It is hardly a secret that the proportion of households in which both parents or the sole custodial parent work outside the home has grown in the 1990s, although the rate of increase has slowed somewhat in recent years. This trend has obvious implications for family income, demand for child care and family routines. But it also poses challenges to schools seeking ways to involve parents in their children's education and to employers facing demands for more "family-friendly" workplace policies and benefits.

The March of Mothers into the Workforce. In 1996, almost two-thirds of mothers with children under 18 worked outside the home. The percentage of mothers in the workforce has increased over the last several decades, although at a slower pace in recent years. The employment rate of mothers with children under 18 increased from 53 percent in 1980 to 66 percent in 1996. While mothers with older children are more likely to work than mothers with younger children, 55 percent of mothers with children under age three were employed in 1996, compared to 37 percent in 1980.

Who's Minding the Kids? In 1995, 60 percent of the nation's children under age six who were not yet in kindergarten received some kind of care from adults other than their parents. (This includes both child care and participation in early childhood education programs.) Eighty-eight percent whose mothers work full-time and 75 percent whose mothers work part-time were receiving care from someone other than a parent.[3]

Child care in the United States is at best an evolving system, reflecting both parental preferences and market forces. Since the mid-1980s, there has been a significant decline in the percentage of young children cared for in family day care (i.e., care by a non-relative in the provider's home). In 1994, 18 percent of children under age five whose mothers worked full time were in family day care, compared to 27 percent in 1984-85. Over the same period, there was a smaller increase in the percentage of children in child care centers or preschools, from 30 percent in 1984-85 to 34 percent in 1994, and a slight increase in care by fathers, from 10 to 13 percent. There was virtually no change in the percentages of children receiving other forms of care, for example, by a relative or a baby-sitter in the home. The decline in family day care could reflect any number of factors, including concern by parents and providers over licensing and liability, growth in the number of child care centers and a strong economy that makes better-paying jobs available to those who previously provided or would have considered providing family day care.

Shrinking Family Time. When two parents or the sole custodial parent work outside the home, parents generally have less time to spend with their children, either in routine activities or special outings. For this or other reasons, between 1988 and 1995, the percentage of mothers and fathers who ate dinner with their children every day decreased slightly, as did that of those who helped their children with homework, or who spent time with their children at home working on a project or in an activity outside the home.[4]

EVOLVING FAMILY STRUCTURE: DADDY DOESN'T LIVE HERE ANYMORE

Children Living with One Parent. Decreases in the percentage of children living with two parents continued in the last decade, although, again, at a slower pace than two decades ago. Indeed, much of the alarming decline in the percentage of children living in two-parent families took place between 1970 and 1985, and has slowed considerably since then. From 1970 to 1985, the percentage of children living with two parents fell from 85 to 74 percent; by 1997, only 68 percent of U.S. children lived with two parents.

While the trend has slowed, it is still deeply troubling that a third of American children live with just one parent, generally a mother. Across a broad range of indicators, starting with poverty, children living with just one parent fare worse than children living with two married parents. Almost half (49 percent) of the children living in female-headed families in 1996 were poor, compared to ten percent of children in married-couple families. Poverty harms children immediately and for years afterward. Even after controlling for the effects of income, race and other background factors, children from single-parent families are still somewhat more likely to use alcohol and drugs, become teen parents and, as adults, earn less.[5] They are also less likely to complete high school.[6]

Differences in family structure by race and ethnicity have also persisted. The rate of decline in the percentage of children in two-parent families has slowed for whites, African Americans and Hispanics, but the percentage of African American children living with two married parents is very low. In 1997, only 35 percent of African American children lived with two parents. In contrast, 64 percent of Hispanic children and 75 percent of white children lived with two parents.[7]

Births Outside of Marriage. The last several decades have witnessed a sharp increase in the percentage of births that occur outside of marriage. What was somewhat rare in 1960 is fairly commonplace today. In 1960, 5.3 percent of all births were to unmarried women. By 1970, this figure doubled to 10.7 percent. It doubled again by 1985, when 22 percent of births were to unmarried women. Since 1994, the percentage of nonmarital births has stabilized at around 32 percent. In other words, about one in three babies born are to unmarried women.

Historically, a higher percentage of African American babies are born out of wedlock. In 1996, 69.8 percent of black births were to unmarried women, compared to 40.9 percent of Hispanic births and 25.7 percent of white births.[8]

FAMILY INCOME: THE ADVANTAGES OF TWO PARENTS

As Samuel Halperin points out in Chapter One, by conventional economic measures, the last decade "can only be described as a boom time." In particular, unemployment and inflation are at their lowest levels in decades. Halperin explores the extent to which this economic good fortune has bypassed many young families. For families in general, however, the income picture is distinctly divided. Two-parent families have reaped the benefits of a strong economy for more than two decades, but single-parent families have not. The same dichotomy exists in the child poverty rate.

***Median Family Income.*[9]** In the aggregate, families with children have not benefited from the nation's economic boom. The median income of *all* families with children was largely unchanged from 1975 to 1996, fluctuating between $39,300 and $41,200 in 1996 dollars.

But this aggregate figure is deceptive, masking important differences and changes among family types. Specifically, it masks the depressive effect that an increase in the percentage of female-headed households with children has had on the median income of families overall. *Median family income for female-headed households with children was slightly lower in 1993 than in 1975.* Between 1993 and 1996, it increased by 12 percent, but at $16,389 was still only 32 percent of the median income of married-couple families with children.

For married-couple families with children, on the other hand, median income has risen steadily, from almost $44,000 in 1975, to $47,000 in 1985, to almost $52,000 in 1996. Some of this increase is attributable to increased maternal employment, described earlier.

Median family income in 1996 was higher for white families than for African American and Hispanic families.[10] Again, family structure plays a large role by accounting for much of the difference between white and African American families. Family structure explains less of the difference in median family income between Hispanics and whites. More than three-quarters of the income difference between Hispanics and whites remains even after considering family type.

Children in Poverty. An extensive body of research documents the immediate and long-term risks that poverty poses to children. Children who are poor do less well than children who are not on a variety of health measures and on assessments of cognitive development, school achievement and emotional well-being.[11] Children who grow up poor are also more likely to become teen parents and, as adults, to earn less and be unemployed more.[12]

One in five children (20 percent) was poor in 1996, the same shameful percentage as in 1985. In the intervening decade, this percentage fluctuated slightly, never going below 19 percent or above 22 percent.[13] *A larger percentage of children are poor in the U.S. today than in 1970*, when the child poverty rate was 15 percent and, until that year, had been falling for at least a decade.

Once again, changes in family structure are at least partly responsible for a stubbornly high child poverty rate. As noted earlier, almost half (49 percent) of the children living in female-headed families in 1996 were poor, compared to ten percent of children in married-couple families, a difference that has persisted for almost three decades.

Persistent racial and ethnic differences in the child poverty rate are also troubling. In 1996, 16 percent of white children were poor, compared to 40 percent of African American and Hispanic children.[14] To a large degree, the black-white differential reflects the greater likelihood that an African American child will live in a female-headed household. The poverty rate for black children in married-couple households in 1996 was 14 percent. This is still higher than the nine percent of white children in married couple households who were poor, but it remains much lower than the overall poverty rate for black children. For Hispanic children, on the other hand, living with married parents does not appear to offer the same degree of protection against poverty. In 1996, 29 percent of Hispanic children in married-couple households were poor. This high poverty rate for Hispanic children in intact families apparently reflects low levels of education and the limited proficiency in English of many recent immigrants.

CHILDREN'S HEALTH AND SAFETY

Many of the traditional indicators of children's health, such as infant and child mortality rates, low birth weight, immunization rates and parents' reports of their children's health, either continued to improve in the last decade or stayed about the same. Today, reckless behaviors have supplanted disease as major threats to young people's health. Rates of youth homicides, for example, have increased substantially, and substance abuse (discussed in a later section) has recently increased among adolescents. In addition, children's access to health care continues to worry policymakers, the general public and parents. While there have been incremental improvements in the percentage of children who are covered by health insurance, a significant portion of children do not have it, and their access to regular and routine health care is thus limited.

Infant Mortality. Since the 1960s, the nation has made tremendous strides in improving birth outcomes, a gain that is illustrated most dramatically by the rapid decrease in the infant mortality rate. The infant death rate in 1960 was 26 deaths per 1000 live births. It was 10.6 in 1985, and 7.2 in 1996.

While this decline occurred among all racial and ethnic groups in the country, there are still differences across groups. African Americans, for example, have an infant mortality rate more than double that for whites and Hispanics. (The African American rate in 1996 was 14.2 deaths per 1,000 live births, compared to 6.0 for whites and 5.8 for Hispanics.)[15]

To a large extent, the decline in infant mortality reflects advances in medical practices and technology that enable many vulnerable newborns to survive. It may also reflect a greater willingness by women to seek and receive early and adequate prenatal care. In 1985, 76 percent of all mothers received prenatal care in the first trimester of their pregnancy; by 1996, almost 82 percent did. For African American and Hispanic mothers, those percentages increased from about 61 percent for both in 1985 to about 71 and 72 percent, respectively, in 1996. The increase for white mothers in the same period was from about 80 percent to about 84 percent.

Child and Youth Mortality. Mortality rates have been falling steadily and dramatically for children under age 15. But for youth ages 15-19 the rate has fluctuated markedly. The 1996 death rate for 15-19 year-olds was 79.2 deaths per 100,000 youth, not much different

Figure 3-1: Homicides, Ages 15-19, 1970-1996

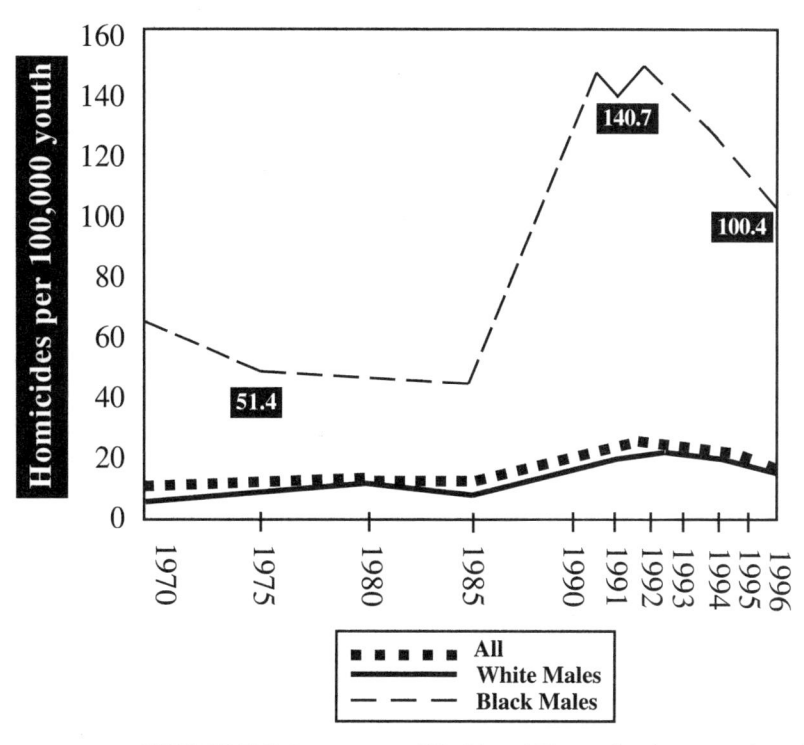

SOURCE: U.S. Department of Health and Human Services. *Trends in the Well-Being of America's Children and Youth: 1998.*

from the 1985 rate of 80.5. However, in the intervening years, the death rate for this group rose to a high of 89 in 1991.

In 1995, the leading causes of death for youth ages 15-19 were injuries from motor vehicles (33 percent of all deaths) and from firearms (29 percent of all deaths).[16] However, deaths from motor vehicle crashes decreased for this age group from 1970 through 1992 and have held steady since then.[17] In stark contrast, the rate of death from homicides more than doubled from 1970 to 1994, from 8.1 to 20.3 deaths per 100,000 youth in the 15-19 bracket. *Almost all of this increase occurred after 1985.* Since 1994, the youth homicide rate has decreased somewhat, to 15.5 deaths per 100,000 in 1996.

The homicide rate for 15-19 year-old black males is perhaps the single most horrifying statistic in the child and family field. It increased threefold, from 46.7 deaths per 100,000 in 1985 to 140.7 in 1993. While it has since decreased by about 30 percent, falling to 100.4 deaths per 100,000 in 1996, this is still more than eight times the homicide rate of 12.1 deaths per 100,000 white males in this age group.

Firearms were involved in 85 percent of all youth homicides in 1995, compared to 66 percent in 1985. Homicides involving firearms were more prevalent among black male youth than white male youth, although the numbers for both — 92 percent and 84 percent, respectively, in 1995 — are unacceptably high.

Health Insurance Coverage. Health insurance is obviously important for the access it provides to health care and for the financial protection it offers families, but it also serves an important preventive function by increasing the likelihood that a child will have a *regular* source of health care. In 1993, 97 percent of children with private health insurance and 94 percent of children with public health insurance had a regular health care provider, compared to 79 percent of children without insurance.[18]

Since 1987, the percentage of American children covered by private or public health insurance has remained relatively stable at 85 to 87 percent. In those 11 years, however, the percentage of children with private insurance decreased, while the percentage with public insurance increased. In 1987, 74 percent of all children had private health insurance; by 1996, only 66 percent did. In contrast, the percentage of all children receiving public health insurance rose from 19 percent in 1987 to 27 percent in 1993, before declining slightly to 25 percent in 1996. To some extent, the increase in the percentage of children receiving public insurance reflects the expansion of eligibility for Medicaid that Congress enacted in the mid-1980s.

Childhood Immunizations. Immunization rates reflect the extent to which children are protected from preventable communicable diseases. Indirectly, they reflect the extent to which children are receiving preventive health care. Between 1991 and 1996, there was a significant increase in the number of children who were fully vaccinated, in part as a result of the Clinton Administration's immunization initiative. Still, at least one million preschool-age children are not fully vaccinated.[19] Poor children are less likely to be fully vaccinated than children who are not poor, and African American and Hispanic children are somewhat less likely than white children to be fully vaccinated.[20]

DILEMMAS OF EDUCATION

Knowledge, skills and achievement — the desired outcomes of education — are the key to economic opportunity. For young people without an established record of on-the-job performance, these attributes are increasingly demonstrated by credentials, particularly baccalaureate and advanced degrees. As reported in Chapters One and Six, there have been notable increases in the percentage of young adults attending college and modest increases in those earning a four-year degree. As discussed in Chapter Five, elementary and high school students' reading achievement scores have shown little change, while math and science scores have improved somewhat. Given the emphasis on education reform during the last decade, these modest outcomes can hardly be cause for celebration. They suggest a need for harder work in the area of school reform and in other environments where children learn — the home, child care settings, early childhood education and after-school programs.

High School Dropout and Completion Rates. High school dropouts earn less, are employed less and are more likely to go to prison or receive welfare than their peers who finish high school.[21] Among white and Hispanic teenage girls, dropping out, especially at a young age, has been found to be associated with a much higher likelihood of a school-age pregnancy. This relationship between dropping out and pregnancy does not hold for African American teens, although other signs of disengagement from school were important predictors of a school-age pregnancy for this group.[22]

The "event dropout rate" for students in grades ten through 12, ages 15 to 24 — i.e., the proportion of students enrolled in these grades in the last year who were not enrolled and had not completed high school in the year in which data are reported — has fluctuated between four and six percent since 1975. Hispanics in this age group had the highest dropout rate in 1996 (nine percent), followed by African Americans (seven percent) and whites (four percent).

Overall high school completion rates for 18-24 year-olds remained between 85 percent and 86 percent between 1985 and 1996. While the overwhelming majority of these young people earned a high school diploma (76 percent in 1996), the percentage earning an equivalent credential such as the GED doubled from five to ten percent between 1990 and 1996.

High school completion rates differ substantially across racial and ethnic groups. Hispanics are much less likely to complete high school than either whites or African Americans. In 1996, 62 percent of Hispanics ages 18-24 had completed high school, less than the 67 percent who had done so in 1985. In comparison, high school completion rates were higher and increasing slightly for both African Americans and whites between 1985 and 1996 — from 81 percent to 83 percent for African Americans, and from 88 percent to 92 percent for whites.

College Attendance and College Completion. The percentage of 25-29 year-olds who have attended at least some college grew substantially between the mid-1980s and the mid-1990s, from 51 percent in 1985 to 65 percent in 1997. Whites have consistently been more likely to attend college than either African Americans or Hispanics. In 1997, 68 percent of whites, 54 percent of African Americans and 54 percent of Hispanics in this age group had some postsecondary education. Over time, the gap between whites and these other two groups has not narrowed.

As Halperin notes, enrollment in college is not the same as college completion. On this latter indicator of educational achievement, the gains are not as impressive. In 1985, 26 percent of 25-29 year-olds had earned a bachelor's degree or higher; by 1997, the percentage had grown to 32 percent. In 1997, whites were about twice as likely as African Americans and Hispanics to complete college — 35 percent of whites compared to 16 percent of African Americans and 18 percent of Hispanics. As with overall college attendance, this gap has not narrowed over time.

Achievement Among Elementary and High School Students. The National Assessment of Educational Progress (NAEP) assesses the reading, math and science performance of 9, 13 and 17 year-olds. In general, scores have either stayed about the same or increased modestly since publication of *TFH*.

Reading proficiency scores among 9 and 13 year-olds showed little change between 1984 and 1996. Average reading scores for these age groups were similar in 1996 to average scores in 1975. Among 17- year-olds, reading scores were stable between 1988 and 1992, and then declined slightly through 1996. Scores in 1996 were similar to those of 1975.

The news is somewhat better for math and science. For all three NAEP age groups, math proficiency scores increased substantially between 1982 and 1994 and were stable through 1996. This same pattern holds for science proficiency scores among 9 and 13 year-olds — increasing through 1994, then remaining stable. Science scores among 17 year-olds continued to improve through 1996.

For reading, math and science, white students on average scored higher than African American and Hispanic students. In each case, however, there were significant gains over time by minority students, so that the gap between whites and blacks and Hispanics has been narrowing.

Perhaps not surprisingly, achievement scores correlated with the educational level of parents. Students whose parents had completed high school scored much higher in reading proficiency than students whose parents had not done so. The highest science and math scores were recorded by students whose parents had completed college; the lowest by those whose parents had not finished high school.

RISK-TAKING BY ADOLESCENTS: WHAT'S THE MATTER WITH KIDS TODAY?

Risk-taking is a hallmark of adolescent development. In moderation, it is healthy and normal.[23] But for some young people, risk-taking becomes excessive and can threaten their own and others' safety and well-being. Of particular concern are those young people who engage in multiple risky behaviors, such as substance abuse *and* unprotected sexual activity *and* delinquent or illegal activity. This accumulation of risky behaviors by a young person heightens his or her risk of long-term negative outcomes.[24]

Smoking, Drinking and Drug Use.

Smoking, drinking, and drug use by adolescents have all followed a similar pattern since 1985 — decreasing until the early 1990s, then increasing through 1997. Among 12th graders in 1985, 19.5 percent reported *daily cigarette smoking*, down from almost 27 percent in 1975. Decreases continued until 1992, when 17.2 percent of high school seniors reported daily smoking. This trend began to reverse itself beginning in 1993 and by 1997 almost one-fourth of all 12th graders reported smoking daily.

In 1985, 36.7 percent of high school seniors reported *binge drinking* (having five or more drinks in a row) in the previous two weeks, down from a high of 41.2 percent in 1980. Decreases continued until 1993, when 27.5 percent reported binge drinking. This trend reversed in 1994. By 1997, 31.3 percent of high school seniors reported binge drinking.

In 1985, 25.7 percent of high school seniors reported *marijuana use* in the previous 30 days, down from 33.7 percent in 1980. Decreases continued through 1992, when 11.9 percent reported recent marijuana use, and then reversed beginning in 1993. By 1997, almost a quarter (23.7 percent) of twelfth graders reported having used marijuana in the previous 30 days.

Data for younger adolescents are only available for the years since 1991, but they too indicate increases in all of these activities from the early 1990s through 1997. In 1997, one in ten eighth graders and one in five tenth graders reported using marijuana in the previous 30 days, and almost as many reported regular smoking. A quarter of tenth graders reported binge drinking in 1997, as did almost 15 percent of eighth graders.

Sexually Active Teens.

Youth who are sexually active risk getting pregnant or causing a pregnancy, becoming a parent at too young an age and contracting or spreading sexually transmitted diseases. Data for 1995 indicate decreases in the percentage of teen girls and boys who had ever had intercourse — the first such decreases in several decades. In 1995, one-half of girls ages 15-19 reported that they had had intercourse, compared to 53 percent in 1988. (In the intervening years, the percentage of girls reporting that they had had intercourse reached a high of 55 percent in 1990 before decreasing.[25]) There was a similarly small but significant decrease in the percentage of teen males who reported ever having had intercourse, from 60 percent in 1988 to 55 percent in 1995.[26]

Contraceptive Use by Teens.

Although the overwhelming majority of sexually experienced teens say they want to avoid pregnancy,[27] and although contraceptive use by teens has increased in recent years, teens still use contraception inconsistently.

Condoms are the most common form of contraception used by teens. In 1995, 67 percent of sexually experienced males ages 15 to 19 reported using a condom at their most recent intercourse, a significant increase from 57 percent in 1988. Male teenagers also reported more consistent use of condoms in 1995 than in 1988. In 1995, 45 percent reported always using a condom during intercourse, compared to 33 percent in 1988. Similarly, the percentage who reported never using a condom decreased over this time period, from 18 percent in 1988 to 10 percent in 1995.[28]

Births to Teens.

The U.S. teen birth rate in 1986 was 50.2 births per 1,000 females ages 15 to 19, the lowest it had been in more than 50 years. The trend then reversed, much to the nation's distress, and the teen birth rate rose by a quarter over the next five years, reaching 62.1 in 1991. Since then, rates fell by about 12 percent. While this downward trend is good news, the 1996 rate of 54.4 births per 1,000 females ages 15-19 is still higher than the 1986 rate,[29] and the U.S. continues to have a much higher teen birth rate than do other industrialized nations.

The teen birth rate fell the most for black teens, declining by almost 21 percent between 1991 and 1996. In contrast, the teen birth rate for white females declined by 13 percent, and by almost five percent for Hispanic teens.[30] The teen birth rate for Hispanics only began to drop in 1996, after staying virtually the same for much of the 1990s.[31]

Still, tremendous disparities remain in teen birth rates across these groups. In 1996, the white birth rate was 37.6 births per 1,000 females ages 15-19, compared to 94.2 for African Americans and 101.8 for Hispanics.[32]

RECENT MAJOR POLICY CHANGES

There have been several notable changes in the last ten years in national policies affecting families' economic security, children's health and parents' ability to balance family and work responsibilities. While each is significant, together they do not add up to a coherent set of policies to support families, but are instead piecemeal responses to prominent issues and concerns. To some extent, this may reflect the lead role that states and localities have traditionally played in some of the major areas of youth policy, such as education policy. It may also reflect a national discomfort with "comprehensive" policy initiatives. With the advent of welfare reform and devolution to the states, there will almost certainly be even more diversity in policies and programs affecting children and families in the next decade.

Family Economic Security

The dominant policy change affecting children and families since publication of *TFH* was the enactment in 1996 of the Personal Responsibility and Work Opportunity Reconciliation Act (PRWORA), a truly radical reform of the nation's welfare policies. This reversal of 60 years of welfare policy did not develop in a vacuum. It was preceded by two other major policy changes: expansion of the Earned Income Tax Credit for working poor families and the Family Support Act of 1988. The latter was swept away by PRWORA; the former was not changed and will presumably take on even greater significance if the number of working poor families increases as a result of welfare reform.

Earned Income Tax Credit. The Earned Income Tax Credit was created in 1975 to supplement the income of low-income working parents. Unlike other tax credits, the EITC is refundable, meaning that if the credit to which a family is entitled exceeds the amount of tax it owes, the family receives a refund of the difference. The refundable nature of the credit was intended to encourage work by increasing the income of low-wage working parents enough to overcome any work disincentives created by welfare.[33]

The EITC has been expanded several times in the last decade. In 1990, for example, the credit was more than doubled from its 1986 level, and some adjustments were made to reflect family size, to offset partially the cost of health insurance for a dependent child and to provide additional income to families with children under age one.[34] As a result of an expansion of EITC in 1993, a low-income worker with two or more children receives a 40 percent subsidy, that is, a worker earning $5 an hour receives a $2 an hour credit.[35] The EITC begins to phase out once a family's earnings rise above a certain threshold ($11,950 in 1997). A family with two children loses eligibility for the EITC when its income exceeds $29,290.[36] In 1997, the maximum credit was $3,656.

For many low-income parents, the EITC provides a powerful work incentive, despite concerns expressed by some economists that it creates work disincentives at the point where the credit begins to phase out.[37] It continues to enjoy bipartisan support, although conservative support has waned somewhat in recent years as the amount of the credit and the number of families claiming it have increased. In 1994, 18 million households claimed the credit, at a cost to the federal government of almost $20 billion.[38] By 1996, its cost rose to about $25 billion.[39] If, as is reasonable to expect, the 1996 welfare reform substantially increases the number of parents in low-wage jobs, the cost of the credit to the government will also increase. This, in turn, may further erode public support for the EITC in the future.

Family Support Act. The 1988 Family Support Act (FSA) was a major policy reflection of public dissatisfaction with the welfare system. It required parents of children older than age three to work, attend school or participate in a job training program. It gave states the option to extend this requirement to parents of children as young as one year old. States were required to make training programs available and to provide child care to parents while they completed their education or training and for 12 months after they started working. In addition to child care, the FSA provided continued Medicaid coverage for one year after a welfare recipient left the welfare rolls for a job. It also strengthened the enforcement of child support requirements.

These reforms were intended to be enacted over a number of years. But before the Family Support Act was fully implemented, public and Congressional sentiment had built for a more radical revision of the nation's welfare system. Always an important and difficult political issue, welfare reform was a dominant theme in the 1992 presidential campaign, with candidate Bill Clinton pledging to "end welfare as we know it." By the end of 1994, control of the Congress shifted to the Republicans, along with a majority of the governorships. The legislation that ultimately passed Congress and was signed by the President in 1996 went much further than the earlier Clinton proposals.

Temporary Assistance for Needy Families. The Personal Responsibility and Work Opportunity Reconciliation Act of 1996 (PRWORA) ended the entitlement to cash assistance that had existed for poor families with children for 60 years, and replaced it with the Temporary Assistance to Needy Families (TANF) program, in other words, block grants to the states. Under TANF, states have broad authority and discretion to design their own welfare programs, with minimal federal requirements. Its major provisions are:[40]

- *Time limits.* Families may receive cash assistance for a maximum of 60 months. This is a lifetime limit and the months need not be consecutive. States may exempt up to 20 percent of families experiencing various hardships from this time limit.
- *Work requirements.* Parents receiving TANF assistance are required to work within two years of beginning assistance. For teenage parents, attending high school or pursuing a GED satisfies this work requirement.
- *Requirements for unmarried teen parents.* A custodial parent under age 18 who is not married must live with her parent, legal guardian or other adult relative in order to receive benefits.
- *State participation rates.* TANF sets specific employment goals for states. For example, 40 percent of a state's welfare recipients must be working by 2000 and 50 percent by 2002. The threshold is higher for two-parent families; from 2000 on, 90 percent of these families must be working. A single custodial parent of a child under age six is exempted from the work requirement if she or he can prove that child care is not available.

PRWORA also has provisions on the fertility behavior of adults and teenagers that, in some cases, go beyond families receiving public assistance.[41] These provisions are explicitly intended to promote marriage; discourage childbearing by unmarried women of any age, whether or not they receive welfare; and promote abstinence outside of marriage for everyone, not just teenagers. Specific provisions related to sexual behavior and childbearing include:

- *"Illegitimacy bonus."* Beginning in Fiscal Year 1999, the federal government will award bonuses of $20 million each to up to five states that demonstrate the largest net decrease in out-of-wedlock births and reduce their abortion rates to below their 1995 level. (If fewer than five states qualify for this bonus, the maximum bonus per state will be $25 million.)[42] This goal applies to *all* women in the state, not just welfare recipients. More generally, states must specify how they plan to prevent nonmarital pregnancies, with a special emphasis on teen pregnancies.[43]
- *Abstinence education.* PRWORA provides $50 million a year for five years to fund state programs that promote abstinence for all unmarried individuals. Abstinence education efforts funded under TANF may not include information about contraception and must be separate from more comprehensive sex education and family planning programs.[44] These programs are not restricted to children and youth.
- *Family caps.* States have the option under TANF to impose a family cap on welfare receipt, that is, they can deny increased benefits to families that have another child while receiving assistance. As of May 1997, at least 19 states had adopted family caps.[45]
- *Teen pregnancy prevention programs.* PRWORA requires the Secretary of the U.S. Department of Health and Human Services to establish national goals to prevent teen pregnancy and to ensure that at least 25 percent of communities have teen pregnancy prevention programs in place.

- *Statutory rape study.* The law directs the Attorney General to study the link between teen pregnancy and statutory rape and to educate state and local law enforcement officers on the prevention and prosecution of statutory rape.

Finally, PRWORA made significant changes in the way federal child care funds are provided to states. The law combines three existing child care programs (AFDC Child Care, Transitional Child Care and At-Risk Child Care) into one block grant, the Child Care and Development Block Grant. Both AFDC Child Care and Transitional Child Care had been entitlements; the federal government matched all state expenditures for child care under these programs. Funding for the new block grant is capped. While the cap in 1998 is at a higher level than the level of spending that was projected for the entitlements, the end result limits the amount of federal child care funds potentially available to states.[46]

It is simply too soon in late 1998 to assess the full impact of TANF on children and families. Welfare caseloads are falling, but are families that leave welfare earning sufficient income to meet their basic material needs? Is the supply of child care adequate to meet increased demand and, more important, is the quality of care sufficiently high to ensure that this population of children is school-ready? Will parents feel depressed and overwhelmed by time pressures, or will welfare reform result in parents with a greater sense of control over their lives, less depression, and improved parenting? Will newly employed parents have jobs that offer health insurance and if they do, will they have sufficient income to pay any employee portion of the premiums? These questions remain to be answered, and compel us to monitor closely the progress of welfare reform in every state.

Martha Zaslow and colleagues at Child Trends applied findings from evaluations of past welfare-to-work programs and broader research on children and families to identify the specific provisions of welfare reform that are most likely to affect child development and family functioning. They warn that children in families who have been on welfare for a long period of time — in the families most likely to reach time limits — are already at high risk of poor development. For example, in one study, long-term recipients were found to provide their children with less intellectual stimulation and emotional support. Their children scored lower on tests of vocabulary and social maturity. The mothers were more likely to display depressive symptoms, to feel less control over their lives and to have fewer social supports than short-term welfare recipients.[47]

Child Trends also warns that the greater flexibility of states under the Child Care and Development Block Grant to determine eligibility for child care subsidies, subsidy levels and the types of care that can be subsidized may lead more families to turn to unlicensed forms of child care. While such care is often less expensive and more flexible than licensed care — and in these respects more attractive to parents in low-wage jobs and jobs with nontraditional hours — research shows that it is also often of lower quality than regulated care, and thus of less benefit to children.[48] This poses a particularly difficult dilemma for states that are seeking to support parental work effort while enhancing the school readiness of children from low-income families.

Balancing Family and Work Responsibilities

The difficulties that many parents face as they seek to balance family and work responsibilities, already evident in 1988, are just as pressing today. While employers offer various "family-friendly" benefits, the only notable federal policy development of the last decade in this area was the enactment in 1993 of the Family and Medical Leave Act. Passed by Congress in earlier years, the legislation was signed by President Clinton upon taking office in January 1993.

The Family and Medical Leave Act (FMLA) requires private sector employers of 50 or more employees to provide up to 12 weeks of job-protected, unpaid leave during any 12-month period to care for a newborn, a newly-adopted child or a foster child; to care for an immediate family member (child, parent or spouse) with a serious health condition; or because an employee has a serious health condition. Health benefits must be continued during that period.

Enactment of the FMLA was a major step forward in the development of a more family-friendly body of employment law. But it pales in comparison to similar policies in other countries. In a survey conducted by the International Labor Organization of maternity leave provisions in 152 countries, the U.S. was one of only six countries that do not require paid maternity leave. (The other five: Australia, New

Zealand, Lesotho, Swaziland and Papua New Guinea.)[49] While there are many historic and political reasons for differences between employment laws in the U.S. and in other countries, the contrast is nonetheless striking. Canada, for example, guarantees a 16-week maternity leave, with more than half pay for 15 of those weeks.[50]

Children's Health

A fierce and ultimately futile battle raged for much of President Clinton's first term over how best to provide health insurance to millions of uninsured Americans. In its aftermath, Congress and the President abandoned efforts to produce a comprehensive health insurance bill, opting instead for incremental reforms. The most significant of these for children is the 1997 Child Health Insurance Program.

The Child Health Insurance Program (CHIP) is a block grant to states of $20.3 billion over five years to provide insurance to uninsured children in families with incomes up to 200 percent of the federal poverty line. Under CHIP, states may expand their existing Medicaid program at an enhanced matching rate, create or expand their own child health insurance programs or do both. Regardless of approach, states must provide matching funds of their own. The law includes safeguards to prevent states from substituting a lower-cost state program for the existing Medicaid program.[51]

At this writing in late 1998, CHIP is just underway. Already, questions have been raised about the extent to which it covers, or could potentially cover, currently uninsured children. According to the Urban Institute, of the 10.6 million children who were uninsured in 1994-95, 7.5 million, or almost three-quarters, lived in families with incomes below the CHIP ceiling of 200 percent of poverty. Of these, 4.5 million are eligible for Medicaid and thus not eligible for CHIP, which leaves about 2.9 million children eligible for CHIP. Yet the Urban Institute estimates that the program has sufficient funding to cover twice that number, or 5.8 million children. Its analysts recommend using some of this funding to enroll children in Medicaid who are currently eligible but not enrolled or, to the extent possible under the new law, expand the CHIP income limit above 200 percent of poverty. (Under CHIP, states set their own standards for calculating family income and could thus choose to disregard certain family assets in calculating income.)[52]

WHAT'S AHEAD FOR FAMILIES AND CHILDREN?

For many of the ills that plague children and families, there are both social and individual, public and private, causes. Public policies and social programs have an essential place in the list of possible remedies, but so do the actions and decisions of parents, adolescents, communities, schools and employers.

In 1991, the National Commission on Children declared that solutions "will require creative public policies and private sector practices, thoughtful investments of public and private resources, and a significant commitment of individual time and attention to the needs of children and their families."[53] Those words are as true at the end of the decade as they were at the beginning.

What direction, then, should public policies, private sector practices and individual decisions take in the next decade? This chapter concludes by suggesting policies and private actions in three broad areas: *investing in early childhood, stronger families, and positive youth development.*

Invest Early

The single smartest investment the nation could make in its children and families would be to support them in a variety of ways in the early years of a child's life. The evidence for doing so is overwhelming: new knowledge of early brain development; years of research on the value of high quality child care and early childhood programs, especially for low-income children; and a documented relationship between family income when a child is young and subsequent school achievement.

Since the late 1980s, science has produced breathtaking new information on early brain development and its links to children's physical, intellectual and emotional growth. A warm, consistent, stimulating environment — in the home and in out-of-home care — promotes development in all of these domains. Babies benefit enormously from being held and touched, talked to, read to and sung to and from having their need for food, comfort and interaction met with care and sensitivity.

With respect to child care, research documents that high-quality child care enhances children's development regardless of their family income, but it appears to contribute the most to children in low-income families. High-quality child care can enhance language development, school readiness and social competence for children of all income levels. Poor children appear to reap the greatest benefits in improved reading and math skills and their ability to relate positively to others.[54]

New research by Greg Duncan and colleagues found that family economic conditions in early childhood had the greatest impact on later school achievement, especially deep and long-term poverty. Family income in early childhood had a bigger impact on completed schooling than did income during middle childhood.[55]

As is evident from the indicators and policies discussed here, family life in contemporary America is anything but simple. How, for example, do employed parents find sufficient time for their children, especially in the critical early months and years? How do they ensure that a caregiver provides appropriate and sufficient stimulation and attention? How does the child care industry, with its notoriously low wages, attract and keep talented staff and ensure low child-to-caregiver ratios? How does a teenage mother, already overwhelmed by the challenges of adolescence, find it in herself to provide consistent and sensitive care to her child? How does an unemployed single father connect with a baby for whom he cannot provide economic support?

Strong, sustained support for families in the early years of a child's life will require a large commitment of public, private and personal resources. Among the approaches suggested from data, research and families' experiences are these:

Enhanced Income for Poor Families with Young Children. Increasing and stabilizing the income of poor families with very young children (perhaps up to age six) could help families in several ways, all of which contribute to children's school readiness. It could provide parents with more time for their children, by allowing a single mother to avoid working two jobs or even to work less than full time. It could enable one parent in a two-parent family to work part-time or stay home. It could help working parents purchase higher quality child care, or enable them to enroll their children in a preschool or other early childhood education program. At the very least, more income makes it more likely that parents can provide their children with toys, books and developmentally stimulating outings and experiences.

The incomes of poor families with children can be enhanced through a number of mechanisms, such as further expansion of the Earned Income Tax Credit, some other tax credit targeted to poor families with children or an increased minimum wage. This income supplement might be limited to poor families with *young* children for a number of reasons. Parents with young children are generally young themselves. As Halperin points out in Chapter One, families with a household head under age 30 saw their inflation-adjusted income decline by more than 14 percent between 1973 and 1996. Almost a quarter of these young families have incomes below the poverty line. The child poverty rate for children in young families was a highly disturbing 38 percent in 1996.

At the same time that their incomes are low, these young families may also have some of their highest child-related expenses. The years before a child enters school are also generally the years when working parents spend the most on child care, both because infant care is the most expensive form of child care and because care is often needed for a greater proportion of the day.

Better Child Care for Low-Income Children. High-quality child care is the product of several features: teachers who are sensitive and responsive to children's needs, low child-to-teacher ratios, small group sizes, well-compensated teachers, and sufficient levels of teacher training.[56] But this kind of care is scarce, especially for low-income families.

Welfare reform could be an opportunity to improve the quality of child care available to poor children. However, at this early stage TANF appears to encourage just the opposite by giving states great leeway to determine the types of care that can be purchased with public subsidies. It seems unlikely that states will require TANF families to seek out high-quality care, although this is precisely the type of care that research indicates would benefit their children the most.

In the near future, increased regulation of child care seems unlikely in this era of less government. Nevertheless, finding ways to enhance the quality, consistency, and affordability of care represent important policy tasks if the younger generation of welfare recipients is to receive the early quality care they need to succeed in school.

An expanded Head Start program — serving more children for more hours each day — may be another vehicle for providing enriched early childhood experiences to low-income children. Despite the program's documented benefits to children (including improvements in their health and social behavior and reductions in the risk that a child will fail a grade or need special education services),[57] Head Start still reached only about a third of eligible children in 1996.[58] In light of this, it may be unrealistic to assume that program hours would be expanded. One way to ensure that low-income children whose parents are employed receive the benefits of Head Start is to encourage these programs to link with child care providers in their community to provide care for that portion of the day when Head Start is not in operation.

Promote Strong Families

Families at all income levels are stressed, even for simple things like more time together. Some evidence indicates families report spending less time together for meals and activities. Some of these developments reflect economic pressures while others reflect personal choices and problems in relationships. There may be little that government can or should do to keep a high-conflict marriage together or to coerce adults to marry. But as a society and a culture, we can take actions and adopt attitudes that promote responsible parenting and strong, stable marriages and that discourage childbearing outside of marriage. For example:

- Employers can voluntarily extend the terms of the Family and Medical Leave Act to allow for longer leaves and paid leaves.[59] They can permit job-sharing, telecommuting, part-time work and other arrangements that give parents more time to meet family responsibilities. They can provide employees with paid time off to volunteer in a child's school, attend a parent-teacher conference or take a child to the doctor. They can subsidize child care and they can provide a wide range of information of value to parents, from guidance on identifying high-quality child care to seminars on child development.
- Private insurers and health maintenance organizations can include parenting education among the covered services available from children's health care providers. Heeding research findings on early brain development, 24 health maintenance organizations announced in 1998 that they would include developmental assessments and parenting information in their basic services to families.[60]
- Religious and social service organizations can do more to provide counseling to individuals and couples both before they marry and afterwards. Medicaid might even cover some of this counseling.
- Community institutions can sponsor family support centers and parent education programs. The Early Head Start program, created in Congress' 1994 reauthorization of Head Start, provides modest federal assistance for family support services to low-income families with children under age three. These services are coordinated with local Head Start programs. In 1996, 10,000 children and their families in 42 states received assistance from Early Head Start.
- State welfare-to-work programs can provide basic parenting education, especially to teen parents. In the New Chance program, teen mothers (all high school dropouts) improved their parenting skills after an average of just 17 hours of parenting education.[61] Improved parenting benefits children and, for mothers who haven't experienced much success in school or the workplace, becoming better parents may provide the motivation to persevere in a job search or job training effort, or in an educational program.
- State welfare reform efforts can also vigorously promote ways for fathers who are not married to the mothers of their children to fulfill TANF's work requirements and support their children in this way. Paying child support can be an important first step for a disengaged or estranged father to connect with his child. Not every couple with a child will or should marry, but every parent who is able to support a child should do so.
- Family planning services should be easily available and affordable to anyone seeking them. This can happen by expanding public family planning services and covering the cost of these services in private health insurance policies.
- The media can send stronger and more consistent messages about responsible sexual behavior, the value to children of living with two parents in a low-conflict

marriage and the costs (to a child and a parent) of childbearing outside of marriage.

Support Positive Youth Development

Reducing excessive risk-taking by adolescents — for example, in their sexual behavior, their use of harmful substances or their decisions about delinquent or illegal actions — remains a challenge to researchers and program designers alike. There are literally thousands of programs for adolescents, especially those considered "at risk." All are presumably well-meaning and some may be very effective, but relatively few have been rigorously evaluated. For all of the public attention to adolescents, we still know very little about how to prevent risky behaviors and promote positive ones. The challenge of the next decade is to expand our knowledge in this area, apply it vigorously, and evaluate the effectiveness carefully.

As a starting point, we have known for some time that supporting adolescent development (indeed, supporting the development of children at every stage), requires a comprehensive approach. Some youth have what they need in their own families and communities. Others need help from programs to fill the gaps. As *TFH* pointed out in 1988, "our society cannot expect to deal successfully with just one aspect of a young person's life and hope to bring focus to every other." The W.T. Grant Foundation Commission wisely reminded us that the influences of the family, school, community and workplace in a young person's life are tightly interwoven and that solutions must therefore be broadly based and integrated.

We also know that the antecedents of at least some risky behaviors go back many years and have roots close to home. Poverty, family dysfunction, early behavior problems and early school failure increase the likelihood of a teen pregnancy[62] — and probably of other forms of risk-taking. This suggests that a strong emphasis on early childhood investments and strengthening families may reap benefits many years later.

Finally, we know from research that youth do best when they have a deep and abiding connection to their parents, their community and their future. Adolescents who feel close to their parents and can communicate openly with them are somewhat protected from a variety of risks, including emotional distress; smoking, drinking and marijuana use; violence; and early sexual behavior. To a lesser extent, youth are also protected from emotional distress when parents are with them at key times of the day and when parents have high expectations for their school achievement.[63] Limited evaluations also suggest that programs for adolescents that focus on school success and that provide apprenticeships and employment and training opportunities appear effective.[64] Further research in this area is certainly warranted.

Tend to Unfinished Business

Many of the indicators reviewed here are troubling in part because they have persisted for so long. Some children and even more parents still lack health insurance. The rate of youth homicide, though declining recently, remains at an alarmingly high level, with most of it attributable to guns. Achievement scores do not reflect the years of public discussion and investment in education reform. In some cases, the approaches suggested below are costly; in almost all cases, they are and have long been highly controversial.

- *Health insurance.* As a nation, we must find a way, either publicly or through private insurers, to provide sufficient health insurance to everyone. While the Child Health Insurance Program will provide urgently needed help to millions of children, it is still an incremental reform that falls far short of the goal of universal coverage. When parents do not have health insurance, children are at risk. A serious illness or injury to an uninsured parent can plunge a family into poverty.
- *Firearms.* Firearms were involved in 85 percent of all youth homicides in 1995. While the roots of youth violence almost certainly go deeper and are more complex than access to guns, youth homicides could almost certainly be reduced by severely limiting young people's access to guns.
- *Greater parental involvement in their children's education.* Other contributors to this volume examine educational issues in detail. I would add only that much more attention is needed to the role of parents in supporting and encouraging their children's learning. For younger children, parental involvement in activities like reading to a child daily, visiting a library at least once a month and telling stories on a regular basis can promote literacy and prepare a child for school.[65] Libraries, pediatricians and even some mayors and governors have already begun to stress the importance of reading to young children on a daily basis. Programs like Parents as Teachers and the

Home Instruction Preschool Program (HIPPY) work directly with parents to build their skills as their children's first teachers. All of these laudable efforts should be expanded. For older children, researchers associate higher levels of parental involvement in their children's schools with closer monitoring of schools, greater parent-teacher contact and coordination, more attention by a teacher to a student and earlier identification of potential learning problems.[66] This suggests that schools must be more creative in involving parents in their children's education, especially noncustodial and employed parents who may not be available during regular school hours. Employers, as suggested above, must be more willing to grant time off for school-related activities. And parents, of course, must take advantage of these opportunities.

> *"[T]he antecedents of at least some risky behaviors go back many years and have roots close to home. Poverty, family dysfunction, early behavior problems and early school failure increase the likelihood of a teen pregnancy — and probably other forms of risk-taking."*

NOTES

The author is indebted to her colleagues at Child Trends, whose work is the basis for the data presented in this chapter. Special thanks go to Kristin Moore and Brett Brown for reviewing drafts of the chapter, and to Laura Gitelson and Michelle Harper for research assistance.

[1] National Commission on Excellence in Education. *A Nation at Risk: The Imperative for Educational Reform.* Washington, DC: U.S. Department of Education, 1983.

[2] Unless otherwise noted, all data in this section are from U.S. Department of Health and Human Services. *Trends in the Well-Being of America's Children and Youth: 1998.* Washington, DC: U.S. Government Printing Office, (forthcoming).

[3] Federal Interagency Forum on Child and Family Statistics. *America's Children: Key National Indicators of Well-Being, 1998.* Washington, DC: U.S. Government Printing Office, p. 55.

[4] Unpublished analyses of the National Survey of Families and Households by Randall Day in "Indicators of Child Well-Being: New Indicators from Existing Data," a report by Kristin A. Moore and Brett V. Brown of Child Trends for the NICHD Family and Child Well-Being Network, December 29, 1997.

[5] Amato, P.R. "Children's Adjustment to Divorce: Theories, Hypotheses, and Empirical Support." *Journal of Marriage and the Family.* 55:23-58.

[6] Ditto.

[7] Data on whites and African Americans include some Hispanics.

[8] Ditto.

[9] I am indebted to Richard Wertheimer, Senior Research Associate at Child Trends, for his analyses of the median income of families with children.

[10] Data on whites and African Americans include some Hispanics.

[11] Brooks-Gunn, Jeanne, Greg J. Duncan and Nancy Maritato. "Poor Families, Poor Outcomes: The Well-Being of Children and Youth." *Consequences of Growing Up Poor.* New York: Russell Sage Foundation, 1997, p. 1.

[12] An, C., R. Haveman and B. Wolfe. "Teen Out-of-Wedlock Births and Welfare Receipt: The Role of Childhood Event and Economic Circumstance." *Review of Economics and Statistics,* 75:195-208.

[13] U.S. Bureau of the Census. *Statistical Abstract of the United States: 1995.* (115th edition.) Washington, DC: 1995, p. 480.

[14] Data on whites and African Americans include some Hispanics.

[15] Ditto.

[16] Federal Interagency Forum on Child and Family Statistics, p. 28.

[17] Ditto.

[18] Simpson, G., B. Bloom, R.A. Cohen and P.E. Parsons. *Access to Health Care. Part 1: Children.* Washington, DC: National Center for Health Statistics. Vital Health Stat 10(196), 1997.

[19] Office of Communication, Division of Media Relations, Centers for Disease Control and Prevention. "Facts About the Childhood Immunization Initiative," 1997.

[20] Ditto.

[21] McMillen, M.E and P. Kaufman. *Dropout rates in the United States: 1996.* Washington, DC: U.S. Department of Education, National Center for Education Statistics, NCES 98-250.

[22] Manlove, J. "The Influence of High School Dropout and School Disengagement on the risk of School-Age Pregnancy," *Journal of Research on Adolescence.* 8(2), 187-220.

[23] National Commission on Children. *Beyond Rhetoric: A New American Agenda for Children and Families.* Washington, DC: U.S. Government Printing Office, 1991, p. 50.

[24] Ditto, pp. 53-54.

[25] Moore, K.A., A.K. Driscoll and L.D. Lindberg. *A Statistical Portrait of Adolescent Sex, Contraception, and Childbearing.* Washington, DC: The National Campaign to Prevent Teen Pregnancy, February 1998, p. 19.

[26] Sonenstein, F.L., L. Ku, L.D. Lindber, C.F. Turner and J.H. Pleck. "Changes in Sexual Behavior and Condom Use among Teenaged Males: 1988 to 1995," *American Journal of Public Health,* June 1988, Vol. 88, No. 6, pp. 956-959.

> "The single smartest investment the nation could make in its children and families would be to support them in a variety of ways in the early years of a child's life. The evidence for doing so is overwhelming: new knowledge of early brain development; years of research on the value of high quality child care and early childhood programs, especially for low-income children; and a documented relationship between family income when a child is young and subsequent school achievement."

[27] Alan Guttmacher Institute. *Sex and America's Teenagers.* New York: Alan Guttmacher Institute, 1994.

[28] Sonenstein, et al.

[29] Moore, K.A., A.D. Romano, L.B. Gitelson and L.C. Connon. *Facts At a Glance, Child Trends.* Washington, DC, October 1997, and Ventura, S.J., T.J. Mathews and S.C. Curtin. "Teenage Births in the United States: State Trends: 1991-96, An Update," *Monthly Vital Statistics Report*, Vol. 46, No. 11, Suppl, 2, June 30, 1998, National Center for Health Statistics, Centers for Disease Control, p. 2.

[30] Calculated from data presented in Ventura et al, p. 5.

[31] Ventura et al.; Moore et al.

[32] Ventura et al., p. 5.

[33] Schiller, Bradley R. *The Economics of Poverty and Discrimination.* New Jersey: Prentice Hall, 1995, p. 273.

[34] National Commission on Children. *Beyond Rhetoric: A New American Agenda for Children and Families.* Washington, DC: U.S. Government Printing Office, 1991, p. 88.

[35] Schiller, p. 273.

[36] Internal Revenue Service. Earned Income Credit (EIC) Table, 1997.

[37] Ditto, pp. 273-274.

[38] Ditto, p. 273.

[39] Blank, Rebecca. *It Takes a Nation: A New Agenda for Fighting Poverty.* New York: Russell Sage Foundation, 1997, p. 113.

[40] Greenberg, M. and S. Savner. "A Brief Summary of Key Provisions of the Temporary Assistance for Needy Families Block Grant of H.R. 3734 (The Personal Responsibility and Work Opportunity Reconciliation Act of 1996)." Washington, DC: Center for Law and Social Policy, August 13, 1996.

[41] Alan Guttmacher Institute. "Welfare Reform, Marriage and Sexual Behavior," *Issues in Brief.* New York and Washington, DC: Alan Guttmacher Institute, 1997.

[42] Greenberg and Savner.

[43] Wertheimer, Richard and Kristin Moore. "Childbearing by Teens: Links to Welfare Reform," *New Federalism: Issues and Options for States.* Washington, DC: The Urban Institute, 1998.

[44] Ditto.

[45] Alan Guttmacher Institute.

[46] Greenberg, M. "A Summary of Key Child Care Provisions of H.R. 3734." Washington, DC: Center for Law and Social Policy, August 1996.

[47] Zaslow, M., K. Tout, C. Botsko and K. Moore. "Welfare Reform and Children: Potential Implications," *New Federalism: Issues and Options for States.* Washington, DC: The Urban Institute, 1998.

[48] Zaslow et al.

[49] Olson, Elizabeth. "U.N. Survey Finds Only Six Nations Don't Offer Paid Maternity Leave," *New York Times.* February 16, 1998.

[50] Press Associates. "Trailing the World on Maternity Leave," *UAW Washington Report.* Vol. 38, No. 5, February 13, 1998.

[51] Mann, Cindy and Jocelyn Guyer. "Overview of the New Child Health Block Grant." Washington, DC: Center on Budget and Policy Priorities, revised August 28, 1997.

[52] Ullman, F., B. Bruen and J. Holahan. *The State Children's Health Insurance Program: A Look at the Numbers.* Washington, DC: The Urban Institute, 1998.

[53] National Commission on Children, p. 12.

[54] Zaslow, Martha and Erin Oldham. "Child Care for Families in the Transition from Welfare to Work: Key Findings from the Research." Presentation given at the Child Care Policy Research Symposium sponsored by the Child Care Bureau, Administration on Children, Youth and Families, Department of Health and Human Services, June 19, 1996, Washington, D.C.

[55] Duncan, Greg, J., J. Brooks-Gunn, W. Jean Yeung and Judith R. Smith. "How Much Does Childhood Poverty Affect the Life Chances of Children?" *American Sociological Review.* Vol. 63, June 1998, pp. 406-423.

[56] Peisner-Feinberg, E.S. "Effects of Child Care on Children by Family Income Level: The Costs, Quality and child Outcomes in Child Care Centers Study." Paper presented at the workshop on child care for low-income families, Washington, DC.,

February 1995 and Whitebook, M., C. Howes and D. Phillips. *Worthy Work, Unlivable Wages. The National Child Care Staffing Study, 1988-1997.* Washington, DC: Center for the Child Care Workforce, 1998.

[57] National Commission on Children, p. 190.

[58] Children's Defense Fund. *Head Start FAQs (frequently asked questions).* Updated September 12, 1997. Washington, DC: Children's Defense Fund.

[59] For example, Child Trends, a nonprofit research organization, provides its employees with six weeks of *paid* family leave at the birth of a child.

[60] Russakoff, Dale. "The 'Millenium Generation' Is Making Its Mark," *The Washington Post.* June 29, 1998.

[61] Zaslow, Martha J. and Carolyn A. Eldred, (eds.). *Parenting Behavior in a Sample of Young Mothers in Poverty: Results of the New Chance Observational Study.* New York: Manpower Demonstration Research Corporation, April 1998.

[62] Moore, Kristin A. and Barbara W. Sugland. *Next Steps and Best Bets: Approaches to Preventing Adolescent Childbearing.* Washington, DC: Child Trends, January 17, 1996.

[63] Blum, Robert, W., and Peggy M. Rinehart. *Reducing the Risk: Connections That Make a Difference in the Lives of Youth.* Minneapolis, MN: Division of General Pediatrics and Adolescent Health, University of Minnesota, 1997.

[64] Moore, Kristin A., Brent C. Miller, Barbara W. Sugland, Donna R. Morrison, Dana A. Glei and C. Blumenthal. *Beginning Too Soon: Adolescent Sexual Behavior, Pregnancy, and Parenthood: Executive Summary.* Washington, DC: Child Trends, June 1995, p. xviii. See also American Youth Policy Forum. *Some Things DO Make a Difference for Youth: A Compendium of Evaluations of Youth Programs and Practices.* Washington, DC, 1997, a review of 69 evaluations of interventions affecting youth.

[65] Wells, C.G. "Preschool Literacy-Related Activities and Success in School," in Olson, D, N. Torrance and A. Hildyard (eds.). *Literacy, Language, and Learning: The Nature and Consequences of Literacy.* Cambridge, England: Cambridge University Press, 1985, pp. 229-255.

[66] Zill, Nicholas and C.W. Nord. *Running in Place: How American Families are Faring in a Changing Economy and Individualistic Society.* Washington, DC: Child Trends, 1994.

"For many of the ills that plague children and families, there are both social and individual, public and private causes. Public policies and social programs have an essential place in the list of possible remedies, but so do the actions and decisions of parents, adolescents, communities, schools and employers."

CHAPTER FOUR

COMMUNITIES: POWERFUL RESOURCES FOR AMERICA'S YOUTH

Martin J. Blank and Carol Steinbach

A decade ago, in bold and unambiguous terms, *The Forgotten Half* challenged our nation to pay attention to the growing social alienation and falling economic prospects of young people, particularly those who do not go to college. Stressing the critical role of communities in nurturing young people, the William T. Grant Foundation Commission urged the creation of strong community-based partnerships to anchor our youth, to ensure that their developmental needs are met, and to inspire them to greater achievement. The reaction was swift. Because policymakers and practitioners had independently reached similar conclusions, the number and variety of youth-oriented community initiatives multiplied rapidly. Communities have increasingly become an important focal point of America's efforts to prepare our youth for the future as well as havens in the often difficult passage to adulthood.

A NEW BREED OF YOUTH-FOCUSED INITIATIVES

Today there are literally thousands of initiatives aimed at connecting local resources in new and more powerful ways to support young people and their families and to build the flexible, diverse, and integrated pathways to success that the Grant Commission envisioned. These efforts represent a variety of purposes and strategies. Some focus primarily on building opportunities for young people to develop their skills and abilities, others on providing better access for whole families to high quality social services, still others on improving academic performance in schools, improving the transition from school to work, or addressing a wide range of community and economic development issues.

Has this burgeoning movement measurably improved outcomes for young Americans? Longitudinal evaluations are only just beginning to be developed even in the most advanced and well-funded initiatives. But early evidence — combined with growing anecdotal experience and the inherent logic of these approaches — suggests that they are moving in the right direction. Knitting together a community's diverse and often rich resources — its people, institutions and values — appears to have powerful impact.

Despite their diversity, current initiatives tend to share several common underpinnings. First, and perhaps most significant, is a new determination to achieve measurable results. As practitioners, funders and civic leaders frequently remind themselves, good intentions are no longer good enough. Their business is making a positive difference in the lives of children and families. At the same time, there is well-placed recognition that complex problems cannot be solved overnight. Measurable improvement depends on a series of near-term changes measured by interim indicators — each one contributing to long-term success.

Second, virtually all community initiatives reflect the conviction that, in order to achieve positive results, policies and programs supported by federal or state government and major private institutions must incorporate community-level creativity and ingenuity. Top-down solutions just don't work. Funders and localities are increasingly entering into more equitable partnerships and, in the process, finding and sustaining better solutions to local needs.

Third, community-based initiatives recognize that no single institution, acting alone, has the capacity to improve results. Contributions from multiple community sectors are essential and collaboration across organizations and systems is their hallmark.

Fourth, these initiatives are distinguished by a belief that results for young people will not improve unless efforts are simultaneously undertaken to support families in their neighborhoods. These initiatives seek to understand and embrace the strengths of the diverse cultures and communities in which young people live. They show a good deal of common sense and "out-of-the-box thinking" — and a minimum of bureaucratic rhetoric.

Many of these youth and community initiatives turn the old social services model on its head. They are working to create a stronger infrastructure for all children and their families, rather than finding dysfunction and trying to stamp it out, individual-by-individual. Today's initiatives promote the view that society as a whole, by better connecting family, neighborhood and community resources, can do more to help all young people access the information, support and opportunities that most affluent families provide on their own.

Finally, these initiatives are distinguished by a new breed of entrepreneurism — they are led by practitioners and community leaders looking for and finding ways to leverage the power of existing resources. "At a time when there is less money, we have to reinvent ourselves," says Jim Mills, executive director of the Juvenile Welfare Board of Pinellas County, Florida. "We have to think about going back to our roots, deal with communities... and go back to where we came from."[1] Public and private seed-money has played an important part in starting many efforts but the local resources, both human and financial, being redirected toward these initiatives are becoming increasingly significant. Even greater inventiveness is needed to finance these efforts as they move past their initial demonstration stages to reach much larger numbers of young people.

The political appeal of community-based programs to foster young people and their families is undeniable. The outlines of this new approach are coming into bolder relief; however, there is no single set of blueprints which prescribe how to build these initiatives or how they should look. They are evolving as they go, each mirroring the people, the persistence, the talents, the challenges and strengths of wherever they take root. This chapter outlines the complex field of youth-focused community initiatives. In Part One, we look at major factors in the policy and political environment within which these initiatives develop and six trends which have contributed to their shape. In Part Two, we sample a few of the wide variety of initiatives underway across the country. Part Three examines the results of this activity to date, summarizing what the evaluators say. Finally, in Part Four, we offer recommendations to strengthen these burgeoning efforts in the decade ahead.

PART ONE: THE POLICY AND POLITICAL ENVIRONMENT

Defining Community

A range of policy and political factors create the environment in which youth-focused community initiatives have developed. Particularly significant has been the emergence of a new consensus on what the term "community" means. Since World War II, considerable attention has been focused on the idea of "community" — deemed by many to be an important aspect of American life but one largely lost in the nation's post-war march to the suburbs. Academics and researchers from a wide spectrum of disciplines approached the term from their sundry perspectives, defining it variously as a geographic place, a political jurisdiction, or a set of interests or relationships created by work, residence or avocation. Unfortunately, definitional differences deflected attention from considering how communities could best be strengthened and used to support children and families. Over the past decade, however, practitioners from a wide spectrum of disciplines have moved toward a shared, multi-faceted definition of the term. Whether in education, housing, health care, economic development, service delivery or policing, a profoundly practical policy focus has reframed the debate and led to a new definition of community in terms of three key roles:

1. Community as keeper of values. Rather than viewing a community as simply a geographic place, a political jurisdiction, or a homogeneous racial, ethnic or religious group, today's practitioners are most likely to focus on the relationships within these settings. The term has broadened to refer to the interests and values of a wide range of people, rooted to a geographic place and committed to safeguarding shared values and achieving common purposes.

2. Community as problem solver. From an operational standpoint, communities are increasingly seen as the social and political level of organization best equipped to deliver solutions to neighborhood problems. This attitude, bubbling up since the 1960s, took firmer hold as a result of the public's growing dissatisfaction with the results of top-down government solutions and reports of successful community-based initiatives, particularly in the areas of housing and community schools.

3. Community as ecosystem. The 1990s also advanced the view that communities are integrated ecosystems, the source of both problems and solutions. Write Michael Timpane and Rob Reich, "the community ecosystem includes families, neighborhood associations, youth programs, social service agencies, teachers and schools. Each ingredient of the system needs to leverage other components to mold a young adult with self esteem, confidence and security."[2]

Practitioners working with children, youth and families in community settings have eagerly embraced this tri-partite view and its promise of new partnerships and shared accountability. Most have long recognized the importance of communities in nurturing young people and in supporting their families. They know well the dangers of failing to create community and allowing young people, as John W. Gardner cautions, to "drift through life without a sense of belonging or allegiance to anything."[3] They know from experience that when caring adults don't work with young people to create supportive environments, young people seek out security and solace wherever they can. As the Grant Commission warned, too many are forgotten — or lost in gangs or other dysfunctional relationships. At the same time, practitioners know that creating community is difficult, complex, long-term work. Thus, most have welcomed the opportunity to link their initiatives with those of other agencies and organizations.

The Impact of Public Attitudes

Other factors have also colored the policy environment in which community initiatives have developed. Even as communities became focal points to address the problems of youth, emerging public opinion dictated to some extent the terms under which these efforts would operate. Chief among these new attitudes have been fading public patience with ineffective social programs and a more punitive response toward young people, especially those involved in serious youth violence.

Welfare reform typifies the enormous impact of the first of these attitudes. In large part, successful efforts to dismantle "welfare as we knew it" came in response to public frustration with social programs, many of which expected too little of families and failed to help them improve their lives. The Personal Responsibility Act of 1996 gave states the authority to tighten eligibility requirements for Aid to Families with Dependent Children. The new law permits states to strengthen sanctions, requires work as a condition of receiving support and imposes a five-year life limit on participation. Sure to have a major impact on the lives of many children and young mothers, the law embodies the growing public demand for a *quid pro quo* from able-bodied recipients of government aid: "We'll help you get a fresh start — but you must work for it." Youth-focused community initiatives, as urged by the Grant Commission, have done their best to build on the positive thrust of this sentiment, emphasizing the reciprocal quality of initiatives in which opportunities are created for young people to contribute to, as well as receive support from, their communities.

A second shift in public opinion — a more punitive response to young people as potential lawbreakers — has also affected the shape and design of youth-focused community initiatives. Youth curfews, for example, gained considerable popularity in the 1990s and have been implemented in numerous cities as a mechanism for dealing with juvenile crime. Across the country, calls for tougher treatment reflect the public's dismay at a rash of high visibility violent youth crime, most recently a tragic wave of schoolhouse murders of children and teachers by fellow students. Many states are considering harsher sentencing for juvenile offenders and increasing the frequency with which juveniles accused of serious crimes are adjudicated in adult courts. At the federal level, legislation is being considered to promote accountability by juvenile criminals and punish and deter violent gang crime. Legislation would amend the Juvenile Justice and Delinquency Prevention Act to make it easier to put young law breakers into adult jails.

The media have contributed significantly to more punitive attitudes toward young people by portraying an inordinately negative picture of youth, especially minorities and young people in low income communities. The negative impact of local television news on public perceptions about youth was chronicled in a 1997 study in the *American Journal of Public Health*.[4] Researchers during several months in 1993 performed a content analysis of 214 hours of local television news in California. Not only did violence dominate the news coverage, but the gruesome details of crimes were typically highlighted. More than half of the stories involved youth violence, often in central cities. With little positive reporting to balance this picture, an electorate dominated by suburban voters has become fearful and suspicious. In recent years, public spending for punishment and incarceration has grown, while dollars for prevention and youth development have been much harder to find.

These trends in welfare, treatment of juvenile crime, curfews and media coverage underscore fundamental tensions in our communities — tensions between punitive approaches and prevention; between individual and community responsibility; between informing the public and fostering an environment of fear. There is enormous controversy among policymakers, researchers, advocates and the public about the impact of these policy choices and opinions are strong on all sides. Within this policy environment youth-focused community initiatives have developed.

Advocates for youth must explicitly recognize the tensions in public attitudes toward youth and the extent to which negative trends affect the willingness of communities to support the healthy development of youth. While we view punitive approaches with extreme caution, we know, as Daniel Yankelovich has argued in Chapter Two, that to dismiss punitive approaches is to ignore the reality of American culture and public opinion. The challenge of youth-focused initiatives must emphasize the rights and responsibilities of both young people *and* adults. Still, as the Grant Commission urged, safe and orderly communities must not come at the expense of creating second-chance opportunities for young people who have dropped out of school, alternative learning settings for young people who need them, and a range of activities after school and on weekends to provide consistent, structured and inviting outlets for young people's energy and enthusiasm.

YOUTH AND COMMUNITIES IN THE 1990s: SIX DRIVING TRENDS

In addition to the broad policy and political environment described above, six trends in the field of community-based strategies for children, youth and families have emerged in the decade since the release of *TFH* and have further shaped today's new breed of youth-focused, community initiatives.

1. A focus on results and performance. Today's collaborations are increasingly motivated by a hard-nosed desire to produce concrete results in measurable terms — from the number of healthy babies born, to the percentage of parents working, to the number of youth ready for productive adulthood. Using outcomes as the starting point for planning enables communities to identify roles for multiple partners in creating the conditions under which those results can be achieved.

The movement to adopt performance measures is reflected in such ambitious initiatives as the *Kids Count Data Book*, published annually by the Annie E. Casey Foundation and replicated at the state and county level across the country. *Kids Count* provides ongoing benchmarks that policymakers can use to assess the well-being of children, youth and families. Included are a wide range of data — from demographic trends to economic statistics, as well as national profiles and state-by-state breakdowns for key indicators of children's well-being.

2. A new stress on building assets. The 1990s brought on a distinctive movement to recognize and build on the assets of low-income communities, both human and financial. In *Building Communities from the Inside Out,* John McKnight and John Kretzmann argue that well-intentioned efforts to help poor communities by focusing on their "needs, deficiencies and problems" have had relatively poor results over half a century. Better outcomes are more likely when initiatives begin with a clear commitment to discovering a community's *positive* capacities.[5] The difference between a needs-based as opposed to a capacity-building approach may sound subtle, but its impact is substantial. According to McKnight and Kretzmann, a needs-based approach highlights — and creates — primarily negative images of a neighborhood. Residents can easily become overwhelmed, feel helpless and see the situation as hopeless. By contrast, an approach which focuses on identifying and reinforcing indigenous capacity is energizing. People want to invest their time in community rebuilding — and outsiders are more likely to contribute resources.

3. A focus on broader stakeholder participation. To a large extent, the move to involve more stakeholders evolved as part of the emerging consensus on community roles and the need to make more effective use of public, private and community resources. Groups that had narrowly conceived their missions began to see themselves as part of a larger constellation of interdependent organizations working together in communities.

Collaboration, though challenging, time-consuming and sometimes frustrating, became essential, requiring a broad range of participation from every sector with responsibility for young people and families.[6] Critical lessons were quickly learned. First, affirmative efforts must be made to enlist broad stakeholder participation — it simply doesn't happen automatically. Second, a new leadership style is required. Those who succeed in guiding today's collaborations are adept synthesizers. They hear what everyone says and can skillfully build consensus and negotiate an agenda for action.

4. *A focus on involving parents, young people and other neighborhood residents.* Today's community initiatives no longer rely as heavily as in the past on professionals or community elites to define problems or implement solutions. Increasingly, the objective is to enable informed participation from residents — on an equal footing with professional partners who also have a stake in improved outcomes. Steps must be taken to ensure that both youth and adult neighborhood residents have the information and skills they need to state their position and to effectively negotiate change strategies — in forums more familiar to elected officials and human service agency leaders. Conversely, professional participants must acquire better understanding and firsthand knowledge of the communities they wish to support. Participants, both residents and professionals, are often skeptical of what they fear will be another wave of token youth and resident "involvement." The most promising initiatives are committed to substantive participation and to striking a new balance of power.

5. *A recognition of the importance of race and culture.* Respect for differences in race, language and culture is increasingly important in the development of today's community-based initiatives. While this attitude reflects appreciation for the strength and untapped resources that arise from diversity and self-determination, it is also motivated by new demographic realities. American youth today represent a wide and rapidly increasing array of ethnicities and cultures. Designing community initiatives that can effectively engage young people and families from many different traditions and perspectives requires a willingness to explore — and respect — the complex social and political issues that can arise from this diversity.

6. *A renewed sense of the importance of building public will*. During the 1990s, advocates for youth and their families became more attuned to the strategic importance of explaining their objectives and accomplishments to the public in terms everyone could understand. Community initiatives have increasingly sought to engage the public in their work and to convince them of its long-term value. Their purpose has been not only to generate financial support but to counter the negative images of youth painted by the media and the trend toward punitive measures. Broad-based awareness of the contributions of young people and the positive results that can occur when communities rally behind and support the efforts of children and families can protect initiatives in a highly politicized environment, especially one where a small but highly organized constituency can thwart even the most positive actions.

Among the tactics that community initiatives have found useful in building public support are:

- The publication of "Community Report Cards" to inform the public about the well-being of their children and youth.
- Having young people speak for themselves. This is increasingly important in an era of public distrust of professional agency leaders and government. It also helps to develop leadership in the community.
- Involving business leaders, who have a distinctive credibility with the public, in community-based initiatives and as advocates for children, youth and families.
- Site visits. Innovative programs, like Child Watch and Walk in My Shoes, have helped leaders to understand better the challenges facing youth and families.[7]

PART TWO: SAMPLING YOUTH AND COMMUNITY INITIATIVES

Today's community initiatives reflect a variety of purposes and strategies. In the next sections, we describe initiatives that have their roots in several distinct advocacy and reform efforts but which all demonstrate important aspects of community-building, including: (1) service reform efforts designed to improve the quality and delivery of health and social services;[8] (2) youth development initiatives to increase opportunities for young people to develop their skills and abilities; (3) community development efforts to strengthen the economic, social and physical vitality of neighborhoods; and (4) school reform initiatives to improve the quality of teaching and learning in schools and the transition of young people from school to work or further education. While differences in the basic

> *Hedy Chang of **California Tomorrow** has crafted nine principles to help community initiatives address the interactions of race, ethnicity, language and cultural diversity.[9] Effective initiatives, she finds, are those that:*
> - Ensure that all institutions support the development of children, youth and adults who have a strong sense of identity, respect for people of diverse backgrounds and a commitment to the community.
> - Provide opportunities to engage in dialogue across ethnic identity groups.
> - Identify and build on the assets of diverse groups and individuals in a community.
> - Use a community lens to assess activities, policies or programs to promote the well-being of children, youth and families.
> - Promote equal access and opportunity based on a solid understanding of the consequences of individual, institutional and structural racism and oppression.
> - Use data broken down by race, language, gender and income to plan initiatives and to hold programs accountable for creating equal opportunity for all children, youth and families.
> - Engage and draw on diverse perspectives at all levels of decision-making.
> - Nurture learning communities which promote deeper individual and collective understanding and support sustained action around issues of equity and diversity.
> - Identify and develop leaders who can be models for a positive approach to diversity and encourage attention to equity.

approach of the initiatives described below are clear, their considerable overlap is evident as well. Experience suggests that as community initiatives mature, the tendency is to incorporate aspects from other approaches while not losing sight of their primary mission.

Service Reform Initiatives

> *We recommend that communities, through public and private cooperation, develop comprehensive and coordinated systems to ensure that all young people and their families have access to a full array of developmental, preventive, and remedial services.*
> *(The Forgotten Half, 1988)*

Community collaboratives aimed at creating new service approaches for children, youth and families grew dramatically in the 1990s. Many began primarily as collaborations of providers of health, education and human services, relate Charles Bruner and Maria Chavez. Over time the strongest collaborations began to move beyond a strictly service approach. Refocusing long-entrenched bureaucratic systems to more effectively deliver education, youth development, human services, housing, economic development and job training goes far beyond service delivery. To be effective, they "had to involve the community and address economic and social issues, as well as human capital development needs."[10]

Practitioners realized that the major barrier to change wasn't a lack of desire for collaboration, but a lack of knowing how to muster the sustained commitment required to bring about lasting change. "We know what works, but we're only doing it at the margins; implementing at the community level requires changes in all systems," Bruner and Chavez reported.[11]

In many communities, the commitment to children and families is strong but too often diffused across numerous community collaboratives. Each is focused on a specific issue, such as infant mortality, school readiness, adolescent pregnancy, violence prevention or welfare reform. Without any communication among them, these individual efforts often find themselves colliding rather than connecting, and exhausting, the same coterie of community leaders who participate in several at the same time.

In other locales, however, collaboratives are noticeably more comprehensive and take on a broader governance role. These governance entities — referred by many different titles, such as community partnerships, authorities or service reform boards — develop and organize services and supports for children and families within a defined geographic area. Rather than focusing on single issues, such collaboratives typically work to organize services across a range of program areas to build more effective systems of support. They bring together public, private, neighborhood and family interests to focus on the basic conditions of child and family well-being: healthy births, school readiness, success in school, community safety, and bringing youth to productive adulthood.

During the 1990s, about two dozen states began developing policy frameworks to support such community collaboratives — including Iowa's

Decategorization and Community Empowerment Boards, Maryland's Local Management Boards, Michigan's Multi-Purpose Collaborative Boards, Minnesota's Family Service Collaboratives, Missouri and Vermont's Community Partnerships, Ohio's Child and Family First Councils, Pennsylvania's Family Service Systems Reform Boards and Washington State's Community Health and Safety Networks. While many of these community collaborations were created at the behest of state leaders, the most effective ones are community driven. They derive their power and influence from the visibility, credibility and legitimacy they can accumulate in their communities. The Local Investment Commission in Kansas City, Missouri and the Youth Futures Authority in Chatham-Savannah, Georgia (discussed later in the context of Community Building) represent two of the most important initiatives of this kind.

The Local Investment Commission (LINC) in Kansas City is a citizen-led reform initiative. The brainchild of a local business leader, Bert Berkley, LINC's membership includes only citizen leaders. Professionals serve on a special advisory cabinet within LINC but have no vote. Gary Stangler, Director of the Missouri Department of Social Services, liked Berkley's approach and empaneled LINC in November 1992 after an extended planning phase.

LINC has responsibility for planning and overseeing the expenditure of Department of Social Service funds in Kansas City and surrounding Jackson County. It has a broad agenda — ranging from welfare reform and comprehensive neighborhood services to health care and early childhood. LINC works to create capacity in all of these systems through its professional development, data and evaluation and communications strategies. Another unusual dimension of LINC's work is its alliances with local community organizers and community development leaders. LINC is outcome-focused and committed to continually assessing and evaluating the results of initiatives as an integral part of its system reform efforts.[12]

At the state level in Missouri, the Family Investment Trust (FIT) supports LINC and a group of 12 other community partnerships. Launched by Governor's Executive Order in 1993, FIT provides a vehicle for state agencies, the private sector and communities to work together to change systems at the state and community level. FIT's board is unique nationally, comprised of leaders of state agencies sitting together with an equivalent number of citizen leaders. FIT staff, supported by foundation and state resources, offers capacity building assistance to local communities and works to make state policy and operations more responsive to local communities.

Each community partnership has its own focus. For example, the Community Task Force in Greene County targets historic preservation, transportation, pollution and physical problems in its neighborhoods. The Jefferson County Community Assistance Network works to improve the delivery of human services by developing a cooperative spirit among service providers, consumers and revenue sources.

Community collaboratives that take on governance roles face many challenges:

- Too many groups are still too dominated by agency professionals, unprepared to share power and resources with community.
- State policy, even in those states that have created such groups, does not fully recognize their broad governance role.

Community collaboratives involved in governance are unique in the community-wide leadership and direction they provide and the broader range of issues they tackle. Among the critical functions of community collaboratives are:

- Developing a shared community vision for children and families
- Building community commitment, support and responsibility for achieving that vision
- Establishing a results-focused accountability system
- Facilitating and negotiating relationships among public, private and community agencies to create systems of supports for children, youth and families — as opposed to providing crisis-oriented services
- Forging a strategy for creative use of public, private, community resources
- Creating an infrastructure to integrate disparate systems, including data systems, interdisciplinary staff and re-engineered budget, personnel and management systems
- Working to change laws, regulations and practices at the federal, state and local levels which may block more effective services and supports.[13]

Some states continue to create competing groups, and too few have decided that these groups will be involved in decision-making and accountability relative to major public funding streams, such as Medicaid, managed care, child care and welfare reform.
- Many neighborhood groups continue to express skepticism about the extent of their involvement in decision making.

Nevertheless, governance groups have real potential to make change and improve results, particularly in large systems. More shared leadership between state and local leaders, with a relentless focus on results, is key to moving this strategy forward.

Youth and Community Development Initiatives

> *We recommend that schools and communities create and revitalize community-based activities that concentrate on the developmental needs of youth, respond to young people's opinions and ideas, and involve youth in the planning and implementation of programs that serve them.*
> *(The Forgotten Half, 1988)*

Community partners across the country have begun to form new systems of support for youth development. Some center on the community as a whole, while others have targeted large institutions, particularly schools. Some communities have chosen to work cooperatively with national organizations to implement youth development strategies. Others have been developed by local community-based organizations; some are faith-based efforts initiated by churches or other religious institutions; still others have emerged from within specific racial or ethnic communities. These initiatives illustrate the overlap between efforts focused primarily on youth development — creating opportunities for young people to develop their talents and abilities — and community development initiatives aimed at improving the economic, social and physical vitality of neighborhoods. This wide array of activity underscores the energy of young people and the positive results that can occur when it is tapped, channelled and encouraged.

An Asset-Based Strategy. In a survey of Seattle high school students in 1997, the Search Institute found that only 14 percent believe their community values them, and only 17 percent believe their schools provide a caring, encouraging environment. The Institute's asset-based youth development framework is designed to respond to attitudes such as these.[14] The Institute identified 40 assets that form the basis of healthy development in adolescence — ranging from perceiving that adults in the community value youth to participating in a meaningful way in such activities as drama clubs and sports.

In 1996, the Institute launched a national ***Healthy Communities - Healthy Youth*** initiative to help communities develop programs that nurture these assets. Today, the Institute reports that about 250 communities have begun to use its approach: Instead of focusing only on reducing risks and intervening in problems, these communities are rallying to rebuild the foundation of development that all young people need.[15]

- *It's About Time . . . for Kids.* This Seattle-based program, launched in 1997, links caring adults with young people who need their support. Program organizers also formed a network of 150 practitioners from youth agencies, schools and churches to stage community town meetings to explain the asset framework to the public.[16]

- *Just Assets.* This Bridgeport, Connecticut initiative works to build young people's trust in adults, as well as their own self-confidence. Youth sit on planning boards and committees and make decisions about budgets and other significant agenda items. "One of the benefits of having youth involved from the beginning in helping to identify positive resources is that they will be more likely to contribute to their own development," says Dale Blythe, former director of strategic initiatives for the Search Institute.[17]

Community Change for Youth Development (CCYD) Strategy. Public/Private Ventures, a Philadelphia-based research and program development organization, created this program concept, now being tested in Savannah, St. Petersburg, Austin, Kansas City, Minneapolis and New York. Working with target groups of 1,000-2,000 teens, the program focuses communities on a set of core concepts.

- *St. Petersburg, Florida.* In the Child's Park neighborhood — lacking a YMCA, Boys and

Girls Club or similar agencies — CCYD decided to create activities for young people and link the city's recreation department with indigenous organizations that could direct specific youth activities. These range from a local arts center helping young people design and install a mural on a large warehouse to the Pinellas County Juvenile Welfare Board, which contributed significantly from its own resources to create full-time jobs for recreation employees previously working only part-time.

● *Austin, Texas.* The CCYD governing body, working with churches, schools and neighborhood associations, focuses on developing neighborhood leadership and expanding youth activities. A new youth development center now serves as a "one-stop shop" for youth and family services, providing information about employment, education and scholarship opportunities, tutoring, counseling and health services. Dennis Campa, assistant city manager and Austin CCYD coordinator, counsels that professionals must be careful not to tell a community what to do. "If we're too quick to find solutions for problems the neighborhoods haven't defined yet, we can devise solutions, but the residents won't buy in. CCYD gives us the chance to stop treating the community as clients, but rather as partners who bring something to the table."[18]

Empowerment Zones and Enterprise Communities. Legislated by Congress in 1993, the Empowerment Zones/Enterprise Communities (EZ/EC) initiative is rooted in a community development approach to collaborative community-building. Some EZ/EC communities focus on youth development as part of a comprehensive strategy to promote economic opportunity and community revitalization. The law provides tax incentives and grants and loans to specified low-income areas to create jobs, expand business opportunities and develop social and human capital. More than 100 urban and rural communities are now participating, including:

● *Lowell, Massachusetts: Healthy Summer Initiative.* This EC initiative provides recreational opportunities, nutritional support, education and summer jobs for Lowell youth through a partnership of local agencies and organizations. More than 5,000 young people have participated thus far.

● *Central Savannah River Area, Georgia: One-Stop Community Center.* This EC came together with the help of community organizers, who coordinated programs within local human development centers. The centers offer youth leadership training, GED classes, tutoring, energy assistance and club activities, such as Boy Scouts and Brownies.

Juvenile Justice Strategies. Community is also becoming a focal point for organizing resources on behalf of youth involved with the juvenile justice system or who are at-risk of such intervention. In several cases, the Office of Justice and Juvenile Delinquency Prevention brought together funding from major categorical programs to enable communities to create more comprehensive strategies. This represents an important effort by a federal agency to try to make categorical resources more accessible and responsive to community needs:

● *Safe Futures* works to control youth crime and victimization. It offers a continuum of services for at-risk youth, including a range of graduated sanctions. Like most of the new breed of youth and community initiatives, Safe Futures works to create community partnerships and integrate information and services across agencies. Safe Futures currently operates in six places — Boston, Contra Costa County (CA), Seattle, St. Louis, Imperial County (CA) and Fort Belknap (MT).

● *Safe Kids/Safe Streets* works to improve community responses to child abuse and neglect. It encourages localities to strengthen their criminal and juvenile justice systems to be more pro-active, implement coordinated management of abuse and neglect cases and develop comprehensive and cross-agency strategies. Local Safe Kids/Safe Streets sponsors reflect the collaborative approach. In Lucas County, Ohio (Toledo), the program is a project of the Lucas County Child Abuse Intervention and Prevention Task Force, a coalition of 18 agencies providing health, welfare and advocacy services for children. The Burlington, Vermont project is managed by the Community Network for Children, Youth and Families.

● *Communities That Care*, pioneered by Development Research and Programs, Inc., identifies the risks young people confront in low-income communities and develops protective factors to mitigate those risks. Communities That Care has been embraced by about 400 communities across the country. In Montgomery County, Maryland, the initiative adopted a school-based strategy to address a rise in violent behavior by middle school students. It provided leadership training, peer mediation and a variety of after-school activities to increase students' commitment to school and to decrease delinquency. The Chesterfield County, Virginia, project works to reduce the recidivism rates of young people in the juvenile court system by getting them involved in community service. It has forged community service agreements with 50 agencies and is developing guidelines for working with young people for use by community service and training supervisors.

Youth Mapping Strategy. In another innovative effort, the Center for Youth Development and Policy Research created a nationwide Youth Mapping program. Like junior surveyors, participating young people walk around their neighborhoods to identify potential trouble spots and come up with ideas for how to improve them. In the South Bronx, it works with the Bronx Overall Economic Development Corporation to make the area "more lively" for young people. In Philadelphia, the Urban Initiative finds friendly adults willing to work with at-risk youth. In Minneapolis, teens have joined with adults from the Search Institute to gather materials on youth activities in neighborhoods and operate a telephone service to provide recreation information to other kids. The Center is now working to create Geographic Information System software applications that will organize data collected through Community Youth Mapping.

School-to-Work Strategies. Community is the focal point for numerous private sector school-to-work programs designed to help students prepare for careers or for college. These multi-partnered initiatives demonstrate the growing view that schools alone cannot turn children into productive adults; the active involvement of other institutions and individuals is essential. School-to-work components range from career academies that provide "real life" experiences during a student's high school years, to school-based enterprises that enable students to start businesses, to service learning projects combining service to community with academic studies.

Local partnerships, typically including employers, local chambers of commerce, school districts, community colleges and other institutions of higher education, community-based organizations and citizens, comprise many school-to-work programs.

Faith-Based Youth Development Strategies. Churches play a vital role in our communities. They bring a spiritual connection that is important to many young people and are often among the few remaining institutional assets that can build and nurture youth programs. In many communities, churches are the most effective vehicle for enlisting community support from members who have moved to the suburbs but still care about and want to maintain connections with the old neighborhood. Some examples:

• *Boston's Ten-Point Coalition.* The Coalition is an ecumenical group of Christian clergy and leaders working on issues affecting black and Latino youth. It seeks to build partnerships with community-based, governmental and private sector institutions committed to the revitalization of families and communities. Key activities in its ten-point plan include establishing four to five church cluster collaborations that adopt gangs and serve as sanctuaries for troubled youth; commissioning missionaries to serve as advocates for minority juveniles in the courts; enlisting youth evangelists for street-level, one-on-one evangelism with youth involved in drug trafficking; establishing accountable, community-based economic development projects; convening Christian brotherhoods and sisterhoods to offer alternatives to violent gang life; and developing an aggressive black and Latino history curriculum with an additional focus on the struggles of women and poor people.

• *Congress of National Black Churches.* Founded in 1978, this ecumenical coalition of denominations, agencies and congregations focuses on empowerment for the African-American community. Among its many activities, the Congress sponsors Project *SPIRIT* — *S*trength *P*erseverance *I*magination *R*esponsibility *I*ntegrity *T*alent — to support the development of youth and strengthen families and communities. Based in churches and usually run by volunteers, *SPIRIT* emphasizes developing self-esteem and the capabilities needed to succeed in school and society. It has four components: after-school tutorial, Saturday school, parent education and pastoral care/counseling. The program targets children ages 6-12 by involving them in numerous activities.

Minority Community Youth Development Strategies. Across the nation, many predominantly minority communities are focusing increasing attention on their own young people. These efforts, and their potential, are too often overlooked by the public, policymakers and funders. Several examples illustrate what is being done:

• *Black Community Crusade for Children (BCCC)*. The mission of the BCCC is to tap into and strengthen the black community traditions of self-help and to rebuild bridges between the middle class and poor people. The program also trains and mobilizes a new generation of black leaders on behalf of children. The Children's Defense Fund coordinates BCCC in partnership with such regional child-serving organizations as the Rheedlen Center for Children and Families in New York City and the Charles Drew Child Development Corporation in Los Angeles. "We want to help our children develop an understanding and appreciation for family, of their own rich heritage derived from African forebears as well as their American experience, the kind of understanding that will simultaneously provide them with roots and wings," says Dr. John Hope Franklin, Honorary Co-Chair of the BCCC.[19]

An echo of the Civil Rights movement, BCCC's Freedom Schools work in partnership with parents, young adults and community leaders to create a new education vision for children. Freedom Schools provide summer options for children where there are none and strengthen parent and community involvement in the year-round achievement of black children. Black college student leaders provide core staff support for the schools. Churches often provide the facilities and volunteer support. The Juvenile and Family Court Judges' Leadership Council is a national network of over 100 African American judges that convenes regularly to design prevention strategies and ensure fair and effective treatment of African American children and youth passing through the child welfare and juvenile justice systems.

• *Concerned Black Men (CBM)*. Founded in Washington, DC, this volunteer organization works in eight cities to provide positive male role models and stronger channels of communication between adults and children in metropolitan areas. CBM adopts elementary schools and works with students in the classroom. Its Rites of Passage Africa Son Rise program helps boys learn skills that help them develop into responsible young men.

• *ASPIRA*. Established by the Puerto Rican-Hispanic Leadership Forum, ASPIRA has offered career counseling to Puerto Rican and other Latino youth since 1961. ASPIRA teaches young people to become aware of their environment and their community, to analyze causes and consequences and to take action for change. It builds pride in Latino culture and brings together students, parents, schools and community members to promote educational success.

The ASPIRACorps Community Service Program operates in several communities. In Bridgeport, Connecticut, its 130 volunteers spend a year tutoring and mentoring middle and high school students working to bring families together in after-school activities.

• *El Centro de la Raza* (The Center for the People). Founded two decades ago in Seattle, the center works to create a sense of community and identifies closely with the philosophy of Dr. Martin Luther King, Jr. El Centro de la Raza's goal is to raise awareness of the needs of the Chicano/Latino community nationwide and to help Seattle's community gain strength and confidence through effective communication among youth, children, and adults of all races and nationalities.

• *America's Promise: The Alliance for Youth.* Led by General Colin Powell, America's Promise unites private sector and community resources to ensure that children and youth have access to five fundamental resources: a healthy start, ongoing relationships with caring adults, safe places and structured activities during non-school hours, marketable skills through effective education, and opportunities to give back through community service. Approximately 350 communities are working in the America's Promise framework.

**School Reform:
Inventing Community Schools**

The past decade has seen an exponential growth in the connections between communities and schools in order to improve the well-being of children and youth. These school-linked initiatives generally originate among the reform and advocacy approaches already discussed, including service reform and youth and community development. They are set apart from the wider universe of community initiatives by a strong connection to the schools, a shared commitment to improved academic outcomes for students, and growing interest in eventually contributing to improvements in the overall quality of teaching and learning. A forthcoming study of school-linked initiatives suggests that while representative of distinct approaches, the field is moving toward complementary approaches

> **"All we are saying...is give youth a chance"**
>
> Recommended by the William T. Grant Foundation Commission and created by the U.S. Congress, Youth Fair Chance helped develop community-wide visions for youth and mobilize resources more strategically. The program provides support for young people to finish high school, get better jobs and address personal and family problems. Congress specified six broad objectives:
> - Saturate neighborhoods with services.
> - Guarantee all youth in the target community access to appropriate education, training and comprehensive support services.
> - Use outreach and recruitment to boost youth participation.
> - Integrate service delivery, assessment and case management.
> - Increase the rates of school completion, enrollment in advanced education and training and employment.
> - Determine the feasibility of offering these services nationwide.
>
> As a national policy initiative, four elements of Youth Fair Chance stand out. The first is a decision to pursue a comprehensive, community-wide strategy, rather than supporting individual programs. The second is to make *all* youth in a delimited community or neighborhood eligible for services. Third, the program capitalizes on the most up-to-date research on effective practice. Finally, Youth Fair Chance defines youth as individuals up to age 30 — recognizing the challenges that many young people have in gaining a firm foothold in the labor market.
>
> The collaborative structure is key. About half of the Youth Fair Chance projects have their own local collaboratives. Others have passed the funding on to existing nonprofit or community-based organizations.
>
> Mathematica Policy Research's evaluation found that Youth Fair Chance is a positive model that works well in involving the community in important decisions about its youth. Universal eligibility helps recruitment, eliminates the potential stigma of participation and is easy to implement.

and strategies.[20] There is a growing level of cohesiveness and common activity across major purposes and strategies, mirroring the trend toward community-building seen in the broader field of community initiatives. Although still developing, a new kind of institution is emerging out of all this activity — the Community School.

In order to implement school-linked initiatives, many communities are creating community-wide collaboratives to provide general direction, set and revise policy where necessary, oversee the long term effectiveness and financial stability of the initiative, and ensure its accountability. At the individual school site, teams including family members, youth, community residents, and school and agency staff provide planning, management and evaluation support to community school initiatives. The site teams are critical to integrating all of the assets of the neighborhood and community into a comprehensive community-based strategy.

As these differing approaches suggest, an array of different organizations are involved with Community Schools — youth development organizations, human service agencies, community development corporations, neighborhood organizations, and business, civic and religious groups, among others. In addition, institutions of higher education, United Ways, community foundations and law enforcement agencies are also playing vital roles. At the University of Pennsylvania, the Center for Community Partnerships is revitalizing curriculum through community-oriented, real world problem solving at schools in West Philadelphia. The Center annually convenes a network of universities pursuing similar initiatives.

As part of their new emphasis on community building, local United Ways, with the support of the United Way of America, are focusing on strengthening relationships between community and school. More than 200 United Ways nationwide report partnerships with schools. Community foundations, supported primarily by local endowments, have been very entrepreneurial in this arena, helping to organize and support community collaboratives and providing financial support. And police departments, in large measure because their leadership recognizes the relationship between after-school programs and reductions in juvenile crime, are working to expand their Police Athletic League programs and advocating for after-school investments through Fight Crime-Invest in Kids, a Washington-based advocacy organization including chiefs of police and prosecutors committed to prevention.

The aforementioned analysis of school-community initiatives concludes that most do not view school reform as their primary purpose. Instead, most see their role as supporting school efforts rather than "telling schools how to do their job." As initiatives mature, however, they are more likely to take an active part in strengthening school functioning, including influencing curriculum and instruction. This capacity builds incrementally and relatively slowly, beginning by fostering positive relations with staff, developing parent participation and leadership, and participating in the school's decision-making process.

Early evaluations of individual school-community initiatives indicate that they are making an important difference to individual students and families. Data suggest that student mobility rates are falling, parent participation is growing and student achievement is increasing, while teen pregnancy and incidents of violence and suspension are being reduced. Much more needs to be learned about what initiatives are accomplishing, for whom, under what conditions and at what cost. In a number of larger, well-funded initiatives, substantial research efforts are underway to answer at least some of these questions.

To advance their efforts, many school-community partnerships are now forming an alliance — the Emerging Coalition for Community Schools. With staff support from the Institute for Educational Leadership, the coalition links leaders in the areas of education, youth development, family support and community development with government at the national, state and local levels, foundations and the private sector. The Coalition's goals are to build a constituency for community schools and inform public policies that affect communities' ability to create these institutions. It faces several challenges:

- It must build stronger connections with education reform and its emphasis on academic standards.
- Public policies and funding streams are too categorical, and make it difficult to create comprehensive Community School initiatives. More education of policymakers is imperative to change these agencies.
- Turf battles, while somewhat diminished, continue to plague efforts to weave together resources around Community Schools.
- The public does not yet have a full understanding of the Community Schools

---

A Shared Vision of Community Schools

Community Schools are partnerships involving school systems, parents, neighborhood groups, government, youth development organizations, human services agencies and other community institutions. They work toward four key results:
- Children and youth are ready to learn every day;
- Children and youth are learning and achieving at high levels;
- Families and communities are safe and supportive; and
- Youth are prepared for productive adulthood and citizenship.

A Community School is a resource to the entire community, and sees the community as integral to its efforts to increase student learning and enhance the development of children and youth. It is open to its community before and after school, evenings, weekends and summers. Four strategies converge in a community school: quality education, youth development, family involvement and support, and community development.
— *Emerging Coalition for Community Schools' Draft Vision Statement, June 1998*

Bridges to Success (BTS), Indianapolis, IN

The United Way of Central Indiana designed Bridges to Success in partnership with the school district to increase the educational success of students by better meeting their non-academic needs and eventually establishing schools as lifelong learning centers and focal points in their communities. Until recently, BTS served about 3,600 students in a six-site pilot project. BTS now works with 28 schools, including seven middle schools and one high school with an enrollment of approximately 20,000.

Oversight is provided by the BTS Council, a collaborative body of institutional partners and service providers, non-profit organizations, business leaders, principals, parents and students. Site teams at each school, involving parent, student, school and community agency leaders, plan and oversee services and connect students and families with a wide range of health and social services and youth development activities.

Texas Interfaith Education Alliance, Texas

The Texas Interfaith Education Alliance Schools initiative includes 89 schools throughout southwest Texas. It reflects the vision of the Industrial Areas Foundation (IAF) to restructure the allocation of power and resources in their communities. Partners include the Texas Interfaith Education Fund, Texas Education Agency, school districts, school staff, parents and community leaders. The Alliance is developing a community-based constituency to strengthen schools by restructuring relationships among school and community stake-holders. As a result, school-community teams have developed neighborhood efforts to counter gang violence and ease racial tensions, introduced tutorial and scholarship opportunities, developed after school and extended day programs, and made substantive changes in curriculum, scheduling and assessment methods.

Children's Aid Society (CAS) Community Schools, New York, NY

CAS Community Schools, centered in two elementary and two middle schools, serve some 7,000 children in New York City's Washington Heights district. CAS Community Schools operate as a full partnership between Children's Aid Society and Community School District Six. A budget of $3.5 million provides a full-time director at each site who works closely with the principal in managing and directing the school. Every student receives at least eight hours of additional instruction each week with content planned by teachers, often working in teams, and with additional materials and supplies frequently provided by CAS.

The original purpose behind the initiative was to reduce the non-academic barriers to school success by bringing health and social services to resource-poor, largely immigrant neighborhoods in a central, school-based location. Over time, however, as the working relationship between CAS and the schools strengthened, the purpose shifted to a direct focus on the quality of education. Currently, an extended day, hands-on learning program designed with school staff to complement classroom experience forms "a school within a school." It is the central part of a full range of activities, including health services, family support and parent involvement that partners say point to a "seamless web" of educational opportunity from 7:00 a.m. to 6:00 p.m.

strategy. The Community Schools movement will have to work hard to sustain and expand its efforts on behalf of children and youth. However, its ranks are swelling and, with continued partnership building at the local level and an emerging national strategy, it is positioned to make a real difference in the decade ahead.

After-School Programs

The evidence is in. The bad news is that when we leave millions of kids without good after-school activities — as we are doing every day — their risk of becoming serious delinquents skyrockets. The good news is that we could dramatically cut crime by making sure kids get good after-school programs while their parents are working.
— Ruben Ortega, Police Chief
Salt Lake City, Utah[21]

A particularly important component of school-community initiatives is after-school programming, often extending into the evening and, in some cases, beginning before school and carrying into the weekend. After-school programs have gained momentum as a way to address crime — the peak hours for violent juvenile crime are between 2:00 p.m.- 8:00 p.m. — and as a way to promote student learning and achievement. Together, parents, law enforcement officials, educators, youth development organizations, churches and government are working to create after-school programs, often linked to Community School initiatives, which involve youth, build on their assets, connect with learning and achieve measurable results, e.g., reduced juvenile crime, increased learning and positive contributions to the community.

Recent data confirm the common sense approach of after-school programs:

- The time children spend in after-school activities is correlated with their academic and conduct grades, peer relations and emotional adjustment.[22]
- A Texas A&M University evaluation found that elementary students who participated in after-school programs showed positive changes in school attendance, grades, behavior and self-esteem. Those who participated in after-school programs scored better on math and reading tests than those who did not.[23]
- *Safe and Smart: Making the After-school Hours Work for Kids* cites eight studies indicating that after-school programs decrease juvenile crime, decrease victimization or decrease vandalism in schools.[24]

Collaborative planning for after-school programs is taking hold. The MOST initiative — *Making the Most of Out of School Time* — brings together youth development groups in a community to forge a clear strategy for quality in after-school programs. Supported by the Dewitt Wallace-Reader's Digest Fund and coordinated by the National Institute for Out-of-School Time, MOST funds programs in Boston, Chicago and Seattle to develop community-based coalitions to start programs, boost the number of children served, strengthen training for providers, raise public awareness of the need for out-of-school care and develop resource streams to sustain the programs. Similar efforts are emerging in other communities as part of broader youth development strategies and to take advantage of the rising interest in after-school programs.

After-school programs received a boost from the Congress in 1997, when lawmakers appropriated $40 million for the *21st Century Community Learning Program,* which awards grants to rural and inner city schools to plan, implement or expand coordinated after-school programs. Schools are obligated to collaborate with other public and nonprofit agencies, local businesses and educational institutions.

Reflecting national trends toward public/private partnerships, the Charles Stewart Mott Foundation has joined with the federal government to support the 21st Century program. The foundation, through the National Center on Community Education and the National Community Education Association, provides support for the grant application process and is planning a training program for new grantees. If Congress approves President Clinton's request for $1 billion over five years for the 21st Century Learning Centers, the Mott Foundation's investment will rise to $55 million over ten years. Foundation resources will support training, technical assistance and evaluation, thus freeing public funds for direct services.

In addition to the increase for the 21st Century Learning Centers Program, a proposed 1998 budget increase of $1.5 billion annually in the Child

West Philadelphia Improvement Corps (WEPIC), Philadelphia, PA

WEPIC was born in 1985 during a University of Pennsylvania seminar on Urban Universities and Community Partnerships. WEPIC evolved from a summer service learning corps into its primary mission, building university-assisted community schools that provide education, recreation, and social and health services for all members of the community, as well as revitalizing the curriculum through community-oriented, real-world problem solving. Thirteen elementary, middle and high schools provide sites for WEPIC activities during and after school hours. Activity areas are chosen by school principals and staff. Each site creates its own projects within WEPIC's general approach that calls for problem-based, hands-on learning focused on community improvement. Focus areas include health, the environment, conflict resolution and peer mediation, desktop publishing and extended day apprenticeships in the construction trades. Extended day and school day programs emphasize the integration of service-learning with academics and job readiness and are often connected to the schools' thematic curricula.

WEPIC "calls for problem-based, hands-on learning focused on community improvement."

"Beacons offer 'safe havens' in school buildings...open seven days a week, 16 hours a day, year-round."

Beacons, New York, NY

Beacons are school-based community centers located throughout all five boroughs of New York City. Beacons emphasize the view that positive outcomes for youth result from opportunities to develop their talents and potential. In combination with community-wide support services and closer connections between home and school, these opportunities are intended to lead to improved educational achievement.

Beacons offer "safe havens" in school buildings for children, youth and families, open seven days a week, 16 hours a day, year-round. Funded by the city's Department of Youth Services (DYS), not-for-profit community-based organizations manage Beacon programs at the school site. Currently, 40 Beacons are in operation and the City is funding 38 new sites to open in fall 1998.

Each site receives City funding of just under $400,000 annually and most leverage much more in in-kind services. Individual centers offer a mix of services, recreation, education and leadership development. Family support and health services, employment preparation and, in some cases, on-site college credit classes and community service activities create an environment full of possibilities for a growing number of students, families and community residents.

Care Block Grant could be used for after-school programs. Local government and private foundations are also investing in this area, but the gap between need and resources remains wide. If passed, these investments will make a significant dent in reducing the number of children who are unsupervised after-school. Still, nearly four million children will remain unserved.

In addition to a lack of financing, after-school programs suffer from the divide that still exists between schools and youth development organizations. While relationships have improved significantly, serious problems remain. Too often school people describe after-school programs as "baby-sitting" or "custodial." Youth development people charge that schools "drill and kill." School policies often shift on short notice with regard to use of school facilities by non-school organizations, wreaking havoc for many youth development and community organizations. If schools and youth development organizations share a commitment to improving the well-being of children and youth, they will move past these divides toward common ground.

Community-Building Takes Hold

By decade's end, the trends discussed in Part One and many of the strategies discussed in Part Two were coming together under an all-inclusive umbrella known as "community-building." Community-building is rooted in the belief that community-based organizations — acting in partnership with residents, each other, and with other local institutions ranging from city government to public schools to major employers — can genuinely improve the social, physical and economic conditions in communities and better support the well-being of children, youth and families.

Whatever their origin and particular goals, community-building initiatives agree that a results-focused, strength-based, collaborative approach — in partnership with the public sector — is inherently superior to the top-down, fragmented manner in which large bureaucratic systems have operated in the past. As journalist Joan Walsh chronicles in her 1997 report, *Stories of Renewal: Community Building and the Future of Urban America*:

> *Community-building rejects a programmatic approach to poverty in favor of efforts that catalyze personal relationships and social networks to improve community life...Today's community-building movement seeks to reckon with all parts of that complicated up-from-poverty story: to strengthen families, churches, schools, small businesses, ethnic associations, employment networks and other community institutions.*[25]

Community-building efforts are spreading rapidly. Organizations ranging from the National League of Cities to the United Way of America and the Bank of America are all involved. The National Community Building Network, now encompassing initiatives in more than two dozen cities and a growing number of national players has been formed to link, support and learn from these burgeoning activities.[26]

There is much to commend today's community-building initiatives as well as many challenges to be overcome. Efforts to integrate disparate organizational and bureaucratic cultures in one common community-building approach generate tensions. Business leaders typically want results overnight.

A Core Issue: Finance

Different community youth strategies represent important efforts to mobilize our communities on behalf of our youth. Each life they nurture is a tribute to their efforts. The questions that must be asked about all of these strategies is whether there are sufficient human and financial resources to achieve the results they seek.

Financing youth programs has proven difficult for local communities. However, a growing number are finding innovative ways to provide funding. These investments — often in the form of increased millage on property tax or a set-aside of funds for youth — recognize that creating an effective system of support for youth requires sustained financial resources and that local communities, must be among the investors.

- In Florida, Children's Services Councils in 12 counties have built on the experience of the Pinellas County Juvenile Welfare Board and now use authority granted by the state to raise youth development resources through a specific portion of county revenue or increased millage. These Children's Services Council — going by different names, depending on the county – allocate more than $100 million for children and youth services. With a growing economy, available funds have been increasing.
- Approximately $16 million is raised annually by a community-based anti-drug sales tax called COMBAT, in Jackson County, Missouri, which includes Kansas City. Voters approved the tax in 1989 in response to a surge of violent crime linked to crack cocaine. Since its implementation, drug pusher arrests have risen and Kansas City's ranking as one of the top ten most violent cities in the nation has fallen. About $9.2 million of the $16 million raised goes to arrests and prosecution of drug criminals, the remainder to prevention.
- With the passage of the Children's Amendment in 1991, San Francisco became the first city in the nation to legislate a baseline fund for services to children and set aside additional dollars for new services. The baseline cannot be touched unless aggregate city appropriations fall. The fund receives 2.5 percent of local property tax revenues to be used for children, youth and families. The measure will provide more than $122 million for children's services between 1992 and 2002. Neighbor Oakland passed a similar provision in 1997.

Community leaders prefer a slower, more deliberative process to build consensus. Government bureaucracies often stress process over results and protection over risk. Race and class divisions are not insignificant. And, too often, fledgling community-based organizations are asked to coordinate a complex web of support activities under the rubric of community-building – without the stable funding mechanisms required to ensure success. Still, the inherent logic of community-building is capturing support. It represents a dynamic confluence of approaches, lessons learned and revitalized commitment.

Two community-building efforts, Banana Kelly, which began as a community development effort, and the Chatham-Savannah Youth Futures Authority, originally a collaborative service reform initiative, illustrate two different approaches to community-building and highlight their unique promise and creativity.

PART THREE: DO YOUTH AND COMMUNITY INITIATIVES IMPROVE OUTCOMES FOR CHILDREN, YOUTH AND YOUNG FAMILIES?

Have the youth and communities initiatives of the 1990s made a difference? Do community-coordinated activities produce better results for children, youth and families than the old-style programmatic approaches? Our sense is "yes" — even though evaluative data are still preliminary. Evaluations that have been completed suggest how difficult these initiatives are to pull off. But most affirm the importance of communities as focal points for strategic planning and implementation of efforts to bolster children and youth. A look at several evaluations of some of the most comprehensive initiatives reveals both the challenges and their potential.

The *New Futures* initiative of the Annie E. Casey Foundation has been instrumental in pioneering youth and community initiatives. Launched in 1988, the ambitious initiative gave grants to five cities — Pittsburgh, Bridgeport, Little Rock, Savannah and Dayton — to encourage a fundamental restructuring in how they planned, financed and delivered educational, health and other services to at-risk youth. Each New Futures city received an average of $10 million over five years. The idea was to form new local governance bodies — community collaboratives — that would devise new policies and practices for meeting the needs of at-risk youth. Participating in the collaboratives were local government officials, administrators from multiple agencies, parents and community representatives.

> **Banana Kelly Embraces Youth Initiatives**
>
> Named for the banana-like shape of Kelly Street where it started, this nonprofit community development corporation (CDC) began in 1977 with a traditional focus on housing and economic development in the South Bronx. Today, Banana Kelly has branched into community-building in the broader sense, including special initiatives to help children and youth.
>
> Banana Kelly has helped transform and renovate portions of the South Bronx by building appealing and affordable row houses for middle- and low-income families. The group provides the South Bronx with community programs such as a pediatric health clinic and an adult vocational training program. It has worked to revive a local commercial strip by providing low-interest loans for businesses and local merchants and, since 1989, has fostered the development of three abandoned industrial parks to provide economic opportunities for the area. The CDC has rehabilitated 2,000 housing units and manages about 1,000 apartments in 47 buildings.
>
> Banana Kelly's YouthBuild program provides economically disadvantaged youth with education and employment skills through opportunities for meaningful work in their communities by helping to meet the housing needs of homeless individuals and members of low income families. The program provides a mix of on-site housing construction, rehabilitation work experience, off-site academic classes, job skill training, leadership development and supportive services for young adults, primarily high school dropouts ages 16-24. Approximately 30 people participate in YouthBuild and avail themselves of a wide variety of social services.

The foundation targeted four outcomes for the New Futures initiative — reducing school dropout rates, improving academic performance, preventing teen pregnancies and increasing the number of youth who go on to a job or college after high school. Each city created a school-based information system to track outcomes.

The lessons we have learned are not brand new insights, concluded Douglas W. Nelson, Casey's executive director.[27] In its own evaluation of New Futures, Casey found that the level of systemic reform required to change outcomes for children, youth and families is very difficult to achieve, and that improving a community's

> **The Chatham-Savannah Youth Futures Authority**
>
> Established in 1988, the Chatham-Savannah Youth Futures Authority (YFA) works to improve outcomes for children and their families in Savannah, Georgia by building systems of support that cut across multiple disciplines. The most successful of the local governing entities created as part of the Annie E. Casey Foundation's New Futures Initiative, YFA focuses on three strategic goals: create and maintain a continuum of supports for children; implement a comprehensive community building initiative for an urban core neighborhood; and maintain and improve the collaborative structure to support planning, implementation and system changes.
>
> YFA started as an effort to integrate multiple services flowing to children and their families. Partners included top business, government and civic leaders who had the clout to help YFA win state authority to enter into multi-year contracts with public and private agencies.
>
> YFA soon moved beyond service integration into community-building. "YFA looked for innovative ways to build supports that enable neighbors to help one another and families to help themselves," Joan Walsh writes in *Stories of Renewal*. Community-building initiatives ranged from family mentoring and seniors programs to community events — all aimed at creating a civic infrastructure strong enough to enable the community to solve its own problems. YFA broadened the constituency for change in Savannah and took on the issue of race with straightforwardness and candor. YFA has yet to become a mechanism for agencies to routinely blend the bulk of their budgets, Walsh notes, but several agencies have adopted YFA's decentralized, community-based approach.
>
> YFA's Family Resource Center is housed in the formerly vacant St. Pius X High School, located in a distressed Savannah neighborhood. "Day and night, the center pulses with activity," writes Walsh. The center features programs galore — from drug prevention to training in African life principles — as well as athletic facilities, a health clinic and a Kids' Café, serving meals to youngsters daily. As a community-building initiative with a clear vision, YFA has become the lead agency for other major youth and community initiatives, including the Comprehensive Community Youth Development (CCYD) program sponsored by Public/Private Ventures and the adaptation of the Beacon Schools program begun in New York City.

economic opportunities and social capital must typically be part of the equation. Casey also found that building community support was harder than envisioned, and that race and ethnicity are critically important issues. Nevertheless, Casey urged participants in youth and community programs to keep at it. Nothing in the experience erodes the validity of this new collaborative approach.[28]

The Center for the Study of Social Policy also weighed in with an evaluation of New Futures. Looking specifically at performance on the four outcomes Casey designated, the Center found mixed results at best. However, the evaluators concluded that New Futures had taken some of the interim steps that may in the longer term lead to improved outcomes for children. The newly-formed collaboratives served as mediating structures to help break down the fragmented categorical systems of services and supports. They raised local awareness of the problems of at-risk youth. They started new dialogues among leaders and community representatives and developed a rich school-based information and tracking system. Each of the collaboratives framed the problems they chose to address in a way that led to cross-system solutions.[29]

In July 1997, the Chapin Hall Center for Children at the University of Chicago released an interim evaluation of the Ford Foundation's *Neighborhood and Family Initiative,* begun in 1992. That initiative seeks to create a working model for integrated neighborhood-based activities in four cities: Detroit, Hartford, Memphis and Milwaukee. Participation by multiple stakeholders and collaboration across agencies and institutions are at the center of the effort, which also attempts to deal comprehensively with social, physical and economic needs. Youth and community initiatives are one piece of the effort.

The 1997 interim evaluation identified several factors within the four communities that tended to influence the shape of the collaboration. Chief among these is whether or not a strong institution exists within the neighborhood to take the lead role. Other key factors include the ethnic, racial and demographic composition and ease of inter-relationships, and the degree to which the neighborhood is economically segregated from the mainstream. Like the Casey initiative, Ford Foundation discovered the difficulties of gaining neighborhood buy-in. After six years, and despite a wide array of outreach activities, three of the four site initiatives had yet to define clearly their goals for increasing their connections with the neighborhood. Resident participation, nevertheless, does appear to be getting stronger, the Chapin Hall Center found.[30]

The Ford evaluation also underscores the difficulty of genuine collaboration. Although all four Neighborhood and Family Initiative sites had thought broadly about their needs and responses across a range of strategic areas, there had been little true integration across disciplines. "In general, program development had followed parallel categorical streams of activity," the Chapin Hall Center found, with projects determined by emerging opportunities in the local environment and based largely on collaborative members' networks.[31]

A 1997 report from Public/Private Ventures also reflects on the early experience of building new collaboratives to change entrenched systems. In *Launching a Resident-Driven Initiative: Community Change for Youth Development (CCYD) from Site Selection to Early Implementation*, P/PV concluded that lead agencies and residents can work through an effective community planning process in a relatively short time period without getting bogged down in process and conflicts. In each of the P/PV evaluated sites, agency staff and residents consistently reported that their willingness to undertake the initiative stemmed from the fact that it was community-driven. They also said the core concepts of CCYD reflected their prime goal — to help young people grow into healthy productive adults. The lead agencies for CCYD implementation sites had strong and widely recognized leadership, stability as organizations, and flexibility of resources — qualities that proved necessary to keep the planning effort moving forward in both community process and strategic content.

From our perspective, these several evaluations suggest that youth and community initiatives in their various forms are building a foundation for making real improvements in the lives of the nation's young people.

PART FOUR: RECOMMENDATIONS

Communities across the nation are demonstrating their capacity and potential to improve results for America's youth. Much remains to be done.

Most importantly, we must sustain and strengthen the focus on community and community building. Youth and community initiatives are beginning to demonstrate results. This approach makes sense to youth, neighborhood residents, practitioners and policymakers. We also believe they make sense to the public and bridge the gap between advocates of individual responsibility and community responsibility.

Nurturing youth to productive adulthood — coupled with the task of moving people from poverty to self-sufficiency — has always been difficult. The work in community integrates much of what we have learned in the past 30 years. Several recommendations should move our efforts forward.

For Communities

1. Promote citizen leadership. Agency leadership still dominates many community initiatives. While these leaders contribute a great deal, some of the most effective youth and community efforts are led by community people — parents, neighborhood residents, business and civic leaders and young people themselves, backed by agency support. This citizen leadership approach has significant value and should be expanded. Citizens are perceived as speaking for the community, not for a particular agency and, as such, have credibility with the public. Community people push agencies to change the way they do their work and can play a major role in building public will for the work. Finally, creating opportunities for citizens to lead can renew people's faith in our democratic institutions and the positive roles that government can play.

2. Focus on results and capacity. The strong emphasis on results is a major step forward in youth and community initiatives. We encourage communities to come to consensus on the outcomes sought and the indicators used to measure progress toward those results. At least annually, communities should publish those results, focus media attention on them and reexamine how well they are accomplishing their objectives.

The focus on results and accountability must apply equally to all organizations — nonprofit and profit-making alike. As more dollars are allocated to private firms to support children, youth and families, they, too, must be accountable. Managed care organizations, residential youth services organizations and child care companies must all demonstrate positive results.

Elected officials at all levels of government must demand accountability across-the-board.

At the same time, we encourage communities to develop a stronger focus on assessing community capacity to achieve the intended results. The work of the Center for Youth Development and Policy Research is an important start in this direction. It proposes measures such as percent of youth doing community service, number of schools open for youth programs until 7:00 p.m., number of youth within walking distance of public transportation, and computer-to-student ratio in schools. In addition to the Center's proposed measures, we suggest communities consider such indicators as availability of good paying jobs, health care, child care, transportation for working parents, affordable housing and after-school program opportunities.

3. Talk to the public in simple, concrete terms. The American people will support clear and cogent policies and programs that they can see responding to specific needs of our youth. All community and youth initiatives should include a component to increase the public will to achieve better results for our youth and make the investments necessary to that end.

4. Pursue specialized local taxing provisions. The increase in the number of communities with special levies on behalf of youth suggests that similar approaches might work in other places. We encourage local leaders of community-based youth initiatives to carefully consider this possibility. Passing a local tax is a daunting task, but the experience of other communities offers encouragement.

5. Remember that communities cannot do it alone. The focus on community is one dimension of the devolution of power and authority over federal programs to states — and through states to local communities. One of our fears is the tendency in some quarters to think that communities alone can produce better results. The experience of the last decade, however, demonstrates that no single institution can achieve better outcomes. It would be regrettable if public policy did not recognize that the federal and state governments have a continuing responsibility to provide sufficient resources to communities so they can improve the well-being of all our children and families. Sustained partnerships between the public, private and nonprofit sectors are essential.

For Advocates and Funders: Public and Private

1. Develop a budget surplus strategy for America's youth. Deficits were once an excuse for limiting government investments in people and community. Even now, with emerging surpluses, there is still no clear investment agenda for young people. While we must avoid competition between the generations, the future of youth cannot be overlooked as America makes investment choices for the 21st Century. Leaders for children and youth, across all systems and interests, should join hands and develop budget proposals and projected outcomes that can be achieved with strategically directed new funding.

2. Invest in After-School programs and Community School strategies. While many youth development areas deserve additional support, we argue for significant investment in two arenas: after-school programs and community schools. Well-designed after-school programs help communities address three important issues: keeping youth safe and out of trouble, giving parents security about their children while they work, and helping youth learn and develop.

Community schools are an extremely promising strategy for weaving together the assets of a community into a coherent and responsive system of support and opportunity. Community school practitioners have been extraordinarily creative in packaging existing funding streams. What they now need most is sufficient core support to sustain these initiatives over time and provide an infrastructure on which to hang a wide range of other programs and services. Some states and communities are creating that infrastructure. We encourage others to do the same, and urge the federal government to do more in this important arena.

For Federal and State Policymakers

1. Let communities decide how funds are used. Laws and regulations related to specific programs are often barriers to the implementation of effective community-based systems of support for youth. If community is to be the fulcrum of planning and oversight of support for youth — as we argue it should be — then funds should flow to communities in ways that empower these collaborative community enterprises. Typically, in the categorical system, federal and state monies flow to specific agencies, which control the resources, leading to turf battles and less effective service delivery strategies.

Rather than funding agencies, federal and state law could fund community collaboratives which meet designated characteristics. These collaboratives, with broad-based citizen-dominated membership, would be expected to: 1) define the vision and results that the community seeks; 2) articulate a set of principles and values that will drive its work; 3) formulate strategies to weave together public, private and community resources; and 4) ensure accountability. The collaboratives would designate their own fiscal agent, and have the authority to select the provider that can most effectively achieve the community's vision and results. Congress tentatively explored such an approach in the idea of a Youth Development Block Grant several years ago. It should be reconsidered.

If shifting funds from agencies to communities is not feasible, then we suggest that all proposals seeking funding, whether from government or private sources, be expected to demonstrate how their plans reflect the vision and results, principles and values, strategy and accountability framework of the community collaborative. This approach should bring agencies to a common table of a community collaborative before they submit proposals, rather than after the fact, and contribute to the design and implementation of effective comprehensive strategies.

2. Pursue policies that support community schools. Community schools seek to organize an array of community assets around learning. Public policy could support this strategy by asking all grant seekers to indicate how they will support learning and development at the school and in the community. Such a provision could be incorporated as part of federal and state government efforts focused on results. This provision would drive agencies and organizations toward a common educational and youth development strategy.

In addition to supporting community schools, we recommend the following:

• *Drive health and mental services toward schools.* We encourage Congress and the states to ensure that primary health care and mental health services become more available at schools. Current Medicaid and child health insurance programs offer few incentives for managed care organizations and other health care providers to offer health services at schools. Yet, these are among the services that educators most often request. School personnel are urgently seeking mental health services for children, especially in the wake of the gun and drug violence which has racked many schools and communities. Communities need more leverage to influence the actions of managed care organizations and providers.

• *Technical assistance and professional development.* Because community schools are not a formally funded program at the federal level and in most states, insufficient technical assistance supports this promising approach to improving results for children and families. We urge Congress and executive branch agencies to build on the commitment of the Mott Foundation and find ways to tap existing technical assistance resources to create a national resource center for community schools and offer technical assistance with an emphasis on creating peer networks of mutual support.

3. Deepen efforts to change the culture of federal and state agencies. Most federal and state agencies still manage programs, rather than work with communities to use program resources in conjunction with other community assets to achieve better results. States should provide the training and support to personnel at all levels so that they, and the programs they fund, can be more effective resources for the community.

For Agencies and Organizations Working With Youth

1. Build common ground. To be effective with individual youth and their families, and to mobilize necessary public will to achieve results, individuals and organizations concerned with the well-being of children and youth must work together. Leaders and practitioners must bridge the many divides that exist, including particularly those between the school and the community, between youth development organizations and educators, between public agencies and neighborhood residents and organizations. Unless these agencies and organizations join forces, it is unlikely that we can build the will of the American people and our political leaders to act in support of our youth and craft workable solutions at the community level.

Communities: Powerful Resource for Youth

For Citizens

1. Talk with young people and really listen to them. Everywhere that Americans gather to do the work of community — in neighborhoods and schools, in houses of worship, at business and civic organizations' meetings, in government forums and in places where youth gather, the voices of youth must be heard. Advocates for our youth must make sure this happens.

2. Think about the kind of community you want for your children and grandchildren and for all of America's children. Work toward it.

NOTES

Illam Askia and Scott Barghaan, interns from Cornell University and the University of Richmond, respectively, and Candice Tollin of the Institute for Educational Leadership provided invaluable research, writing and editing support in the preparation of this paper.

[1] "Community Change for Youth Development: The Process Begins," *Public/Private Ventures News*, Special Edition, vol. 11, no. 3, p. 8.
[2] Timpane, Michael and Rob Reich. "Revitalizing the Ecosystem for Youth," *Phi Delta Kappan*, February 1997, p. 465.
[3] Gardner, John W. *Building Community*. Washington, DC: Independent Sector, 1991, p. 8.
[4] Dorfman, Lori, Katie Woodruff, Vivian Chavez and Lawrence Wallack. "Youth in Balance of Local Television News in California," *American Journal of Public Health*, August 1997, vol. 87, no. 8.
[5] Kretzmann, John P. and John L. McKnight. *Building Communities From The Inside Out*. Chicago, IL: ACTA Publications, 1993, p. 1.
[6] Pierce, Neal and Curtis Johnson. *Lessons for Community Builders: Citizen Leadership for the 21st Century*. College Park, MD: Academy of Leadership, 1997.
[7] Contact the ChildWatch Program at the Children's Defense Fund: 202-628-8787.
[8] Melaville, Atelia I. *Learning Together: The Developing Field of School-Community Initiatives*. Flint, MI: Charles S. Mott Foundation and Institute for Educational Leadership, 1998.
[9] Chang, Hedy. *Community Building and Diversity: Nine Principles*. San Francisco, CA: California Tomorrow, 1997, p. 7.
[10] Bruner, Charles and Maria Chavez. *Getting to the Grassroots*. Des Moines, IA: NCSI Clearinghouse, Community Collaboration Guidebook Series, 1998, p. 1.
[11] Ditto, p. iii.
[12] Further information about LINC can be found at www.kclinc.org. Also see Center for the Study of Social Policy. *Toward New Forms of Local Governance*. Washington, DC: 1996 and Martin J. Blank and Jacqueline P. Danzberger. *Developing Collaborative Community Governing Bodies*. Washington, DC: Institute for Educational Leadership, 1994.
[13] Blank, Martin and Jacqueline Danzberger. *Developing Collaborative Community Governing Bodies: Implications for Federal Policy*. Washington, DC: Institute for Educational Leadership, 1994.
[14] Howard, Bill. "Assets vs. Risks," *Youth Today*, September/October 1997, p. 18.
[15] Search Institute website: www.search-institute.org
[16] Howard, Bill, op. cit., p. 18.
[17] Fisher, Deborah. *Listen Up! Integrating Youth Voices Into Asset-Building Efforts, Assets*. Minneapolis, MN: Search Institute, Winter 1997, pp. 3-4.
[18] *Public/Private Ventures News*, Special Edition, Summer 1996, vol. 11, no. 3.
[19] "The Black Community Crusade for Children." Freedom Schools brochure. Washington, DC: Children's Defense Fund.
[20] Melaville, Atelia, op. cit.
[21] "Major Cities Police Chiefs Organization Calls for Child Care, After-School Programs: Investments in Kids 'Powerful Weapons Against Crime,'" *Major Cities Chiefs*, February 19, 1998, p. 1.
[22] Posner, J. and D. Vandell. "Low income children's after-school care: Are there beneficial effects of after-school programs?" *Child Development*, 1994, p. 440.
[23] Hatch, Tom and Tina Blythe. *More Than a Place to Go: Creating and Sustaining Effective After-School Programs*. Cambridge, MA: Harvard Project Zero, 1997.
[24] *Safe and Smart: Making the After-School Hours Work for Kids*, U.S. Department of Education and U.S. Department of Justice, June 1998.
[25] Walsh, Joan. *Stories of Renewal: Community Building and the Future of Urban America*. New York, NY: The Rockefeller Foundation, 1996, p. 1.
[26] National Community Building Network, 839 Temple Terrace, Los Angeles, CA 90042; 213-254-2121.
[27] *The Path of Most Resistance*. Baltimore, MD: Annie E. Casey Foundation, 1995, p. vi.
[28] Ditto, p. 27.
[29] *Building New Futures for At-Risk Youth*. Washington, DC: Center for the Study of Social Policy, pp. x-xi.
[30] Chaskin, Robert, Selma Chipenda Dansoko and Mark Joseph. *The Ford Foundation's Neighborhood and Family Initiatives: The Challenge of Sustainability; An Interim Report*. Chicago, IL: Chapin Hall Center for Children, University of Chicago, July 1977.
[31] Ditto, p. 5.

CHAPTER FIVE

YOUTH AND SCHOOL REFORM: FROM THE FORGOTTEN HALF TO THE FORGOTTEN THIRD

Jack Jennings and Diane Stark Rentner

Ten years ago, *The Forgotten Half* report focused much-needed attention on a generation of 16-24 year-olds whose future did not include college. Today, a decade later, it is very appropriate to reflect on what is different for teenagers in general, and especially for those highlighted in *TFH*.

During that decade the world has changed substantially and, therefore, today's youngsters face different prospects in their lives than did the youth of the late 1980s. During that momentous ten-year span, Communism collapsed in the U.S.S.R. and eastern Europe. As a result, dozens of nations turned to democracy as a form of government and to capitalism as the driving economic force. The former Russian empire embodied in the Union of Soviet Socialist Republics imploded and left the United States as the world's only super power. The economic threat of a surging Japanese economy receded as that country slipped into economic doldrums, and the United States emerged as the world's most competitive economy.

American military, economic, and political supremacy have been accompanied by social changes in the United States — many positive but some with negative side-effects. A smaller military, reduced in size because of the collapse of communism, has meant fewer opportunities for economic and social advancement for youth, especially minority youngsters. A competitive American economy has come about — in part — through layoffs and a shift to part time and contracted employment which does not offer health care, retirement, and other benefits.

We cannot as yet understand all the effects of these monumental changes in politics, economics, and sociology; but we can see that the lives that today's youngsters will lead will be different from the past, even the near past of the 1980s. One clear effect is greater economic insecurity which is leading young people — and their parents — to place a greater value on gaining more years of formal education. This chapter will concentrate on changes in the education system during the last ten years, while acknowledging fully that changes in the economy, in communities and in families have a great effect on how well children succeed in school. Other chapters of this report also explore these important changes.

Since the late 1980s, millions of words have been spoken and thousands of newspaper articles and reports have been written on the status of public elementary and secondary education. Moreover, hundreds of school reform laws have been enacted by legislatures, and numerous innovations tried in many schools. In fact, the period from the early 1980s to the late 1990s could be called the time of "the Great Debate" of the twentieth century on American public schooling. A major cause of this debate is concern about the quality of American education due to greater worldwide economic competitiveness and resulting domestic job insecurity.

A major consequence of this debate has been that many students in The Forgotten Half of the late 1980s were helped to learn more and encouraged to gain further education and training. Therefore, today there is only a "forgotten third," in the sense that only about one-third of high school graduates end their education at the termination of secondary school (See Figure 5-7). That is the good news. The bad news is that the ones left behind — those who do not gain any education or training after high school and those who do not even earn a high school degree — face a bleaker economic future than those of the The Forgotten Half" of the late 1980s.

This chapter discusses what has happened for the better in schooling and describes what needs to be done to help the ones left behind. Our focus is on the K-12 school system, since other chapters deal with related developments affecting families, communities, and preparation for employment.

COMPREHENSIVE REFORMS

In 1983, anxiety about the condition of public education crystallized when the report titled *A Nation at Risk* was released. In language unusually bold for a government-sponsored document, it asserted: "If an unfriendly foreign power had attempted to impose on America the mediocre educational performance that exists today, we might well have viewed it as an act of war. As it stands, we have allowed this to happen to ourselves." Although labeled unduly alarmist by some educators, the report put into words what many leaders in business and government then felt about the condition of American public schools — and those conclusions resonated with the public and the Reagan Administration. As already mentioned, many of those fears in the early 1980s resulted from a concern about declining American economic competitiveness in a world economy.

Making It Tougher to Graduate

The greatest immediate impact of that reformist mood on the schools and students was the toughening in the mid- to late-1980s of high school graduation requirements by state legislatures and state boards of education. A majority of the states raised their demands for the minimum course-work needed for graduation from secondary school. This was the first of two major comprehensive reforms in American public education during the last ten years.

As a direct result of this reform, high schoolers now are taking much more demanding course-work than their predecessors did in the early 1980s (See Figure 5-1). In 1994 fifty-one percent of students were taking what *A Nation at Risk* called a minimum program: four years of English and three years each of science, mathematics, and social studies. This contrasts with only 14 percent of students taking such course-work in 1982. Enrollments in algebra, geometry, trigonometry, calculus, advanced sciences and Advanced Placement courses are significantly higher than they were a decade ago.

Even if one were skeptically to assume some relabeling of courses by school officials, the overall differences are marked. It is clear that many more high school students have recently been taking more difficult academic course-work. Further, despite concerns that increased demands would result in higher dropout rates for high schoolers, the exact opposite has happened. More teenagers are staying in school or returning for their equivalency degrees than ever before. In 1996, only 11% of persons ages 16 to 24 had <u>not</u> completed high school or an equivalency degree, compared to over 14% in 1980.

High school vocational education has experienced the downside of this push for more academic content in the secondary school curriculum. Compared to the early 1980s, today's vocational student enrollments are notably reduced as a result of this emphasis on

Figure 5-1: Percentage of High School Graduates Earning the Minimum Number of Course Units in Core Courses, 1982, 1987, 1990 and 1994

Characteristics	"New Basics" curriculum			
	1982	1987	1990	1994
Total	14.0	28.3	39.6	50.6
Race/ethnicity				
White	15.5	29.3	40.6	53.6
Black	11.5	24.1	41.5	44.7
Hispanic	6.7	16.8	30.4	43.8
Asian/Pacific Islander	21.3	45.6	48.7	56.6
American Indian/Alaskan Native	6.5	24.6	21.6	43.6

SOURCE: U.S. Department of Education, National Center for Education Statistics, *The 1994 High School Transcript Study Tabulations: Comparative Data on Credits Earned and Demographics for 1994, 1990, 1987 and 1982 High School Graduates,* 1996; *The Condition of Education* 1996, p. 98.

more demanding academic course-work. In 1982, 26.9% of high school seniors reported that they were in a vocational program, while only 11.7% reported such enrollment ten years later. A basic reason for this shift away from vocational education is that high school vocational courses frequently are electives; and with increased academic demands being placed on students without an increase in the length of the school day, many students do not have enough time to enroll in vocational courses in addition to the newly-mandated academic course-work.

Standards-Based Reform*

In 1988, when *TFH* was published, these requirements for more academically demanding high school course work were beginning to result in a shift of students to more challenging subjects, but since the changes had only recently been enacted by state legislatures or mandated by state boards, the evidence of change was not as dramatic as can be seen today. In the absence of signs of dramatic change and in the face of stagnating national test scores, many political and business leaders — and some educators — became anxious about the lack of progress being made in improving the public schools. Therefore, leaders began a push for states and local school districts to hold students to higher academic standards.

Raising academic quality thus came to mean not only prescribing the completion of more rigorous course work for graduation from high school, but also defining the levels of academic content that students should master at particular grade levels. Kentucky, Delaware, Maryland, and Vermont were early leaders in writing clearer and more demanding standards for what they expected their schoolchildren to know and be able to do. By 1996 forty-nine states had begun to write academic standards or to implement them in their public schools. These changes have come to be known as *standards-based reform,* the second comprehensive school improvement movement of the last ten years in American public education.

National encouragement to raise academic standards resulted from the adoption by the nation's governors of the first-ever national goals for education in 1990 and Presidents George Bush and Bill Clinton's proposals for national standards and tests, as well as for modest federal aid to states and school districts to raise the quality of their education. These national efforts were complementary to state and local efforts to raise standards, reinforcing what the states were initiating on their own with prodding from their governors, business leaders, and the media.

Today, the states are at far different stages of standards-based reform. Some have not even finished writing their standards, while some have been testing schoolchildren for seven to eight years based on the higher expectations contained in more rigorous standards. Despite their varying progress in implementing higher standards, the future for many states — as they continue with standards-based reform — can be discerned from what is occurring in the leaders.

Kentucky rewards schools with grants if they have raised student achievement and plans soon to penalize them if they have not. Maryland determines which schools should be placed on a watch list for state intervention based on student results from the state assessment. Using student performance on the Texas Assessment of Academic Skills (TAAS), along with attendance rates and dropout rates, schools in Texas are rated as "exemplary," "recognized," "acceptable," or "low-performing." At least 35% of a school's students--including 35% of the school's black, Hispanic, and low-income students--must pass each component of TAAS or it will fall into the "low-performing" category. If a school continues to be low-performing for several years in a row, the state can "reconstitute" the school.

After holding schools accountable for the results of their students on state tests, the next step is for students to be held accountable individually for meeting higher standards. Such accountability reforms will have direct and substantial effects on teenagers in high schools. For example, the Maryland State Board of Education recently adopted a requirement that high school students, early in the new century, will have to pass a set number of examinations in order to graduate. Michigan will soon require that high-schoolers pass a demanding exit examination if they are to earn a diploma, and the New York State Board of Regents voted to require that *all* students will have to pass the "Regents Exam" which has traditionally been taken only by college-going students. Virginia and other states are moving in the same direction.

---

*For a fuller discussion of the national debate surrounding standards and assessments, see *Why National Standards and Tests* by John F. Jennings. Thousand Oaks, CA: Sage Publications, 1998.

In early 1998, it is too early to tell exactly how the course of standards-based reform will go. In Maryland and other states, parents have voiced concerns that students will be held to higher standards and denied a high school diploma without being adequately prepared for the examinations and without having several chances to pass the tests. As a result of these complaints, the Maryland State Board of Education adopted a policy to improve teaching and learning when it adopted its requirements for exit examinations from high school. In Michigan, the state legislature made some modifications in the provisions of the exit examination because some students opted out of taking the test, but the state legislature still retained the test. In Virginia, many educators complained that the more demanding requirements are being instituted without adequate teacher training and other aids.

To summarize, there have been two comprehensive school reforms during the last ten years and these are having, or will have, major effects on high school students. The course work requirements for graduation from high school have been increased in many states and school districts, and higher academic standards are being implemented in most states to measure the success of schools and students in mastering knowledge. The first reform is far advanced with direct results already evident among the students highlighted in *The Forgotten Half*. The second reform is still evolving with its major effects on students yet to be seen, as states grapple with issues of testing, accountability, teacher preparation, and equity. Although not fully implemented as yet, standards-based reform—if it continues on track—will have even greater impact on high school students than have the increased demands for academic course-work.

Both of these comprehensive reforms are meant to prod the public schools to improvement, through the first reform's requirements for completion of more demanding course work for graduation and through the second reform's raising the rigor of the academic content of schooling and measuring achievement of that content in tests. Increasing requirements and raising expectations for students can be very helpful in improving schools, but they must be accompanied by changes in the quality of teachers, fairer distributions of funding, and additional opportunities for students to master the curriculum.

The severe problems faced by many large city school systems are a particular drag on comprehensive school reform. As the January 1998 *Quality Counts '98* from *Education Week* pointed out, while over 60 percent of students in non-urban school districts scored at the "basic" level on the National Assessment of Educational Progress's reading, mathematics, and science exams, only about 40 percent of students in urban districts met that standard. Indicative of broader equity concerns and the effects of poverty, an Educational Testing Service study found that, in schools with minority enrollments of over 90 percent, the ratio of students to computers is 17 to 1, while schools nationally have about one computer for every ten students. Further, the study includes a survey of seniors from the Class of 1996 which found that 54 percent of white students had taken courses in computer literacy compared with 41 percent of black and Puerto Rican students.

Those facts about inequities in educational opportunity show some of the serious challenges facing the implementation of comprehensive reforms. The next sections will discuss some of the changes which reformers have sought to bring about in schools, in funding, and in the preparation of teachers. These should be seen as complementary to comprehensive reforms as, in many respects, they are meant to address the inequities inherent in American education.

SCHOOL-BASED REFORMS

During the last ten years, while the two comprehensive, system-wide reforms were being implemented, particular schools were the focus of other efforts to bring about change. These included networks such as the Coalition for Essential Schools and the High Schools That Work project. Other reform efforts involved linkages between high schools and community colleges fostered by the Tech-Prep program and schools involved in the "choice movement."

Coalition of Essential Schools

One of the most interesting phenomena of the last decade has been the creation of reform "networks" among schools and school districts. Often organized by a university professor who advocates a particular way to bring about improvement in schools, these leaders have sought to broaden the effects of these changes by connecting with like-minded teachers, principals, and superintendents in other schools and school districts.

Most of these networks involve elementary schools, because reformers' experiences have shown that it is easier to change an elementary school than it is a high school, in part because of the departmental nature of secondary education. The Coalition of Essential Schools, organized in 1984 by Theodore Sizer of Brown University, took on a more difficult set of problems by focusing on high schools, although elementary and middle schools have since joined. The Coalition seeks to bring about improvement by dealing with the relationship among students, teachers, parents and the curriculum, plus the structural changes needed to make that relationship work better. The Coalition emphasizes that change must come from within the school, that there is no other way to bring about improvement. Sizer explains his philosophy thus: "Our research suggests that you're not going to get significant, long-term reform unless you have subtle but powerful support and collaboration among teachers, students, and the families of those students in a particular community." Approximately 800 schools participate in the Coalition.

High Schools That Work

The High Schools That Work (HSTW) project deals exclusively with secondary schools. Initiated by Gene Bottoms of the Southern Regional Education Board, HSTW began in the southern states and has now spread to every region of the country, involving about 550 high schools. The idea behind HSTW is that schools blend the best from the college preparatory curriculum with vocational and technical studies of high quality. Schools join this network if they agree to raise the academic rigor of course-work for all students, especially those who are in a vocational track, and to give those students who need it extra assistance to meet the higher standards. Schools must also agree to eliminate the general track and to improve counseling on careers for all students. Every year, test scores are collected to determine the effectiveness of the project as well as to provide schools with valuable information that they will use to make improvements in the program.

The Tech-Prep Movement

A broader and looser movement than the HSTW project and the Coalition for Essential Schools is Tech-Prep. Its basic concept is to coordinate education and training in high schools and postsecondary institutions, such as community colleges and technical colleges, in order to allow a student to proceed smoothly from courses that are less complex to those that are more demanding and which build on what has been learned earlier. Articulation agreements about course work are entered into by high schools and postsecondary institutions as the way to achieve this progression of academic and skill training. Although such agreements had been used prior to 1990 in some states and localities, Tech-Prep received a major boost that year when the Carl Perkins Vocational Education Act was amended to provide federal financial assistance to all states to carry out such programs. In the fall of 1995 there were more than 1,000 Tech-Prep consortia of high schools and postsecondary institutions with approximately 740,000 students participating in school year 1994-95.

The School Choice and Charter Movements

The "choice movement," another effort to change individual schools, has several facets. Open enrollment among public schools in one school district allows students to opt to attend whatever school he or she wishes within certain restraints, such as space and racial balance. Thousands of school districts throughout the country now permit this choice for students, especially high schoolers. Magnet schools, frequently organized around a theme such as science and technology or arts, are a form of open enrollment.

Charter schools are a more advanced form of choice. These schools vary greatly by state in their structures, with some states only permitting charters which are controlled by local school districts and with others permitting charters to operate independently of school districts. The concept is that all of these public schools will be freer to experiment, being bound by fewer regulations and administrative strictures than regular public schools. Charter schools are growing in popularity as more state legislatures authorize them or enlarge the number permitted. In 1998, there were 784 charter schools in 32 states and the District of Columbia. Sixteen states allow charter schools to operate as independent entities. In 12 states, only local school boards can grant a charter; in the 13 other states and the District of Columbia, many agencies have the authority to grant charters. The U.S. Department of Education estimated that less than a quarter of charter schools were secondary schools in the 1995-6 school year, although it cautioned that some charters were ungraded or kindergarten through grade 12 (K-12).

To summarize again, the system-wide movements for change of the last decade have been occurring at the same time as efforts to improve individual schools. These efforts have operated separately from one another since they are premised on different approaches to reform. The systemic reformers generally believe that change must occur throughout the whole system and that the levers of change are state laws, regulations and assessment systems. The individual school reformers, by contrast, believe that true improvement in schooling only occurs when teachers and administrators change the way they act within the school buildings and that this new way of thinking must come about through their desire to change, not through state laws, tests or regulations.

Although these two mechanisms approach reform from different perspectives, they should be seen as complementary. System-wide efforts to bring about change will flounder if individual teachers and administrators are resistant. Changing schools one-by-one may not be possible due to a lack of motivation on the part of some teachers and administrators. Furthermore, system-wide changes are having a broad impact; but mandates for change have their limits, since teacher training and student assistance must be brought in as a complementary set of activities. Individual schools can change, but "light-house" schools frequently do not help to improve whole systems, and so a broader effort can help to spread good practices. The years ahead will show if it is possible to merge these two movements to bring about both widespread and consistent improvement in elementary and secondary education.

Furthermore, comprehensive academic reforms and school-based reforms — even if more fully implemented — would still not be enough to help all children to succeed. Some schools have a "culture of failure" which must be changed. Many states have unfair systems of school finance which deprive children of adequate classrooms and science laboratories. Too many teachers do not have a major or even a minor in the subjects they teach. Consequently, even more changes are needed than those described to this point.

OTHER APPROACHES TO REFORM
State Takeovers of School Districts

In some states, concern about the poor performance of some school districts has led to direct state action to bring about improvement. In New Jersey, the state has taken over the Newark and Jersey City school districts; in New York the state took over the Roosevelt school district; and in Ohio, Cleveland was placed under the control of a state administrator. Although the districts in these three states have all been large urban districts, two rural county school districts in Kentucky have also been placed under state control.

In other states, the legislatures have enacted laws which place failing urban districts under the control of the mayors. In Illinois the mayor of Chicago was given near complete control of the public schools, and in Cleveland the state is trying to extricate itself from direct control of the schools by giving the responsibility to the mayor. In Boston, the mayor led a successful effort to do away with the elected school board and to have a board under his control so that he could make major changes in the schools. The opposite happened in Baltimore, where the mayor had control of the schools, and the state legislature injected the state board of education into the process of appointing the school board and in changing the administrative structure of the school district. The theme of all these various changes is that large urban school systems are not adequately educating youngsters and therefore there must be major changes to improve the schools.

School District Intervention in Failing Schools

Continuing with the same theme, within some large urban school districts the school board or the school superintendent have taken over failing schools and "reconstituted" them. This local takeover varies by district, but it usually involves removing the principal and reassigning at least some of the teachers. The idea is to administer shock therapy to the school to change the culture of the school from one of failure to one of success. Many of these local takeovers have been of high schools, since they are frequently the poorest-performing schools in a district. For instance, in San Francisco and in Philadelphia several high schools were reconstituted, causing an uproar from the teachers' unions.

The state takeovers of school districts and other shifts in governance and the reconstitution of schools have all occurred relatively recently. These changes have also affected relatively few school districts and schools. Therefore, it is too early to draw any general conclusions about their effects on students highlighted in *TFH*. However, since high schools, and especially large urban schools are becoming objects of increasing concern, the effects could be substantial in years ahead as more schools and districts face the prospect of takeover or reconstitution.

Improved Teacher Quality

Another major education reform of the last decade is to raise the quality of the teaching force. To illustrate the need for improvement, in 1993-94, 24 percent of all mathematics teachers and 17 percent of science teachers were not certified to teach in those fields. The reform of teacher education and of training of current teachers is occurring on several fronts.

Since 1994, the National Board for Professional Teaching Standards has been constructing an assessment system which awards a certificate to teachers as "board-certified." The idea is to have a voluntary and vigorous national system of recognition for outstanding teachers, with the hope that they will receive monetary and other rewards for being so recognized. In North Carolina, board-certified teachers are now given salary increases of 4%. It has taken years to organize this certification system and so, in May 1998, there were only 912 certified teachers in the whole country. The numbers may soon grow significantly, especially since some states and school districts are paying for the costs of the process of certification.

Other improvements are coming to teacher preparation and training. The states are cooperating in a project to make state licensure more meaningful and the accreditation system for colleges of education is being gradually overhauled. With a million new teachers needed in the next decade due to retirements among current teachers and to increased pupil enrollments, the recommendations of reform groups, like the National Commission on Teaching and America's Future are carrying weight. The Commission contends that now is the opportune time to raise the quality of teaching. Although it is too soon to draw conclusions on the affects of these reforms on high school students, it is fair to predict that the eventual impact will be major.

Equitable Funding of School Districts

Another reform in education is the ongoing effort to secure more adequate and fairer funding of elementary and secondary education within the states. Since 1971, most of the states have been sued in state courts for unfair systems of school finance. In 16 of these cases, state supreme courts have found the finance systems unconstitutional; many states are still in litigation. For example, in *Abbott v. Burke*, the court found that New Jersey's finance system was unconstitutional for poor urban districts, and the state was ordered to fund those school districts at a level commensurate with wealthier districts. In addition, the state was directed to provide additional funds to meet the needs of at risk students in those districts.

The New Jersey case is especially interesting because the state had prescribed higher academic standards for all children and said it was providing enough funding to help them achieve to the level of those standards. The Supreme Court held that, at least as regards the poorer urban districts, the state was not providing enough for children to have an opportunity to meet those standards. This case could be an indication of the future direction of litigation as courts evaluate the level of funding provided for education with the expectations for students embodied in higher standards.

Service Learning

To this point, we have discussed increasing course work, raising academic standards, changing individual schools, improving the quality of teaching, and more fairly distributing funding. Much of the motivation for these changes has come from a concern to improve education so that children will have a chance to be better prepared for an economic future of greater insecurity than was faced by their parents. The emphasis on the need for greater American economic competitiveness runs through the debate leading to many of these changes.

An entirely different reform involves encouraging students to volunteer in their communities. The motivation for this reform is not economic at all. Rather, it is rooted in a concern that youth must be taught to think of the needs of others in society. According to the Association for Supervision and Curriculum Development, learning through serving in the community is a fast-growing phenomenon. Only Maryland requires community service for a student to graduate from high school, but ten other states allow districts to award credit for service. Ten more states encourage student service, such as Hawaii's inclusion of service-learning in the curriculum framework for middle school students. Some school districts are also taking action. For instance, the Chicago Public Schools announced in 1997 that 60 hours of community service will be required for high school students to graduate.

HOW REFORM IS AFFECTING STUDENTS

Those have been the major reforms in elementary and secondary education over the course of the last decade or so. The first two —

increasing course work required for high school graduation and standards-based reform — are aimed at bringing about comprehensive, system-wide change among all schools within a state. The school-oriented reforms take the opposite approach by focusing on bringing about change building-by-building. The governance changes are meant to reform whole school districts while takeover strategies are aimed at particular districts or schools within districts. The movement to improve teacher quality is obviously intended to have a wide impact, as is the effort to require state legislatures to fund the schools more equitably.

While no one has yet demonstrated the connection between each of these education reforms and the desired higher academic achievement, there are some encouraging signs, even in our largest urban school districts. According to the data gathered by the Council of Great City Schools, significant achievement gains have been registered in San Francisco, Seattle, Philadelphia, Milwaukee and other cities. For example, Milwaukee reported that the pass rate on its comprehensive math test had risen from 21 to 98 percent. Major declines in the dropout rate — some as much as 40 percent from just few years ago — have also been recorded in Broward County, Florida, Denver, Fresno and El Paso.

One additional measure of progress in major school systems is the rising public support for new bond issues and higher operating levies, sometimes with approval margins of 70 percent. Among the cities where this has recently happened are Los Angeles, Detroit, Tulsa, Oakland, Las Vegas, San Antonio, Charlotte, Cleveland, Columbus and Seattle. While the crisis in urban education is far from over, the public's increasing vote of confidence in their schools is still worthy of note.

The 1980s and the 1990s have been years of rhetoric and specific actions calling for improvement in public schooling. Our description indicates how many reforms there have been and how varied they are. Many schools have tried to improve. School districts have implemented changes. State legislatures have mandated increased course-work and permitted charter schools. The federal government has funded innovative programs, encouraged states to raise their academic standards, and funded voluntary national certification of teachers.

In this description of changes in schooling, we have tried to show the effects of particular reforms on students in middle and high schools but, frequently, the discrete reforms are too new, too isolated, or too hard to quantify to show a direct effect on students due to any specific change. Consequently, it might be better to look at the condition of students more broadly, especially those students who were the

National Assessment of Educational Progress

Figure 5-2: Average Mathematics Proficiency of 13-Year Olds By Race/Ethnicity, 1978 and 1992

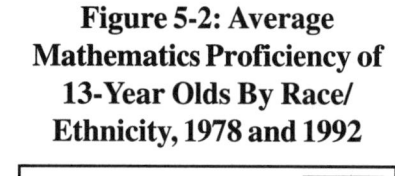

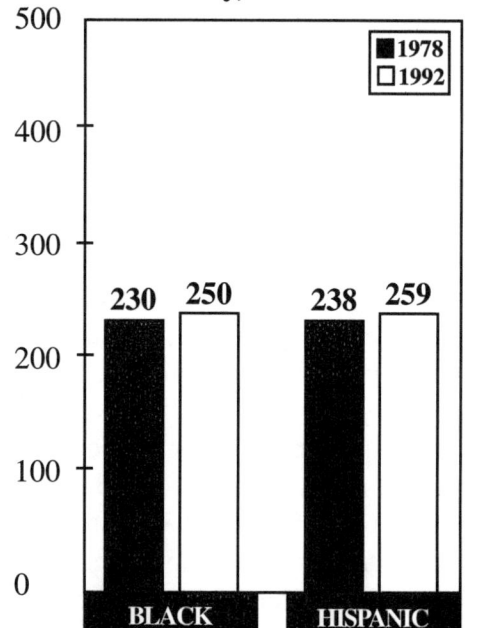

Race/Ethnicity	1978	1992
BLACK	230	250
HISPANIC	238	259

Figure 5-3: Average Science Proficiency of 13-Year Olds By Race/Ethnicity, 1977 and 1992

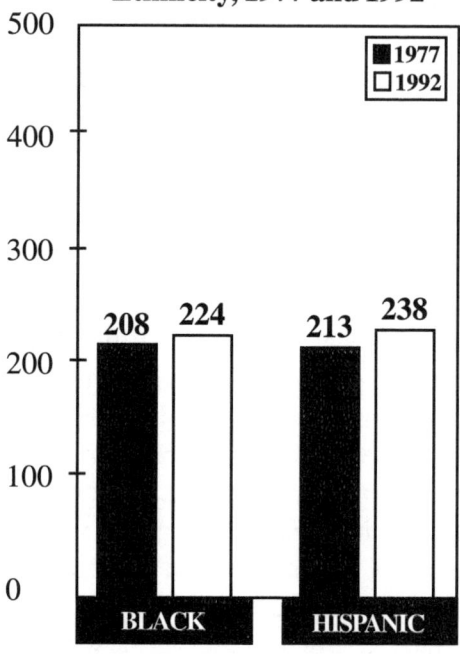

Race/Ethnicity	1977	1992
BLACK	208	224
HISPANIC	213	238

SOURCE: Center on Education Policy, *The Good — and the Not-So-Good — News About American Schools,* p. 19.

Figure 5-4: Percentage of High School Graduates Who Took the SAT

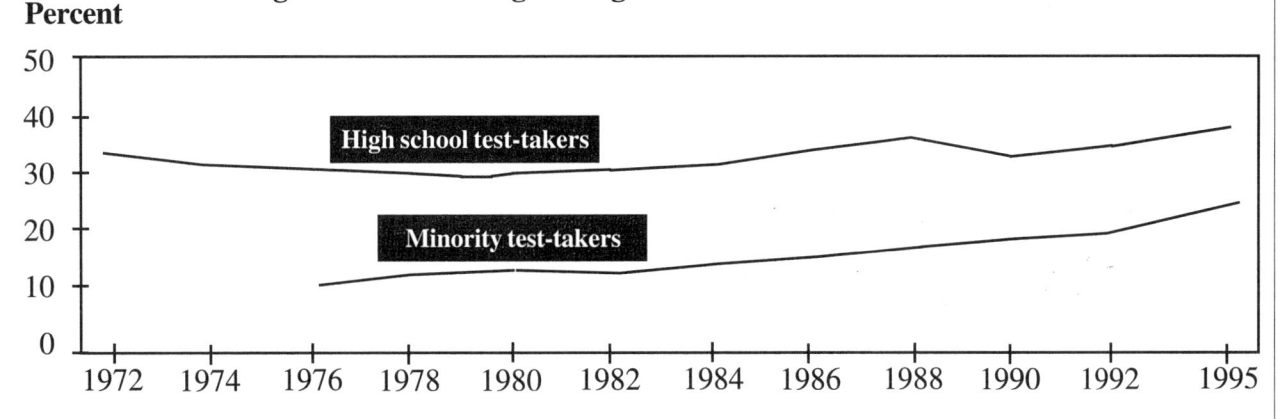

[Line graph showing Percent on y-axis (0-50) and years 1972-1995 on x-axis. "High school test-takers" line stays around 30-38%, and "Minority test-takers" line rises from about 10% to 25%.]

SOURCE: U.S. Department of Education, *Condition of Education 1996*, p. 87.

focus of *TFH*. That is the important question because change is not meant to be achieved for itself; it is meant to bring about improvement in educational opportunities. The question, then, is: Are teenagers, and especially those who would not have formerly gone on to college, better or worse off today due to all these reforms of the last fifteen years?

We will not include data on the increasing numbers of poor children and the rising numbers of minority students and immigrants because that data has been included in earlier chapters. The point must be made, though, that increasing test scores and related indicators are noteworthy achievements because today's student body presents greater challenges than did those of the past.

Course-Taking

We have already seen the effects on course-taking of the legal changes mandated in the 1980s and early 1990s, but they are worth repeating since they are so dramatic. Several states are currently taking further action to increase the requirements for graduation from high school.

NAEP Scores

The National Assessment of Educational Progress, the only reliable national test we now have, shows progress in mathematics and science reflecting increased demands for more difficult course-work but NAEP does not show much improvement for reading and writing. When broken out by racial and ethnic groups, the results show improvements for African-Americans and Hispanics in all subject areas.

Scholastic Aptitude Tests

The tests which high school students take as they apply for college are not nationally representative since students opt each year whether to take them or not, and so the pool of students varies by year. The general trend though is for gradual improvement in these scores, especially for minority groups. An important point to be emphasized is that more students traditionally not considered college-bound are taking these tests, which may be due to raised expectations of college-going and also to these students taking more difficult course work in high school. Both the College Board (which sponsors the SATs) and ACT, Inc. (which sponsors the ACTs) have pointed to students taking more demanding high school courses as the reason for higher SAT and ACT scores.

International Comparisons

A note of caution about increasing test scores comes from the Third International Mathematics and Science Study (TIMSS). In that comprehensive international comparison, American twelfth graders scored lower than the students of most participating countries in general knowledge of both mathematics and science. Even advanced American students scored below advanced students in other countries.

These findings about twelfth graders are especially disturbing because American fourth graders were found by the same study to be at or near the top of all countries in the same subjects, and eighth graders were shown to be in the middle. Deterioration happens between fourth and eighth grade and then again between eighth and twelfth, leading to a downward trend in test scores using this international comparison.

The experts have not as yet reached definite conclusions, but preliminary evidence points to the sequence of courses and their timing in

American schools and also to the lack of depth of content in these courses. In other words, the curriculum may have to be altered to expose American students to more difficult subjects earlier and to teach them in more depth than is now evident.

Dropout Rates

Earlier reference was made to the rates showing dropouts from high school. Improvements in school retention were made in the late 1980s but since the early 1990s the rate appears to have leveled off.

College-Going Rates

A dramatic change has occurred in the last ten years in terms of high school graduates going on to postsecondary education. In 1987, 57 percent of such students enrolled in two- or four-year colleges, and in 1997 over two-thirds (67%) of such students began higher education studies. (See the next chapter.)

"In that comprehensive international comparison, American twelfth graders scored lower than the students of most participating countries in general knowledge of both mathematics and science. Even advanced American students scored below advanced students in other countries."

Figure 5-5: Mathematics General Knowledge Achievement of 12th Grade Students

NATIONS WITH AVERAGE SCORES SIGNIFICANTLY HIGHER THAN THE U.S.	
NATION	AVERAGE
(NETHERLANDS)	560
SWEDEN	552
(DENMARK)	547
SWITZERLAND	540
(ICELAND)	534
(NORWAY)	528
(FRANCE)	523
NEW ZEALAND	522
(AUSTRALIA)	522
(CANADA)	519
(AUSTRIA)	518
(SLOVENIA)	512
(GERMANY)	495
HUNGARY	483

NATIONS WITH AVERAGE SCORES NOT SIGNIFICANTLY DIFFERENT THAN THE U.S.	
NATION	
(ITALY)	476
(RUSSIAN FEDERATION)	471
(LITHUANIA)	469
CZECH REPUBLIC	466
(UNITED STATES)	**461**

NATIONS WITH AVERAGE SCORES SIGNIFICANTLY LOWER THAN THE U.S.	
NATION	
(CYPRUS)	446
(SOUTH AFRICA)	356

INTERNATIONAL AVERAGE = 500

NOTE: Nations not meeting international sampling and other guidelines are shown in parenthesis.
SOURCE: *Pursuing Excellence, A Study of U.S. Twelfth-grade Mathematics and Science Achievement in International Context*, Office of Educational Research and Improvement, U.S. Department of Education, February 1998, p. 26.

Figure 5-6: Science General Knowledge Achievement of 12th Grade Students

NATIONS WITH AVERAGE SCORES SIGNIFICANTLY HIGHER THAN THE U.S.	
NATION	**AVERAGE**
SWEDEN	559
(NETHERLANDS)	558
(ICELAND)	549
(NORWAY)	544
(CANADA)	532
NEW ZEALAND	529
(AUSTRALIA)	527
SWITZERLAND	523
(AUSTRIA)	520
(SLOVENIA)	517
(DENMARK)	509

INTERNATIONAL AVERAGE = 500

NATIONS WITH AVERAGE SCORES NOT SIGNIFICANTLY DIFFERENT THAN THE U.S.	
NATION	
(GERMANY)	497
(FRANCE)	487
CZECH REPUBLIC	487
(RUSSIAN FEDERATION)	481
(UNITED STATES)	**480**
(ITALY)	475
HUNGARY	471
(LITHUANIA)	461

NATIONS WITH AVERAGE SCORES SIGNIFICANTLY LOWER THAN THE U.S.	
NATION	
(CYPRUS)	448
(SOUTH AFRICA)	349

NOTE: Nations not meeting international sampling and other guidelines are shown in parenthesis.
SOURCE: *Pursuing Excellence, A Study of U.S. Twelfth-grade Mathematics and Science Achievement in International Context,* Office of Educational Research and Improvement, U.S. Department of Education, February 1998, p. 31.

"Deterioration happens between fourth and eighth grade and then again between eighth and twelfth, leading to a downward trend in test scores using this international comparison."

Figure 5-7: Percentage of High School Graduates, Ages 16-24, Enrolled in College the October Following Graduation, by Type of College: Selected Octobers 1972-97

		Type of college	
October	Total	2-year	4-year
1972	49.2	—	—
1973	46.6	14.9	31.7
1975	50.7	18.2	32.6
1977	50.6	17.5	33.1
1979	49.3	17.5	31.8
1981	53.9	20.5	33.5
1983	52.7	19.2	33.5
1985	57.7	19.6	38.1
1987	56.8	18.9	37.9
1989	59.6	20.7	38.9
1990	60.1	20.1	40.0
1991	62.5	24.9	37.7
1992	61.9	23.0	38.9
1993	61.5	22.4	39.1
1994	61.9	21.0	40.9
1995	61.9	21.5	40.4
1996	65.0	23.1	41.9
1997	67.0	22.8	44.2

SOURCE: U.S. Department of Commerce, Bureau of the Census, October Current Population Surveys, *The Condition of Education 1996,* p. 52; Bureau of Labor Statistics Web Page.

"A dramatic change has occurred in the last ten years in terms of high school graduates going on to postsecondary education."

Figure 5-8: Average Annual Income by Educational Attainment for Persons Age 18 and Over, March 1995

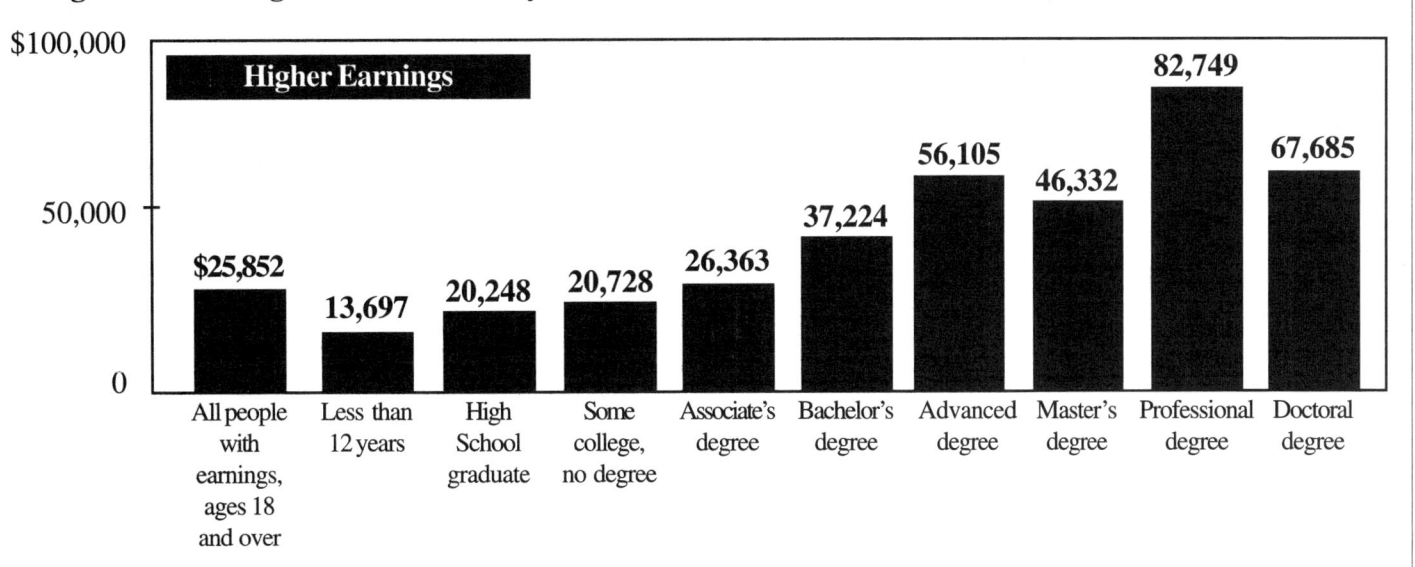

Higher Earnings

All people with earnings, ages 18 and over	$25,852
Less than 12 years	13,697
High School graduate	20,248
Some college, no degree	20,728
Associate's degree	26,363
Bachelor's degree	37,224
Advanced degree	56,105
Master's degree	46,332
Professional degree	82,749
Doctoral degree	67,685

Figure 5-9: Unemployment Rate by Educational Attainment, March 1995

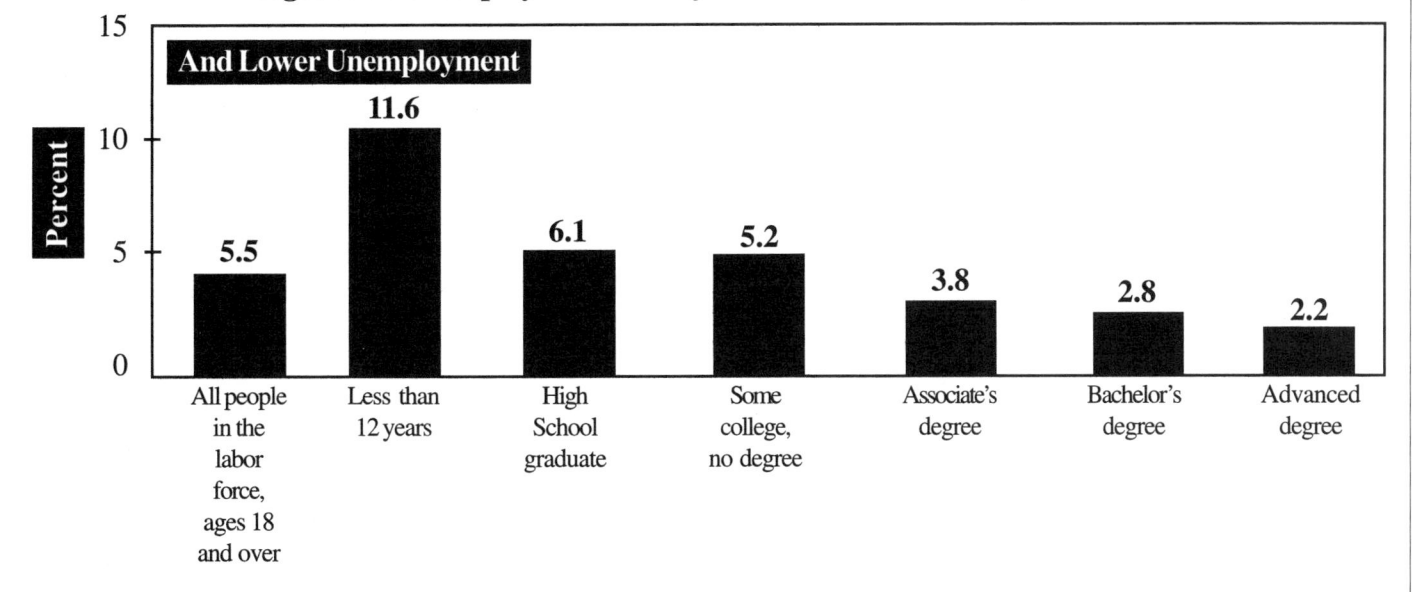

And Lower Unemployment (Percent)

Category	Percent
All people in the labor force, ages 18 and over	5.5
Less than 12 years	11.6
High School graduate	6.1
Some college, no degree	5.2
Associate's degree	3.8
Bachelor's degree	2.8
Advanced degree	2.2

SOURCE (for both figures): U.S. Department of Labor, Bureau of Labor Statistics, *Occuapational Outlook Quarterly.* Winter 1996-97, p. 52.

"Those students not going on to postsecondary education or training are facing low-paying jobs."

CONCLUSIONS AND RECOMMENDATIONS

During the last ten years, there has been general improvement in the test scores of students in elementary and secondary schools in the areas of mathematics and science. In other subject-matter areas, such as reading, there has been no major improvement, but, contrary to popular impressions, there have been no major declines. In addition, students from racial and ethnic minority groups have improved their scores in all subject areas, especially in mathematics and science.

These broad improvements by racial and ethnic minorities and these increases in mathematics and science by the general student population result from the requirements for more demanding coursework in high school, the movement to raise academic standards in elementary and secondary education, and the curricular reforms in mathematics and science.

Furthermore, many more high school graduates are going on to some postsecondary education and there has been no increase in the dropout rate from high school, despite a more demanding curriculum. As with the increases in test scores, the most noteworthy improvements in high school retention and in college-going have been made by students from racial and ethnic minority groups.

A note of caution about the increases in test scores in mathematics and science comes from the TIMSS study which revealed a relative decline in the scores of American students in those subjects as they progress in school, compared to the scores of students in other countries. In other words, American scores in mathematics and science may be getting better, but we have a way to go compared to what students are learning in other countries.

Looking at these results in the aggregate, we can conclude that many of the students whom *TFH* highlighted for attention ten years ago have increased their educational achievement and have raised their aspirations for further education. Those students took, and their successors are taking, more demanding academic course work, and their test scores are better in mathematics and science. Furthermore, many more are going on to some form of postsecondary education. These accomplishments are occurring in a student body which has more poor students, more minorities, and more immigrants than a decade ago. That is the good news.

At the other extreme there is the bad news: those who are now dropping out of high school or who are not going on to postsecondary education are facing job prospects with lower earnings than their predecessors did a decade ago when they dropped out or terminated their education with a high school diploma. So, we have solved part of the problem by raising the aspirations of many youngsters to acquire more education and training after finishing high school, but we still have not found a way to help those who drop out of high school or who end their formal education with a high school degree.

There is a third conclusion that is both good and bad news. The Forgotten Half has indeed shrunk to the "forgotten third" because about two-thirds of high school graduates now continue formal study after they finish high school. But too many of those going on to some institution of postsecondary education leave without finishing the course work needed for an associate degree, a skill certificate, or a bachelor's degree. Half of all students leave postsecondary institutions in their first year of attendance and only about one-fourth of all high school students eventually attain a college degree.

To state it differently, while the college-going rate has substantially increased, the rate at which young adults achieve a bachelor's degree has not increased as much. To illustrate, in 1994 60 percent of 25-29 year-olds had completed one or more years of college, compared to 44 percent in 1971. But only 27 percent completed four or more years of college compared with 22 percent in 1971. In other words, many more high school completers are going on to some college but there has not been a proportionate increase in the number completing.

Many of those students who leave these postsecondary schools in the first year do so because they were not adequately prepared in high school or because they find that postsecondary education is not for them. Other students leaving before finishing a degree or certificate do so for lack of financial resources. All these students may have somewhat improved their chances of getting a good job, but their odds may not have appreciably improved with this smattering of postsecondary education. In a way, these students from the former Forgotten Half are in between the success of the degree attainers and the serious earnings problems facing today's high school completers and dropouts.

The challenge ahead is more daunting because of the demographic changes which are now occurring in our elementary and secondary schools. Total public school enrollment is expected to increase from 46.4 million students in 1997 to 48.3 million by 2007. Hispanic Americans and Asian Americans, many of them from families with limited financial resources, will be the fastest growing segments of this student population.

In creating greater educational opportunities for all American students, we still must pay special attention to helping those highlighted in 1989 in *TFH:* those students who drop out of high school and those who terminate their formal education with only a high school diploma. Such students are a smaller percentage of the general student population than they were ten years ago, but their job prospects are bleaker than those faced then by earlier cohorts.

We should also pay attention to the "in-betweens"—those who begin postsecondary education and leave before obtaining a degree. Often with just a smattering of postsecondary education, many of these people are not adequately prepared for employment.

Solutions to these problems will, in part, build on the reforms in elementary and secondary education that we have outlined earlier, but they will also depart from them in some respects. Although most of these changes will have to come from the actions of the states, local school districts, employers, teachers, and others, the federal government due to its historic involvement in the area of work-related education is in a unique position to be of assistance.

The "In-Betweens"

As with the students who have succeeded in attaining a degree or certificate, those who have gone after high school to further education and training but who are leaving without attaining a degree or certificate have been helped by the increasing demands for academic coursework and by raising academic standards in elementary and secondary education. But they must be leaving postsecondary education for one of three reasons: they can't afford it, they are not adequately prepared, or they find that college does not interest them.

If they are leaving school due to financial reasons, then the next chapter, which addresses postsecondary education, has recommendations that can help them. In addition to existing federal student aid programs, a new tax credit, the Hope Scholarship, was enacted in 1997 which enables adult learners to claim a tax credit of 20 percent of the first $5,000 of the costs of education and training. Students who began postsecondary study but did not complete it should be encouraged to return to school. Federal student aid programs and tax credits and deductions will help them.

If the reasons that these students didn't complete their postsecondary study are that they were not adequately prepared for higher education or that they did not understand what they were getting into, then we must look for changes in elementary and secondary schools to help future students avoid the same pitfalls. First, the movements to raise academic standards and the number of required courses must be continued so that students will be adequately prepared for the academic demands of postsecondary education. But raising standards is not sufficient in itself. More qualified teachers, greater fairness in funding and changing the cultures of schools are also necessary reforms. In addition, students should be counseled early on about the proper sequence of courses that must be taken in middle and high school in order to qualify for enrollment in postsecondary course work. Higher academic standards and counseling will not only help students to succeed in postsecondary education, but will also greatly reduce the number of students who must take remedial courses in college because they lack a necessary mathematics or science course they should have taken in high school.

Other students leave postsecondary schools because they did not understand what is required to be able to get an associate degree or a bachelor's degree. They had little concept of the demands of postsecondary education. These deficiencies argue for more and better counseling in middle and high school about what it means to go to college, both in terms of what they should be doing to prepare for further education and what will be expected of them in postsecondary studies. There should be a much more structured way for students and parents to think about education through middle and high school into college as a progression of academic studies. Unfortunately, too many students do not receive that assistance today.

The "in-betweens" can be especially helped in this regard if Tech-Prep were substantially expanded. The purpose of that effort is precisely to connect high schools and postsecondary institutions so that they can provide a coherent sequence of courses leading to an associate's degree or a skill certificate.

Since the federal Tech-Prep program in the Perkins Act was so influential in the early 1990s in expanding such opportunities throughout the country, it would seem to be a perfect vehicle to encourage further work by school districts, community colleges, and other postsecondary institutions to mesh secondary and postsecondary education. For that reason, the President and the Congress should provide greatly increased appropriations for Tech-Prep and retain it as a separate program at the federal level.

"The Forgotten Third"

There may come a point when "the forgotten third" shrinks to "the forgotten fourth" or some other fraction, since the number of students completing high school and going on to some form of postsecondary education is rising. But whatever number of students that is left behind, high school dropouts and high school graduates without any further education or training will face a future of jobs paying low wages and the prospect of higher unemployment than for those who attain an advanced degree or skill certificate. Those students are truly the forgotten ones. Much more needs to be done to help them.

Some of these students are not interested in schooling. Some just want to get a job, and some have to get a job to support the family. We should accept the fact that not everyone should, or wants to, go on to college. This would be a major change in our current culture which devalues those who don't pursue postsecondary education.

We should also acknowledge that people who choose to enter the labor market after high school do benefit from having learned more mathematics, science, and other rigorous subjects while in school. Furthermore, many of these people can be helped in gaining good job skills while they are in high school, particularly if they develop computer skills demanded in today's workplace.

Two recent surveys confirm the need to raise the academic skills of all students and to provide an opportunity for them to gain good job skills. A survey of IBM managers found that the job skills they seek in entry-level employees include the ability to do mathematics, solve problems, communicate effectively, follow directions, and work as part of a team. Further, a National Association of Manufacturers survey indicates that many employers do not feel that current workers possess necessary job skills: 60 percent of manufacturers say that current workers lack basic math skills; 55 percent believe that current works have serious deficiencies in their basic writing and comprehension skills; and 63 percent report that current workers lack basic job skills, such as showing up at work on time and staying the whole day.

In a nutshell, what is needed for the "forgotten" is a good high school education with solid academic content. It must *not* be a watered-down curriculum which is what is being offered to many young people today in the form of a general course of studies.

The High Schools That Work program is an excellent model for what should be available to students everywhere in the country. That program is not universally successful, but its objectives are right on target. It is aiming for mastery of college-preparatory academic content by all students, including those who are job- rather than college-oriented. Furthermore, it often provides this content in applied academic settings which makes education more realistic to those who are not interested in abstract presentations. The program also demands the end of the general track, insists on counseling for both students and parents on the sequence of courses and on the goals of education and training, and emphasizes the integration of academic and vocational education.

High Schools That Work, when it is fully implemented, is an updated and improved form of vocational education, preparing students for employment after high school as well as for further education and training. Since the federal government has been very influential in funding and shaping vocational education since the early part of the century, the enactment of a revised Perkins Vocational Education Act, incorporating the essential elements of the High Schools That Work approach, would have a dramatic impact on the type of programs being offered in thousands of high schools across the country. An increased federal appropriation would help to spread that impact.

* * *

Often we get so involved in arguing among ourselves about what is wrong that we overlook what has gone right. Progress has indeed been made in the last decade in helping many high schoolers who would have been forgotten to go on to further education and training. We should take pleasure in that. As a country, we did something right.

The tasks remaining are to help those who do not continue far enough after high school to gain sufficient education and training to improve their prospects in life and to assist those who do not want to go on to any further education after high school. We can succeed with those tasks as we did with helping those who are now succeeding. All it takes is the will to do so with the application of sufficient determination and persistence.

We should not forget, though, that education is not meant solely to prepare one for employment. Education is also meant to help create a better society. Consequently, we should encourage students, parents, and other adults to think of opportunities for national and community service as an integral part of growing up. Education is more than being prepared to earn dollars and cents, it is also about learning to be a responsible citizen.

SOURCES

Center on Education Policy. *The Good — and the Not So Good — News About American Schools.* Bloomington, IN: Phi Delta Kappa, 1996.

Center on Education Policy and American Youth Policy Forum. *A Young Person's Guide to Earning and Learning, Preparing for College, Preparing for Careers.* Washington, D.C.: American Youth Policy Forum, 1998.

Center for the Future of America's Children and the David and Lucile Packard Foundation. *The Future of Children: Financing Schools*, Vol. 7, No. 3, Winter 1997.

Council of the Great City Schools. *Urban Education,* March 1998, Vol. 7, No. 2. Washington, D.C.: Council of the Great City Schools, March 1998.

Education Daily, "IBM Carefully Weighs Work Needs, Academics," November 19, 1997, Vol 30, No. 224. Alexandria, VA: Capitol Publications, November 1997.

Education Week. *Quality Counts '98*, January 1998. Bethesda, MD: Editorial Projects in Education, Inc., January 1998.

Educational Testing Service. *ETS Developments*, Volume 43, Number 1, Fall 1997. Princeton, NJ: Educational Testing Service, 1997.

Forgione, Pascal D. "Achievement in the United States: Progress Since A Nation At Risk?" Remarks delivered before the Center for Education Reform and Empower America, April 13, 1998.

National Association of Manufacturers. *News Alert* "Major New Survey Sounds Alarm: America's Competitive Edge At Risk as Qualified Employees Become Precious Commodity," November 14, 1997.

National Commission on Teaching and America's Future. *What Matters Most: Teaching for America's Future.* New York: National Commission on Teaching and America's Future, September 1996. *Note: Updated information on the number of NBPTS-certified teachers comes from the National Board for Professional Teaching Standards.*

Public Agenda. *Assignment Incomplete: The Unfinished Business of Education Reform*, 1995. New York: Public Agenda, 1995.

Steinberg, Laurence. *Beyond the Classroom: Why School Reform Has Failed and What Parents Need to Do*, 1996. New York: Public Agenda, 1995.

U.S. Department of Education, National Center for Education Statistics. *A Back to School Special Report: The Baby Boom Echo.* Washington, D.C.: U.S. Government Printing Office, August 1996.

_____. *The Condition of Education 1995; 1996; 1997 editions.*

_____. *Digest of Education Statistics 1994.* Washington, D.C.: U.S. Government Printing Office, April 1983.

_____. National Commission on Excellence in Education, *A Nation At-Risk: The Imperative for Educational Reform.* Washington, D.C.: U.S. Government Printing Office, April 1983.

_____. Office of Educational Research and Improvement, *Dropout Rates in the United States: 1996.* Washington, D.C.: U.S. Government Printing Office, 1997.

_____. *The Emergence of Tech-Prep at the State and Local Levels.* Washington, D.C.: U.S. Government Printing Office, 1995. *Note: Updated information on the number of Tech-Prep consortia and the number of students participating in Tech-Prep programs comes from Mathematica Policy Research, Inc.*

_____. *A Study of Charter Schools: First Year Report - May 1997.* Washington, D.C.: U.S. Government Printing Office, 1997. *Note: Updated information on the number of states which grant charters and the number of charter schools comes from the Center for Education Reform, Washington, D.C.*

_____. Office of Educational Research and Improvement, *Pursuing Excellence: A Study of U.S. Twelfth-Grade Mathematics and Science Achievement in International Context.* Washington, D.C.: U.S. Government Printing Office, February 1998.

_____. *Urban and Suburban/Rural: Special Strategies for Educating Disadvantaged Children, First Year Report.* Washington, D.C.: Government Printing Office, February 1998.

U.S. Department of Labor, Bureau of Labor Statistics. "College Enrollment and Work Activity of 1997 High School Graduates," Press Release, May 1, 1998

CHAPTER SIX

POSTSECONDARY EDUCATION: STUDENT *SUCCESS*, NOT JUST ACCESS

Lawrence E. Gladieux and Watson Scott Swail

As the previous chapter argued, if ten years ago "The Forgotten Half" was shorthand language for non-college-bound youth and young adults, the fraction today is surely more like one-third. Earlier chapters of this book have noted the rising tide of educational aspirations and college enrollments among young Americans over the past decade and more. Access to some form of postsecondary education has been growing steadily — overall, and for just about every economic and racial or ethnic group. Sheer economic incentives have primarily driven this growth in postsecondary participation. Forces running deep in our economy have ratcheted up skill and credential requirements in the job market, putting a premium on education beyond high school.

There are no guarantees in life, with or without a diploma — high school, college or advanced degree. But, as Chapter One has repeatedly demonstrated, the odds are increasingly stacked against those with the least education and training. The more years of formal education one has, the more, on average, one earns. More important, the earnings advantage or "premium" paid to the most highly educated workers increased during the 1980s and 1990s. And such trends have become conventional wisdom. People understand: who goes to college, and often which college and which course of study, determines more than ever who has entree to the best jobs and the best life chances.

This is the good news of past decade — more people are attaining higher levels of education and filling millions of skilled, high-paying jobs generated by America's booming, globally competitive economy. This "winner-take-all" society, however, means that the stakes have gotten bigger. So while more of The Forgotten Half may be finding upward mobility through postsecondary education than a decade ago, those who are left behind today have lower pay and less security in an increasingly volatile job market. As Chapter One and this chapter demonstrate, the past ten years highlight two troubling issues: *1) the least educated and skilled are getting a smaller piece of the pie, evidenced by unequal opportunities for education beyond high school and unprecedented extremes in wage and wealth disparities, and 2) even for those who do go to college, their prior preparation, the college they choose, and their specific course of study affect, now more than ever, who has access to the best jobs and best living standards.*

Education and training alone will not solve structural problems in the employment system that are tending to widen gaps between rich and poor. Yet it is clear that postsecondary education is more important than ever, to the individual and to our society. Estimates vary from 70 to 90 percent on the proportion of future jobs that will require postsecondary training, but the demand for high skills shows no sign of abating.

This chapter begins by answering with statistics the following questions: who goes to college, who goes where and who gets a degree. We then examine recent policy trends, look at the roots of unequal educational opportunity, and suggest strategies to address some of the underlying problems. *Our most important message to policy makers and postsecondary leaders is to focus on student success, not just access — persistence to completing the degree, not just getting students in the door.*

WHO GOES TO COLLEGE?

More than 50 years ago the original GI Bill demonstrated to skeptics in both government and academia that higher education could and should serve a much wider segment of society. More than 30 years ago, in the heyday of the civil rights movement and the war on poverty, Congress passed the Higher Education Act of 1965 and committed the federal government to the goal of opening college doors to all, regardless of family income or wealth.

Federal student aid and related efforts have helped fuel a half century of explosive growth in college attendance and educational attainment. Yet large gaps persist, by income and race, in who benefits from higher education in America. In virtually every country of the world, participation in higher education — rates of entry and completion, as well as type and prestige of institution attended — is closely associated with socio-economic status. This association may be less pronounced in the US, as we have surely created the most open, diverse, and accessible postsecondary system in the world. But the gaps are large and persistent nonetheless.

The most clear-cut advance in postsecondary opportunity in recent decades has been gender parity. The rise of women's educational attainment has been a spectacular achievement. Women closed the enrollment gap in 1978 and have since constituted a majority of total graduate and undergraduate students. By discipline and courses taken, there remain differential rates of participation. For example, women are still significantly underrepresented in hard sciences and engineering. Nonetheless, today women of all ages make up more than 55 percent of total postsecondary population, and women aged 25 to 29 are slightly more likely than men to have attained at least a baccalaureate degree.[1]

Put another way, The Forgotten Half is now disproportionately male. In fact, a serious but little acknowledged problem today is the relative underperformance of males in school and the workforce. Young women tend to have stronger high school records and educational aspirations, and to move more easily into postsecondary education and into the labor market than do their male counterparts. And thousands of men who in previous decades would have received valuable education and training in the armed services do not have this option because of military cutbacks in the 1990s.

Figure 6-1: College Participation Rates by Family Income Quartile for Unmarried 18-24 Year-old High School Graduates, 1970-1994

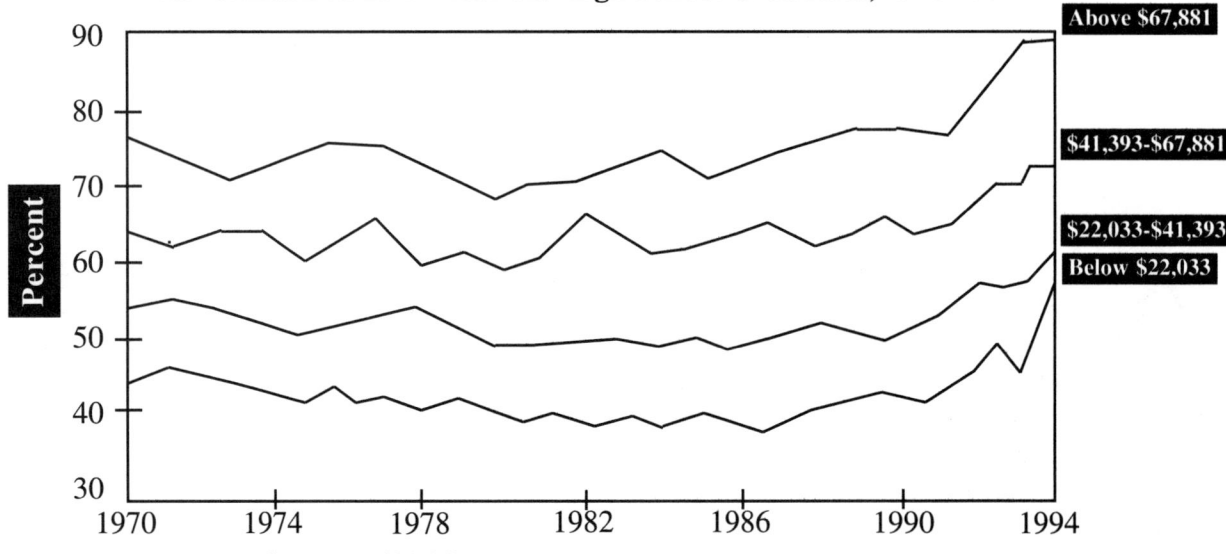

Note: Income figures are 1994 dollars.
SOURCE: *Postsecondary Education Opportunity.* Iowa City, IA: Thomas G. Mortenson, Publisher, November 1995, p.6.

Overall, public policy has done a good job of boosting entry into the postsecondary system during the past quarter century. Figure 6-1 traces a broad index of postsecondary participation based on Census data for 18-to-24 year-old high school graduates. All income groups show gains. But low-income 18-to-24 year olds attend college at much lower rates than those with high incomes, and participation gaps are about as wide today as they were in 1972.

Census figures have limitations and tend to be volatile from year to year. Yet other data sources yield basically similar results. According to the Department of Education's longitudinal studies of high school seniors, three out of four high school graduates in 1992 gained access

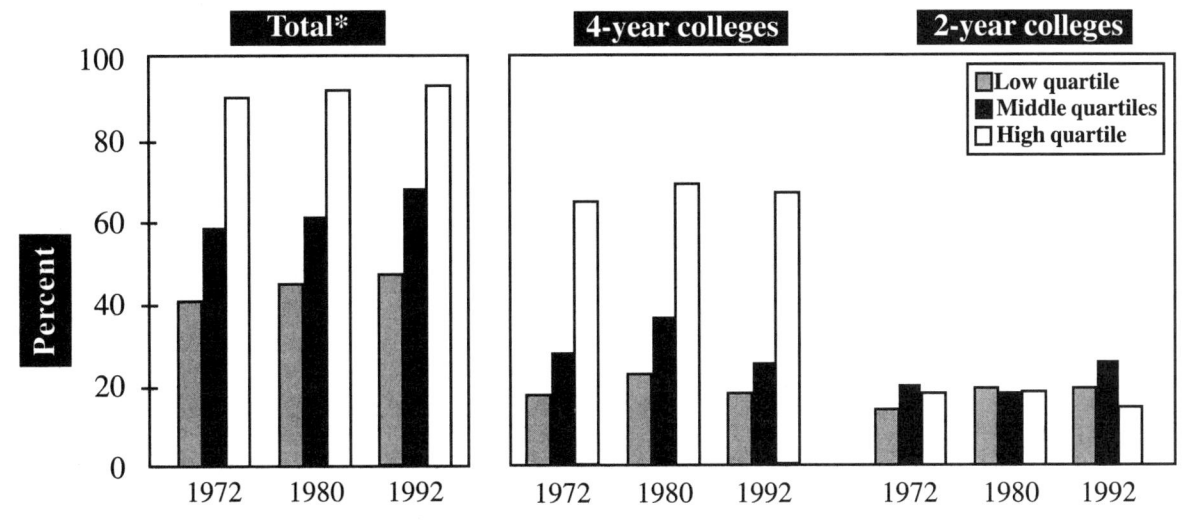

Figure 6-2: Percentage of Students Who Attended a Postsecondary Institution Within Two Years Following Scheduled High School Graduation in 1972, 1980 and 1992, by Highest Level of Institution Attended and Socio-economic Status

*Included in the total but not shown separately are those students who attended vocational, technical and trade schools.

SOURCE: *The Condition of Education 1997*. Washington, DC: U.S. Department of Education, National Center for Education Statistics, 1998, p. 65, Indicator 9.

to higher education by 1994, up from 70 per cent for the Class of 1980 and 60 percent for the Class of 1972.[2] However, as shown in Figure 6-2, 1992 graduates from high socio-economic backgrounds were still nearly twice as likely to enroll as those of low socio-economic origins.

WHO GOES WHERE?

Where students enroll can be as important as whether they go to college at all. Average returns to education rise with institutional level. Students attending less than four-year schools are less likely to receive the same rewards — at least economically — as those who earn a bachelor's degree or higher.

This is not at all to say that the B.A. is the only measure of parity — far from it. "Going to college" means many things and produces many outcomes. We need a range of sub-baccalaureate postsecondary opportunities, providing skills and credentials for survival and success in a complex economy. And as a culture we need to attach more status and value to non-baccalaureate education. (See Center for Education Policy and American Youth Policy Forum, *A Young Person's Guide to Learning and Earning,* 1998.)

It is nonetheless a reality that institutional choice is closely linked to family income and background. Figure 6-2 shows enrollment patterns and trends by socio-economic status using the high school senior cohorts of 1972, 1980 and 1992. In the most recent cohort, *only one of five students from the lowest socio-economic quartile enrolled in a four-year institution, compared to two of three from the highest quartile. The gaps between the lowest and highest quartiles are about as wide as they were two decades ago. Meanwhile, the most disadvantaged students are more likely to enroll in two-year colleges.*

Michael McPherson and Morton Schapiro conclude in a recent study that, while institutional choice is often viewed in terms of public versus private alternatives, the opportunity to attend a four-year public institution is constrained by income in many states. They found that the percentages of middle- and higher-income students attending two-year colleges decreased significantly between 1980 and 1994, while the percentage of the lowest-income students attending these institutions increased slightly during the same period.[3]

Thus, not only do students from disadvantaged backgrounds enroll in higher education at rates less than those of other groups, but their enrollment appears to be increasingly concentrated at two-year institutions.

This said about "choice," we hasten to add that postsecondary enrollment patterns have become increasingly complex. Many students are stretching out their education, attending part-time, balancing study with work and family responsibilities, attending intermittently and attending more than one institution before finally graduating. Nothing is easy to categorize anymore, especially in the community college sector:

- At least five percent (estimates vary) of bachelor's degree recipients subsequently attend a community college at some point.
- Another five percent of students who started at four-year institutions are reverse transfers, that is, they transferred to a community college without completing a bachelor's degree first. (Meanwhile, the transfer rate in the other, traditional direction — from two-year to four-year — has been running at about 30 percent for the past 25 years.)
- Another eight percent of college students are simultaneously enrolled in two-and four-year colleges.
- A minimum of three percent (estimates vary and depend on state policy) of high school students currently have dual-enrollment status in community colleges.

For increasing numbers of students, postsecondary education is no longer a straight shot. And if students increasingly defy categorization, so do institutions. A range of unconventional providers have entered the postsecondary marketplace, offering instruction and credentials in new settings, on flexible schedules, often by way of new telecommunications media.

For example, many corporations are essentially bringing postsecondary education in-house, thus the rise of the "corporate university" (Motorola and Xerox among the most noted). By establishing their own campuses, corporations are able to provide focused opportunities for their employees to upgrade technological skills and knowledge, while the company benefits through increased competitiveness. Then there is the new breed of far-flung, profit-making, customer-oriented enterprises that are tapping into a growing market for career retraining and advanced degrees. The University of Phoenix is the leading prototype and, in fact, is now the largest private university in the country, delivering business and other applied degree programs to 48,000 students at 50-plus sites nationwide.

Increasingly, students may be able to get postsecondary training without setting foot on a campus or entering a classroom. Pennsylvania State University, University of Wisconsin and other land-grant universities have pioneered distance education. Mind Extension University (among others) has been offering courses over cable TV since 1991. Other providers are pioneering "virtual instruction" on the Internet. The University of Phoenix now serves 3,600 students on-line, while California Virtual University, Penn State's "World Campus" and others are preparing to go on-line. The Western Governors University, slated for operation in late 1998, will be the nation's first exclusively virtual university.

Yet, it is not at all clear that such new institutions and delivery systems will significantly expand opportunities for The Forgotten Half. While there has been growth in employer-provided basic skills training for workers who do not have college degrees, most corporate, on-the-job training helps to upgrade the skills of those who already have postsecondary experience. Those who have get more. As for electronic modes of instruction, while virtual space is infinite, it does not promise universality or equity.[4] Ninety-four percent of the University of Phoenix' On-line Campus students are in technical, professional, managerial or executive positions, with an average age of 38. Not exactly fresh, not exactly needy and surely not "forgotten."

Virtual instruction will not address the needs of all students, least of all those who have limited experience with technology or lack ready access to the required equipment. Such students might benefit far more from traditional delivery systems.

WHO COMPLETES?

We have summarized the record and described changing patterns of postsecondary access and choice. The more important question is whether students *complete* their programs — at whatever level — and receive their degree or certificate. Some students fall short, yet go on to productive careers. But we live in a credentials-driven economy and labor market.

Postsecondary enrollments have soared during the past quarter century, yet the proportion of college students completing degrees of any kind has remained flat. Given the growing diversity of students and the increasing complexity of their attendance patterns as noted

Figure 6-3: Percent of 1989 Beginning Postsecondary Students Who Received a Bachelor's Degree or Higher as of 1994, by Socioeconomic Status and Race/Ethnicity

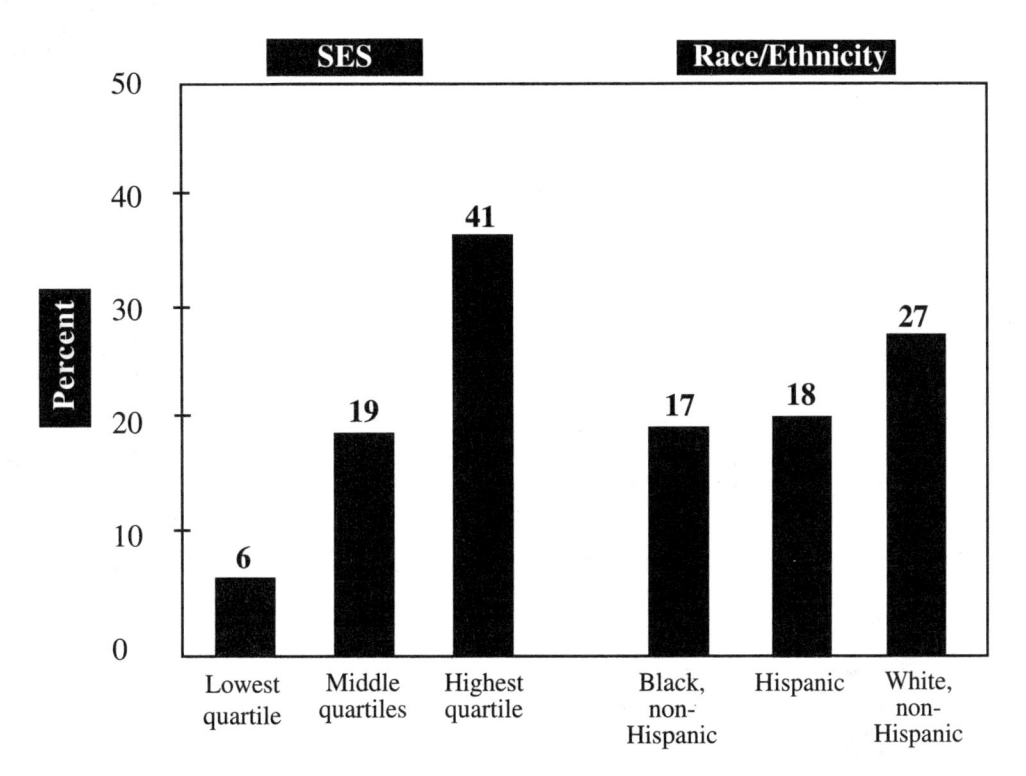

	Percent
SES	
Lowest quartile	6
Middle quartiles	19
Highest quartile	41
Race/Ethnicity	
Black, non-Hispanic	17
Hispanic	18
White, non-Hispanic	27

SOURCE: *Descriptive Summary of 1989-90 Beginning Postsecondary Students: 5 Years Later.* Washington, DC: U.S. Department of Education, National Center for Education Statistics, 1996, p. 34, Table 1.3.

above, stable completion rates may be more than we could have reasonably expected. But we need to do much better.

There are wide disparities by socioeconomic status and race in who actually receives a degree. Of students who began postsecondary study in the 1989-90 academic year, half received some type of degree by 1994, and about one-quarter received a bachelor's degree or higher. As shown in Figure 6-3, more than 40 percent of the most advantaged students received a bachelor's degree or higher within five years, compared to only six percent from the least advantaged group. And white students were considerably more likely to receive a bachelor's degree than black and Hispanic students. While these degree completion rates rise for all groups in the sixth, seventh, and subsequent years, long-term attainment gaps for white as compared to black and Hispanic stu-

dents who attend four-year colleges have remained steady at 20 to 25 percent.

Students who go to college directly after high school and attend full-time complete their programs in much higher proportions than other students. Delayed entry and other deviations from this traditional path result in lower persistence rates, and disadvantaged students are much more likely than not to fall into a less traditional path. At the sub-baccalaureate level, these patterns are magnified. Associate's degree completion rates are in the 20-25 percent range, and these rates have changed little over the past 25 years.

Getting students in the college door is not good enough. Along with young people who do not finish high school and those who stop their education with a high school diploma, many postsecondary non-completers surely fall into The Forgotten Half. In fact, some of these students may be left worse off if they have borrowed to finance their studies — increasingly the case for low-income students — and do not complete their programs. They leave college with no degree, no skills and a debt to repay. Most will find a place in our economy, but at a low level, and will have difficulty supporting a family.

WHY HAVEN'T WE DONE BETTER?

Why do gaps in postsecondary opportunity remain so stubbornly wide? National policy has focused for the better part of four decades on *access* to the system. As we have seen, there has been progress, but there remains a long way to go to equalize access. As we have also suggested, the greater challenge is to increase the likelihood that students actually *succeed* in reaching their goals, which in most cases means completing a degree.

Enrollment and success in higher education are influenced by many factors: prior schooling and academic achievement, the rigor and pattern of courses taken in secondary school, family and cultural attitudes, motivation and awareness of opportunities — as well as ability to pay, which has been the primary emphasis of federal policy. For low- and moderate-income students, removing financial barriers is critical, but so are many other things starting much earlier in both life and the educational pipeline.

In the past decade, the media, policymakers and the general public have focused much attention on the difficulties of financing higher education, and with good reason. Public alarm about college affordability is rooted in real economic trends since 1980, which we shall review below. Shifts in tuition, income and aid policy have fallen hardest on those least able to afford postsecondary education. But we believe that addressing these financial issues is not enough. Equalizing college opportunities requires more fundamental and complementary strategies.

We first summarize recent trends in affordability and financial aid, then turn to the core issues of student motivation and readiness for postsecondary education.

Figure 6-4: Average Undergraduate Tuition at Private 4-Year, Public 4-Year and Public 2-Year Institutions, Adjusted for Inflation (With Total Percentage Change in Parentheses)

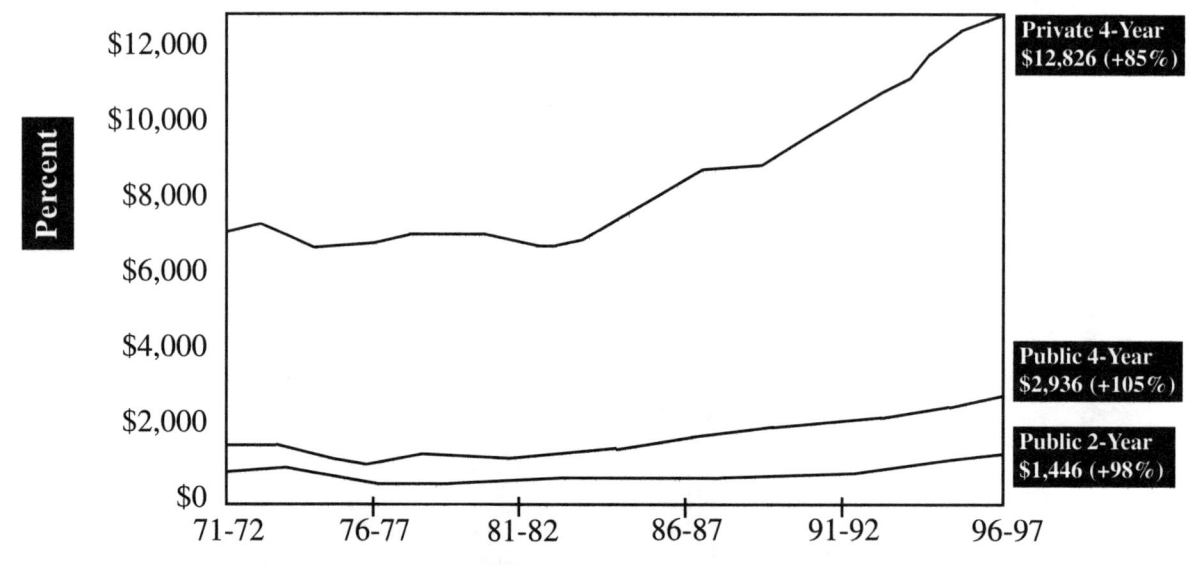

Private 4-Year: $12,826 (+85%)
Public 4-Year: $2,936 (+105%)
Public 2-Year: $1,446 (+98%)

Figure 6-5: 15-Year Changes in Tuition, Family Income and Student Aid, 1981 to 1996

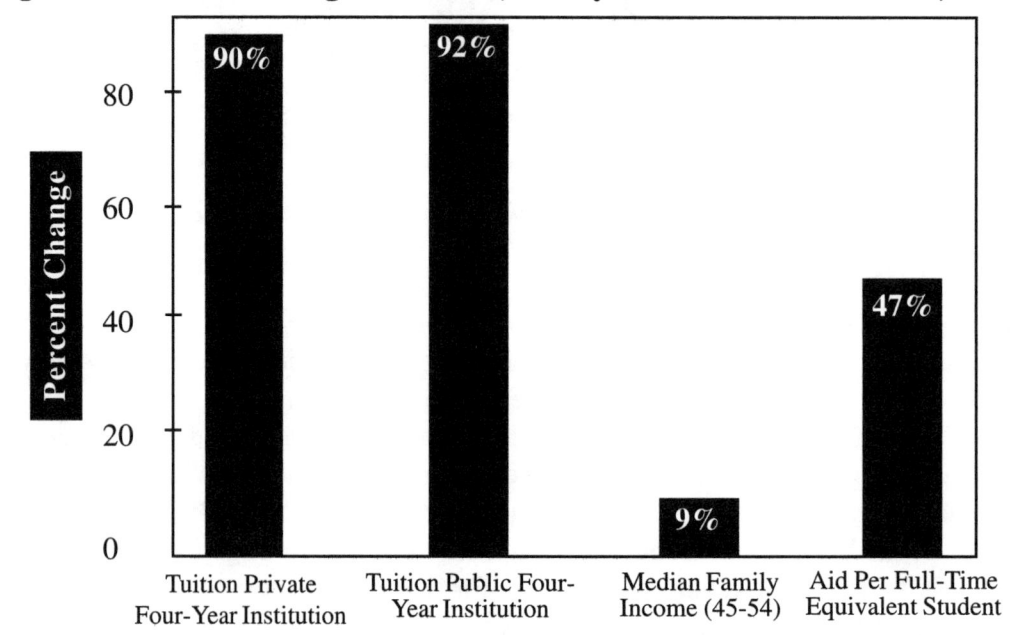

- Tuition Private Four-Year Institution: 90%
- Tuition Public Four-Year Institution: 92%
- Median Family Income (45-54): 9%
- Aid Per Full-Time Equivalent Student: 47%

SOURCE: *Trends in Student Aid: 1987 to 1997,* The College Board; U.S. Bureau of Labor Statistics; Digest of Education Statistics 1997, NCES.

College Affordability

Figure 6-4 traces the growth of tuition after adjusting for inflation. While tuition was nearly flat in the 1970s, prices charged by both public and private four-year institutions soared after 1980. Private college tuition rose most sharply in the early and mid-1980s, while the price of public higher education increased the fastest in the early 1990s, rising at three times the rate of inflation as the economy and tax revenues declined in most states. Tuition increases have moderated somewhat in the mid-1990s, but on average are still running well ahead of the Consumer Price Index.

Figure 6-5 compares increases in tuition, family income and student aid from 1981 to 1996. Average, inflation-adjusted tuition has nearly doubled at both public and private institutions during this period, while median family income has been stagnant, growing only nine percent after inflation. Median income, however, tells only part of the story, because incomes have grown steadily less equal during the 1980s and 1990s. As indicated in Figure 6-6, the share of family income required to pay college costs has increased for all families, but it has gone up the most for those on the bottom rungs of the economic ladder.

Student financial aid, meanwhile, has failed to close the gap between family income and college costs. The real value of total aid available to students *has* increased, but not enough to keep pace with growth in either tuition levels or in the eligible student population. Also, student aid has evolved from a grant-based to a loan-based system.

Figure 6-6: Cost of Attendance at Public Four-Year Institutions as a Share of Family Income, 1976 to 1992

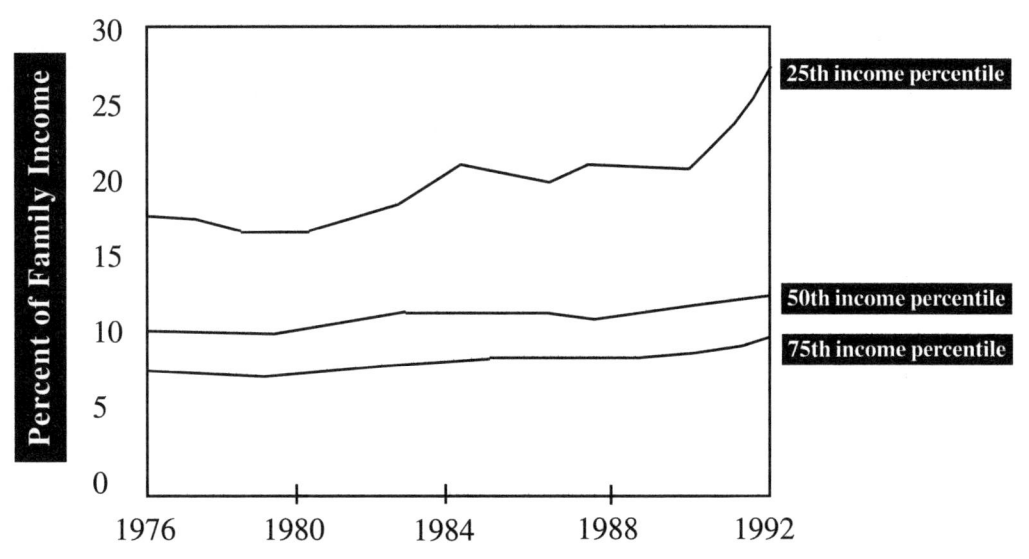

SOURCES: The College Board. *Trends in Student Aid: 1987 to 1997*, U.S. Bureau of Labor Statistics; *The Digest of Education Statistics 1997*, NCES.

Figure 6-7: Percent Share of Grants vs. Loans, 1980-81 to 1996-97

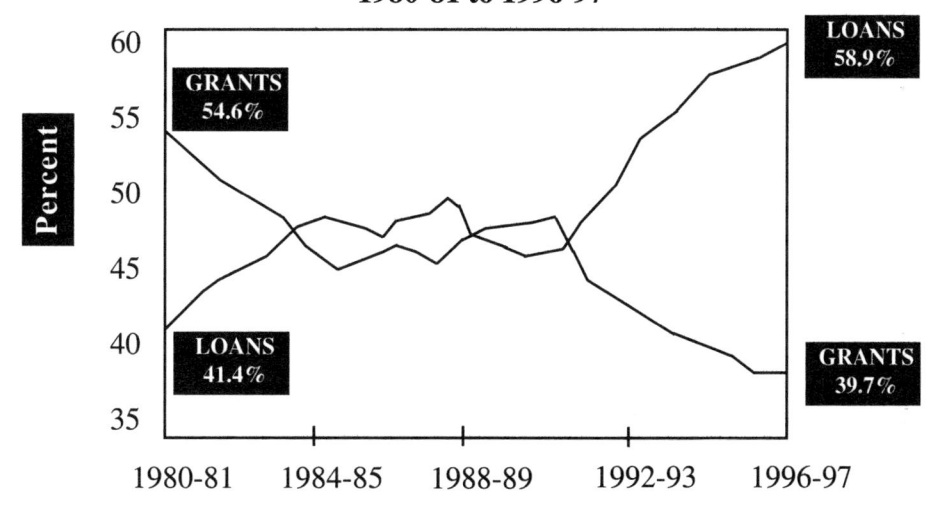

SOURCES: The College Board. *Trends in Student Aid: 1987 to 1997*.

Loans now provide by far the most aid (see Figure 6-7). In 1996-97, federally-sponsored programs generated more than $30 billion in student and parent loans, five times the size of the Pell Grant program that was meant to be the system's foundation for the neediest students. Even those who are most at-risk — low-income students, students in remediation, students taking short-term training with uncertain returns — increasingly must borrow to gain postsecondary access. More than two-thirds of low-income B.A. recipients use loans to offset college costs, compared to one-fourth of those from high-income backgrounds. And the low-income student's debt burden is about $3,000 higher on average than that of a high-income student (see Figure 6-8).

Effects of the shift to loan financing are difficult to ascertain, but the prospect of debt probably discourages many young people — and almost certainly those of The Forgotten Half — from considering postsecondary education. And there is evidence that financial assistance in the form of loans is less effective than grant aid in helping students to stay in college and get their degrees.[5]

Not only has the aid system gravitated toward loans, but the primary federal focus has evolved from helping students who "but for such aid" would not be able to attend college, to relieving the burden for those who probably would go without such support. The anti-poverty origins of the 1960s legislation have faded into history as eligibility for federal student assistance has been extended up the economic scale. Most recently, the Taxpayer Relief Act of 1997 has created new benefits for middle- and upper-middle-income students and their families, while doing little or nothing for low- and moderate-income students who have insufficient tax liability to benefit from tuition tax breaks in the form of credits and deductions.

In fact, *the entire aid system seems to be moving away from need-based principles, becoming less responsive to The Forgotten Half and reducing opportunities for students with the least resources.* Not only has federal policy shifted, but the states are investing more heavily in merit scholarships as well as tuition savings and pre-paid plans oriented to the middle class. And the colleges themselves have increasingly turned to merit-based aid and preferential packaging not always based on need.

Figure 6-8: Percent of B.A. Recipients with Federal Student Loan Debt and Average Amount Borrowed, by Family Income, 1995-96

Family Income	PUBLIC FOUR-YEAR Percent Who Had Borrowed	PUBLIC FOUR-YEAR Average Amount Borrowed	PRIVATE FOUR-YEAR Percent Who Had Borrowed	PRIVATE FOUR-YEAR Average Amount Borrowed	TOTAL Percent Distribution of B.A. Recipients Who Borrowed
Less than $30,000	66	12,550	70	15,240	45
$30,000 to $49,999	56	12,370	62	13,790	18
$50,000 to $69,999	40	10,320	42	13,500	16
$70,000 or more	24	9,290	29	12,360	21
All income levels	52	11,950	54	14,290	100

SOURCE: American Council on Education analysis of National Postsecondary Student Aid Study: 1995-96.

The Deeper Roots of Unequal Opportunity

The problem of unequal opportunity has proved more intractable than anyone anticipated in the early years of the Higher Education Act of 1965. As originally conceived, federal student aid was meant to send an early signal to young people and their families that college was a realistic goal. Sponsors of the Pell Grant, in particular, hoped that the promise of aid would have a powerful motivational effect.

The reality of today's patchwork student aid system falls short of such visions. As we have also seen, student aid has not been able to keep pace with the rising costs of attendance in higher education, and the drift of aid policy is increasingly toward cost relief for the middle class. This is not to say that the aid programs have failed, but rather that too much may have been expected of them. *Financial aid is a necessary but not sufficient*

Figure 6-9: Percentage of All 1992 High School Graduates Considered College Qualified,* by Income and Race/Ethnicity

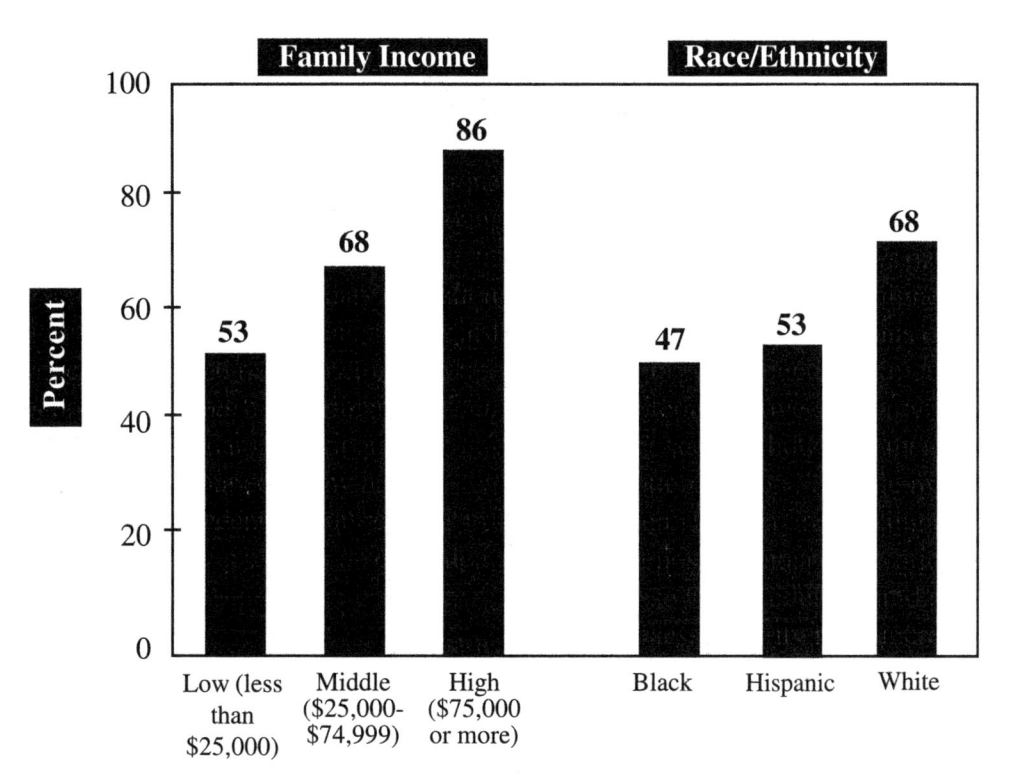

Category	Percent
Low (less than $25,000)	53
Middle ($25,000-$74,999)	68
High ($75,000 or more)	86
Black	47
Hispanic	53
White	68

* 4-year college qualification index developed for NCES based on high school GPA, senior class rank, NELS 1992 aptitude test, SAT and ACT scores and academic coursework.
SOURCE: *Access to Postsecondary Education for the 1992 High School Graduates.* Washington, DC: U.S. Department of Education, National Center for Education Statistics, 1997, p. 29, Table 15.

condition for the college attendance and success of disadvantaged students.

Of all the variables that influence who enters and who succeeds in higher education, aspirations and academic preparation are the most powerful. Both must start early. "By the time students reach the 12th grade, it is too late to ... increase the numbers of students who are ready for college," according to Laura Rendón. "In fact, it could be said that students begin to drop out of college in grade school."[6]

Research has repeatedly shown that students who take rigorous, progressively more challenging coursework through high school are far more likely to plan for and enroll in college. Based on data from the U.S. Department of Education's longitudinal studies on high school seniors, the answer to who finishes college and why is always the same: those who are best prepared, regardless of race, income or financial aid.[7]

For many students, the die is cast by the eighth grade. Students without the appropriate math and reading skills by that grade are unlikely to acquire them by the end of high school. One of the most publicized gatekeepers in the secondary school curriculum is course-taking in mathematics. A study by the U.S. Department of Education found that high school students who take algebra and geometry are much more likely to go on to college than students who did not take these courses. The early course-taking sets the pattern. Sixty percent of students who completed algebra I by the end of the eighth grade also took calculus in high school.[8]

Nearly all eighth-graders say they expect to go to college, and even low-income students overwhelmingly envision postsecondary education in their future. Aspirations, however, must be acted upon. Almost all high-income students meet their expectations, yet only two-thirds of low-income students do so.[9]

The problem is that the course-taking patterns of low-income and minority students make it difficult to meet their expectations. As a result, they are left less well prepared, on average, than higher-income, majority students. Tracking policies, school resources and quality, societal conditions and expectations all have a part in creating these disparities.

The stark reality is reflected in Figures 6-9 and 6-10. According to a college-qualification index developed for the National Center for Education Statistics, only half of low-income high school graduates are qualified to go to college, compared to 86 percent of high-income students. And by this index, black and Hispanic students are also far less qualified than white students.[10]

Among high school graduates who actually enrolled in a four-year institution, less than half of low-income students were judged to be highly or very highly qualified, compared to two-thirds of high-income students. Twenty-nine percent of black students and 44 percent of Hispanic students were similarly qualified, compared to 61 percent of white students. Starkest of all may be the fact that 30 percent of black students were considered marginally or not qualified for college — almost twice the percentage of low-income students in this category.

Two problems are evident in these data: 1) low-income and minority high school graduates are less well prepared in general, and 2) a significant percentage of those who actually do go on to four-year higher education may not have the basic academic skills required to succeed. Unfortunately, these students may be set up for disappointment.

WHITHER PUBLIC POLICY?

The easy thing to conclude is that we need comprehensive reform of K-12 American education to lift student performance and reduce the disparities in academic preparation documented above. And we do. Some form of state and national standards are surely needed to set clear benchmarks of what students should know and be able to do. Current expectations often are too low. We have noted that students who took algebra I and geometry were much more likely to take higher-level courses and enroll in college. The reality is that only 28 states currently require algebra and geometry for high school graduation.[11]

Figure 6-10: Percentage Distribution of All 1992 High School Graduates Who Enrolled in a Four-year Institution by 1994, by Level of College Qualifications, Income and Race/Ethnicity*

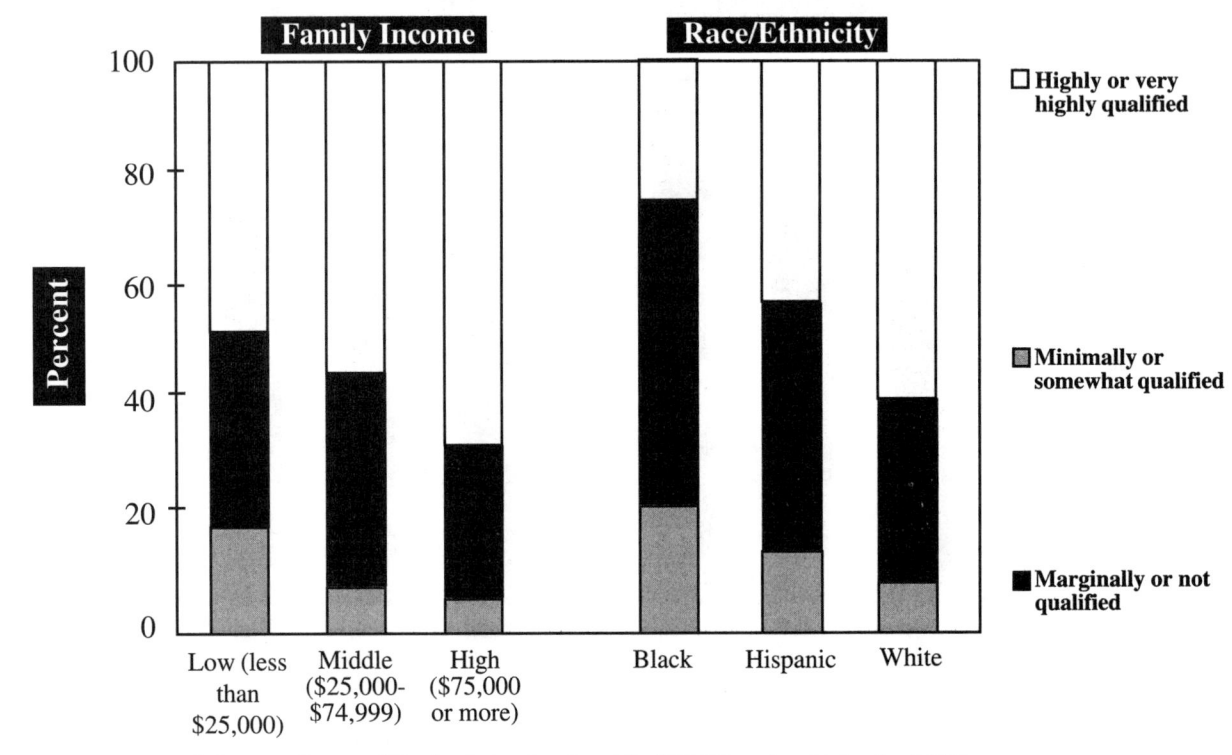

* 4-year college qualification index developed for NCES based on high school GPA, senior class rank, NELS 1992 aptitude test, SAT and ACT scores and academic coursework.
SOURCE: *Access to Postsecondary Education for the 1992 High School Graduates.* Washington, DC: U.S. Department of Education, National Center for Education Statistics, 1997, p. 28, Table 14.

But standards — much less testing — alone will not raise the achievement of low-income, black and Hispanic students. Safety nets must be in place to ensure a supportive environment for learning. Students must have opportunities to learn in secure settings, with up-to-date materials and the encouragement to believe that they can achieve at high levels.

Neither, surely, can all of the problems of educational failure be laid at schoolhouse doors. Learning is hardly exclusive to the classroom. In fact, only one-tenth of a child's hours are spent in school. We need to look far beyond classroom walls — to parents, families and community resources — to increase the motivation and academic performance of students. What happens to kids during *non-school time* is at least as important as what happens in school (see Chapters Three and Four, above).

Chapter Five of this book discusses a variety of educational improvement strategies. For the long haul, broad school reforms will hopefully effect change and benefit generations to come. For the short haul, we need direct outreach to more of the current generation: intervention programs that make a difference in the lives of young, disadvantaged kids early in their schooling — widening their horizons and encouraging them to stay in school, study hard, take the right courses and keep their options open. Early and sustained guidance and support are needed to make postsecondary education a realistic possibility later on.

Research and experience tell us that when a student from disadvantaged circumstances beats the odds by enrolling and succeeding in college, the critical difference can often be traced to a particular individual who touched or changed the student's life at some point along the way, someone who served as a role model or otherwise sparked a sense of possibility for the future. That individual might be a relative, a neighbor, a counselor, a teacher, a coach, a tutor — anyone who cares enough to try to make a difference.

Getting poor people prepared and into college, Levine and Nidiffer suggest, "is retail, not wholesale, work in the sense that it requires intensive involvement with individuals rather than passing contact with larger numbers." According to their study:

> In simplest terms, the recipe for getting to college is mentorship — one arm around one child... What mattered most is not carefully constructed educational policy but rather the intervention by one person... Sometimes the mentor was a loving relative; other times it was someone paid to offer expert advice. In either case, it was the human contact that made the difference.[12]

Scores of early intervention and mentoring programs have developed across the country. More than 15 years ago, Eugene Lang started a movement with his "I Have a Dream" promise to 60 East Harlem sixth-graders that he would pay their college tuition if they graduated from high school. Today, Lang and other philanthropists are investing considerable wealth and personal commitment in such programs, including not just the tuition guarantee but the critical mentoring, counseling, tutoring and other support to keep students from falling between the cracks. Many of these programs work, but for the millions of youngsters whose life chances are dim and might be lifted by an "I Have a Dream" or similar program, the movement is almost like a wheel of fortune. A youngster must be lucky enough to be in the right city, the right school, the right classroom.

The challenge for public policy is to leverage such programs that work to a vastly larger scale. Upward Bound, Talent Search and other so-called TRIO programs have been a companion to federal student aid policy since the Higher Education Act was first enacted in 1965, providing information, outreach, counseling, encouragement and academic support for students from the lowest socio-economic levels. TRIO appropriations have grown over the years to more than a half billion dollars, yet these programs are estimated to serve less than ten percent of the eligible student population. And only a small proportion of TRIO services is dedicated to intervening with kids and their families at middle school or earlier.

The Clinton administration's proposed "High Hopes" program reflects a growing recognition by public policymakers of what is required to make a difference. This federal initiative tries to build on the "I Have a Dream" model, aiming to reach over a million kids in 2,500 middle or junior high schools with mentoring and related support over the next five years. The High Hopes proposal also borrows from legislation introduced by Representative Chaka Fattah of Pennsylvania that aims to promote early awareness of college opportunities. The Congressman's "21st Century Scholars" program would provide notice to low-income sixth-graders of their potential Pell Grant eligibility upon high school graduation and acceptance into college.

Just as we need to reach kids earlier, we need to do a better job helping students once they have enrolled in college to persist and complete their degrees. Again, the TRIO programs provide support here. But public policy, federal in particular, has focused too narrowly on access to the system. More attention and incentives should be directed at persistence among students who are economically and academically at-risk. Some analysts, for example, have suggested that students who complete their degrees should receive a financial aid bonus, perhaps in the form of loan forgiveness. Others have suggested that TRIO funds be allocated to institutions based on the number of Pell Grant recipients they graduate. Both proposals have drawbacks. The first would tend to penalize those most at risk of dropping out, those who can least afford the cost of higher education. The second might encourage institutions to lower graduation standards.

The point is, we need a new debate. Public policy has done a fairly good job of facilitating initial entry into the system. We need to do a better job promoting persistence and completion.

HIGHER EDUCATION'S RESPONSIBILITY

According to a 1995 report from the National Center for Education Statistics, only one-third of colleges and universities sponsor pre-collegiate outreach programs for disadvantaged students, most such programs rely on federal funds and faculty involvement is thin. Yet, postsecondary institutions have a direct stake in such efforts, especially given the coming generation of students.

Looking toward the year 2010, Samuel Kipp projects:

> While the potential pool of high school graduates and college students will increase substantially, the only thing that will be traditional about this growing cohort will be its age. The nation's college-age population will be even more ethnically diverse than the general population because of differential birthrates and migration patterns. Furthermore, the most rapid growth will occur among groups traditionally more likely to drop out of school, less likely to enroll in college-preparatory course work, less likely to graduate from high school, less likely to enroll in college, and least likely to persist to earn a baccalaureate degree.[13]

If demography is destiny, colleges have their work cut out for them heading into the next century. America is still an ongoing experiment in diversity, and American higher education's part of the social contract has been to help extend the possibility of a better life to new groups in society. It will be in the enlightened self-interest of institutions to invest more heavily in partnerships with school systems to expand the potential college-bound — and qualified — pool. Reaching out to help motivate and prepare more students for college is a long-term investment that will pay off for higher education and for the nation.

Outstanding models of pre-collegiate intervention exist where colleges have taken the initiative to collaborate with schools and communities. Programs like the University of North Carolina's MSEN program (grades 6-12), California's MESA program (grades 4-12), and Xavier University's ChemStar, BioStar, and MathStar programs (high school) have had great success in motivating and preparing under-represented students for college. These college/school/community partnerships work. But much more extensive commitments are needed.

A boost to such efforts could emerge, ironically, from the rollback of affirmative action. Affirmative action as we know it may be scaled back, restructured, even abandoned. Techniques and terminology may change. But, as necessity is the mother of ingenuity, surely new strategies will evolve to advance the same broad goals of campus diversity. One example may be the University of California's response to the Regents' decision to end race preferences in admission (and subsequent approval of Proposition 209 by California voters). The University has adopted a system-wide "new directions for outreach" program, and has committed $60 million to the effort. Other states are beginning to follow California's lead. The state of Wisconsin recently unveiled "Plan 2008" to double the number of pre-college programs sponsored by its universities.

Perhaps new forms of affirmative action will evolve — reaching disadvantaged schools and populations, those in the inner city, those with educational handicaps, those with academic potential but poor preparation — without using explicit racial or ethnic classifications. Minorities and underrepresented groups would nonetheless surely benefit, as would society in general.

Institutions likewise have a stake and a responsibility in assuring that more students who arrive on their campuses persist and complete degrees. This is a matter of enlightened self-interest for colleges. One university has estimated that it costs more to recruit students than to keep them. The institution invests an estimated $1,400 to recruit each of its incoming freshmen, and for every student who leaves after a week, month, or even a semester, that investment is lost.

Again, there already are effective models around the country, incorporating student orientation, advisement, support and mentoring designed to boost persistence and degree completion.[14] Much deeper and wider commitments are needed.

Many years ago, former U.S. Commissioner of Education Harold Howe II asked, "Do institutions serve the needs of students, or is it the other way around?"[15] It was a rhetorical question with an everlasting ring.

* * *

Debates on postsecondary aid policy tend to be insular. It is easier to focus on program mechanics, eligibility formulas, delivery systems and funding levels for the student aid programs, all of which are important — but often obscure the larger challenge. The roots of unequal educational opportunity are deep. There appear to be huge and growing disparities in the capacity of K-12 educational systems to prepare young people for the world beyond high school. Higher education, even with more generous student aid as a financing strategy, cannot by itself redress social deficits and imbalances that appear to threaten our country's future. But neither can colleges stand apart. All of us — policymakers, educators, analysts, citizens — are challenged to try to make a difference.

> "The cost-shifting from taxpayers to students that began about 1980 has reintroduced price barriers to student enrollment. Students face very much higher prices in both public and private higher education today. For those who need financial aid to help pay these attendance costs, the financial aid provided by the federal government is much more expensive. The combined effects have been to reimpose price barriers to higher education that had been substantially reduced in the 1960s and 1970s. These price barriers affect the affluent least, and the poorest the most.
>
> These price barriers are neither equitable nor just. Nor are they in society's long-term interest where economic changes require far broader and deeper and continuing education and training than has ever been required by the labor market before."
>
> — *Thomas G. Mortenson,*
> *Postsecondary Education OPPORTUNITY,*
> *July 1998*

NOTES

[1] *Women and Men of the Engineering Path: A Model for Analyses of Undergraduate Careers.* Washington, DC: Office of Educational Research and Improvement, 1998; *Digest of Education Statistics 1997.* Washington, DC: U.S. Department of Education, National Center for Education Statistics, 1997, p. 185, Table 175; p. 324, Table 310.

[2] 1992 data extracted from *Access to Postsecondary Education for the 1992 High School Graduates.* Washington, DC: U.S. Department of Education, National Center for Education Statistics, 1997, Table 2, p. 7; earlier data based on transcript studies collected from 1972 and 1982 high school seniors by age 30. *The Condition of Education 1996*, p. 25.

[3] McPherson, Michael and Morton Schapiro. *The Student Aid Game.* Princeton: Princeton University Press, 1998.

[4] The stated mission of Western Governors University is to "expand educational opportunities for learners everywhere" and provide access to a "dispersed population of students who might not otherwise have access to higher education and to those needing workplace training." This is the basic tenet of most on-line and distance education operations. However, there is no current evidence to support that these delivery systems will expand access to non-traditional populations. To the contrary, it may be argued that virtual systems serve the highly skilled and those with greater access to technology, characteristics not generally attributable to disadvantaged students.

[5] *Higher Education: Restructuring Student Aid Could Reduce Low-Income Student Dropout Rate.* GAO/HRD-93-47, March 23, 1995.

[6] Rendón, Laura I. *Access in a Democracy: Narrowing the Opportunity Gap.* Unpublished paper presented at the Policy Panel on Access, National Postsecondary Education Cooperative, September 9, 1997, p. 7.

[7] Adelman, Clifford. "Diversity: Walk the Walk, and Drop the Talk," *Change,* July/August 1997, p. 41.

[8] *Mathematics Equals Opportunity.* Washington, DC: U.S. Department of Education, 1997, a White Paper prepared for U.S. Secretary of Education Richard Riley. The College Board's EQUITY 2000 program is a mathematics-based school reform strategy that grew out of similar research. In EQUITY 2000 school districts, students are required to complete algebra I by the ninth grade and geometry by the tenth grade, and are provided with safety net programs (such as Saturday Academies) to help them succeed.

[9] *Access to Postsecondary Education for the 1992 High School Graduates.* Washington, DC: U.S. Department of Education, p. 16, Table 8; p. 17, Table 9.

[10] MPR Associates of Berkeley, California, developed a four-year college qualification index for the National Coalition on Education Statistics based on high school GPA, senior class rank, NELS 1992 aptitude test, SAT and ACT scores and academic coursework. The index is used in *Access to Postsecondary Education for the 1992 High School Graduates,* previously cited.

[11] *Content Standards, Graduation, Teacher Licensure, Time and Attendance: A 50-State Report.* Washington, DC: Council of Chief State School Officers, 1996.

[12] Levine, Arthur and Jana Nidiffer. *Beating the Odds: How the Poor Get to College.* San Francisco: Jossey-Bass, 1996, pp. 139, 143. See also American Youth Policy Forum. *Some Things DO Make a Difference for Youth: A Compendium of Evaluations of Youth Programs and Practices.* Washington, DC, 1997, especially pp. 7-12.

[13] Kipp III, Samuel M. "Demographic Trends and Their Impact on the Future of the Pell Grant Program," in *Memory, Reason, and Imagination: A Quarter Century of Pell Grants.* New York: The College Board, 1998.

[14] Some prominent examples include: the Emerging Scholars Program based at the University of Texas at Austin, which utilizes peer groups and interaction to form strong, cohesive study groups that encourage academic excellence and problem solving; the Supplemental Instruction program developed at University of Missouri-Kansas City and now in place on over 1,100 campuses, providing tutoring-like experiences for students on campus; and the University of South Carolina's Freshman Seminar Program (entitled University 101) originally developed to help retain African-American students through their freshman year.

[15] Quoted in Gladieux, Lawrence E. and Thomas R. Wolanin. *Congress and the Colleges.* Lexington, MA: Lexington Books, 1976, p. 28.

CHAPTER SEVEN

PREPARING YOUTH FOR THE WORLD OF WORK

Thomas Bailey and Vanessa Smith Morest

Our national preoccupation with the international competitive position of the American economy has fueled an extensive discussion of our workforce development system. Policymakers, employers and even some educators have argued that some of the economic problems that the country experienced, especially during the 1980s, were due, in part, to shortcomings in our educational system. These views were highlighted in a series of widely read reports, including *The Forgotten Half*, published between the early 1980s and mid-1990s.

This chapter analyzes developments in workforce preparation since the publication of *TFH* and suggests possible future directions. We begin with a brief description of the traditional workforce development system in the United States. We then show how *TFH* and other significant reports published in the last 15 years, taken together, have defined a new model for reforming this system. Finally, we discuss federal legislation that responded to these reports and assess how it has altered the ways in which future workers are trained and educated. We end with some conclusions and suggestions for future research and policy development.

THE U.S. WORKFORCE DEVELOPMENT SYSTEM

The basic structure of the U.S. workforce development system is straightforward. Theoretically, all students are expected to learn basic academic skills in a uniform public education "system" that runs through middle school. Curricula, however, vary by state and even region, students are often tracked by their "ability" and profound social class distinctions abound. Although education is normally compulsory only through age 16, there is a general presumption that all students will graduate from high school. By the time they get to high school, students often find themselves in one of three distinct "tracks" or ability groupings: academic, general or vocational. The academic track is for college-bound students and has few, if any, components of workforce development. The vocational track is designed to prepare students for work after high school (and sometimes after some occupationally specific postsecondary training). The general track is for students who have no specific occupational interest (and thus are not on the vocational track) and are not headed for college. This track has been much criticized for providing watered-down, tedious curricula that weaken students' motivation to learn and to continue their schooling. Criticism of the general track is a key focus of most discussions of education reform.

As a rule, young people have three choices after high school: work, community college or four-year college. (In the past, the military was an important option.) In a rough way, these three options represent paths to different levels of the occupational hierarchy: low-level and unskilled jobs for those with only a high school diploma (or less); skilled, craft and technician-level jobs for community college graduates; and professional and managerial jobs for college graduates. Unlike in many other countries, these three possibilities do not, at least in principle, represent definitive occupational paths. Many people who work after high school eventually go back to school, some community college students transfer to four-year institutions, and even some four-year graduates return to community colleges for a variety of reasons, including learning specific work-related skills. Overall, in 1997, 6.6 percent of the adult population had earned a graduate or professional degree, 14.4 percent had a bachelor's degree, 6.6 percent had an associate's degree or technical certificate, 18.7 percent had some college but no degree, 32.1 percent stopped their formal schooling on high school graduation and 21.6 percent had no high school diploma, although some were still in school.[1]

Finally, a large network of institutions provide supplementary education and workforce development. Their clientele includes students who have dropped out of school as well as adults who are changing careers, reentering the labor force or upgrading their skills, often to help them cope with technological change. "Second-chance" programs for out-of-school youth generally provide counseling and some training to help them find employment, attain a high school equivalency degree or return to school.[2] Programs for adults are offered by community colleges, community-based organizations, consultants, private sector providers and businesses. Estimates for company-based training suggest that, in 1991, employers provided some formal training for about 20 percent of all workers (mostly managerial and sales personnel, much less for frontline workers) and spent about $63 billion (in 1991 dollars).[3] In addition, employment and training programs for adults who are unemployed or face particularly serious problems in finding a job are generally available.[4] As changes in the welfare system take hold around the country, such programs are increasingly directed to the needs of welfare recipients.

This rather loose "system" for preparing young people for work is characterized by extreme flexibility and wide variations in quality. There are usually several possible paths into most occupations. In principle, doors to particular occupations are almost never completely closed although, in practice, options are often limited. The other side of flexibility, though, is confusion, and students often have very little idea about what is necessary to establish themselves in a particular occupation. Also, as *TFH* pointed out in 1988, young people spend a great deal of time drifting or floundering among a variety of low-wage, low-skill jobs before finding more or less stable employment.[5] Recent evidence suggests that it takes more time than formerly for young people to finally end up in stable jobs that pay enough to support a family.[6]

IMPROVING THE WORKFORCE DEVELOPMENT SYSTEM

Before 1980 there was little criticism of the country's system for preparing workers for jobs. The economy was strong until the early 1970s and the oil crisis seemed to be an adequate explanation for the stagflation of the 1970s. As late as 1980, when a popular article in the *Harvard Business Review* suggested that we were "Managing Our Way to Economic Decline,"[7] education was not considered a cause of America's apparently growing vulnerability to international competition. Furthermore, many books and articles, including *The Overeducated American* by Richard Freeman[8] and *Education and Jobs: The Great Training Robbery* by Ivar Berg,[9] argued that the U.S. workforce in the 1970s was *overeducated*.

The publication of the official federal government report *A Nation at Risk*[10] in 1983 marked a turning point in stirring up popular anxieties about the education-economy connection. (It and the four subsequent reports discussed below are summarized in Figure 7-1.) *A Nation at Risk* argued that profound weaknesses in the education system were undermining U.S. productivity and competitiveness and threatening the American standard of living. Although it provided no evidence to connect education and economic performance, it concluded that the primary cause of the nation's faltering international competitiveness was a weakened commitment to basic and traditional academic skills. The major flaw in the system was said to be in the secondary schools, so *A Nation at Risk* proposed strengthening academic course requirements for graduation.

The 1980s also saw a growing literature suggesting that employers' skill requirements were rising. The influential U.S. Department of Labor/Hudson Institute report *Workforce 2000*[11] predicted that a majority of the jobs generated between 1987 and 2000 would require at least some college education. This was not as dramatic a change as the language of the report implied; nevertheless, based on this and other research reports of the 1980s, most policymakers were convinced that skill requirements were escalating rapidly.[12]

This was the context in which *TFH* reports of 1988 were written — a conviction of rapidly growing skill demands and growing anxiety about the international economic position of the United States. Unlike *A Nation at Risk* and other influential education reports of the last two decades, *TFH* did not emphasize problems with workforce development. In a tone somewhat at odds with much of the education discussion of the decade, it focused more directly on the problems of those who were either not in the labor force or who were at the lower levels of the employment ladder — the Forgotten Half. Even though it was not preoccupied with the country's economic position, *TFH* clearly argued that the education and training system was failing a large segment of the country's young people. It concluded that they were not being adequately

Figure 7-1: Five Major Reports Dealing with Workforce Development (1983-1991)

Report	Recommendations
A Nation at Risk (1983)	Called for a commitment to improve the basic academic skills of secondary school students by raising academic course requirements for graduation.
Workforce 2000 (1987)	Claimed that skill requirements are escalating rapidly and that the majority of new jobs between 1987 and 2000 will require college education.
The Forgotten Half (1988)	Recommended that all segments of society work together to strengthen the education and general development of young people. Educators should provide better support to those not going to 4-year college by providing high-quality vocational education programs and expanding and improving second-chance programs.
America's Choice: High Skills or Low Wages! (1990)	Recommended an emphasis on standards and clear educational pathways to particular careers combined with increased involvement of employers, especially through the provision of work-based learning.
Report of the Secretary's Commission on Achieving Necessary Skills (SCANS) (1991)	Proposed a classification of workplace skills that are neither traditionally academic nor specifically vocational, including five "competencies"— resources, interpersonal skills, information, systems and technology — and three "foundation" skills (basic skills, thinking skills and personal qualities).

prepared for good jobs, and it warned that this was a problem for the entire society:

> *Education and training thus remain the Forgotten Half's most fundamental and reliable pathways to success.* Knowledge and skills open doors to current employment opportunities that would otherwise remain closed. More important, advanced skills and competencies (particularly the ability to think flexibly and creatively about new technologies and emerging problems) make it possible for both the individual and society to adapt in a world of endlessly wrenching change. And with such skills and competencies come the earnings that make it possible to have a decent living, to support one's family, and to contribute responsibly to the community.[13]

From this perspective, what did *TFH* see as the problem with the U.S. workforce development system? First, it stated that U.S. educators over-emphasized those headed for college:

Despite the very real benefits of non-collegiate post-high school education and training, such opportunities are considered "second best" by many policymakers and by much of the educational establishment whose major priority is college education. Far too many of our young people are not encouraged to pursue such non-collegiate education, nor are the financial and counseling supports in place to make such learning a viable possibility.[14]

The Forgotten Half pointed out further that society invested much more in those who went to college than in the Forgotten Half. It argued that secondary schools needed more high-quality vocational education programs, especially those that were tied to subsequent preparation in community colleges.

Second, *TFH* concluded that all segments of society needed to work together more effectively to strengthen the education and general development of young people. Pointing out that youth did not have enough close contact with adults and that employers, among others, should be much more involved with the education of young people, it called for an expansion of partnerships between schools and other educational institutions, and employers and business groups. It also suggested that employers should be willing to provide good entry-level jobs to high school graduates and to support apprenticeships and internships.

Third, *TFH* concluded that instruction should be improved. Based on Howard Gardner's theory of multiple intelligences,[15] it called for "a mixture of abstract and experiential learning opportunities, a combination of conceptual study and concrete applications and practical problem solving."[16]

Finally, *TFH* called for an expansion and improvement of the second-chance system for young people. It pointed out that "by any reasonable calculation, federal, state and local governments provide only token support for second-chance remediation and employment training programs that assist a small fraction of American youth."[17] As a partial solution, it recommended the passage of the *Fair Chance: Youth Opportunities Demonstration Act,* "a state-administered national demonstration designed to increase access to education and training opportunities, through the provision of financial aid, counseling and academic support programs for out-of-school youth living in targeted Demonstration Act areas."[18] Throughout its analysis and recommendations, *TFH* emphasized that solutions required a more integrated system of education and youth development that involved school, family, employers, churches, the public sector and community organizations in the support of America's youth.

To understand policy developments since the publication of *TFH,* it is necessary to review the subsequent workforce-focused reports. In 1990, two years after *TFH,* the Commission on Skills in the American Workforce published *America's Choice: High Skills or Low Wages!*[19] which further pursued many of these themes. Written in the alarmist style of *A Nation at Risk, America's Choice* charged that the U.S. was failing to prepare its workforce adequately and that, if this continued, it would have dire economic consequences — such as descent to a status as a second-class power with growing inequality and consequent social disruptions. It particularly emphasized the inadequacies of the workforce preparation system for production, or frontline, workers. While *A Nation at Risk* claimed that other countries would surpass the U.S., *America's Choice* tried to draw lessons from the education systems in those countries. Three central points emerged: (1) setting high standards and holding young people to those standards, (2) creating clear educational pathways to particular careers and (3) getting employers involved, especially through providing work-based learning experiences.

In addition, both *TFH* and *America's Choice,* as well as other reports of the late 1980s, implied that efforts should be made to integrate academic and vocational education. There are many ways to do this, especially by using the industrial or occupational context of vocational training to teach academic skills. Thus, the student

Figure 7-2: The SCANS Skills

A THREE-PART FOUNDATION	FIVE COMPETENCIES
Basic Skills: A. Reading B. Writing C. Arithmetic/Mathematics D. Listening E. Speaking	1. **Resources:** Identifies, organizes, plans and allocates resources 2. **Interpersonal:** Works well with others
Thinking Skills: A. Creative Thinking B. Decision Making C. Problem Solving D. Visualizing E. Knowing How to Learn F. Reasoning	3. **Information:** Acquires and uses information 4. **Systems:** Understands complex interrelations
Personal Qualities: Displays responsibility, self-esteem, sociability, self-management and integrity and honesty A. Responsibility B. Self-Esteem C. Sociability D. Self-Management E. Integrity/Honesty	5. **Technology:** Works with a variety of technologies

Figure 7-3: Workforce Development Strategies Defined by the Five Major Reports

Skills and the Measurement of Skills

1. Improved academic skills for production workers and the Forgotten Half
2. Strengthened SCANS skills
3. A greater emphasis on standards

Enhancing the Connection between School and Work

4. Innovative pedagogies, including the integration of academic and vocational instruction and work-based learning
5. Participation of many institutions, including employers, in education

Enhancing the Transition to Postsecondary Education and Work

6. Making pathways into particular occupations more transparent (relevant to the entire labor force)
7. Facilitation of the transition of The Forgotten Half to postsecondary education (focused on students not traditionally headed for college)
8. Continued emphasis on second-chance efforts to help young people continue their education or find employment (focused on those people with the most serious educational and labor market problems)

who is learning vocational skills also acquires a strong base of academic skills. Furthermore, many analysts have suggested that this approach is such an effective way to teach academic skills that it can be used to enhance adacemic performance even for students who do not plan to work in the particular vocational area being used as a context.[20]

Finally, the 1991 *Report of the Secretary's Commission on Achieving Necessary Skills (SCANS)*[21] defined a set of broad skills that were neither traditionally academic nor specifically vocational. These more or less "generic" skills included broad competencies that the SCANS Commission judged were increasingly necessary for almost all work. (See Figure 7-2 for a summary of these skills.)

The SCANS report estimated that fewer than half of all young adults had achieved the needed reading and writing minimums; even fewer could handle the mathematics it proposed. The report saw schools as only indirectly addressing the need for listening and speaking skills.[22] It suggested that students lack motivation to perform well in school, and it emphasized the need for youth to have a well-developed mind, a passion to learn and the ability to put knowledge to work if they are to succeed in employment and contribute to the economic well-being of the nation.

PROPOSED WORKFORCE DEVELOPMENT STRATEGIES

Taken together, these five reports gradually defined a model, consisting of the eight strategies displayed in Figure 7-3, for reforming the workforce development system. These strategies in turn can be divided into three broad groups. The first emphasizes skills and the measurement of those skills. The second involves approaches to teaching that strengthen the linkage between school learning and the world outside the classroom, with an emphasis on enhancing the connection between school and work. And the third involves specific approaches to enhancing the transition to postsecondary education and work.

Within the model for workforce development that emerged in the early 1990s, the eighth element—strengthening second-chance programs—received the least emphasis. But *TFH*, which put programs for young people with very serious problems at the center of its analysis and recommendations, was an exception to this indifference. The relatively light attention these programs have attracted over the last decade is probably a result of an excessively narrow focus on workforce development as an approach to education reform. If one accepts the premise that the workforce preparation system for production workers is weak, then considerable progress is possible through improvements in the education of those who stay in school. Thus from a strict workforce development perspective, attention to young people with serious education and employment problems is of secondary importance. The Workforce Investment Act of 1998 (WIA), the Personal Responsibility and Work Opportunity Reconciliation Act of 1996 (i.e., "welfare reform") and the relatively low unemployment rates of the late 1990s have refocused attention on second-chance-type training programs.

POLICY CHANGES IN THE 1990s

Many of the recommendations of the reports discussed above found their way into federal legislation during the 1990s. In this section, we review the four most important of these initiatives and evaluate the extent to which they implement the eight workforce development strategies outlined in Figure 7-3. Specifically, we examine the 1990 Carl D. Perkins Vocational and Applied Technology Education Act, the 1994 School-to-Work Opportunities Act, the 1994 Goals 2000: Educate America Act (especially the establishment of the National Skill Standards Board) and the 1998 Workforce Investment Act, including the One-Stop Career Centers.[23] (These initiatives and their relationship to the eight workforce development strategies are displayed in Figure 7-4.) In addition, we include a section on developments in community colleges. Although there is no particular legislation devoted primarily to community colleges, they merit serious attention because the discussion about them has not been commensurate with their growing importance as workforce development institutions.

CARL D. PERKINS VOCATIONAL AND APPLIED TECHNOLOGY EDUCATION ACT (1990)

The Forgotten Half was published during the discussions leading up to the 1990

Figure 7-4: Workforce Development Strategies Incorporated into Federal Legislation

Strategy	Perkins (1990)	STWOA (1994)	Goals 2000 (1994)	WIA (1998)
Skills and the Measurement of Skills				
1. Improved academic skills for production workers and the Forgotten Half		✓	✓	
2. Strengthened SCANS skills		✓	✓	
3. A greater emphasis on standards		✓	✓	✓
Enhancing the Connection between School and Work				
4. Innovative pedagogies including the integration of academic and vocational instruction and work-based learning	✓	✓		
5. Participation of many institutions, including employers, in education	✓	✓	✓	✓
Enhancing the Transition to Postsecondary Education and Work				
6. Making pathways into particular occupations more transparent (relevant to the entire labor force)	✓	✓	✓	✓
7. Facilitation of the transition of the forgotten half to postsecondary education (focused on students not traditionally headed for college)	✓	✓	✓	✓
8. Continued emphasis on second-chance efforts to help young people continue their education or find employment (focused on those persons with the most serious educational and labor market problems)				✓

reauthorization of the Carl D. Perkins Vocational and Applied Technology Education Act. Indeed, several of *TFH's* recommendations found their way into the Act. Two of its most important objectives were the integration of academic and vocational education and the development of Tech Prep, a program to strengthen the link between high school and community college.

Integrating academic and vocational education: Historically, support for vocational education has tended to be narrowly defined and tied directly to the development of occupational skills for non-college-bound students. The 1990 amendments to the Perkins Act, however, called for the integration of academic and vocational education; vocational instruction should be infused with academic content so that students in occupational programs would be assured of a solid foundation of academic skills.[24] As there has been no recent specific evaluation of the integration of academic and vocational education, it is difficult to assess how much this initiative has influenced high school or community college curricula and pedagogy. In 1991, Grubb et al. found that many different approaches were being used to integrate academic and vocational education, but they were not able to determine either the extent or the effectiveness of such integration. According to the National Assessment of Vocational Education, approximately 84 percent of the local districts surveyed in the 1991-92 school year reported having taken at least some steps towards integrating academic and vocational curricula.[25]

Tech Prep: The primary goals of the Tech Prep movement are to enhance the preparation of high school students for postsecondary education and to improve the transition between high schools and community colleges. *The Forgotten Half* called for this linkage. The program model for Tech Prep was originally conceived in the early 1980s by Dale Parnell[26] and was intended to offer students planned career pathways linking high school classes to advanced technical education in community colleges. Tech Prep programs begin during the last two years of high school and continue into the first two years of college. Their focus is on "articulation" between secondary and postsecondary schooling, allowing for coordination between majors as well as courses. At the local level, Tech Prep is organized by consortia of businesses and secondary and postsecondary educational institutions.

Tech Prep was proposed as a high-quality alternative to the academic track in high school. Previously, students who were not planning to go to four-year college took either a vocational or a general track. Both, but especially the latter, have been widely criticized for their low quality. Tech Prep was designed to give the non-college-bound student a rigorous, technically oriented education leading to a community college.

The infrastructure of Tech Prep, which began receiving federal funding in 1990, has grown considerably. According to a 1993 survey by Mathematica, 69 percent of all school districts reported membership in a consortium.[27] The number of community college and postsecondary school consortia members has grown considerably during the mid-1990s.[28]

The implementation of Tech Prep faces a number of challenges. Research has shown that the diversity of programs and students they reach make it difficult for consortia to build a consensus regarding its fundamental purpose. Although Tech Prep was designed to be a joint activity between community colleges and secondary schools, the integration of academic and vocational curricula, which is fundamental to Tech Prep programs, is occurring predominantly at the secondary school level. Community colleges often seem to be cheerleaders or spectators rather than team players even though the idea of Tech Prep came from Parnell, a leading figure in community college circles.

Despite these difficulties, Tech Prep appears to be moving in the right direction. The Mathematica survey of Tech Prep in 1993 and another in 1995 indicated continuing growth in education plans spanning secondary and postsecondary programs and in career development activities such as the preparation of career counseling materials. Tech Prep programs are increasingly promoting programs of study that encourage students to focus on career clusters covering broad occupational areas such as business and health rather than on specific occupations or technical fields. In 1995, almost all Tech Prep programs reported implementing applied learning curricula, and more than 40 percent of consortia resources were spent on either curriculum or staff development.[29]

Since Tech Prep consortia were located in some of the most populous areas of the U.S., the 1995 survey found that Tech Prep was potentially available to 88 percent of secondary school students. However, only 8.4 percent (740,000) actually participated in these programs. Although this was a substantial increase over the 1992-1993 participation rate of 4.7 percent,[30] the original conception of Tech Prep as a way to reach the forgotten majority of students whose performance falls in the middle range, was, by 1995, far from fulfilled.

SCHOOL-TO-WORK OPPORTUNITIES ACT (1994)

The School-to-Work Opportunities Act of 1994 (STWOA) was the most comprehensive attempt to implement the new workforce development model. Indeed, it included every element of that model, although, despite providing links to such programs as the Job Training Partnership Act, it did not place particular emphasis on second-chance programs. It centered instead on encouraging the integration of academic and vocational education. States were asked to accomplish this by clarifying the educational pathways to particular occupations, by promoting the involvement of businesses and other institutions in the education of young people and by utilizing more extensive skill standards.

Unlike Tech Prep, funding under STWOA is provided in the form of grants to states and local partnerships, which have latitude in structuring their programs to meet the demands of their constituencies. The funding is also considered to be "venture capital," as the Act expires in 2001. STWOA calls for programs that incorporate a variety of structural principles. With respect to governance, it promotes the inclusion of a spectrum of community members, including employers, students and parents. In addition, states must coordinate their school-to-work efforts with other federally funded programs, such as the Job Training Partnership Act, Elementary and Secondary Education Act, Adult Education Act, Perkins Act and Individuals with Disabilities Education Act. Furthermore, institutional linkages must be forged between all levels of schooling, from elementary through postsecondary, thereby making STWOA a considerably broader initiative than its predecessors.

School-to-work is characterized by a comprehensive program of reform that includes three broad components: school-based learning, work-based learning and connecting activities. The school-based component emphasizes career awareness, exploration and counseling, followed by the selection of a career major. Unlike earlier initiatives, this legislation requires that vocational students meet the standards of academic content that apply to all of a state's students. In addition to integrating vocational and academic training, the curriculum must facilitate the entrance of students into employment, additional training or postsecondary education programs.

The work-based component of school-to-work programs includes a planned program of job training and work experience that is coordinated with learning in the school-based component and mentoring at the workplace. Students acquire work-based skills through participation in paid work experience, job shadowing, a school-sponsored enterprise or on-the-job training. Their workplace training also embraces general competencies, such as the development of positive work attitudes and the skills outlined by SCANS.

The third component of school-to-work programs comprises activities that connect the school- and work-based programs. For example, a school-site mentor might be appointed to act as a liaison between the employer and a student's teacher, school administrator and parents. Other activities might include providing technical assistance to aid employers and other parties in designing school-based learning components and in training teachers, workplace mentors and counselors. The most important element of this connecting component is that the active participation of the employer should be encouraged, as well as that of the school; graduates must be assisted in finding a job, continuing their education or entering into additional training.

Success rates under the third or fourth year of STWOA funding vary greatly among the states. Indeed, the Act's encouragement of flexibility has yielded a large number of models in secondary and postsecondary institutions around the country. They span a gamut that includes cooperative education, school-based enterprise (i.e., student-created and operated businesses), career academies, youth apprenticeship and many less comprehensive initiatives.[31]

Funding for STWOA was awarded to all 50 states, the District of Columbia and seven U.S. territories in the form of noncompetitive development grants to be used for designing statewide school-to-work programs.[32] Implementation grants were then awarded on a competitive basis to states which had developed viable programs.

By April 1998, 40 states had received these implementation grants.[33]

The assumption behind STWOA was that federal "venture capital" funding would enable states to build statewide school-to-work infrastructures that would include high-level governance and administrative support, statewide marketing of school-to-work concepts, training and technical assistance for local partnerships, integrated curriculum models, a skill certification process and improved systems of labor market information.[34] By mid-1998, most states had taken steps toward creating such a statewide infrastructure, but implementation was still in the early stages. The infrastructures include such features as:

- Incentives for employer participation, such as tax credits or wage subsidies for hiring youth apprentices;
- Comprehensive career development models for age-appropriate activities in the elementary, middle and high school years;
- New institutional linkages, including aligning college admission criteria with high school assessments and easing the transfer from two-year to four-year institutions;
- Defined career clusters that identify industries as the focus of school-to-work career pathways or majors; and
- State technical assistance to local partnerships.

Based on these categories, state technical assistance to local partnerships turned out to be the most common policy feature of the first eight implementation states. Most states had also defined comprehensive career development models spanning various school levels and specific career clusters.[35]

The first states to implement statewide school-to-work systems have grafted various elements of the new legislation onto existing programs, which explains why local partnerships have become widespread. In Michigan, for example, partnerships have been subsumed under established Workforce Development Boards. The expansion of work-based activities has depended largely upon whether administrative responsibility for school-to-work has been placed under the jurisdiction of preexisting agencies. In some states, workforce development agencies or state departments of education have provided a locus for the new reforms, while in other states, such as Ohio and Massachusetts, independent school-to-work offices have been created.

The major hurdle that states face is the formation of a cohesive school-to-work system. This is a complex process requiring understanding and agreement between state and local policymakers. Most states still have not been able to produce a comprehensive document or legislation that sets forth a seamless system of workforce development. The majority of reforms thus far have focused on the school-based elements of implementation. Work-based reform has proved to be a greater challenge, since the more widespread and inclusive the system, the greater the demands on employers.

STWOA is due to expire on October 1, 2001, by which time states are expected to have created and implemented sustainable school-to-work programs. The National School-to-Work Office reported in 1997 that 13 states had created strong, sustainable systems,[36] while ten states never sought STWOA funds. To some extent, the shortcomings of STWOA should be viewed in context, because the legislation's aims are extremely ambitious. In many ways, STWOA has been quite successful compared to previous educational reforms.

Determining the effectiveness of the activities funded by STWOA is difficult. In 1998, the track records were at most only four years old. An ongoing process evaluation by Mathematica has shown widespread implementation of elements of the model, but there are very few examples of comprehensive programs that use all of the components called for. The Act emphasizes the need to use the funds to initiate systemic changes within school systems, that is, it discourages the use of the money for small isolated projects. But in most states systemwide change has not yet occurred.

What we know about the effectiveness of school-to-work activities comes from evaluations of programs that resemble school-to-work, such as cooperative education and career academies, that existed before the enactment of STWOA. Overall, the academic outcomes of students involved in such programs appear to be mixed, with some initiatives resulting in academic gains[37] and others finding no gains.[38] Crain's study of New York City's career magnet schools found that graduates engaged in significantly fewer risk behaviors, such as drinking and drug use, than comprehensive high school students in the control group. Other studies have found higher rates of college attendance, faster credit accumulation in college, higher post-high school wages and higher rates of employment.[39] Evaluations of career academies, which are distinct from career magnet schools, have also found positive results, including slight but statistically significant increases in levels of attendance and school engagement and lower dropout rates in comparison with their nonacademy counterparts.[40] Postgraduate employment records for academy students were also better than those of graduates of comprehensive schools.[41] Although much more information is needed, these results are beginning to document some of the benefits of the school-to-work model.

GOALS 2000: EDUCATE AMERICA AND THE NATIONAL SKILL STANDARDS BOARD (1994)

A series of meetings among educators, governors and legislators beginning in the late 1980s produced *Goals 2000: Educate America Act of 1994,* which set a number of goals for the American educational system to achieve by the year 2000. Although creating benchmarks for student achievement in academic subject areas was the centerpiece of Goals 2000, the legislation also called for lowering the dropout rate and promoting adult literacy and lifelong learning. In addition, it established the National Skill Standards Board (NSSB), charged with creating and promoting a national (not federal) system of skill standards. In response to continuing concern over our international status, these standards were intended to enhance America's ability to compete effectively in the global economy. The authors of the Act hoped that states would voluntarily adopt these skill standards with encouragement from the NSSB. The standards themselves were to be developed through a partnership between industry, education, labor and community stakeholders. As with the 1990 Perkins reauthorization and STWOA, this represented an attempt to build a system of workforce development with meaningful connections to education.

The broad and ambitious voluntary national system of standards envisioned in Goals 2000 was intended to facilitate the nation's transition to more flexible and productive approaches to organizing work, increase opportunities for minorities and women and improve linkages between other components of the national strategy to enhance workforce skills, such as welfare-to-work, job training and apprenticeship programs. Like the 1990 Perkins Act reauthorization and STWOA, the Goals 2000 legislation calls for integrating academic and vocational learning. Specifically, these legislative acts support the concept of career clusters that group related occupations together. While vocational education formerly trained students for specific entry-level occupations, it envisioned that students in the 1990s would acquire a set of skills that they could apply to any job in a particular industry cluster. The authors of the Act expected that broadening the concept of an occupation in this way would prevent youth from being trained for jobs that might soon be obsolete. The NSSB developed 16 economic sectors,[42] but it is uncertain how closely they will match up with the career majors developed by various states. Advocates of the Board hope that its broad industry and occupational clusters will work to strengthen the concept of career majors that is central to STWOA.

At this writing in mid-1998, the NSSB does not appear to have met its ambitious goals. Given the brief time that it has been in operation, this is hardly a criticism. The Board faces two significant problems in developing the new system: (1) it must interact with the many state systems, and (2) political considerations dictate that its standards be voluntary.[43] It is still much too early to tell whether the standards that it establishes will ultimately become broadly used benchmarks.

ONE-STOP CAREER CENTERS

The U.S. Department of Labor-funded One-Stop Career Centers represent an attempt to centralize information about the large array of federal, state and local employment and training programs. They are designed to provide integrated services for both job seekers and employers. For example, the One-Stop system has developed America's Job Bank on the Internet (www.ajb.dni.us), which by the spring of 1997 had listed more than 750,000 job openings. Employers are offered an equivalent posting of resumes submitted by job seekers via America's Talent Bank (www.atb.org). In the future, these two sites will be supplemented with local and national occupational projections along with the qualifications needed for each occupation. The One-Stops also serve as referral centers for job seekers, helping them find appropriate training and educational institutions in their local area.

The One-Stop system is still developing. Through the 1997 fiscal year, 33 states received funds to implement the system and others were in the planning stage. It is thus premature to judge the effectiveness of the centers. Traditionally, the U.S. Department of Labor's intermediary functions, such as the Employment Service (which is being folded into the One-Stop Centers), primarily served workers in the lower levels of the occupational hierarchy. The challenge for the One-Stop system will be to encompass a much wider segment of the labor market. If this does not happen, One-Stops will continue to be associated with the second-chance system and will not become a central developmental resource for the broad array of production-level workers.

WORKFORCE INVESTMENT ACT (1998)

President Clinton signed the Workforce Investment Act into law on August 7, 1998. The legislation is fundamentally a reform of the second chance programs for youth and adults who have serious barriers to employment or to further education. Built primarily on the Job Training Partnership Act (JTPA), one of its goals is to integrate the types of services provided by the JTPA with the rest of the workforce development system. However, the new law does not include vocational education, which is addressed in separate legislation.

The allocation of funds provided by the new Act consolidates resources previously contained in several federal laws into three separate funding streams for adults, dislocated workers and youth — three distinct target populations. Eighty-five percent of the funds for adults and youth are allocated to local areas, with the remainder reserved for statewide activities. The legislation authorizes $1.25 billion annually for youth programs.

To be eligible for funds from the Workforce Investment Act, states must establish state workforce investment boards. These must include the governor of the state, two members of each chamber of the state legislature and appointed board members comprised primarily of business representatives, but also including representatives of chief local elected officials, labor organizations, and individuals and organizations with experience in the delivery of workforce investment and youth activities. The law also calls for the governor to designate local workforce investment areas. Activities within those areas will be overseen by local workforce investment boards also comprised primarily of business representatives. Each local area will also establish a youth council appointed by the local board. This legislation is structured to provide for a strong private sector emphasis and local decision making in targeted areas.

A key element of the Workforce Investment Act is the institutionalization and expansion of One-Stop Centers, the local hub of the system. Eligible adults, 18 years of age and older, will be provided with Individual Training Accounts, in essence a training voucher, which can be used for training at any certified educational provider. Training providers must make core measures of performance available to service recipients. These measures relate to the rates of completion, job placement, job retention, attainment of skills and wage rates.

Even though most of the funding based on the Act is aimed at adults and youth with serious barriers to employment and further education, some aspects of the Act are designed to encourage better coordination among all aspects of each state's workforce development system. For example, the Act permits and encourages, although it does not require, state workforce development boards to submit a "unified" state plan to ensure coordination of, and avoid duplication among, workforce development activities. Aspects of the One-Stop system are designed to provide labor market intermediation for all job seekers, not just those who face particular barriers to employment. Also, although vocational education was not included in the Workforce Investment Act, the certification process for eligibility to provide training paid from Individual Training Accounts favors traditional occupational education providers, such as community colleges. This will further integrate WIA-funded activities into the broader workforce development system. Finally, to further help coordinate the broader workforce development efforts, the Act calls for the development of a national employment statistics system.

Another key element of the Workforce Investment Act is its reform of programs for 14-21 year-old youth. The WIA has separate funding for youth and a distinct youth council within the local workforce development boards. To receive services under the Act, youth must have incomes below a set limit and be in one of the following categories: deficient in basic literacy skills; a school dropout; homeless, runaway or foster child; pregnant or a parent; an offender; or require additional assistance to complete an educational program or to secure and hold employment. The legislation encourages the provision of comprehensive services to these youth, including assessment of skills levels and service needs, a services strategy, preparation for postsecondary educational opportunities or unsubsidized employment, strong linkages between academic and occupational training, and effective connections to intermediaries with strong links to the job market and employers. The Act mandates follow-up services after job placement, particularly encouraging activities, such as mentoring, which promote stronger ties between youth and responsible adults. It also contains provisions that recognize the developmental differences between under-18 and over-18 youth. WIA also extends and expands the Job Corps, the intensive residential training and educational program for disadvantaged youth.

One of the two major changes in youth services is the extension of Youth Opportunity Area grants. During the two years before the passage of the WIA, the Department of Labor had developed and funded six pilot projects called Opportunity Areas for Out-of-School Youth (OASY or "Kulick" grants) in Chicago, Houston, Los Angeles, Boston, The Bronx and Kentucky. The programs comprising these projects focus on getting seriously disadvantaged, out-of-school youth into private sector employment.

Summary

The Workforce Investment Act does not establish a comprehensive workforce development system for the country. Most preparation of the country's labor force takes place in public high schools, community colleges, four-year colleges and workplaces. Most of the activities occurring in these institutions will only be marginally influenced by the WIA. In the end, education and workforce development is a state function. Nevertheless, the Act does have a chance to refocus attention on the nation's second chance workforce development system. And it does contain several provisions that could potentially spread its influence more broadly throughout the labor market. Of course, it is much too early to predict any effects; at this writing, appropriations have not yet been passed. Moreoever, experience suggests that it is very difficult to broaden the scope of activities that are perceived to be primarily oriented towards a second chance function.

The WIA's emphasis on youth is perhaps its most significant feature from the point of view of the legacy of The Forgotten Half. This emphasis addresses long-standing criticisms of the Job Training Partnership Act and other second-chance initiatives. The call for comprehensive services that take account of the changing developmental needs of youth and the encouragement of follow up services and stronger relationships to responsible adults particularly resonate with the recommendations of *TFH* a decade earlier.

COMMUNITY COLLEGES

The most prominent education reform documents of the 1980s and early 1990s put little emphasis on community colleges, even though they play an extensive and important role in workforce development. Enrolling about half of the students entering college each year, community colleges account for about 40 percent of all college students at any given time. While academic education and transfer to four-year colleges are still important roles, the large majority of community college students are enrolled in either one-year or two-year occupational programs. The colleges also have extensive contacts with local employers. As a result, they have become increasingly involved with customized training programs.

Clearly, community colleges are one of the key institutions for workforce preparation, and yet there has been nowhere near the imperative to reform them that there has been for secondary schools. To the extent that community colleges have been part of the national debate on reform, the following points are relevant:

- Tech Prep has encouraged high schools to coordinate their programs with community college curricula. While the implications of the Tech Prep model for community college reform are not entirely clear, thus far it has not had a profound effect.
- STWOA calls for the full participation of community colleges in local school-to-work partnerships and activities, but there remains a greater emphasis upon secondary schools in the discussion and implementation of school-to-work.
- Although plans for standards-based education could apply to occupational programs in community colleges, the work of the National Skill Standards

Board has not had much influence on these programs, in spite of the fact that community colleges have been involved for many years with standards for many of their occupational programs.
- Community college curricula could also promote the integration of academic and vocational education. Although some of this certainly goes on, much of the emphasis on integration so far has taken place at the secondary school level.

Of the points raised in the literature on reforming workforce development, one that has perhaps been embraced most enthusiastically by community colleges is the importance of fostering greater cooperation among schools and businesses. Indeed, declining enrollment during the mid to late 1990s and decreasing public funding have encouraged community colleges to seek new niches in the public postsecondary education marketplace. While certificates in health careers, business and technology are still the most popular courses of study, community colleges are increasingly working closely with companies and industries to provide job training in other areas. This broadened economic role includes providing company-specific curricula through contract training, encouraging new businesses through incubation and assistance and aiding state and local governments in regional economic planning.

Grubb et al. have termed this new role the "entrepreneurial college," referring to a "college functioning within the traditional community college which operates with the intention of creating conditions of economic and community well-being and demand for services, rather than simply responding to the need for educational programs."[44] By identifying the training needs of industry clusters, the entrepreneurial college can also promote economic development in the community or state by providing a steady source of workers trained in relevant industry skills. Some states, notably the Carolinas, have used the training provided by community colleges to attract employers.

It is not clear how prevalent the entrepreneurial college is compared with the traditional community college. Contract training is by far the most popular entrepreneurial role of the community college, although the number of students involved is difficult to gauge. A 1994 survey found that 90 percent of community colleges offered contract training.[45] Grubb and his colleagues estimate that the proportion of students involved in contract training is around 22 percent.[46] Other estimates suggested a participation rate of 10 to 20 percent.[47] It is difficult to track student enrollment in these training courses because they are often noncredit and students are likely to attend part-time for only a few weeks. What is clear, however, is that these contract relationships are beneficial to both community colleges and to businesses. Their success as a vehicle for workforce development remains in question; today we have only a rough idea of the size or impact of the entrepreneurial college.

Community colleges in general have also been criticized for very low graduation rates in their degree programs. According to data collected on 1989 entering community college students, within five years of their matriculation, almost half are no longer enrolled and have earned no degree, 37 percent have earned a degree and 15 percent are still enrolled.[48] It is possible that many of the students who did not complete their degrees enrolled to learn specific skills and left when they had achieved them. But there is little information on that hypothesis.

Thus, community colleges are central institutions in the nation's workforce development system and they deserve much more attention than they have received. About one-half of all first-time freshmen enroll in community colleges, and a majority of community college students are in occupational programs. Certainly, their efforts to prepare the nation's workforce have generated a great deal of interest and enthusiasm. Indeed, educators from many countries are visiting our community colleges to see what they can learn. Still, we need to know much more before we can definitively evaluate the role of community colleges in the nation's workforce development system.

ASSESSMENT OF PROGRESS AND IMPLEMENTATION

The Forgotten Half is a decade old. What have we learned in the past decade about the overall approach to workforce development that *TFH* helped define? We return now to the eight strategies listed in Figure 7-3 and discuss the extent to which each has been implemented.

1) Improved academic skills for production workers and the Forgotten Half

After a great deal of discussion about academic skills, many states have strengthened their academic skill requirements for high school graduation. But the continued emphasis on academic skills does not appear to be driven primarily by concerns about preparing the nation's workforce. Indeed, many people believe that an emphasis on workforce development might reduce the essential emphasis on academic skills. Moreover, it is particularly difficult to judge the extent to which the workforce has been strengthened by stronger academic skills, since we still lack a concrete understanding of exactly how academic skills relate to work requirements in particular and economic performance in general. For example, although research shows a strong relationship between individual earnings and years of schooling, the measured relationships between earnings and specific academic skills are much weaker.[49]

Results from the Third International Mathematics and Science Study (TIMSS) also cast doubt on our understanding of the relationship between academic skills and economic performance. In tests of twelfth graders in 23 countries, TIMSS found that U.S. students scored significantly lower than students in most other countries, including Russia, Lithuania, Greece and Italy. These results are puzzling in light of the continued dominance of the U.S. in science and technology.

Some of the initial reactions to the TIMSS results raised alarms about the country's future ability to compete internationally. Soon, however, other commentators began to question whether the skills measured by these tests were in fact vital to the economic strength of the country. Still others have claimed that it is the very flexibility and lack of structure criticized by many reformers that account for the apparent anomaly. This is illustrated by the headline in a March 2, 1998 *New York Times* article: "Freedom in Math Class May Outweigh Tests."[50] Experts quoted assert that the quality and accessibility of postsecondary education in the U.S. may actually compensate for the supposed inadequacies of secondary schools. It may also be that academic skills are crucial but that TIMSS did not measure the right ones. In any case, all of this simply indicates the level of our ignorance about the relationship between specific academic skills and economic performance. While this is a difficult problem, one approach would be to encourage much more interaction among the different industry and academic groups trying to understand required skills and abilities.

2) Strengthened SCANS skills

The conviction that students need to learn a set of skills that are neither academic nor vocational, such as problem solving and teamwork, has now been widely accepted and plays a part in many discussions of education reform. Indeed, if U.S. schools do a particularly good job of teaching these types of skills, that might help account for U.S. technological success despite poor performance on traditional academic tests. Most of the systems of industry skill standards that have been developed recently include SCANS skills, and even standards developed for the academic disciplines include process skills, such as critical thinking and problem-solving, that are not strictly within a discipline.

But there is much less agreement about how to teach and assess these skills. Some analysts argue that they can be taught within the traditional academic disciplines, while others favor teaching them within the context of authentic situations, for example, through work-based learning. Thus, while SCANS skills have become a staple in debates on education reform, the practical implications of the discussion have yet to be determined, and much work remains to be done on teaching and assessing them.

3) A greater emphasis on standards

Standards have become a watchword of educational reform in the 1990s, and there has been a great deal of discussion about setting them and demanding more from our students. While most people agree with this at a conceptual level, the establishment and assessment of specific standards are much more controversial. Opposition to a centralized system has thwarted national testing, and technical and conceptual difficulties have created barriers for assessment. The National Skill Standards Board has made some progress in defining a framework for industries to follow in the development of their standards, but it remains to be seen whether their work will catch on and have a widespread effect, given that standards set under NSSB auspices have to be voluntary. So far, what has been most valuable in this area are discussions about the notion of standards and about what skills and knowledge are needed for work. These discussions have also created many useful opportunities for employers and educators to work together.

4) Innovative pedagogies, including the integration of academic and vocational instruction and work-based learning

The last decade has seen a significant increase in experimentation with both the integration of academic and vocational education and work-based learning. Of the various strategies educators employ to combine the instruction of academic and vocational material, perhaps the most common is the use of applied learning curricula. In general, these have been introduced more as reforms of vocational education than as fundamental reforms of education in general. The most important problem here is that, despite some studies that suggest that these approaches can work, we still lack definitive evidence about their effectiveness for teaching and learning.

Much the same can be said about work-based learning. Case studies suggest that it has many benefits. Indeed, internships and other types of structured work experience are central components of almost all professional training, and apprenticeship is accepted as an effective way to teach many occupational skills. But the use of work-based learning as an element of a general education for young people who have not already chosen a specific profession or occupation is much more controversial. Advocates argue that learning skills in the context of particular applications has important motivational effects and gives coherence and relevance to otherwise abstract academic skills. Critics say that it diverts students from a focus on studying core academic skills.

Thus, both integrated curricula and work-based learning are effective ways to teach specific occupational skills, but we still need a better understanding of their role in broad educational reform.

5) Participation of many institutions, including employers, in education

School-to-Work, Tech Prep, the National Skill Standards Board, the Workforce Investment Act, developments at community colleges and other efforts focus on getting employers involved in schools and colleges. While there has been considerable skepticism about the feasibility of large-scale, intensive employer participation in educating young people, recent research suggests that a reasonably large number of employers already have some contact with schools. It appears that substantial minorities of employers in several cities provide students with some type of internship.[51] We know less about the content and impact of the experiences that young people get at these worksites, although anecdotal information from case studies of the implementation of STWOA suggests that young people in these programs develop useful and productive relationships with adults outside of their families. Overall, the discussion and legislation of the last decade have moved the concept of school-employer partnerships beyond such superficial efforts as participation in "adopt-a-school" programs or occasional service on school advisory boards. The current discussion involves employers becoming serious players in the education of young people and in working with schools and educators to determine what types of education are necessary to prepare students for the world of work.

A principal barrier to broader-based and more intensive employer involvement is the weak tradition in the U.S. of employer participation in education. Unlike some other countries, the U.S. lacks an institutional structure that empowers employer organizations to participate in education and set skill requirements. As a result, developing a stronger foundation of employer participation is likely to be a gradual process and will probably come about through incremental locally-based activities.

6) Making pathways into particular occupations more transparent

In the flexible and diverse U.S. labor market, young people often have no realistic sense of what they must do to prepare themselves for particular jobs or occupations; the career development system is "opaque," in the language of the labor market. As a result, school-to-work advocates and the NSSB have worked toward establishing broader occupational clusters and have promoted discussion about the education and experience that would be necessary to develop careers in those areas. There has also been discussion of improvements in counseling in secondary schools and of how Tech Prep encourages young people to engage in more systematic thinking about the future. The work-based learning experiences promoted by STWOA are expected to give young people a better idea of what it takes to get a job in a field that interests them. The Department of Labor's One-Stop Centers are also designed to clarify career pathways by providing information about the training and educational requirements of particular jobs. Yet it is still too early to tell whether these developments will lead to a more systematic and "transparent" labor market experience for young people.

While computerized systems increase the amount of information available, more regular and systematized labor markets still seem a long way off. Indeed, it is probably unrealistic to expect to define with much specificity the educational and experiential pathways leading to particular occupations. Two problems thwart the development of a clear sense of what young people must do to enter a particular occupation. First, informal networks, "connections" and contacts are of paramount importance in the U.S. labor market. Institutionalizing these networks, especially under the auspices of the public sector, is extremely difficult, and attempts to do so have generally been confined to lower levels of the employment hierarchy. Second, clarification requires more than information; it also depends on stronger regulation of the labor market. However, if anything, political trends are leading in the opposite direction — towards less regulation. Other countries, such as Germany and Austria, have a more understandable system of career development and also have considerably more government regulation and intervention in the labor market. Career progression is clearest when there are legal restrictions and related educational regulations for practicing particular professions. If a young person wants to become a doctor or a lawyer, the required educational steps are easy to explain. Although many young people may not know them, this is a problem that can be solved with better information. How to become a software developer or to build a successful business is much less obvious because there are so many possible routes to these occupations.

Thus, it certainly makes sense to provide young people with more information about what they need to do to achieve their goals. It also makes sense to help them figure out what their interests are and what they might like to do. At the same time, the nature of the U.S. economy places severe limits on the extent to which occupational pathways can be made navigable or "transparent."

7) Facilitation of the transition of The Forgotten Half to postsecondary education

The Forgotten Half argued that too much emphasis had been placed on college-bound students and that, as a result, the large majority of young people who would never earn a bachelor's degree had been neglected. Two trends have emerged. First, the discussion and legislation of the past decade have succeeded in focusing some attention on the education of the non-college-bound. The elimination of the general track, increased rigor in vocational programs and the development of career clusters and magnet schools have all created discussion and ferment. Thanks to *TFH* and other publications, the training and education of the non-college-bound is no longer "forgotten." But at the same time, there has been a movement away from using the college-bound/non-college-bound distinction. Research on education and earnings (as summarized in Chapter One), shows that students with no more than a high school diploma (the non-college bound) have trouble making enough money to support a family. Therefore, reformers and policymakers now emphasize the importance of at least some postsecondary education for all students.

Although the focus on the non-college-bound has certainly been useful, it is unrealistic to try to develop a system that is explicitly designed to prepare young people for work immediately after high school. There certainly are many jobs, some reasonably well paid, that do not require the skills learned in college. Nevertheless, programs that foreclose or appear to foreclose the college option will either be viewed as second-class or run into strong political opposition. This shifts the justification for occupationally-oriented education in high school from direct preparation for work to an argument that such an orientation can in fact do a good, or even superior, job of teaching academic skills. Educational strategies at the secondary and community college levels can be designed to prepare people for relatively specific work, but they must explicitly hold open the option for further education.

This approach will work most effectively if a case can be made that work-oriented education, perhaps including a work-based learning component, can be an effective means of teaching broad academic and SCANS-type skills. Although there are many examples of school-to-work programs that send their graduates to college,[52] there is still no systematic understanding of how effective a work-oriented approach, including work-based learning, is as a general educational strategy.

While keeping postsecondary options open for students, we must pay more attention to what happens in postsecondary institutions. Low completion rates in both two- and four-year colleges need to be addressed more seriously. (See Chapter Six.) And in general, we need to focus much more attention on the role of community colleges in the workforce development system. The research and analysis devoted to these institutions is not commensurate with the important role that they already play.

8) Continued emphasis on second-chance efforts to help young people continue their education or find employment

Despite the emphasis *TFH* placed on second-chance programs, such efforts have not been a significant part of the workforce development agenda during most of the 1990s. This was partly a result of pessimistic assessments of the effectiveness of such programs. In addition, a widespread impression prevails that the nation's educational system was not doing a good job in preparing even those workers who did not appear to have serious educational problems and who presumably were not in need of a second chance. The recent welfare legislation and the long economic boom and low unemployment rate have brought "employment and training" back to the national workforce development agenda. Passage of the Workforce Investment Act may revitalize second chance efforts, although it will not take effect for several years.

Perhaps one lesson to be learned from this experience is that workforce development may not be the best justification for programs designed to strengthen the educational background and preparation for work of people who have serious employment problems. Except at times of very low unemployment, the economy can function effectively without the participation of at least some people. Thus a workforce development justification for second-chance programs loses force when unemployment rises. Second-chance policy should not rise and fall with the business cycle.

SUMMING UP AND LOOKING AHEAD

The Forgotten Half and related reports defined a broad set of workforce development strategies. Implementing them has had a profound effect on the discussion of education reform in the United States. It has also led to a new focus on the education of production-level workers as well as to extensive discussion about what skills are needed for work and how people can acquire those skills. Higher standards and better benchmarks for student progress have also come into prominence, as have new ways to help young people make transitions to both additional education and work. Out of this decade have also come alternative approaches to teaching both academic and occupational skills.

While these developments have resulted in some general progress and many individual successes, the structure of the American educational system has remained essentially intact. None of these policies and programs have penetrated the core of schooling and pedagogy. Tech Prep and school-to-work remain specialized approaches that have made significant progress in some areas, but they are still outside mainstream education. It is much too early to tell whether the work of the National Skill Standards Board will have a significant effect on how the country understands and documents the skills needed for particular jobs and occupations. Despite many encouraging efforts afoot in the states, it is still difficult to discern a broad, consistent national movement. Community colleges are deeply involved with workforce development, yet this seems to be more a long-standing trend than a response to the policy discussions of the last decade.

Why has it been so difficult to penetrate the core of the education system despite widespread discussion and important new national legislation? First, many of the proposals call for a more structured and centralized education system and a more regulated labor market. Such efforts invariably run into political opposition. Second, greater employer involvement and more widespread work-based learning are thwarted by the absence of a tradition of employer participation in education and an institutional structure that could be used to organize and oversee that participation. Third, many Americans believe that a work-oriented education will inevitably force young people to make early career decisions and thereby restrict their future opportunities. Fourth, systematic evidence about the effectiveness of some of these strategies remains elusive. We know little about the effectiveness of integrated curricula or work-based learning in teaching academic skills; we have difficulty defining, measuring and assessing SCANS skills; and we have a surprisingly weak understanding of how academic skills are used on the job. Without this type of information, it will be difficult to convince skeptics that the workforce development strategies outlined here will strengthen young people's choices and opportunities, rather than restrict them.

Recent developments in the economy have also diverted attention from the workforce development strategies. Many Americans have always opposed a more centralized, regulated and differentiated education system. At the same time, however, the economic weakness in the 1980s and the strength of Germany, Japan and other countries on the Pacific Rim gave credibility to more regulated systems for preparing the workforce; people were asking whether the U.S. was sacrificing its competitive position and standard of living to maintain its flexible, college-oriented workforce preparation system. In the 1990s, public preoccupation with our economic competitors has changed. The Japanese economy, formerly perceived as a threat to the strength of America's economic position, has been experiencing severe difficulties. Japanese and Korean businesses are conceding that their version of capitalism, in which government regulations and loyalty determine the market, has been unsuccessful.[53] Likewise, the formidable German system of workforce development has been challenged. In the past, approximately 60 percent of German youth were prepared for the workforce through an extensive apprenticeship program. During this decade, fewer German students are choosing to move through the apprenticeship program into full-time employment. Rather, they prefer to enter the more academic *Gymnasia* or the *Realschulen,* hoping to obtain entry into the university system. Furthermore, the juxtaposition of U.S. economic strength and educational weakness (at least as measured by the TIMSS) suggests that the more structured and centralized education systems that produce high test scores in other countries may not provide a clear path to economic success.

This reasoning illustrates the danger of relying too much on economic competitiveness as a reason for undertaking education reform. Indeed, alarmists never had strong evidence that educational problems caused the particular economic ills faced by the United States in the 1980s. *A Nation at Risk* made the argument without presenting evidence that linked changing economic fortunes to educational practices or outcomes. To its credit, *TFH* did not rely primarily on an economic argument to motivate its call for reform.

In the end, a strong international position does not obviate the need to analyze and improve the nation's workforce development system. It makes no more sense for Americans to be complacent in 1998 than it did for the Japanese to be complacent in 1988. *TFH* warned that large numbers of people were left behind despite strong economic growth. While we have begun to pay more attention to the education of this group, *TFH's* warning has come to pass. During the last 20 years, the U.S. has experienced an unprecedented increase in inequality — the top 20 percent of the workforce has gained at the expense of the lower 60 percent.[54] Furthermore, there is evidence that school does not interest or engage all students — many evidently apply very little effort.[55] Murnane and Levy[56] argue that students have to finish college in order to learn what they should be able to learn in high school. The very high dropout rate in four-year and community colleges continues. What is more, many of the country's top graduate programs in technical fields have large numbers of foreign students, as U.S. students are either uninterested or unqualified, and many computer and other high-tech firms depend heavily on foreign-trained technical personnel. At the very least, all of this suggests that a tremendous amount of human and financial resources are being wasted and that young Americans are still losing many opportunities.

What, then, has the past decade of policy discussion and practice taught us about building a workforce development system that can address these problems? *Returning for a moment to TFH, it appears that many of its recommendations are still useful: Focus on the non-college-bound, involve many of society's institutions in the education of the young, work to facilitate the movement of the non-college-bound into postsecondary education and continue to develop programs to address the employment and educational problems of young people who have not had success in the mainstream educational system. Some progress has been made in responding to all of these recommendations, with the possible exception of the last. All continue to make sense.*

Indeed, although it is still too early to make a definitive judgement, the overall experience of the past decade suggests that the eight workforce development strategies continue to provide a reasonable framework for reform. Three points need to be emphasized nevertheless.

First, it is unrealistic to design a strategy that would depend on increased labor market regulation, educational centralization or earlier occupational selection by teenagers. Reformers should take on these political battles only if alternative approaches are shown to be out of the question. It is currently popular to tout the advantages of the flexibility of the American education system. While this may be reasonable, we need to know much more before we can draw any definitive conclusions.

Second, the full implementation of the workforce development approach outlined here requires much more information than we have so far. Many questions remain to be answered: What is the relationship between academic skills taught in school and effectiveness at work? How does the United States continue to lead in science and technology-based industry while American students fare so poorly on science and mathematics tests? Why do innovation and creativity in software and computer design flourish while the number of computer science majors drops? How can we measure and teach SCANS skills? How effective are integrated curricula and work-based learning at teaching academic skills? What other skills do young people learn in work-based learning, and are they worth the effort needed to recruit and work with employers? Many of the policies proposed during the last decade have some support from research and can draw on a growing body of examples and case studies that suggest that they are effective. Nevertheless, more systematic evidence is necessary both to improve program design and to allay many of the reasonable fears of skeptics.

Finally, one central implication of the experience of the last decade is that, certainly at the secondary school level, *we should dispense with the distinction between educational policy and workforce development policy. The funda-mental goal of both is that high school students should be actively engaged by their studies and that they should leave secondary school with a solid base of academic and SCANS skills that will enable them to succeed in occupational or academic education at the postsecondary level. Whatever the performance of the economy may be, our society is far from achieving that goal.*

All of the policies and strategies that we have discussed in this chapter, such as the integration of academic and vocational education, work-based learning, Tech Prep and even second-chance programs, need to be looked at from the point of view of this goal. This does not mean that occupationally-oriented education will not take place in high school, but rather that when it does, its primary goal will be to provide motivation and a context for acquiring foundation skills. Armed with this perspective, workforce development advocates should join forces with a broad range of educational reformers.

> *"...we should dispense with the distinction between educational policy and workforce development policy. The fundamental goal of both is that high school students should be actively engaged by their studies and that they should leave secondary school with a solid base of academic and SCANS skills that will enable them to succeed in occupational or academic education at the postsecondary level. Whatever the performance of the economy may be, our society is far from achieving that goal."*

NOTES

[1] National Center for Education Statistics. *Digest of Education Statistics. 1996.* Washington, DC: Government Printing Office, 1996, Table 259.

[2] Urquiola, Miquel, David Stern, Ilana Horn, Carolyn Dornsife, Bernadette Chi, Lea Williams, Donna Merritt, Katherine Hughes and Thomas Bailey. *School to Work, College and Career.* Berkeley, CA: National Center for Research in Vocational Education, 1997; American Youth Policy Forum. *Some Things DO Make a Difference for Youth: A Compendium of Evaluations of Youth Programs and Practices.* Washington, DC: American Youth Policy Forum, 1997.

[3] Carnevale, Anthony P. *Education and Training for America's Future.* Washington, DC: Manufacturing Institute, National Association of Manufacturers, 1998, pp. 24-26.

[4] Grubb, W. Norton. *Learning to Work: The Case of Re-Integrating Education and Job Training.* New York: Russell Sage Foundation, 1996.

[5] See also Osterman, Paul. *Getting Started: The Youth Labor Market.* Cambridge, MA: MIT Press, 1980.

[6] Bernhardt, Annette, Martina Morris, Mark Handcock and Marc Scott. *Work and Opportunity in the Post-Industrial Labor Market, Final Report to the Russell Sage Foundation and the Rockefeller Foundation.* New York: Institute on Education and the Economy, Teachers College, Columbia University, 1997; Duncan, Greg, Johanne Boisjoly and Timothy Smeeding. "Economic Mobility of Young Workers in the 1970s and 1980s," *Demography* 33 (4): pp. 497-509.

[7] Hayes, Robert H. and William J. Abernathy. "Managing Our Way to Economic Decline," *Harvard Business Review* 58 (4): pp. 67-77.

[8] Freeman, Richard B. *The Overeducated American.* New York: Academic Press, 1976.

[9] Berg, Ivar E. *Education and Jobs: The Great Training Robbery.* New York: Praeger Publishing, 1970.

[10] National Commission on Excellence in Education. *A Nation at Risk: The Imperative for Educational Reform.* Washington DC: U.S. Government Printing Office, 1983.

[11] Johnston, William B. and Arnold E. Packer. *Workforce 2000: Work And Workers For the Twenty-First Century.* Washington DC: U.S. Department of Labor, 1987.

[12] Bailey, Thomas. *Changes in the Nature and Structure of Work: Implications for Skill Requirements and Skill Foundations.* New York: Institute on Education and the Economy, 1989.

[13] *The Forgotten Half: Pathways to Success for America's Youth and Young Families.* Washington, DC: 1988, p. 127.

[14] Ditto, p. 130.

[15] Gardner, Howard. *NASSP Bulletin* (1996).

[16] *The Forgotten Half*, p. 131.

[17] Ditto, p. 127.

[18] Ditto, p. 136.

[19] National Center on Education and the Economy. *America's Choice: High Skills or Low Wages!* Rochester, NY: National Center on Education and the Economy, 1990.

[20] Grubb, W. Norton, G. Davis, G. Lum, J. Plihal and C. Morgaine. *The Cunning Hand, the Cultured Mind: Models for Integrating Vocational and Academic Education.* Berkeley, CA: National Center for Research in Vocational Education, 1991; Berryman, Susan and Thomas Bailey. *The Double Helix of Education and the Economy.* New York: Institute on Education and the Economy, Teachers College, Columbia University, 1992.

[21] The Secretary's Commission on Achieving Necessary Skills, U.S. Department of Labor. *What Work Requires of Schools: A SCANS Report for America 2000.* Washington DC: U.S. Government Printing Office, 1991.

[22] Ditto, p. xix.

[23] Although the system was first established through seed funding from the U.S. Department of Labor, One-Stop Career Centers were institutionalized in the Workforce Development Act of 1998.

[24] Urquiola et al., 1997.

[25] National School-to-Work Office, U.S. Department of Education. *National Assessment of Vocational Education: Interim Report to Congress.* Washington DC: U.S. Government Printing Office, 1994, p. 313.

[26] Parnell, Dale. *The Neglected Majority.* Washington, DC: Community College Press, American Association of Community Colleges, 1985.

[27] Silverberg, Marsha K., Lara K. Hulsey and Alan M. Hershey. *Heading Students toward Career Horizons: Tech-Prep Implementation Progress, 1993-1995.* Princeton, NJ: Mathematica Policy Research, 1997, p. xiii.

> "There is no doubt that anyone without a high school diploma has a hard time finding a job today — and will have an even harder time in the years ahead as jobs require an even higher degree of skill and training to perform."
> — *President John F. Kennedy*
> *Labor Day 1962*
>
> "Over the last twenty years, high school graduates have seen their real wages slide by more than 10 percent. High school dropouts have had a real wage decline of over 25 percent.
> ...a majority of the out-of-school youth population in high poverty areas don't have a job...Twenty years ago...the annual unemployment rate for black teens was over 30 percent. Twenty years later...that statistic hasn't gone anywhere."
>
> "The message is clear: the new global economy is unlimited to those with the right skills — and unforgiving to those without...when young people cannot fulfill their potential, America cannot fulfill its promise."
> — *U.S. Secretary of Labor Alexis M. Herman*
> *Labor Day 1998*

[28] Ditto, p. xiii.
[29] Ditto, p. xvii.
[30] Ditto, p. xiii.
[31] Urquiola et al., 1997.
[32] Urquiola et al., 1997, p. 18; National School-to-Work Office, U.S. Department of Education. *Report to Congress: Implementation of the School-to-Work Opportunities Act*. Washington, DC: U. S. Government Printing Office, 1997.
[33] U.S. Department of Education, National School-to-Work Office, 1998. (http://www.stw.ed.gov/grants/grants.html).
[34] Hershey et al., 1997.
[35] Ditto, p. xix.
[36] Geotz, Branden, Scott Barstow and Patty Farrell. "School-to-Work Implementation Falls Short of Expectations," *Counseling Today*. February 24, 1998. (http://www.counseling.org.)
[37] Orr, Margaret Terry. *Wisconsin Youth Apprenticeship Program in Printing: Evaluation 1993-1995*. Boston, MA: Jobs for the Future, 1996.
[38] Kopp, Goldberger, Morales. *The Evaluation of a Youth Apprenticeship Model: A Second Year Evaluation of Boston's Pro Tech*. Cambridge, MA: Jobs for the Future, 1994; Crain, Robert et al., *The Effects of Career Magnet Education on High Schools and Their Graduates*, MDS-779. Berkeley, CA: National Center for Research in Vocational Education, University of California, 1997.
[39] Crain, R., 1997; T. Orr, 1996; and D. Hollenbeck. *An Evaluation of the Manufacturing Technology Partnership (MTP) Program*, Upjohn Institute Technical Report No. 96-007. Kalamazoo, MI: Upjohn Institute, 1996.
[40] Kemple, J.J. *Career Academies: Communities of Support for Teachers and Students*. New York: Manpower Demonstration Research Corporation, 1997.
[41] Stern, David, M. Raby, and C. Dayton. *Career Academies: Partnerships for Reconstructing American High Schools*. San Francisco: Jossey-Bass, 1992.
[42] The 16 economic sectors that the NSSB has developed are agricultural production and natural resource management; mining and extraction operations; construction operations; manufacturing, installation, and repair; energy and utilities operations; transportation operations; communications; wholesale/retail sales; hospitality and tourism services; financial services; health and social services; education and training services; public administration, legal, and protective services; business and administrative services; property management and building maintenance services; and research, development, and technical services.
[43] Bailey, Thomas and Donna Merritt. *School-to-Work for the College Bound*. Berkeley, CA: National Center for Research in Vocational Education, University of California at Berkeley, MDS-799, 1997.
[44] Grubb, W. Norton, N. Badway, D. Bell, D. Bragg and M. Russman. *Workforce, Economic, and Community Development: The Changing Landscape of the "Entrepreneurial" Community College*. (A Report of The Center for Research in Vocational Education, The League for Innovation in the Community College and The National Council on Occupational Education, forthcoming), p. 22.
[45] Johnson, S.L. "Organizational Structure and the Performance of Contract Training Operations in American Community Colleges," Ph.D. dissertation, University of Texas, 1995, pp. 88, 90.
[46] Grubb, et al., 1997, p. 47.
[47] Johnson, S. L., 1995, p. 100.
[48] National Center for Education Statistics. *Descriptive Summary of 1989-90 Beginning Postsecondary Students: 5 Years Later*. Washington, DC: U.S. Government Printing Office, 1996, p. 32.
[49] Levin, Henry. "Mapping the Economics of Education: An Introduction," *Educational Researcher*, May 1989, pp. 13-16, 73.
[50] Bronner, Ethan. "Freedom in Math Class May Outweigh Tests," *New York Times*, March 2, 1998. p. A1.
[51] Bailey, Katherine Hughes and Travis Barr. *Achieving Scale and Quality in School-to-Work Internships: Findings from an Employer Survey*. Berkeley, CA: National Center for Research in Vocational Education, 1998.
[52] Bailey and Merritt, 1997.
[53] Kristof, Nicholas D. "Crisis Pushing Asian Capitalism Closer to U.S.-Style Free Market," *New York Times*, January 17, 1998. p. A1.
[54] Danziger, Sheldon and Peter Gottschalk. *America Unequal*. Cambridge, MA: Harvard University Press, 1995, p. 23.
[55] Newmann, Fred M. and Gary G. Wehlage. *Successful School Restructuring: A Report to the Public and Educators by the Center on Organization and Restructuring of Schools*. Madison, WI: Wisconsin Center for Education Research, 1995.
[56] Murnane, Richard J. and Frank Levy. "A Civil Society Demands Education for Good Jobs," *Educational Leadership* 54 (5): 34-36.

CHAPTER EIGHT

TEN YEARS OF YOUTH IN SERVICE TO AMERICA

Shirley Sagawa

Tozerria Haywood was just 11 years old when he started volunteering. "I was goofing off, getting into trouble at the beginning of the summer," he recalls. His parents signed him up for the Detroit Youth Volunteer Corps. Since that time, he has donated more than 2,500 hours to volunteer work -- tutoring young children, visiting senior citizens, and working with visually impaired children. Today he is an AmeriCorps member planning to go to college in the fall. "The most important thing volunteering has taught me is that you must love yourself before others can love you," Tozerria says.

Frankie Gomez had always faced challenges and emerged a star. Born to a teenage mother who was incarcerated when Frankie was in her sophomore year, Frankie raised her three-year-old brother while finishing high school. Although she excelled in school, Frankie lacked direction and dropped out of college. When she heard about City Year, the idea of giving a year of full-time service appealed to her. She served one year as a City Year AmeriCorps member, and then another, and then began her own program, The Little Big Citizens, an afterschool program serving 80 children in a lower-income neighborhood in San Jose. "Without national service, I would be afraid of what the world would look like," says Frankie.

At 13, Victor Burgos dropped out of school. With little else to do, he began hanging out on the streets of Roxbury in Boston. By age 15, he was a single father struggling to make ends meet. "Having a son changed everything," he says. But for Victor, finding work to support his family quickly translated into a series of dead-end, low-paying jobs. "Without an education or marketable skills, I had no future." Then he heard about YouthBuild. His decision to join the program changed his life. Today, Victor is a junior drafter at one of Boston's leading design engineering firms.

In *The Forgotten Half*, the William T. Grant Foundation Commission promoted service as a "pathway to success" for young people and an antidote to the "debilitating sense of powerlessness" that they often feel. By redirecting a sense of futility and preoccupation with self towards an ethic of service and a commitment toward others, young people would become active citizens and important resources for the community. Service was thought to be an effective way to expand learning through experience beyond the classroom, connect young people to careers and their communities, teach responsibility and basic life skills, and provide useful services to others.

Based on these assumptions, *TFH*'s chapter on service recommended a number of measures. It named the creation of quality student service opportunities as central to the educational program of every public school. It called on states to support this effort and recommended using federal funds to expand youth service programs and revitalize existing service programs, such as VISTA and the Peace Corps. And it asked that business, local foundations, cities, states and organizations whose constituencies could be served by youth provide financial backing. *The Forgotten Half* further recommended creation of a national commission to study national service and urged the many organizations interested in expanding youth service to join together into one nationwide service federation to speak with greater authority.

In the 1990s, Americans made substantial progress toward these objectives. In 1988, the corps that Tozerria, Frankie and Victor served with were small demonstration programs. Ten years later, YouthBuild enrolls 4,600 mostly low-income corpsmembers in 108 sites who earn their GEDs while building housing for low-income families; City Year fields a diverse cadre of 850 young adults performing a range of education and human services in nine cities. And the Youth Volunteer Corps of America's 55 affiliates involve 25,000 11-18 year-olds in various kinds of community service. In 1988, AmeriCorps, YouthBuild and other federal funding authorizations for youth service did not exist. Ten years later, they supply more than $600 million dollars for these programs. A decade ago, just a handful of states supported service programs. Today, 48 states have bipartisan state commissions on service and almost every state educational agency administers service-learning funds. A decade ago, a national commission was a legislative proposal. Today, the work of the National and Community Service Commission, established by Congress in 1990, is continued by the larger and more visible federal Corporation for National Service, which Congress authorized in 1993. A decade ago, a few visionary foundations supported youth service. Today, the Grantmaker Forum, first convened in 1993, serves as a communication tool for funders interested in service programs and consists of more than 700 grantmakers bound together by a belief that citizen service is a core value of American democracy.

SUPPORT FOR SERVICE GROWS

Support for youth service has grown in part because it offers a strategy for achieving several diverse goals:[1]

- Increase academic performance, either directly, by reaching students who learn more effectively through experiential, hands-on education than through traditional methods, or indirectly, by motivating students to achieve as they connect classroom learning to the real world;
- Teach lifeskills, develop problem-solving abilities and increase understanding of the community;
- Prepare young people for the world of work, expose them to careers and develop specific skills leading to employment;
- "Get things done" that would not otherwise be addressed by existing public programs or the private sector;
- Bridge gaps in understanding among people of different backgrounds;
- Develop active citizens who are engaged in the community through their volunteer service and other forms of civic involvement, such as voting and awareness of current affairs; and
- Help young people learn that with rights come responsibilities.

Some of these theories were tested in earlier decades by the federal government, with the Depression-era Civilian Conservation Corps and National Youth Administration, the Peace Corps and VISTA founded in the 1960s, the Youth Conservation Corps and Young Adult Conservation Corps piloted during the 1970s, and even the military draft. Some, like state-sponsored youth corps, urban service corps, college campus-based programs and service programs organized by religious organizations, schools and community groups, grew at the local or state level. The early 1980s saw the founding of new national organizations whose mission was to expand and support service by young people, among them such groups as Campus Compact, Campus Outreach Opportunity League (COOL), Youth Service America and the National Association of Service and Conservation Corps (NASCC). And during this same decade, new models were developed, including City Year, YouthBuild and the Youth Volunteer Corps. Early support from the Ford Foundation, W.K. Kellogg Foundation, Echoing Green and other philanthropic foundations helped establish the programs and the infrastructure of the service field.[2]

As the number of models grew, advocates for youth development, civic activism and education began to organize in support of federal funding for service. The Potomac Institute's 1979 report, *Youth and the Needs of the Nation*, called for a move toward universal voluntary national service linked to educational scholarships.[3] Youth Service America, which had incubated many of the new model programs, including City Year and the Youth Volunteer Corps, and had begun to train many young service leaders through its New Generation Training Program, organized a working group to discuss policy issues affecting youth service and build an advocacy base for all streams of service. In 1989, the Democratic Leadership Council took this proposal a step further, advocating a $15 billion national program combining civilian and military options that would replace existing student financial aid for higher education with a requirement to render a period of service.[4] In 1988 and 1989, more than a dozen bills were introduced in Congress and both major party candidates in the 1988 election proposed expanding service opportunities for young people. A foundation was being built.

A large bipartisan majority in Congress passed the National and Community Service Act of 1990, introduced by Senator Edward M. Kennedy and signed by President George Bush. This legislation created the Commission on National and Community Service and provided federal funding for four types of programs: school- and community-based programs for school-age youth; campus-based programs; youth service and conservation corps; and demonstration programs to test the idea of linking service to money for college studies. It also provided funding for the Points of Light

Foundation, a nonprofit organization proposed by President Bush to promote volunteer service as a strategy to solve community problems.

The relatively modest federal funds provided through the Commission on National and Community Service helped to jumpstart fledgling programs. They also began to create a state-level infrastructure for service, including independent state service commissions and service-learning offices in state education agencies. The Commission's January 1993 report, *What You Can Do For Your Country*, recommended service as a central practice in schools and colleges and increases in the quality and number of youth corps opportunities. It also posited that it would be "feasible to expand the number of worthwhile [full-time] national service opportunities to approximately 100,000 within a few years," although it did not go so far as to recommend this course of action.[5]

The Points of Light Foundation proposed by President Bush was established as a nonpartisan, nonprofit organization in 1990 to promote volunteering. Its mission, to engage more people more effectively in volunteer service to help solve serious social problems, is manifested through efforts to create workplace volunteer programs, develop youth service leaders, encourage family volunteering and, after merging with the Volunteer Action Centers, provide support to volunteer management professionals and local volunteer centers. The Foundation, with the cooperation of volunteer centers, has recently continued the practice begun by President Bush of selecting an exemplary volunteer each day to be the "daily point of light."

DEVELOPMENT OF AMERICORPS

In 1993, President Clinton took office after pledging in his election campaign to provide Americans the opportunity to pay for college through service. In September, he signed the National and Community Service Trust Act of 1993, which updated earlier legislation and provided substantially more funding for all the streams of service. The Act also consolidated the National and Community Service Commission and ACTION, the agency administering VISTA and several senior volunteer programs, into a new federal Corporation for National Service. It expanded funding for school- and college-based service-learning programs, now known as "Learn and Serve America" and folded the dedicated funding stream for youth corps into a larger program which came to be known as "AmeriCorps." Funding for AmeriCorps would flow through bipartisan state commissions appointed by the governor in each state, with local organizations competing for funding. Finally, the Act brought VISTA and the recently authorized National Civilian Community Corps, a residential youth corps intended to be operated on former military bases, under the AmeriCorps umbrella.

AmeriCorps's roots were in the earlier Democratic Leadership Council proposal but it differed in several important ways. Although AmeriCorps members would receive "education awards," in the form of a scholarship or loan forgiveness, the award would not affect their federal financial aid, nor would individuals who did not serve be penalized. Federal student aid programs would continue, rather than be ended as the DLC had proposed. Secondly, the amount of the award, $4,725, was significantly less than proposed by the DLC. Thirdly, the program, although far larger than the earlier demonstration effort funded by the Commission, would allow only a limited number to serve full-time, rather than the almost universal program contemplated by the DLC. And there would be no formal ties to the military.

In 1993, 48 out of 50 states appointed state commissions or identified appropriate alternatives to administer AmeriCorps, and more than 250 programs received funding after competing at the state or national levels. The first AmeriCorps members began their service in September 1994, just a year after the legislation was signed into law. A year later, more than 20,000 members were serving, and Congress appropriated additional funding to expand the program.

AmeriCorps became a prime target of some Congressional Republicans because of its close identification with President Clinton, as well as philosophical opposition to the idea of providing stipends to "volunteers" and antipathy towards expanding the federal role in the social sector.[7] The controversy intensified in 1994, when Republicans gained a majority in both houses of the Congress. AmeriCorps and the Corporation for National Service were the subject of six highly contentious oversight hearings from 1995 through 1997. Opponents charged that the program was excessively expensive. They alleged that it allowed AmeriCorps members to engage in political activity and favored nontraditional nonprofit organizations. They also cited irregularities in the grantmaking process and a lack of adequate financial controls. Amendments taking money from AmeriCorps and giving it to the Department of Veterans Affairs were offered on several spending bills, resulting in the elimination or dramatic reduction of funding for the program in the House appropriations bill on several occasions.

In response to these criticisms, the Corporation undertook reforms to improve its grantmaking and financial processes, and worked aggressively to correct misinformation about AmeriCorps. The Corporation funded programs in every state and many governors of both parties rallied to its support. Backing also came in favorable editorials and through advocacy by friends of national service, including the business community and nonprofit leaders as well as through strong public support[8] and the President's unwavering commitment to AmeriCorps. All of these helped ensure the survival of the agency and its programs. Discussion of their demise has gradually diminished but still persists in some Congressional quarters. Authorizing legislation for the Corporation and its programs expired in 1997, but Congress continued to provide funding. In fiscal year 1998, $485 million was appropriated to support 50,000 AmeriCorps members and one million students through Learn and Serve America. President Clinton has proposed reauthorization legislation to extend the Corporation's programs through 2002.

PRESIDENTS' SUMMIT OF 1997

"The Presidents' Summit for America's Future" of April 1997 provided further evidence of a growing national consensus in favor of youth service, as well as the power of service and philanthropy to assist youth. Organized jointly by the Corporation for National Service and the Points of Light Foundation and chaired by General Colin Powell, the Summit brought together a dazzling array of national leaders: all of the living Presidents and First Ladies (Nancy Reagan represented her husband), entertainers from Oprah Winfrey to Tony Bennett to LL Cool J, corporate and nonprofit leaders, more than 30 governors and 100 mayors, and delegations from all 50 states and 150 selected communities. Those organizations represented at the Summit, whether Fortune 500 businesses or grassroots nonprofits, made "commitments" to support the Summit goals, which together represent a comprehensive view of what children need: a caring adult, role model or mentor; safe places to learn and grow during non-school hours; a healthy start; a marketable skill through effective education; and an opportunity to "give back" to the community through their own service. Commitments included Denny's Restaurants' promise to support Save the Children's out-of-school-time initiative, the National Association of Head Start Centers' plan to place Foster Grandparents and Retired Senior Volunteer Program (RSVP) volunteers in 45,000 Head Start Centers, and a Navy and Marine Corps proposal to establish partnerships reaching 700,000 youth.

Some critics questioned whether America's Promise, the nonprofit organization set up to continue the work of the Summit, would compete with other youth and volunteer organizations. They also raised concerns about measurement and the accountability of those making commitments. Other critics complained about a lack of coordination between the national and local levels and argued that few nonprofits expecting to attract new funders through the Summit had actually done so. Most observers agreed, however, that the Summit succeeded in raising the visibility of service and increased the involvement of individuals and organizations, particularly the business community, and that many new partnerships were created as a result of the effort.[9]

One of five Summit goals, "to assure that all young Americans have an opportunity to give back to their communities through their own service," continues to be a major part of followup conducted by America's Promise. A task force assembled to assist with implementation of the Summit goals set targets for the year 2000: two million additional young people providing at least 100 hours of service each year through high quality programs; 100,000 young people becoming service leaders by providing 1,000 hours or more of high quality service each year; and colleges and universities committing at least half of the nearly one million work-study positions to service to the community.[10]

Today, thanks in part to *TFH*, there are tens of thousands of service leaders around the country, and any table of advocates for youth service would include former presidents from both parties, General Colin Powell, governors in dozens of states, and mayors in hundreds of cities. As a result of the support of foundations, corporations, churches, federal, state and local government and thousands of individuals, today 46,000 young people serve in youth corps around the country, an additional 40,000 Americans are part of the AmeriCorps national service program, three million young people participate in the annual National Youth Service Day, and more than 15 million young people serve through schools, colleges and community organizations. This strong foundation brings us closer to the reality contemplated by the W.T. Grant Foundation Commission: that all young people —whether college-bound or not — have opportunities to render needed service.

SCHOOL-BASED SERVICE-LEARNING

"Service-Learning answers the question I am most frequently asked by students: When am I ever going to use this stuff?" Teacher Connie Smithson, Hixon High School, Tennessee

"It's like messing up your room; if you messed it up, you've got to clean it." Sheldon, Vermont elementary student Lydia Kennison participates in the River Keepers effort to clean up Vermont's polluted Mississquoi river.

Through the National Literacy Corps, more than 1,000 high school juniors and seniors are tutoring elementary school students in reading and writing with significant results. At Lincoln High School in Philadelphia, for example, 80 percent of the second graders at a nearby elementary school are now reading at their grade level, compared with just 57 percent before the Lincoln High tutors began. Teachers report an increase in positive behavior and higher motivation among students being tutored. The tutors themselves have benefited through increased academic achievement, attendance and plans to continue their education.

Many advocates of youth service look to schools as a way to make service the universal experience of children growing up in America. *The Forgotten Half* specifically called for the

[c]reation of quality student service opportunities as central to the fundamental educational program of every public school, including (a) either a requirement that each school provide opportunities to every student for a voluntary service-learning program eligible for elective credit toward graduation, or a graduation requirement of a specified amount of service; and (b) age-appropriate curricula and instruction, including both service and class-based reflection, during each year from kindergarten through twelfth grade." It also called for "[s]tate-level encouragement of local school jurisdiction efforts to enlist the young in serving their communities, including the provision of sufficient financial and technical assistance to ensure high quality programs. (p.85).

Service-learning is a method:
(1) For students to learn and develop through active participation in organized service experiences that meet actual community needs and that are coordinated in collaboration with the school and community;
(2) That is integrated into the students' academic curriculum or provides structured time for a student to think, talk, or write about what the student did and saw during the actual service activity;
(3) That provides students with opportunities to use newly acquired skills and knowledge in real-life situations in their own communities; and
(4) That enhances what is taught in school by extending student learning beyond the classroom and into the community and helps to foster the development of a sense of caring for others.[11]

Once the passion of a handful of isolated educators and pioneering foundation officers prior to the federal government's involvement, service-learning has gained widespread support as a strategy to build sound character and values, develop civic awareness and involvement and improve student learning. Several recent national efforts, such as the Partnering Initiative, have galvanized support from mainstream educators and community organizations. These new efforts join national groups that have long been advocates for service-learning, such as National Youth Leadership Council, National Society for Experiential Education, Community Service Learning Center, Council of Chief State School Officers, National Association of Partners in Education and American Youth Policy Forum.

With funding from the Corporation for National Service, 48 states are administering service-learning programs through state education agencies. In 1998, however, Maryland was still the only state to *require* all public school students to engage in service-learning in order to graduate, and the class of 1997 was the first to be affected by a state-decreed mandate to complete 75 hours of service. In Minnesota, state funds enabled the number of school-age students involved in service to grow from 30,000 in 1989 to over 173,000 in 1994.[12]

Other states have begun to integrate service-learning into state educational standards or to connect service-learning to the state's education reform initiative. Colorado is integrating service-learning into its New Standards Project by developing a "how to" manual for connecting service-learning with performance-based assessment strategies for reading, writing, mathematics, science, history and the social sciences. Vermont has linked its service-learning initiatives to such reform efforts as the state's Common Core of Learning,

Goals 2000, and school-to-work transition. Moreover, it required that districts engage in a state-led pilot portfolio assessment project using service-learning as a primary strategy.[13]

The number of schools and students engaged in service-learning is difficult to tabulate. U.S. Department of Education statistics for 1996 suggest that about half the students in grades six through 12 performed some community service (although not necessarily service-learning) during the past year. This proportion was significantly higher for Catholic and other private school students than for public school students, higher for wealthier schools than for those with large numbers of low-income students, and higher for students whose adult family members volunteered than for those whose families did not. Eighty-six percent of students were in schools that encouraged community service and of those who participated in service, more than half reported it was incorporated into the curriculum. Sixteen percent of public school students and 42 percent of private school students reported that their schools required community service.[14] In comparison, a 1992 Department of Education study found that 44 percent of high school seniors had performed service in the previous two years and that less than eight percent of seniors said they did so because it was required by their schools.[15] A follow-up study of 1992 high school seniors found that those young adults who had performed community service in high school were significantly more likely to continue to volunteer than those who did not.[16]

The annual nationwide survey of college freshmen conducted by UCLA confirms that the number of high school students performing service is growing slowly but steadily. The UCLA study found that, in 1997, the percentage of students performing volunteer work in their last year in high school had reached a new high, 73 percent compared with 62 percent in 1989. But at the same time, the study found that the nation's college freshmen demonstrated the lowest levels of political interest in the history of the survey, with just 27 percent believing that "keeping up to date with political affairs" is an important life goal. Similarly, the number of freshmen surveyed saying they hope to become involved in programs to clean up the environment, help to promote racial understanding, or participate in a community action program also declined.[17]

Authors of the UCLA study attribute the growth in the number volunteering to the increasing number of schools making service a requirement for graduation. While this rise in volunteer service by young people is a positive development, the decline in political and social activism is cause for concern. These seemingly incongruous results may suggest that youth may see service as an alternative to political action, and that many schools requiring service do not support service-learning that incorporates sufficient programmatic content for students to understand its significance in a larger educational and civic context. The differential impact on young people of volunteer service and service-learning is worthy of further study.

The Forgotten Half argued that "[o]nly programs that properly train and engage the participants and provide an atmosphere for serious reflection on the meaning and impact of the experience are ultimately worthwhile." Recent research supports this conviction. The 1997 evaluation of Learn and Serve America found that well-designed, fully implemented service-learning programs increase students' sense of responsibility, acceptance of cultural diversity, work orientation, college aspirations and school achievement.[18] Importantly, this study, which examined only programs that met specific quality criteria found far stronger results than an earlier evaluation that looked at a larger set of programs of mixed quality. Another study found that students participating in Learn and Serve America-funded programs in Florida had better attendance, higher grade point averages and fewer discipline referrals than prior to their participation.[19] Unfortunately, however, there is very little high quality research on service-learning, and much of what is available does not tell us whether the programs studied met accepted quality standards.[20]

The kind of sustained commitment implicit in a program based on a significant number of hours of service is one element of a quality program. The Learn and Serve America evaluation reported that the programs studied involved an average of 77 hours per student. However, experts believe that a high quality service-learning program involves not just a significant number of service hours, but is connected to an organized curriculum, involves students in planning the projects, engages them in reflection that enables them to process what they have observed, and involves meaningful service that students can see benefits others.[21]

In order to emphasize the importance of quality and to reward schools that implement exemplary programs, President Clinton proposed that middle and high schools meeting specified criteria be honored through the President's Leader School Initiative. The Service-Learning Clearinghouse, operated by a consortium led by the National Youth Leadership Council, offers technical assistance to schools and community-organizations looking to implement service-learning programs. These and other efforts to encourage high quality are needed to help programs and students achieve their full potential.

While well-designed, well-run programs can be done at minimal cost, some resources are essential. Teachers must be trained to integrate service into the curriculum. Costs of insurance and transportation must be covered. And programs must be able to hire service-learning coordinators to help design service projects. Resource-strapped schools, particularly those serving large numbers of low-income children, may be least able to direct even modest resources to support service-learning. Yet, there may be the students who have the most to gain from an experiential curriculum that defines them as valued resources instead of future failures. Studies tend to show the greatest impact of service-learning occurring among "at-risk" and minority youth.[22]

Fortunately, the kinds of reforms needed to support quality service-learning go hand-in-hand with changes advocated by experts concerned with improving student achievement. Providing teachers more time to prepare lessons, decreasing class size, providing flexible scheduling options, adopting team teaching and multidisciplinary approaches, as well as increasing connections between the school and community all create an environment conducive to service-learning approaches.

In addition, schools should recognize students as a valuable resource who can help the school respond to a variety of needs. Organizations hosting Learn and Serve America students reported high levels of satisfaction with the young volunteers, with 90 percent stating that they had helped the agency improve their services and 96 percent saying they would participate in the program again.[23] Creative schools will find ways to use service to address priority needs. They can involve high school students in tutoring younger children, which has been shown to increase the achievement levels of both youth-tutored and tutoring.[24] Schools can connect service projects with school-to-career programming, which is appropriate because of the experiential nature of both approaches. They can use conflict resolution and peer counseling to decrease violence and drug use among students. And schools can use service as a strategy to offer enriching programming for out-of-school hours, a period when millions of children spend time supervised only by their television set or a distracted older sibling. By engaging students in service related to the priorities of the school, service-learning need not compete with basic programs, but can become a cost-effective way to address important needs.

COMMUNITY-BASED SERVICE

"To know that people need me does a lot for me. It has given me a sense of wanting to be successful. Sometimes people you're helping depend on you." Shanekha Young, a freshman at Western New England College and 1997 National Service Scholar, began volunteering with Save Our Kids as a peer tutor, mediator and mentor while in high school.

Since 1991, the National Crime Prevention Council's Youth As Resources (YAR) program has helped juvenile offenders become successfully reintegrated with their communities. "I had a bad attitude for a while, but YAR kept me looking forward to something... Now I have staff coming up to me all the time who used to say stuff like, 'You better be good,' and now they're telling me, 'You are going places soon.'... Helping people, that helps me too," says one young volunteer. Christopher Debruyn, former commission of the Indiana Department of Corrections, confirms the power of the program to turn lives around: "It has shown us grizzled veterans in corrections that there is a better way to do things."

Through the YMCA Earth Service Corps, children at 56 Y's in 22 states are building their leadership skills and learning that environmental problems often have an impact close to home. Whether organizing beach cleanups, promoting recycling, or keeping a local animal shelter from closing, teenage members of the Corps are learning that they can have a positive effect on their neighborhoods.

Service by young people has always been a central feature of the youth programs of religious institutions, YMCAs, 4-H, Girl and Boy Scouts, Red Cross, civic groups and many other youth-serving organizations. While some community-based organizations have developed high quality service-learning programs, linked to schools or to nonacademic curricula, others fall into a volunteer service model, in which learning outcomes may be secondary to community benefits.

It is difficult to tell how many young people are involved in service through community-based organizations. According to Independent Sector,[25] 59 percent of teenagers engage in service. Seventy-five percent of young people who belonged to a youth group volunteer, as do 80 percent of those youth active in a religious organization. The Big Help, an annual campaign sponsored by the Nickelodeon cable TV channel, urges children to pledge volunteer hours and, in 1996, 8.5 million children pledged 92.5 million hours of community service.[26] These efforts support an important point borne out by studies: that children who are asked to serve are likely to do so, while those who aren't asked, don't.[27]

Community-based service-learning programs offer many of the benefits of school-based programs. Similarly, the elements that create high quality school-based programs should also be present in community-based programs in order to ensure positive results.

Twenty-four million children ages 5-14 spend unsupervised time during out-of-school hours.[28] These hours, in comparison to the tightly scheduled school day, offer an excellent opportunity for regular service activities. Youth who are too old for child care and too young for paid employment need structured activities after school, weekends and summers.

Many young people are already involved in community-based organizations in their neighborhoods, through their places of worship, or with their families. Integrating service into existing youth programs can be a cost-effective way to engage more youth in service. Doing so will help to avoid imparting to young people the sense that they are "clients" being served and, instead, build their self-esteem and belief in their ability to have a positive effect on their communities. Recognizing the potential of youth service, Big Brothers Big Sisters recently called for each "big" to help their "little" become a volunteer, pledging during the Presidents' Summit 100 percent participation by the year 2000. A recently formed alliance of civic organizations, including Boy Scouts, Girls Scouts, Veterans of Foreign Wars, Future Farmers of America and Lions Clubs International have pledged, as part of their drug prevention strategies, to invest "time and resources to assist young people to learn the importance of volunteer service."

Because they offer the opportunity for full-time, intensive service experiences and help fill the need for supervised, constructive activities when school is not in session, summer service programs hold great potential. Summer service programs combining elements of service-learning, civic responsibility, career exploration and youth development could have a dramatic impact on young people during early adolescence. Youth corps and other community organizations meet this need in some communities, but they engage only a small fraction of school-age youth. There continues to be a great need for summer programming, particularly for children too young for paid employment.

COLLEGE CAMPUS-BASED SERVICE

Zayannab Abdu-Shaahid heard about JumpStart through the Work Study office in her first year at City College. It was "something to explore," and she liked the people. Now she is hooked. "It's not just a job — I'm trying to get my parents to understand it," she says. "It's a commitment." A 21-year-old education major, Zayannab thinks her one-on-one service at a Head Start Center in West Harlem will be good preparation not just for her future career, but for her role as mother to a two-year-old daughter. "Everyday I'm thinking, 'what can I use on her?'" Zayannab says.

"I used to think volunteers were saps," says Val Joseph, the 25-year-old founder of Inner Strength. "In seventh grade, my principal said I was stupid — 'ain't never going to be nothing.' I thought I would die by 16," explains Val. With the help of caring adults, Val was able to go on to college, despite his experience living homeless, belonging to a gang, and getting kicked out of four different high schools. While a student at Morehouse College he met a kid selling drugs. "We just talked — he's my first," says Val, whose personal experience helped him connect with the youth. Val applied for fellowships from echoing green and Southern Community Partners to help him start Inner Strength, which deploys student volunteers from six Atlanta colleges to mentor, tutor, and teach conflict resolution to more than 100 youth, including 30 who are currently incarcerated. Val sees evidence that it's working: among youth in the program attendance is up, violence is down, and attitudes have improved.

While service has been part of campus life for the better part of this century, the 1980s brought new energy to postsecondary student service. At a time when students were thought to be self-interested and apathetic, young people played a leading role in sparking a service movement on college campuses. In the mid-1980s, organizations like COOL (Campus Outreach Opportunity League), which promotes student leadership in campus service, and specialized groups like the National Student Campaign Against Hunger and Homelessness, Student Coalition for Action in Literacy Education and Student Environmental Action Coalition were created to provide a national network and visibility for student-led service. The Bonner

Scholars Program provides scholarships to selected students with strong records of service, financial need and good academic records who commit to serving ten hours a week during college.

Also in the mid-1980s, higher education leaders, including Harvard's Derek Bok, Frank Newman and the late Ernest Boyer challenged colleges and universities to become more actively engaged in responding to the country's pressing needs.[29] Campus Compact, a network of college presidents, was created in 1984 to "cultivate discourse and support" for service. Since its founding, 20 state-level compacts have been formed and the number of national member institutions has grown from about 100 to more than 570 campuses involving 837,000 students in service each year.

Support for campus-based service-learning has also grown. Higher education institutions, particularly graduate and professional programs, have traditionally placed students in internships or clinical settings to provide practical experience to apply what they learned. In the 1980s, campuses began to extend this integration of service and learning to undergraduate liberal arts courses. The three-volume resource book, *Combining Service and Learning,* published by the National Society for Experiential Education in 1990: the widely disseminated "Principles of Good Practice for Combining Service and Learning," published following a Wingspread conference in Racine, Wisconsin; and other resources both legitimized service as a learning strategy and offered guidance for the development of quality programs. In 1994, a group of faculty members convened by Campus Compact created the "Invisible College," educators committed to sharing service-learning information with others. An 18-volume monograph published by the American Association for Higher Education is one product of the Invisible College; for the first time, this series provides discipline-specific information about service-learning for a wide-range of subjects.[30]

These developments — involving students, college administrators and faculty — combined to increase service opportunities dramatically on many campuses. Service programs took many forms. Some campuses created service centers. Others hired "green deans" (recent graduates hired to help organize service programs). Some provided support for student-led service organizations. Still others expanded the range of course offerings to include those with service components linked to academic course work.[31]

Federal funding for campus-based service, even after passage of the National and Community Service Act, has been limited. Federal Work Study funds, however, have the potential to augment greatly the $10 million in Learn and Serve America funding set aside for campus-based service. Work Study funds have been available for community service since 1964, although the amount used for off-campus service placements was less than one percent until 1994, when amendments to the Higher Education Act sponsored by then-Senator Harris Wofford required a minimum of five percent.

In 1997, President Clinton announced the America Reads Challenge, an effort to ensure that all American children would be able to read well by the end of third grade. He asked that colleges meet this challenge by voluntarily deploying 50 percent of any increase in federal Work Study funding to literacy efforts. As of February 1998, 915 institutions had pledged to meet the challenge. The President also asked Congress to expand the Work Study program to more than $1 billion and one million positions a year, an increase of 250,000 positions over 1995 levels.

Although Work Study provides millions in stipends for community service, it does not provide the program support funds that are so often necessary to ensure quality placements. Entrepreneurial service programs have sought to make good use of Work-Study by marrying these funds to Bonner Scholarships, AmeriCorps or Learn and Serve America program funds. For example, JumpStart places Work Study and other students in Head Start centers to provide one-on-one attention to low-income preschoolers. AmeriCorps provides education awards and, together with private sector donors, funds a training program so extensive that JumpStart members qualify for their Child Development Associate (CDA) credential when they complete their service. Most Work-Study community service programs, however, do not provide training or program support.

Because of the wide-range of different program structures found on campuses, it is hard to assess the benefits to the students themselves. As with school-age programs, some campus-based programs focus solely on benefits to the community while others are intended to enhance students' leadership abilities, civic responsibility and academic learning. A 1996 evaluation of Learn and Serve America's Higher Education program[32] which compared program participants to a control group found that service increases commitment to helping others, while promoting racial understanding and influencing social values and political structures. It also found that student service-providers exhibit higher levels of academic achievement, aspiration and involvement. On life skills measures, the study found that student volunteers had greater social self-confidence, interpersonal skills, understanding of community problems, knowledge and acceptance of other races and cultures, and self-perceived leadership ability than other students. A nine-year longitudinal study by Campus Compact and the Higher Education Research Institute (HERI) at UCLA confirms that college students who participate in community service are more likely to socialize with persons from different racial and ethnic groups and participate in community service work after college.[33] Other studies have found that volunteering by college students increases their appreciation for democratic participation and significantly increases their civic skills.[34]

Clearly, these benefits are desirable for at-risk and low income students. But these students may face barriers that make it difficult for them to become involved in service. Lower-income students may need to seek paid employment in addition to their academic load, which leaves little time for service. They may be older with significant family responsibilities. They are underrepresented at private, liberal arts colleges which are most likely to encourage service, and overrepresented at community colleges, which have been slower to embrace curricular-based service programs.

The provision of stipends through Work-Study or other sources, along with greater integration of service into academic learning may increase involvement by members of the Forgotten Half in campus-based service. It may also prove attractive to use service to build connections between schools and colleges in several ways. It can offer a valuable resource to schools in the form of tutors, mentors, or service-learning coordinators. It can expose younger children to positive role models. And, it has the potential to increase the number of students who go on to college and become engaged in service on campus and after they graduate.

FULL-TIME SERVICE
AmeriCorps

"I saw my dream dying until this came along." Former AmeriCorps member Janelle McGee's hope was to finish her college degree and teach high school English once her kids were in school. After serving with the Simpson County, Kentucky SLICE Corps, a tutoring program which raises children's reading levels an average of three levels in one year, McGee returned to college with an education award of $4,725 and the confidence to pursue her dream.

Ernest Azebedo was an active gang member in San Jose and served time in jail before joining Public Allies. Now he finds jobs and other alternatives for young people to release the grip of gangs. Azebedo's work has been recognized by the Mayor's Task Force on Gangs.

Sharon Holmes was homeless for 2 1/2 years because of drug and alcohol problems. Now sober for four years as an AmeriCorps member in Augusta, Georgia, she helps the homeless obtain birth certificates, housing, and medical care. "I can point to a number of people whose lives she's changed this year by making them face up to their own situation," says Reverend David Clay, director of Augusta Urban Ministries. "How can you put a dollar amount on someone getting back into society?"

Mateo, from a Native American community in Southern Colorado, grew up poor and fatherless in East Los Angeles. When he "fell into the negative attitudes and actions" of his peers in middle school, mentors and family helped steer him back in the right direction. With their support, Mateo went on to graduate from Stanford University. "I wanted to be able to afford an opportunity to work with my community full-time while still paying rent, bills and a burrito or two on the side," says Mateo. "I wanted an experience that would bring me back to the 'real deal.' This is what brought me to AmeriCorps." He joined the San Francisco Urban Service Corps as a service-learning coordinator; three years later, he is a new father, senior project director with the Corps, and a volunteer with numerous youth organizations.

Several hundred AmeriCorps members serving with more than 50 Habitat for Humanity affiliates help to recruit, train and organize thousands of local volunteers. In Miami, Florida, 23 members engaged thousands of college students, professionals and senior citizens to rebuild more than 70 houses following Hurricane Andrew. In Philadelphia, 11 AmeriCorps members provided crew leadership for short-term volunteers, enabling seven families to move into new or renovated houses in 1997; before AmeriCorps's involvement, just one house was completed annually. "We at Habitat for Humanity feel privileged and honored to have the AmeriCorps people with us, and we want more of them," says Millard Fuller, Habitat Founder and President.

Nearly 200 corpsmembers from the National School and Community Corps serve in Philadelphia and New York City schools providing before school, afterschool, Saturday and summer programs. Funded by schools, parent associations and AmeriCorps, the Corps has involved 200 teachers and 2,500 students in service-learning projects, as well as another 20,000 students and adults in other activities -- including tutoring, book clubs, safety and fitness programs. "They are so thoroughly involved I wonder how we managed without them," according to one teacher. Parents agree: "When you ask for help, you get it," says one. "The NSCC is the best thing that ever happened to us," according to another. For corpsmembers, the reward is immediate: "It does a lot for your heart."

Ten years ago, *TFH* called for "legislation that would provide federal funding to launch youth service programs." The report cautioned that states and communities should "retain wide latitude in the design of programs that meet local needs." It proposed the revitalization of the Peace Corps and VISTA and it suggested a National Youth Conservation Corps to work primarily in national parks, wilderness areas and national forests.

A decade later these recommendations had become reality. More than 44,000 Americans are expected to serve in AmeriCorps in 1998, which is federally-funded but locally-controlled. VISTA, now part of AmeriCorps, has grown by more than 50 percent. President Clinton also proposed to expand the Peace Corps from 6,500 volunteers to 10,000 by 2000. In 1994, AmeriCorps's National Civilian Community Corps, a residential national youth corps with an emphasis on the environment, was launched. In 1998, it numbered 1,000 members on five campuses.

AmeriCorps funding has both expanded existing programs and seeded new ones. AmeriCorps funding, supplementing private-sector support, assists diverse programs such as Public Allies, which trains young community leaders from diverse backgrounds, Teach for America, which recruits talented recent college graduates to teach in urban and rural schools, and Volunteer Maryland, which uses AmeriCorps members to recruit volunteers to serve in local nonprofit organizations.

Federal legislation requires all national service programs to meet educational, public safety, environmental and other human needs. In keeping with the Corporation's encouragement of focused programs with measurable objectives, new programs selected for funding often target a single community need. For example, San Francisco's Partners in School Innovation places teams of AmeriCorps members in schools undergoing major reforms. Action for Children Today, a national program sponsored by the National Association of Child Care Resource and Referral Agencies, trains AmeriCorps members to increase the supply and quality of infant/toddler and school-age child care. In 14 New Hampshire counties, AmeriCorps members assist victims of stalking, domestic violence and sexual abuse.

The AmeriCorps motto is *"Getting Things Done,"* which underscores the importance of serving the community. However, AmeriCorps sponsors are also required to develop outcome-based objectives for strengthening the community and developing participant opportunities. Regulations require that grantees provide GED assistance to members who have dropped out of school, help those completing the program to make the transition to education or employment, and provide skills training needed for performance of service. Providing child care and health care benefits in addition to the poverty-level living allowances, along with the option of half-time service (for half-time stipends), helps make it possible for individuals from low-income backgrounds to participate.

One in ten AmeriCorps members has dropped out of high school and two in ten have not attended college. One in four is under age 21, and one in two is between the ages of 22 and 29. Two in ten have a household family income of less than $10,000, and more than half have household incomes of less than $30,000. Twenty-nine percent are African American, 16 percent Hispanic and 42 percent white.[35]

The demographics of AmeriCorps members are directly related to the types of programs that are part of the AmeriCorps National Service Network. More than 3,000 organizations — state and local governments, schools, colleges and nonprofit institutions — recruit and place or supervise AmeriCorps members who are selected based on locally-determined criteria. For example, the National Service Legal Corps fields teams of attorneys, social workers and paralegals at legal services offices nationwide. Action for the Homeless in Baltimore recruits individuals who were formerly homeless, college graduates, and a range of individuals from 20 to 50 years old to help homeless families obtain housing and services. The Catholic Community Services program in Newark, New Jersey, deploys community members, including ex-inmates, to assist adjudicated youth make the transition from probation to jobs or school. This system has yielded a diverse mix of

AmeriCorps members nationwide. At individual service sites, however, one often finds a homogenous group of members. This lack of diversity at the program site has occurred despite regulations requiring that programs "[a]gree to seek actively to include participants and staff from the communities in which projects are conducted and ... of different races and ethnicities, socioeconomic backgrounds, educational levels and genders, as well as individuals with disabilities, unless a program design requires emphasizing the recruitment of staff and participants who share a specific characteristic or background."[36] Diversity at the site level is a valued goal. It helps break down barriers between different racial and ethnic groups and enables local members who know the community to work alongside individuals from other places who have needed skills. The Corporation's 1997 - 2002 strategic plan calls for increasing the number of people of different backgrounds serving side-by-side.[37]

In order to make the federal dollar go further, and as an indicator of local or private sector buy-in or support, AmeriCorps programs are required to raise matching funds, including a portion from private sector sources. To respond to Congressional criticism concerning the cost of each AmeriCorps member, the Corporation agreed to reduce the federal share of the budgeted average cost per member to $15,000 by 1999. (AmeriCorps opponents charged that annual per member costs were as high as $70,000 when, in fact, the General Accounting Office of the U.S. Congress determined that real costs were under $19,000.[38]) In addition, the Corporation allocated a share of education awards to AmeriCorps members serving with nonprofit programs that provide living allowances and programmatic support without a grant from the Corporation. These "education awards only" sponsors include such organizations as the National Council of Churches, Boys and Girls Clubs and the United Negro College Fund. Fourteen thousand such AmeriCorps positions have been approved with more than 5,000 sponsored by faith-based organizations.

Now in its fourth year, AmeriCorps has demonstrated benefits that more than equal the costs. Several analyses, validated by the General Accounting Office, found that every dollar spent on AmeriCorps programs returned from $1.60 to $2.60 in benefits.[39] AmeriCorps has touched the lives of more than 4.5 million Americans, including the 700,000 students who were tutored or otherwise assisted, the two million Americans who live in cleaned-up neighborhoods, and the more than 100,000 homeless people who were given food or shelter in AmeriCorps's first year alone.[40] Ninety-seven percent of community representatives surveyed in a national evaluation believed that AmeriCorps members were making a difference in the day-to-day lives of residents of their communities.[41] More than 70 percent of placement sponsors reported that AmeriCorps members were performing service that was extremely useful to their communities, with only eight percent believing there was any overlap or conflict between AmeriCorps and the work of other community organizations.[42] The General Accounting Office confirmed that AmeriCorps is achieving valued results in communities.[43]

Although opponents contended that a living allowance would somehow reduce the nation's volunteer spirit, the evaluation found that AmeriCorps members engage as many as eight non-stipended volunteers for every AmeriCorps member.[44] Traditional volunteer organizations have reported that the program has been "an enormously beneficial addition to the traditional voluntary sector... [R]ather than replacing volunteers or diminishing volunteerism, we are finding over and over again that national service participants are helping draw more volunteers into service in communities across the country."[45] Red Cross President Elizabeth Dole concurred that national service "will enlarge the means by which individuals can make a difference in their community."[46]

Furthermore, AmeriCorps has had a significant positive impact on the organizations where members serve.[47] The national AmeriCorps evaluation found that 80 percent of community representatives interviewed thought AmeriCorps programs had succeeded in promoting collaboration.[48] A University of Minnesota study also confirmed that AmeriCorps created:

> a culture of cooperation and collaboration. In community after community it became a catalyst for people to work together to find new ways to solve problems... Organizations became more aware of the services and operations of their counterparts ... thus enabling them to avoid duplication and improve the quality of service delivered.[49]

AmeriCorps has also played a role in helping community-based nonprofits become more aware of and responsive to the needs and views of those they serve. "AmeriCorps, it would appear, is a program that gives service clients a friend in power, a voice to speak for them within the agency, an interpreter of their struggles with the larger world," according to a study by Rutgers University and the George H. Gallup International Institute.[50]

AmeriCorps appears successful at benefiting those who help others, including increasing the civic commitment, educational opportunities and life skills of members. The evaluation found strong evidence of civic responsibility in members and reported that they rated "contributing to the well being of their communities and the people who live in them" as the most important aspect of their experience.[51] As for educational opportunity, although 16 percent of AmeriCorps members entered the program without a high school diploma or GED, the evaluation found that 97 percent said they intend to pursue higher education, and 70 percent said they felt the education award was necessary for their future studies. Those programs in the survey that had enrolled members without a high school diploma or its equivalent provided assistance to help these members earn their GED. Most program sponsors tried to help members plan for their lives after AmeriCorps, with nine out of ten providing training to promote awareness of opportunities for college and a similar percentage offering training to help members set more long-term educational goals. The study reported, however, that programs "did not always offer under-represented members the kind of intensive forms of intervention that are necessary if 'at risk' youth are to make a successful transition to college."[52] Finally, the evaluation found evidence that the program increased members' communication skills, ability to work within an organizational structure, self-discipline, teamwork, self-confidence and ability to deal with people unlike themselves.

In his book, *The Bill*, Steven Waldman describes AmeriCorps as a Swiss-army knife "performing numerous useful functions in one affordable package."[53] Because of the program's ability to provide needed services and strengthen communities while developing participants' skills, citizenship and educational opportunity, AmeriCorps holds great promise for America's young people. As the program matures, it will be important to study what has been effective, and to refine AmeriCorps' approach to achieving each of these goals, keeping them in balance.

YOUTH CORPS & YOUTHBUILD

Back in 1988, as a high-school dropout and member of the Crips, a notorious Los Angeles street gang, Arthur Bonner sold drugs, stole cars, cracked heads and soon ended up spending over six years in juvenile detention and prison. Upon his release from jail at the age of 22, Bonner signed up with one of the "good gangs" — the Los Angeles Conservation Corps. Through his work on environmental service projects, he discovered the El Segundo Butterfly Habitat, home to the "Palos Verdes Blue," a rare and fragile species of butterfly found nowhere else on earth. Intrigued, he began to volunteer at the Habitat on weekends and, after completing his year in the Corps, he landed a $26,000 a year job to help save "the Blues." Now 27 and the recent winner of a National Wildlife Federation award for outstanding work in conservation, Arthur leads inner-city kids on field trips and spends the weekends with his four-year-old son.

Vicki Young joined Serve Houston to gain more experience after unsuccessful applications to medical school. Her service at Casa de Esperanza de los Ninos, which operates group homes for children who are HIV-infected or at high risk for abuse or neglect gave her the experience she needed to realize her dream of becoming a doctor.

The Milwaukee Community Service Corps (MCSC) in partnership with the Milwaukee Housing Authority (MHA), created an on-the-job training program in urban rehabilitation and construction. The goals of the program are to: 1) help young adults develop the skills and experience needed for successful employment and 2) successfully complete non-routine maintenance and modernization work. MHA awarded MCSC a $500,000 contract in 1993 for training and construction. Corpsmembers replace windows, learn basic masonry techniques, fit new dryer vents, and perform modernization work and cosmetic landscaping. Crew supervisors train corpsmembers in the use of a wide assortment of tools and techniques. Many of the corpsmembers are recruited from the housing projects where the work is to be performed. The program serves as a pre-apprenticeship component for future employment of corpsmembers. Approximately 60 corpsmembers go through MCSC programs each year with a placement rate of 56 percent (working or in school full time).

The past ten years have witnessed the expansion and strengthening of youth conservation and service corps which specifically engage "the forgotten half" of America's young people in meaningful service. This progress results not so much from targeted federal funding as it does to a growing recognition at the grassroots level that service is an effective strategy for using the same dollar — whether public or private — to address multiple social goals simultaneously.

Among the oldest and largest full-time service programs in the country, youth conservation corps are heirs to the legacy of the Civilian Conservation Corps (CCC), a Depression-era public jobs program. From 1933-42, the CCC employed six million young men in conservation work that dramatically improved the nation's public lands, while also providing President Franklin Delano Roosevelt's "CCC boys" with food, shelter, education and a precious $30-a-month stipend that literally saved many of their families from hunger in tough times. For many Americans times are still tough and — like the legendary CCC of the 1930s — today's youth corps are a proven strategy for giving educationally and economically disadvantaged, out-of-school young men and women the chance to improve their communities, their own lives and those of their families for the better.

Beginning with the establishment of the mighty California Conservation Corps back in 1976, the corps movement has evolved into a diverse patchwork quilt of state and local programs stitched together by a shared commitment to youth development and community service. In 1988, *The Forgotten Half* reported on 50 youth corps; a decade later there are 110 corps operating in 33 states and the District of Columbia, enrolling over 20,000 young people in year-round and summer programs and delivering 13 million hours of service annually.

Some corps are part of state government agencies and focus primarily on conservation projects, often in wilderness areas; the majority, however, are community-based nonprofits which perform environmental work in an urban setting and address an array of neighborhood revitalization and human service needs as well. Among other things, corps protect and restore the fragile ecosystems on public lands, revive green spaces and play places in urban neighborhoods, and buttress the efforts of paid staff in health clinics, youth centers, residential care facilities for the elderly and countless other human service delivery settings.

While the organizational structure and kind of service projects performed vary considerably from corps to corps, most share a common framework:

- Corps accomplish tangible, visible projects that otherwise would not be done.
- Corps organize young people ages 16-25 into crews that work under the supervision of an adult leader.
- The young people who participate in corps receive stipends approximating minimum wage; they generally devote 32 hours or more each week to service projects and another 8-10 hours to education and life skills development.
- Because 60 percent of corpsmembers arrive without a high school diploma, corps provide GED classes and offer other educational activities to improve the math and literacy of those who do have a diploma.
- Corps also improve basic skills through work-based learning so that corpsmembers gain the reading, writing, and critical thinking abilities that employers demand.
- Corps ensure that young people acquire valuable work skills, preparing them for future employment in the public and private sectors.

A case-control study of youth corps completed by Abt Associates/Brandeis University in 1996 determined that corps yield $1.04 in monetary benefits *over and above costs* for each hour of service they perform. (Cost efficiency increases as corps grow larger and gain experience. This figure does not include *non*-monetary benefits such as workforce preparation and diversion from less productive pursuits.) Eighty percent of project sponsors polled rated corps' work as "good" or "excellent." Most notably, the researchers found that — compared to the control group of similar individuals not enrolled in corps — corpsmembers worked more, earned more and were less likely to be arrested. The outcomes reported for young African-American men who participate in corps are particularly striking: they work more, earn more, vote more often and earn more associate degrees than a comparable group of their peers. This evaluation confirmed earlier studies by Public/Private Ventures which determined that youth corps are highly successful in promoting youth development.

YouthBuild programs, mentioned earlier, are a subset of the conservation and service corps. Eighty percent of YouthBuild members dropped out of high school, 40 percent come from families on public assistance, 30 percent have been adjudicated, and all are poor. But YouthBuild's history, program design, funding pattern, outcomes, national network structure and strategies for expansion are different from corps in several important respects.

YouthBuild was invented at the grassroots level, in East Harlem, between 1978 and 1984. It started as an effort by former school teachers to organize teenagers to think of themselves as potential leaders and to take responsibility for their community by creating tangible community improvement projects. The program did not grow out of the Depression-era CCC, but out of the civil rights movement and antipoverty programs of the 1960s, and the community development movement of the 1970s.

YouthBuild members split their time between building affordable housing and preparing for the GED or obtaining a high school diploma in a YouthBuild alternative school. Leadership development through program governance and community involvement is a core tenet of YouthBuild while personal and group counseling is built into the program. Placement in jobs and college at the end of the program is another program objective, often accomplished in partnership with employers and local trade unions. With such strong supports, 83 percent of YouthBuild graduates are placed in jobs with a wage average above $7.50, and 18 percent go on to college.

A 1993 evaluation carried out at MIT of early YouthBuild programs found that the program was successful in helping youth manage their time, develop leadership skills, become responsible parents and avoid drugs and crime. The study found that YouthBuild helps large numbers of corpsmembers obtain their GED and go on to further schooling or employment. These results were particularly dramatic given the population enrolled in the demonstration programs evaluated: 65 percent had prior dealings with the criminal justice system and one-third had been convicted and incarcerated for felonies.

Understanding the potential of corps, including YouthBuild, private grantmakers made investments in the late 1980s and early 1990s that significantly strengthened and expanded the field. Foundations collectively invested more than $10 million to capture the best practices of existing corps and infuse them into new urban corps in 15 cities through the Urban Corps Expansion Project. Foundation grants were also responsible for supporting the establishment of YouthBuild USA in the early 1990s to serve as a national support center and the replication of YouthBuild in ten cities.

Shortly thereafter, new Federal funds — authorized by Subtitle C of the National and Community Service Act of 1990 — prompted unprecedented growth within the youth corps field. A June 1992 survey of the corps, undertaken by the National Association of Service and Conservation Corps (NASCC), identified 63 "pre-Federal funding" youth corps; the follow-up 1993 survey identified 104 corps programs, many of which had been in existence for less than one year. While these earmarked Federal funds, totaling $22 million annually, lasted for only two years, they did help many corps to start-up, stabilize their operations and build alternative sources of support. In 1993, $40 million was appropriated under the Housing and Community Development Act of 1992 for YouthBuild, enabling the network to grow from 15 programs engaging 600 members in 1993 to 108 programs engaging 4,600 in 1996. Congress has made an appropriation for YouthBuild every year since 1993.

By and large, however, the youth corps movement has grown and matured without a dedicated source of Federal funds and has done so during years marked by a spiraling downturn in support for youth and young adult job training at the federal, state, and local levels. As a result, corps have become skilled at accessing public resources not necessarily intended for services to out-of-school youth and captured under the umbrella of "work-based" funding. Even the large state conservation corps, which receive appropriations from their state legislatures, have begun to diversify their base of financial support.

As recently as 1992, federal funds accounted for just 9.3 percent of total corps operating budgets and came from only two sources — JTPA, administered by the U.S. Department of Labor (DOL), and the Community Development Block Grant Program (CDBG), administered by the U.S. Department of Housing and Urban Development (HUD). A few of the state conservation corps also earned federal revenue through contract work with the U.S. Forest Service.

By 1997, federal grants and contracts — most received through competitive processes at the state and local level — accounted for over 25 percent of the $193 million in total corps funding and came from the Environmental Protection Agency's watershed restoration and air quality programs; HUD's HOPE VI Urban Revitalization, Youth Apprenticeship and YouthBuild Programs as well as CDBG; the Department of Transportation's "enhancements" program; the US Department of

Agriculture's Food and Nutrition Service; and DOL's "Kulick Grants" demonstration program, as well as Job Training Partnership Act.

The long-standing relationship between the Forest Service and the corps continues to generate both work and revenue, particularly for those in the Western states. Most recently, corps all over the country are benefiting from cooperative agreements with the National Park Service, which earmarked new "user fee" revenue to enlist corps to tackle the backlog of conservation projects under the banner of the Public Lands Corps Act.

Fifty corps programs also receive AmeriCorps funds and/or educational awards — mostly through the competitive process managed by state Commissions. In 1997, AmeriCorps funds represented about $40 million or 20 percent of total corps revenue. Almost 5,000 corpsmembers are now co-enrolled in AmeriCorps and benefit from an educational award upon the completion of their service. Thirty-two YouthBuild programs receive AmeriCorps support as half-time programs because program time is split evenly between service and education.

While it is too soon to tell, the new Welfare-to-Work block grants may well become another source of considerable funding for corps. Within the past year, a dozen corps — both state and local — have entered into formal contracts with government agencies to provide services to the recipients of public assistance. Because the corps offer intense, structured work experience as well as education and training, they are well suited to the task of helping young adults move toward economic self-sufficiency.

In terms of financial sustainability for the corps, however, no trend is more encouraging than the consistent growth in non-federal sponsored work revenue which the corps earn through contracts with public agencies and nonprofit organizations in their own communities. This source of earned income represented just 16 percent of total corps budgets in 1992 but exceeded 23 percent in 1997.

The corps have always embraced their role as comprehensive youth development programs. In their infancy and adolescence they survived by concentrating relentlessly on delivering good services to the community and providing solid work and education experiences for the corpsmembers. Now — having matured and secured greater financial stability — the corps have moved the goal of enhanced educational and employment outcomes for corpsmembers to the front burner. A few, including YouthBuild programs in Texas, Pennsylvania, and Massachusetts and the East Bay and Los Angeles Conservation Corps, are already designated as charter schools or are affiliated with one; several have relationships with local community colleges which get corpsmembers started on the road to college degrees and better careers. Spurred on in part by the urgency of welfare reform requirements, many corps are adding new job development and placement staff as well as post-program support services to help their graduates secure and retain decent-paying jobs.

Over the past ten years, the corps have pursued more sophisticated service projects, enriched the educational and youth development content of their programs and mastered the art of juggling multiple funding sources. They have stayed in the business of giving a "second chance" to young people who did not have much of a first, and held fast to the belief that the projects which corpsmembers accomplish in their communities — whether viewed as work training or service — are key to the success of the corps experience.

THE FUTURE: A NATIONAL COMMITMENT

It is within our reach to make service the common experience of every child growing up in America and an abiding ethic valued by our most important public and private institutions. There are opportunities today that seemed impossible in 1988. An infrastructure has been established. We are witnessing rising interest from many philosophical perspectives about ensuring a "civil society" of active citizens. More and more, public interest in service as a strategy to respond to many of today's challenges offers opportunities beyond what appeared possible just a decade ago.

Service can begin in the earliest grades and be integrated into the curriculum at every level. Every child old enough to serve but not old enough to work for pay can serve after school or weekends, and every group that serves youth — through tutoring, mentoring or recreational activities — can help youth to serve. All middle school children can have the chance for a "summer of service" in their own community. Young people who need a "second chance," or who want to make a full-time commitment to service after high school, can join youth corps that offer them education and skills training while they serve their communities. Those who go on to college can put their earlier experience to good use, providing needed services, practicing leadership and teamwork skills, and connecting what they learn in class to real situations. After college, full-time service is again an option for those who want to make a significant commitment. Alumni networks and other organizations can help keep the spirit of service alive for young adults as they begin their careers.

While the groundwork for this system has been laid, to make it a reality would require the nation to make several important commitments. Funders of all sorts must be challenged to look comprehensively at their approaches to youth development, civic engagement and service delivery and to explore how youth service serves these goals. If policymakers consider young people as potential resources, understand service as a strategy to respond to community needs, and appreciate the ways in which high quality service programs can improve the lives of those who serve them, they should see no trade-off between funding for service and support for other programs. Secondly, all youth-serving institutions and organizations that use volunteers to deliver services to youth must learn to "turn it around" and help youth serve others.

Thirdly, education institutions at all levels should connect service to learning from the earliest grades, while reaffirming the mission of schools and colleges to prepare young people to be productive citizens as well as productive workers. A great opportunity exists to make the senior year of high school a year of service. An intensive year of service-learning could build a bridge from school to career and give young adults the "life experience" that will help them get more out of college while connecting schools and communities in important ways.

Finally, communities need to build a new American institution: the "Summer of Service" — especially for middle school-age youth. Using AmeriCorps members, high school and college students and older volunteers to organize youth can help minimize the cost of the program while providing excellent role models for younger children. A ten-week summer program, using AmeriCorps members to lead teams of ten young people, could cost as little as $500 per young volunteer. For a national investment of under $1 billion annually, half of all eighth graders in the country could become part of such programs. Exposing young people early on to service through an intensive learning experience can have a profound effect on their self-esteem, career goals, motivation for learning and sense of community at a time when many youth fall into antisocial or dangerous activities. Connecting their service to money for college could also pay dividends; efforts to get at-risk children on a college track need to begin by the middle grades. Service activities should continue after the summer through after-school clubs or service-learning at the high school level, helping to fill the critical need for constructive activities for young people during out-of-school hours.

FUNDING SOURCES

Creating universally available service opportunities spanning the period from childhood to young adulthood would require a major national commitment, with support from new and existing federal funds, as well as significant contributions from other public and private sources. Federal agencies other than the Corporation for National Service — such as the Departments of Housing and Urban Development, Transportation, Education and Agriculture — today support service programs that address the missions of these agencies in a cost-effective manner. As service gains more and more legitimacy as a strategy to respond to community needs, additional federal, state and local funds may become available from existing social service, education, public safety or environmental programs.

Funding sources like College Work-Study, school-to-work, or welfare reform can be used to support service positions consistent with their legislated purposes. Further, communities can develop partnerships that allow for "cascading" service programs, where AmeriCorps members, senior corps members, college student volunteers or even high school students lead younger children in service.

Service can be integrated into existing youth programs. A teacher or youth worker can be trained in service-learning methods at a modest cost. The teacher or youth worker may also serve as a peer trainer, which is another cost-effective way to expand service opportunities. Pre-service preparation and inservice professional development in service-learning methods should be a priority for funding. In addition, if the promise of the Summit for America's Future is realized, the business community should make available significant resources — both cash and in-kind.

As more nonprofit organizations become convinced of the value of AmeriCorps, they may decide to support the members themselves, with the Corporation for National Service providing just the education award without a living allowance. With two million nonprofit and educational organizations across the country, this strategy for expansion presents great potential. AmeriCorps should continue to encourage program sponsors to pursue private sector funds, with a goal of increasing the matching of federal funds with nonfederal dollars. Providing multi-year rather than annual grants to proven programs will help them attract other funders concerned about sustainability.

Youth corps, including YouthBuild, should be made available in every major city and in every state. Residential programs, which offer a change of environment and more intensive experience, should be expanded. Funding should come from several sources. Initially school districts should consider supporting youth corps as alternative schools for youth having difficulty in a regular classroom setting and those who have completed course work needed for college and who could benefit from a greater understanding of the community. Second, Congress should consider dedicated funds for these programs and continue to expand the YouthBuild program. Third, youth corps should continue to pursue fee-for-service funds; all federal, state and local public agencies should be challenged to contract with corps to perform needed services. Finally, youth corps should be eligible for job training and other dollars dedicated to youth development, whether these funds are from are local, state or federal sources.

As important as expanding service opportunities is strengthening the infrastructure that supports them. It is critical to expand the capacity of state commissions to assist and connect service programs of all kinds within the state, not just those receiving AmeriCorps and Learn and Serve America funds. To perform this task, these small organizations will need additional resources. Funders should support the development and strengthening of a national network of state commissions and other national and regional networks of service organizations. Technology should be supported as a way to connect these networks and speed the sharing of information more broadly. SERVEnet, sponsored by Youth Service America, provides an important foundation for this effort — the website receives 100,000 hits a month — but this and other efforts to explore the potential use of the internet to increase youth service opportunities should be greatly expanded.

All programs should examine their operations to find ways to be more inclusive, particularly of disadvantaged youth. AmeriCorps should continue the core elements that have made it possible for disadvantaged young people to participate, including child care and health care benefits, a livable stipend, provision of GED training and other supportive services, and policies that encourage recruitment of members from the communities served. However, the Corporation should do more to meet the needs of disadvantaged youth, and should carefully monitor and seek to increase the number of such youth enrolled as AmeriCorps members.

STRENGTHENING QUALITY

Finally, major attention and resources ought to be directed at strengthening the quality of youth service programs through the application of high-quality research and evaluation. This effort by the Corporation, foundations, state commissions, research institutions, service programs and others should begin by analyzing existing data. Where high-quality research suggests clear directions, this information should be widely disseminated through publications, training and other means in forms that make it easy for program leaders to incorporate the findings into their practice. Where gaps exist, they should be identified as priorities for future research.

More needs to be known about when diversity is appropriate to achieve specific participant development and community-strengthening goals, and how best to achieve it. Evaluations of AmeriCorps have already suggested the need for more information about how to support and retain "at-risk" corpsmembers, including former welfare recipients. Effective practices for helping members make the transition into education or employment after their term of service are also needed. More research is needed to determine how service-learning programs can best achieve academic impacts, including the effectiveness of specific curricula. Ways to ensure that service leads to other forms of civic engagement should be studied. How service programs of all types can be more effective "getting things done" in specific issue areas should also be explored, beginning with national priority areas likely to receive additional funding. Areas for study might include the use of volunteers as reading tutors, for delivering afterschool child care, to increase access to information technology and to assist in the transition from welfare-to-work.

A top-quality task force composed of researchers, funders, policymakers, and practitioners could be convened to develop a research agenda and a plan for seeing that research results are applied in practice. A project of the task force could be revision of the "Principles of High Quality Practice" developed by the Corporation for National Service before the creation of AmeriCorps. Much has been learned since that time, and the document needs to be updated based on actual experience and evaluation.

This emphasis on using proven practices to improve programs does not mean that program leaders should not draw on their own experience and instincts, which are essential to making programs work well. The rich range of backgrounds of current service program leaders enables the service field to incorporate the knowledge base of many different disciplines, from education and job training to business and law. Service programs should continue to involve people and practices from many fields to contribute to the success of national service. At the same time, efforts should be made to develop career tracks and expand training for professionals within the service field.

Increasing professionalism within the field should not come at the expense of opportunities for young people to assume leadership roles. Consistent with the spirit of youth service, programs should find ways to give them a genuine voice in decisionmaking, to involve them in designing service projects and to represent the program to the public. Every youth service program should have at least two young people on its governing board, and these younger board members should be supported so they can fulfill this role responsibly and learn from the experience. Organizations of youth and young adults in service — such as AmeriCorps Alums and COOL — should be supported and looked to for leadership in the field.

Greater attention to research should not discourage innovation. On the contrary, funders and national organizations should do more to support "social entrepreneurs" — founders of innovative new ventures, usually with a combination of public and private support. In addition, greater attention should be given to the successful replication of proven programs. The current field of AmeriCorps programs includes at least a dozen that, like City Year, YouthBuild, and Youth Volunteer Corps of America, have experience with a "franchise" model. These should be examined to determine what lessons other programs can learn from their experience.

* * *

If we are successful at building the capacity, quality and leadership of the service field, service can become an experience that defines growing up in America. With the strong foundation of the last decade, service can become a part of the life of every child who begins school. And if it works, we can expect that more people will be attracted to the helping professions, and that those who pursue other careers will nonetheless keep the needs of the broader community in view. Americans will volunteer throughout their lives, in both formal and informal ways, and our democracy should grow stronger as civic engagement becomes the norm. As the nation expects more of its young people, they will expect more from themselves, becoming adults who are better prepared to contribute to the economy, democracy and sense of community of our nation.

"If we are successful at building the capacity, quality and leadership of the service field, service can become an experience that defines growing up in America."

NOTES

[1] Sagawa, Shirley and Samuel Halperin, eds. *Visions of Service: The Future of the National and Community Service Act.* Washington, DC: National Women's Law Center and American Youth Policy Forum, 1993.

[2] Sagawa and Halperin; Shapiro, Peter, ed. *A History of National Service in America.* College Park, MD: Center for Political Leadership and Participation, 1994; Waldman, Steven. *The Bill.* New York, NY: Viking, 1995.

[3] Wexler, Jacqueline Grennar and Harris Wofford, co-chairs. *Youth and the Needs of the Nation,* Washington, DC: Potomac Institute, 1979.

[4] Democratic Leadership Council. *Citizenship and National Service: A Blueprint for Civic Enterprise.* Washington, DC: May 1988.

[5] Commission on National and Community Service. *What You Can Do For Your Country.* Washington, DC, 1993.

[6] Blair, Jill. *The Philanthropic Perspective on Community and National Service.* San Francisco, CA: Grantmaker Forum on Community and National Service, 1996.

[7] "The New Volunteerism," *CQ Researcher,* December 13, 1996.

[8] 85 percent of Americans support the use of taxpayer dollars to help fund AmeriCorps, according to a national telephone survey by Wirthlin Worldwide, October 1996.

[9] Dundjerski, Marina and Holly Hall. "America Answers Call to Help Kids," *Chronicle of Philanthropy,* Vol. X, No. 13, April 23, 1998, p. 1.

[10] "Goal 5 Progress Report for America's Promise," Washington, DC: Corporation for National Service, February 5, 1998.

[11] 45 Code of Federal Regulations 2500.2(a)(29).

[12] Kielsmeier, James C. "Harnessing the Trojan Horse: Future Directions in Service-Learning," *Generator,* Vol. 17, No. 1, Winter 1997, p. 4.

[13] National Association of State Boards of Education, *Policy Update,* Vol. 5, No. 17, October 1997.

[14] Nolin, Mary Jo, Bradford Chaney and Chris Chapman. *Student Participation in Community Service Activity.* NCES 97-331. Washington, DC: U.S. Department of Education, 1997.

[15] U.S. Department of Education, National Center for Education Statistics. *The Condition of Education 1996,* p. 146.

[16] U.S. Department of Education, National Center for Education Statistics. *The Condition of Education 1997,* pp. 124-125.

[17] Sax, L.J., A.W. Astin, W.S. Korn and K.M. Mahoney. *The American Freshman: National Norms for Fall 1997.* Los Angeles, CA: Higher Education Research Institute, UCLA Graduate School of Education and Information Studies, 1998.

[18] Melchior, Alan. *National Evaluation of Learn and Serve America School and Community-Based Programs: Interim Report.* Waltham, MA: Brandeis University, 1997.

[19] Follman, Joe and Kate Muldoon. *Florida Learn and Serve 1995-96: What Were the Outcomes?, NASSP Bulletin,* October 1997, pp. 29-36.

[20] Scales, Peter C. and Dale A. Blyth. "Effects of Service-Learning on Youth: What We Know and What We Need to Know," *Generator,* Vol. 17, No. 1, Winter 1997, p. 6.

[21] Alliance for Service-Learning in Education Reform (ASLER). *"Standards of Quality for School-Based Service Learning,"* 1993; Honnet, Ellen Porter and Susan J. Poulsen, *"Principles of Good Practice for Combining Service and Learning,"* 1989.

[22] Drug, James Leonard. *"Select changes in high school students' self-esteem and attitudes toward their school and community by their participation in service learning activities at a Rocky Mountain high school."* Doctoral dissertation, Michigan State University, cited in Scales and Blyth, p. 8.

[23] Melchoir, p. 42.

[24] Scales and Blyth, p. 6.

[25] Statistics can be found on the Independent Sector website, www.indepsec.org

[26] Verzemnieks, Inara. "Volunteers, Never Too Young; Getting Children Involved in Public Service." *Washington Post,* November 4, 1996, p. C5.

[27] Independent Sector found that 93 percent of teenagers who were asked to volunteer did so, compared with just 24 percent of those who were not asked. See the Independent Sector website, www.indepsec.org

[28] Corporation for National Service and the National Institute on Out-of-School Time. *Service As a Strategy in Out-Of-School Time: A How-To Manual.* Washington, DC, October 1997.

[29] Jacoby, Barbara, ed. *Service-Learning in Higher Education: Concepts and Practices.* San Francisco, CA: Jossey-Bass, 1996.

[30] Zlotkowski, Edward, ed. *AAHE Series on Service Learning in the Disciplines,* Washington, DC: American Association for Higher Education, 1997-98.

[31] Liu, Godwin. "Origins, Evolution, and Progress: Reflections on a Movement," Providence, RI: Feinstein Institute for Public Service, Providence College, 1995.

[32] Gray, Maryann Jacobi, Sandra Geschwind, Elizabeth Heneghan Ondaatje, Abby Robyn, Stephan P. Klein, Linda J. Sax, Alexander W. Astin and Helen S. Astin. *Evaluation of Learn and Serve America, Higher Education: First Year Report,* Vol. I. Santa Monica, CA: Rand, May 1996.

[33] Astin, Alexander W., Linda J. Sax and Juan Avalos. "Long Term Effects of Volunteerism During the Undergraduate Years," *Review of Higher Education,* 1998, in press.

[34] Barber, Benjamin R., Robert R. Higgins, Jeffrey K. Smith, Janice Ballou. *"Democratic Theory and Civic Measurement: A Report on the Measuring Citizenship Project."* New Brunswick, NJ: The Walt Whitman Center for the Culture and Politics of Democracy, Rutgers University, April 30, 1997.

[35] Unpublished data, Corporation for National Service Office of Evaluation, February 19, 1998.

[36] 45 Code of Federal Regulations 2522.100.

[37] p. 18

[38] General Accounting Office. *National Service Programs: AmeriCorps*USA — Early Program Resource and Costs of National Service: Methods for Benefit Assessment with Application to Three AmeriCorps Programs,"* June 1995.

[39] Neumann, George R., Roger C. Kormendi, Robert T. Tamura and Cyrus J. Gardner. *The Benefits and Costs of National Service: Methods for Benefit Assessment with Application to the Three AmeriCorps Programs,* June 1995.

[40] Aguirre International. *AmeriCorps State/National Programs Impact Evaluation: First Year Report,* June 12, 1997, p. 20.

[41, 42] Aguirre, p. vi.

[43] General Accounting Office.

[44] Aguirre, p. 39.

[45] *Letter to Members of Congress from Sara Melendez, President, Independent Sector, and others,* April 6, 1995.

[46] *Letter from Elizabeth Dole to Chairman William Ford,* July 9, 1993.

[47] Aguirre, p. v.

[48] Aguirre, pp. vi, 37.

[49] Shumer, R. & Maland Cady, et al. *YouthWorks-AmeriCorps first year evaluation report.* St. Paul, MN: Department of Work, Community, and Family Education, University of Minnesota, 1995.

[50] Van Til, Jon and George H. Gallup, Jr. *AmeriCorps: Twenty Questions and their Answers from a National Study,* 1997, p. 31.

[51] Aguirre, p. 49.

[52] Aguirre, p. vii.

[53] Steven Waldman. *The Bill,* op. cit., p. 20.

CHAPTER NINE

REFLECTIONS ON A DECADE OF PROMOTING YOUTH DEVELOPMENT

Karen Pittman and Merita Irby

The central themes of youth development were articulated ten years ago. The main accomplishment of the past decade has been giving them a name. The youth development language and philosophy have caught on; the policy uptake has been uneven at best. However, the call for a "paradigm shift" from deterrence to development has generated a surprising amount of energy and enthusiasm in Washington and across the country. If used strategically, this positive, normalizing language could foster a national conscience that propels us to do better by *all* our young people, especially those who have been aptly called The Forgotten Half.

THE CALL FOR A COHESIVE STRATEGY FOR PREPARING YOUNG PEOPLE FOR ADULTHOOD

Within a year of each other, two commissions, the Grant Foundation Commission on Work, Family and Citizenship and the Carnegie Council on Adolescent Development, issued reports that reframed the challenges for coming decades.

From the Carnegie Commission's *Turning Points* (1989):

> What qualities do we envision in the 15-year-old who has been well served in the middle years of schooling? What do we want every young adolescent to know, to feel, to be able to do upon emerging from that educational and school-related experience?
>
> Our answer is embodied in the five characteristics associated with being an effective human being. Our 15-year-old will be:
>
> - An intellectually reflective person;
> - A person enroute to a lifetime of meaningful work;
> - A good citizen;
> - A caring and ethical individual; and
> - A healthy person.
>
> The challenge of the 1990s is to define and create the structures of teaching and learning for young adolescents 10 to 15 years old that will yield mature young people of competence, compassion, and promise.

From the Grant Commission's *The Forgotten Half: Pathways to Success for America's Youth and Young Families* (1988):

> Young people's experiences at home, at school, in the community, and at work are strongly interconnected, and our response to problems that arise in any of these domains must be equally well integrated... All young people need:

- more constructive contact with adults who can help them guide their talents into useful and satisfying paths;
- opportunities to participate in community activities that they and adults value, especially giving service to others;
- special help with particularly difficult problems ranging from learning disabilities to substance addiction; and
- initial jobs, no matter how modest, that offer a path to accomplishment and to career opportunity.

These commissions focused on different age groups and, to some extent, different systems. *The Forgotten Half* helped focus the country's attention on a vulnerable population – non-college bound youth – simultaneously pushing age boundaries for support and challenging the adequacy of social, economic and vocational supports for those not in trouble, but not in college. The Carnegie reports focused on a younger age group and the systems that serve them – schools, health, community-based organizations. Both offered lists of desired youth outcomes and critical community resources that spanned systems and levels. Both offered broad agendas calling for systemic and social reforms. And most importantly, both focused on the preparation of young people, rather than solely on the prevention or amelioration of their problems. Other reports have followed since, but these two reports set the stage for a decade of work focused on building on youth's potential.

The number of programs, policies and initiatives addressing these challenges that were proposed, started or expanded since the publication of these two reports is too numerous to count. With the assistance of HUD funding, YouthBuild – a training and leadership program employing out-of-school young adults in housing rehabilitation – has become replicated nationally. Boys and Girls Clubs of America have developed a foothold in low-income housing projects. Dedicated youth development taxes or authorities have been established in a number of cities as diverse as San Francisco and Savannah. The Youth Development Community Block Grant – a bill reallocating existing federal prevention funding into a dedicated funding stream – was introduced but not passed in Congress. There have been significant wins and losses.

But numbers aren't really the issue. There were plenty of high quality youth programs in 1988. *The most significant change over the past decade has not been in the quality or quantity of programs or policies that promote youth development, although there have been improvements in both. It is in the increased acceptance of youth development as a broad goal requiring intentional monitoring and intervention.*

"Youth development is not a happenstance matter." This simple statement, made more than a decade ago by the Youth Committee of the Lilly Endowment, sums up the progress that has been made in the last decade in focusing attention on the need to promote healthy youth development. There is now, much more so than a decade ago, a strong public sense that youth development is not a happenstance matter: a general awareness that society will not reap the youth outcomes desired without a greater and more intentional investment not only in deterrence, but in development. Without a doubt, there are those who believe that youth violence and teen childbearing are happenstance matters, subject only to swift and harsh deterrence strategies. But most of the public believes that growing up is much harder than it was a generation ago. And most adults have a nagging sense that deterrence is not enough – that we leave youth development to chance at our own peril.

Increased access to drugs, weapons, X-rated materials; decreased access to supportive adults, summer jobs, libraries – all these make it easy to understand why young people's development should not be left to chance. The introduction of a framework that a) doesn't vilify young people and b) simultaneously validates the role that community organizations and adults play in youth development has been met with enormous enthusiasm around the country.

As Blank and Steinbach related in Chapter Four, the past decade has seen significant enactments of this philosophy. Public/Private Ventures embarked upon a multi-year, multi-site demonstration project designed to strengthen community supports for youth. The Search Institute engaged over 400 communities in using its Asset Building model. The Coalition of Community Foundations for Youth embraced youth development as the over-arching approach to promote among its members. The Center for Youth Development launched a multi-city mobilization campaign. The National Network for Runaway and Youth Services (now the National Network for Youth) and the National 4-H rewrote their mission statements to underscore a commitment to community youth development. The Department of Health and Human Services and the Office of Juvenile Justice and Delinquency Prevention fully embraced the concept, shifting research and program dollars toward community supports for youth development. Localities from San Francisco, California, to Pinellas County, Florida, leveraged public dollars to support broad, developmentally-focused youth services and activities. And grandest in reach, if not yet in impact, The Presidents' Summit for America's Future sounded a clarion call to everyone from multinational corporations to individual citizens to step up their commitments to provide American youth with the fundamental resources they need to succeed: caring adults, safe places, healthy starts, education for marketable skills, opportunities to serve.

The phrase "youth development" is now fairly well ingrained in the U.S. policy lexicon, undergirded by the bumper sticker phrase "problem-free is not fully prepared." But the overall impact of this language shift is uneven. What has really been accomplished in the last decade? What hasn't? What is needed in the next decade?

THE PARADIGM SHIFT: SIX ASSERTIONS

"Paradigm shift" is one of the many overused terms of the 1990s. In this case, however, it is the appropriate term. The decade spawned the development of a number of frameworks put forth as either descriptive or predictive youth development frameworks. Behind them all are six fundamental assertions about the goals, process, inputs, settings and strategies required for positive youth development, as well as about young people themselves. When taken together, these assertions remind us of things we know, and call into question the youth-related goals, strategies and priorities of everyone from policymakers to philanthropists to pollsters. They suggest that we have to focus beyond prevention, quick fixes, basic services, overburdened schools and yet more calls for coordination to develop a reality-based vision of what youth need and how, where and when they need it that is both universal (applicable to all youth) and pragmatic (targeting those whose circumstances place them in danger of faultering).

The goal: Beyond prevention. Problem-free isn't fully prepared. Addressing youth problems is critical, but defining goals exclusively in terms of problem-preventing is limiting. We should be as articulate about the attitudes, skills, behaviors and values we wish young people to have as we are about those we do not want. Academic competence is important, but not sufficient. Social, health (emotional and physical), vocational and civic competence are all needed to be fully prepared. But competence in and of itself is not sufficient. Young people need skills and they also need confidence, character, connection to family, peers and community.

The process: Beyond quick fixes. Development doesn't occur in a vacuum and it doesn't stop because program funds run out. Adolescent development, like human development, is ongoing, uneven and complex. It is difficult to address one aspect of development without at least acknowledging, if not addressing, the others. Equally important, development requires engagement. It is fostered through relationships, influenced by environments and triggered by participation. Adults can provide services to young people without their engagement, but they cannot foster their development.

The inputs: Beyond basic services. Young people need affordable, accessible care and services (e.g., health, transportation), safe and stable places and high quality instruction and training. They also need supports — relationships and networks that provide nurturing, standards and guidance — and opportunities to try new roles, master challenges and contribute to family and community.

The settings: Beyond schools. Schools are pivotal institutions in most young people's lives. Young people also grow up in families, in neighborhoods, with community-based organizations, workplaces and employers, and service agencies. All of these are settings for interactions and, consequently, settings that can contribute to or undermine development.

The strategies: Beyond coordination. Promoting youth development requires more than the coordination of fragmented, problem-focused services. It requires vision. Efforts have to be early and sustained. It is futile to ask at what age it is best to intervene. Development is ongoing and so must be the services, supports and opportunities. No one program, organization or setting can provide everything that young people need. Joint accountability is essential.

The youth: Beyond labeling. All young people are engaged in development. Most need additional support in navigating choices and assessing options. A growing number need significant expansion in their supports, choices and options. All may be at risk, but the risks are not equal, and risks do not define potential. Targeting is fine, labeling isn't.

Beyond recipients. Young people need services, supports and training. They also need opportunities to be contributors. The best preparation for tomorrow is participation today. Young people's participation should not be seen only as contributing to their personal development. They can and do play critical roles as change agents in their communities.

Taken together, these assertions are both comforting and disconcerting. They make enormous logical sense, confirming things that we know about ourselves and our children. They help us quickly understand why the childhoods of the majority of Americans over 40 are remembered as supportive, regardless of race, ethnicity, income or geography. And they are supported by a growing body of research.

We entered the 1990s well armed with the knowledge that problems vary. Young people who are doing poorly in school are also more likely to be young people who drink, smoke, use drugs, have unprotected sex and commit crimes and misdemeanors. As we end the 1990s, we have not only an increasing amount of evidence about the characteristics of resilient youth, but also growing survey data bolstering the argument that the best way to prevent problems is not to narrowly reduce risks, but to broadly strengthen the individual, family and community assets that young people have in their lives.

Bonnie Bernard at the Northwest Regional Educational Laboratory has taken the research on young people who, by virtue of their backgrounds, should have faltered but did not and boiled it down to three factors in their lives: *caring adults, high expectations and opportunities to participate.* In addition, these successful young people have some common individual assets: good social skills, problem-solving skills, a sense of purpose and a sense of independence. Peter Benson and his colleagues at the Search Institute have done pioneering survey research on sixth through twelfth graders, generating amazingly consistent data that show that the more assets young people have in their lives the more likely it is that they will engage in positive behaviors and the less likely it is that they will engage in negative ones. And the federal government has underwritten one of the largest adolescent surveys ever – the AddHealth Study – to further document the relationship between assets, risk factors and adolescent behaviors, and to explore the roles of families, schools and communities.

THE PRIORITIES DRIFT

The paradigm shift has both sparked and been reinforced by a wealth of research and demonstration studies. But from a policy-making perspective, the shift has muddied the waters. The lists of outcomes, outputs and strategies embedded within the six assertions are inviting when seen as options lists. Policymakers and planners can choose which things to support. But they are daunting if presented as a package. To be effective, they must be a package.

Promoting youth development isn't about picking any one of these things. It is about supporting all of them – protecting those that are strong and compensating for those that are weak. The ambitiousness (and diffuseness) of the prescription stifles planning and implementation. In the real world, especially the policy world, choices have to be made in order to get things done. No program can be truly comprehensive (addressing all outcomes with equal weight), no initiative completely integrated (coordinating efforts across all settings). It is a sad truth that overly ambitious programs, policies or initiatives stall or die under their own weight.

Youth development proponents (ourselves included) made several strategic choices over the decade that, in hindsight, may have diffused energy and resources. First, we argued for too long that everything could be done. We offered insufficient guidance to communities, program planners and policymakers who agreed with the vision but wanted assistance in prioritizing the work – leaving many feeling guilty that they could not deliver "the whole works."

Second, once we realized that everything really couldn't be done, we began to pick and choose among the listed items. The criteria, however, were more personal than strategic. Subtly but steadily, the youth development movement became less about promoting broad, critical use of the framework by the broadest range of actors engaged in improving the lives of young people and more about promoting youth-serving organizations and their issues and strategies. There is no doubt that the role of community-based youth-serving organizations in promoting youth development has been underfunded, underpromoted and undervalued. But advocacy on their behalf, sparked in large part by the success of *A Matter of Time,* the Carnegie Council on Adolescent Development report that focused on the voluntary youth-serving organizations, has been so strong that the term "youth development" has become most closely identified with the specific sub-areas for which these organizations are known: the younger age group, the non-academic competencies, the non-school hours, the less vulnerable populations, the softer inputs (e.g., caring relationships, opportunities to participate). The architecture of the field began to take precedence over the advancement of the approach.

Third, we confused logic with evidence. In part because youth development advocates turned their attention inward toward the critical tasks of field-building, there was insufficient attention paid to fortifying the evidence base. We were embarrassingly unprepared for the "prevention is pork" arguments that were flung freely during the 1994 federal Crime Bill debates and the 1995 appropriations rescission battles. The American Youth

Policy Forum's compendium, *Some Things DO Make a Difference* (1997) amassed a powerful collection of evidence, but it came too late to make a difference in the struggle of 1994-95. (It was, however, cited in the Senate's 1998 work leading to the Workforce Investment Act.)

There are easily twice as many examples of things done well. As we think about the next decade, however, the shortfalls are more instructive. They are shortfalls, not wrong decisions. All of the choices were and are still valid. Combined, however, they drained the movement of some of its momentum. Articulation of common sense proved to be a powerful motivator, but an inadequate guide for action. We have not forged a clear path from enlightenment to investment in sensible public policies or sustained public support.

AN EMERGING AGENDA

The youth development movement is like a truckload of hothouse plants – lush colors, plentiful blossoms, shallow roots. If youth development is to be useful as a galvanizing theme, these plants will have to be pruned, fed and landscaped. More importantly, they will have to be taken out of their pots and trained to grow not only in their own hothouse, but in the fields and along the fences that define the major public policy areas that affect young people's lives – education, family support, juvenile justice, health, child care, social services, housing, employment, economic and community development, income support and so on.

There are some specific opportunities on the horizon, like the current interest in expanding after-school programming and community schools, that can be built upon, as Blank and Steinbach have elaborated in Chapter Four. And some ongoing battles (e.g., in juvenile justice) still need to be fought. Stepping back from these, however, there are six broad suggestions that might aid the transplanting process:

1. Put the primary focus on the young people, not on the programs. A youth-focused definition of youth development could go as follows: *Youth development is the ongoing process in which young people are engaged in building the skills, attitudes, knowledge and experiences that prepare them for the present and the future. The youth development process is smoothed and youth development outcomes enhanced when adults (as individuals and professionals) work with young people to help them set and monitor their course <u>and</u> work with youth and each other to ensure that the course options are plentiful, positive and varied.*

The first sentence reinforces the role of young people as key actors in their own development. The second sentence has two parts. The first part (direct work with young people) ensures the success of some young people by helping individual youth beat the odds. The second part maximizes the success of the majority of young people by helping communities change the odds.

Youth organizations have stellar track records in the first part – bringing together the right mix of adult supports and opportunities to help individual young people beat the odds. But most youth organizations do not have the wherewithal – financial, political and human resource – to help the majority consistently. Doing so requires changes beyond their doors – in schools, crime-fighting, housing, jobs. Youth organizations have to figure out – honestly – what role they can play in helping to set community goals for youth and to deliver on community inputs. In the end, this may mean that youth-serving organizations take on more monitoring and coordinating functions and make fewer big ticket claims on implementing.

These organizations can, and should, go after some key pieces, such as after-school programming. Doing so effectively will require very clear articulation of the financial and programmatic advantages they bring. It will probably also require assuming partial responsibility for improving academic outcomes.

2. Engage the public systems, connect to popular public issues. There are strong elements of the youth development message in many of the school reform, juvenile justice, youth employment, adolescent health and prevention initiatives and policies developed over the past decade. The National Youth Employment Coalition, for example, has embraced youth development, making adherence to sound youth development one of three areas in which programs self-assess. (The other two are organizational effectiveness and youth employment and training practices.) Prevention curricula coordinators in state and local public school systems used the paradigm shift to argue for consolidation of the separate prevention curricula and better integration with the core academic curricula. Everyone acknowledges that these systems are slow to change. But they are where the young people and the resources are. We need to rekindle early efforts to tailor the presentation and language of the framework to these institutions and work with them as they engage in their own reform efforts. Youth development advocates should bear the burden of translation.

The same advice applies to youth development advocates' connection to popular issues and strategies. Ones that address positively stated needs and opportunities, such as mentoring, after-school programming and community service, as well as ones such as teen pregnancy, smoking and violence prevention that address risk behaviors.

3. Link with larger community development and change efforts. As previously mentioned, five years ago the National Network for Youth coined the term "community youth development" to reflect the challenge to its members to go beyond their commitments to high-quality programs and services to make commitments to link themselves and the young people they serve more firmly to the communities in which they live. The Network's formal language reflects a growing recognition that young people, especially adolescents and young adults, cannot and will not (unless forced) grow up in programs. Community supports are critical to their development. As we refocus on the approach, we need to look aggressively for ways to learn from and link with efforts to strengthen and engage families, residents, citizens and communities. Increasingly, experts in the range of community-building strategies – community development, community organizing, neighborhood revitalization, economic development and family support – are recognizing the importance of young people as service recipients, residents and occasionally resources. Community development corporations are steadily increasing their interest in and commitment to providing youth services and engaging youth leaders. Community organizers, especially in immigrant neighborhoods, are finding young people a valuable resource. Economic development experts are wooing young people as the next wave of entrepreneurs. And there are a growing number of efforts to rekindle civic pride and community ownership by engaging the younger generations.

If it is to move, the youth development philosophy – which may in many cases boil down to a commitment to see young people as resources and investments, not as threats or cost-centers – has to find its way into a broader set of discussions about rebuilding communities.

4. Promote ongoing efforts to define youth indicators. The current selection of indicators for tracking youth progress is decidedly negative. Whatever the titles (e.g., *Kids Count; Indicators of Child Well-Being*), the data reported are about problems and services. It is absolutely true that problem-free isn't fully prepared. But it is also true that problem-free is also an accomplishment. The challenge is not to replace the current indicators – which focus on problems and on long-term outcomes like graduation and employment – it is to expand and, equally important, to organize them. The new additions (e.g., volunteer hours) have to be clearly linked to the old. And all of the indicators need to be grounded in a framework that makes sense.

In 1998, the federal government recently released the second annual indicators report on children and youth, *America's Children: Key National Indicators of Well-Being.* While there are dozens of factbooks and compendia of national and state data, this report is the product of an interagency working group that came together to select the official indicators for the country. Marketed correctly, the release of these numbers could carry at least a fraction of the authoritative weight that the government's release of leading economic indicators does. Youth development advocates may write off the exercise because it doesn't capture enough positives. But we could also work to expand the positives that are monitored.

Many indicators beg for international comparisons. Such comparisons lit a fire under Americans in the 1980s when the international teenage pregnancy and childbearing data were reported by the Alan Guttmacher Institute, and they continue to generate sparks in education. And most of the categories (e.g., education, health, family security) beg for a consistent mix of indicators. The current mix of *resource indicators* (e.g., available college scholarships, clinics, dentists), *status indicators* (e.g., poverty, immunization, enrollment), and *behavior indicators* (e.g., pregnancies, test scores) is not even across the categories. Whatever the quality of the indicators, the youth development cause would be better served if the public could catch on to the idea that, in every basic category, *resources* connect to *status conditions* connect to *behaviors*. If poor children continue to go to poor schools they will achieve and attain poorly.

5. Reinforce the importance and wisdom of parents. Interestingly, a good portion of what we know about early childhood care and development was learned by observing parents – both good parents and troubled parents. The centrality and intuition of parents in the early development of their children is non-debatable. But how often are the parents of adolescents consulted or observed? The youth development framework, on the one hand, is common sense with footnotes. On the other hand, there is relatively little appreciation of the wisdom and centrality of parents, even though year after year, polls show that a majority of young people either do (or want to) talk with their parents as key advisors and look to their parents as role models. While true that, developmentally, early childhood is the time for bonding and adolescence is the time for separation, we should not let the superficial differences in parent-child relationships (early adoration vs. adolescent antagonism) lead us to the conclusion that the parents of adolescents and young adults are clueless. We could learn much from observing and reflecting on their balancing act.

Hugh Price, President and CEO of the National Urban League, has stated, "youth development is what you'd do for your own kid on a good day. We don't need a fancy definition to know what to do." He is right. Growing fully prepared youth isn't as simple as A + B = C. But it isn't rocket science, either. Probably only one in 20 parents could label the steps they take, and only two in a thousand would label them the same way. But it is quite likely that parents would quickly develop a common list if interviewed.

There are six steps most parents or guardians take to support their children and, in fact, that most young people take to protect, prepare and promote themselves:
- ✓ **Reality check.** Where are they developmentally — cognitively, emotionally, socially, physically, spiritually?
- ✓ **Goals check.** Where are they aiming? What knowledge, attitudes, skills and behaviors do parents and children want to achieve? Avoid?
- ✓ **Progress check.** Where are they now? What progress? Are the goals still realistic targets?
- ✓ **Inputs check.** Are they getting what they need? Is the fuel supply adequate? Is the fuel mix correct?
- ✓ **Settings check.** What are the possible sources of needed fuels? Are they adequate? Marginal? Dangerous?
- ✓ **Overall community check.** Is the overall settings mix right? Is it easy to piece together a steady diet of needed inputs or is it necessary to bypass or compensate major settings (like schools, neighborhood blocks) that are not functioning well?

These six "checks" for parents are not interchangeable, but they are interlinked. While policymakers and programmers may arbitrarily select among them, parents work them together more organically in ongoing assessment of their child's needs. But even when parents have a strong sense of what is needed, they often cannot find (or afford) the supports they seek. Community supports need to be developed in such a way that they help parents to help their kids. This is the place where youth development advocates have misjudged public opinion. There is a strong, long-standing belief in this country that youth development starts with families – not programs or initiatives. Consistently (especially but not exclusively around issues of reproductive health), the public pulls back when programs seem to be less interested in helping families help their children than in helping young people help themselves.

Youth development advocates have, understandably, taken an approach biased towards encouraging young people as independent actors and, more importantly, protecting young people from hazardous or punitive home situations. These elements should not be lost, but, rather, balanced with a recognition of the wisdom of parents and the central role they play in the lives of young people. As with early childhood, a major support for parents could be the teaching of good parenting skills for adolescents based upon lessons learned from parents and backed up by research and practice in youth development.

6. Shift from lists to lenses. There is an algebra to youth development that parents and young people intuitively use. It is one that we have yet to translate into powerful, policy-adaptable equations. The current language of youth development is at once too broad and too narrow; too dense and too thin. Broad and dense, but getting sharper, in its definitions of outcomes, progress indicators and inputs. Thin and erratically broad and narrow in its definitions of settings and communities. At times, "community" means everything and everyone associated with or in proximity to a young person. At other times "community" is used quite narrowly to refer to the nonprofit organizations that have youth development as a primary goal. Neither reference is solid ground for building policy or articulating practice.

If young people are to get the services, opportunities and supports they need in this country, policy planners, organizers and researchers must find ways to assess the fuel mix as it is supplied by all of the fuel sources in a community (families, schools, CBOs, peer groups, faith organizations, gangs, etc.). Parents do this every day. Poor fuel mixes are one of the primary reasons parents move residences when they can afford to.

Why push for formulas? *Because youth development **requires** multiple inputs from multiple sources over a sustained period of time.* Formulas are the way to show concrete interrelationships between multiple variables. Lists (of desired outcomes, essential inputs, etc.) inform, but they don't instruct. More importantly, they give funders, practitioners and policymakers a false sense that they can choose to support their favorite outputs, inputs or settings at whatever levels they feel comfortable.

Example: A community-based organization with a "good fuel" output of three units a day can complement the mix offered by an adequately functioning school or family. But it cannot compensate for the fuel mix dosed out by a poorly functioning school or family or neighborhood that pumps out 15 to 25 units of fuel that is not only thin but also harmful. Equally important, that organization may not have the capacity (even with increased funding) to provide the right mix at the right volume to help all of the students in need. Pushing it or allowing it to claim as much in order to receive grant funds isn't helpful.

Communities, in the geographic sense, are combinations of families, neighbors, schools, faith and civic organizations and community-based organizations, businesses, public and private services which include basic places like parks and ball fields. What we need are concrete ways to talk about and gauge how key settings interconnect to improve or contaminate the fuel mix for the kids they touch. Each setting should be 1) held accountable for providing the inputs needed to produce the outcomes it claims are its primary goal, 2) pushed to provide other inputs that could be added without averting resources from that goal and 3) monitored to ensure that, they are doing no harm in any area.

The first lesson learned by youth development advocates was that it is unproductive to insist that everything be done simultaneously. The more recent lesson is that it is equally unproductive to insinuate that anything can be done in any order or at any level of scale and consistency. There is a logic to the list of assertions. And there is an internal logic to how the outcomes, inputs and settings fit together. We may never get to formulas (and probably really shouldn't try except in rhetorical ways), but we should be able to craft rough lenses that help communities assess their strengths and weakness (or force them to confront them) and push them to prioritize responsibly.

A SUCCESS STORY

The youth development framework has served community-based youth organizations well. It has helped define their role, promote the youth work profession and quantify the need for expanded reach and resources. But the framework has the potential to work across systems. It must be adapted and integrated more broadly if there is any hope for meeting the increasing needs of young people, their families and their communities. Only by expanding and integrating beyond what have become the more traditional confines of youth development can this increased reach be achieved.

Any attempt to expand the reach of the youth development philosophy and approach must be balanced with attention to ensuring the quality of the efforts as well as strategic decision-making about how to sustain them over time. Effectiveness, scale and sustainability – a troika of goals called for by the International Youth Foundation and others – are useful lenses for strategic decision-making about the youth development framework. All of the pieces of the framework are integrally related and important. Policymakers and planners must think strategically about the full complement of goals, settings, resources and strategies. And they must do so in such a way that clearly addresses the hopes and concerns of the broader public. But how to avoid the trap of picking and choosing among hot topics and single-focused, silver bullet approaches? At any given point, the strategy visible in a city, county or state initiative should be only the tip of an iceberg. Two questions should be asked: Is the rest of the framework intact below the surface? Are the pieces visible above the surface the ones that strategically achieve the broader goals of effectiveness, scale and sustainability?

Success is possible when these questions are both answered affirmatively. Consider, for example, the Beacon Schools in New York City of which there were to be 78 by the end of 1998. The number alone is impressive – suggesting a level of scale in publicly-funded youth programs rarely reached in American cities. The Beacons are one of the field's clear success stories for the decade. But the story is not in the number; it is in the strategy that led to it – a strategy that, at every turn, opted to promote the goals and principles of youth development while intentionally working to ensure the quality, reach and longevity of the effort. By using the lenses of effectiveness, scale and sustainability, we are able to see how they triangulated on a highly visible, politically savvy strategy for achieving scale and sustainability while keeping the overall approach of youth development intact.

Beyond Prevention. The focus was on positives – people, places, possibilities – but with crime prevention as the hook. Funding was secured as part of a comprehensive anti-drug and crime strategy for New York City. Nine centers were proposed instead of an additional prison. Notably, a substance abuse prevention curriculum was not proposed, and funding did not hinge on promised reductions in youth crime and drug use. Instead, the publicly-stated focus was on improving community inputs – increasing the number of safe and stimulating places for young people to go, things to do and people to talk to in neighborhoods where the streets and those on them were the only after-school alternatives. Achieving a full range of positive youth and community outcomes, while not touted for accountability purposes, remains the underlying and ultimate goal.

Beyond Quick Fixes. Within the Beacons are any number of short-term, targeted activities – summer service programs, six-week prevention courses – but specific programming for targeted issues and age groups is embedded within a permanent institution committed to building relationships and the ongoing engagement of young people with ample opportunities to contribute and benefit. Community engagement and ownership was key from the beginning. Young people, parents, residents, community associations and councils were engaged in planning their Beacon. The broad blueprints were filled in by the community. The neighborhood, not the school, was the focal point. Centers serve, support and challenge the children, youth and families of the neighborhood, not only the student body.

Beyond Services. Beacons were designed to provide a full array of services, supports and opportunities for young people and for the full age range in communities. Institutions committed to broad-based development – schools and community-based organizations – were made the key players. Young people and their families were brought in at the beginning to shape the programming and were critical to ensuring that there was a mix of engaging activities and opportunities for participation and leadership both within the Beacon and throughout the community. Parents and young people both teach and take classes (in everything from aerobics to English as a Second Language) and are key planners of and actors in community initiatives. Social services, child welfare, law enforcement and health were brought in later, once the tone had been set.

Beyond Schools. The driving idea behind the Beacons was to expand the hours, activities and actors involved in young people's lives beyond what they find in school. But the commitment was also to do this in permanent, accessible places. School buildings were quickly identified as universal, yet underutilized, settings. While community-based organizations were essential to ensure community ownership and flexible operation, the partnership with schools and government was essential for securing and sustaining resources. Selecting schools as the actual settings for this work did more than open up unused facilities in the before- and after-school hours. From the outset, it laid the foundation for a savvy scale and sustainability strategy. Starting with ten Beacons in 1991, there was a clear realization that going to scale meant starting big enough to capture attention across school districts. The initial placement of these ten Beacons was also strategic. Putting positively-pitched programming in the worst neighborhoods allowed the political process to work for expansion. Parents in less distressed neighborhoods clamored for their Beacons. The publicly-stated goal of at least one in every school district was quickly met and there were 40 Beacons by 1996 with an increase to 78 projected by early 1999.

Beyond coordination. Joint accountability was essential. Schools, along with established community-based organizations and the Department of Youth Services were key members of an unusually well balanced partnership. No single partner wielded excessive power. Schools (selected based on location not interest) provided space. CBOs (selected competitively based on capacity and established neighborhood ties) provided the staffing and basic programming. DYS provided management and funding. The Youth Development Institute at the Fund for the City of New York – a then-young intermediary organization – coordinated the privately-funded technical assistance and evaluation. Private foundations came in as quiet partners supporting training, technical assistance and evaluation.

Beyond Labeling. Initially targeting neighborhoods most in need, the Beacons opened their doors to all members of the community. While activities are most often what brought people through the doors, Beacon staff were prepared to do assessments of the full range of needs and to coordinate services. Over time, as Beacons were able to demonstrate that they could attract large numbers of youth and families that needed critical services, they were able to bring services or the service dollars on-site.

Beyond Recipients. Young people are engaged as significant, if not primary, change agents in their communities – doing everything from physical revitalization of housing and parks to voter registration and political advocacy.

The Beacons are one of the best examples of beginning with a clear blueprint based on the youth development framework – the full set of "beyonds" – to ensure effectiveness, scale and sustainability. Politics was never ignored. Positioning and additional public systems funding and integration were always goals. The strategies were not all successful, but the diligence never let up – in city hall, in the school buildings, in the communities. Parents, the public and the press were key stakeholders to keep the political pressure on. The simple name (Beacons), simple goal (people, places, possibilities) and simple plan (one per district), allowed the media to track progress, parents to label what they knew they wanted for their children and themselves, and the public to rally when the going got hard. Had DYS simply let 40 contracts for substance and delinquency prevention to 40 separate CBOs with different names, not just the expansion but the existence of Beacons would be in question. The public and the press saved them from the chopping block after the change in New York's city administration.

Effectiveness, scale and sustainability. Beacons schools rate high on all three. On effectiveness, they have not only done a good job of adopting the philosophy but training to it and evaluating against it. But they might not have achieved the triple crown had they taken the traditional route – prove effectiveness, slowly increase scale, then (and only then) begin to plan for long-term sustainability. Beacons' master crafters took the best of what is known, pitched it straight – did not overpromise on outcomes – and planned for rapid but sustainable growth from the beginning, building on what already existed. This is the lesson. There is no doubt that the quality of Beacons varies from center to center. But the number of Beacons would not be pushing 100 if these centers had had to be established, funded and evaluated one at a time. We didn't build a public school system or a public health system or a public corrections system that way. And we certainly won't link and blend these systems with the existing community-based infrastructure (for youth and community development) this way.

In an increasingly complex society – where families are becoming more fragmented, working hours of working parents are on the upswing, gun and drug availability is rampant – affluent as well as distressed families are less able to coordinate, much less personally deliver the supports that they once provided. Our challenge now is to help develop healthy and engaged young people by supporting families and communities in their efforts to identify and maintain the right mix of fuel suppliers in their neighborhoods.

Success stories like the Beacons suggest that there are ways to build on and link to services and professionals that exist in neighborhoods while actively engaging parents and young people in securing the supports and opportunities they need. Growing individually and in number, each Beacon school is a dynamic part of the community, responsive to young people, families and service providers. Much more effective than opening up dozens of cookie-cutter service centers that all provide the same menu of supports, the network of community-based Beacon sites is primed to promote the full youth development framework.

They dynamically engage the full range of actors – families, school and human service officials, community members, teachers, service providers, law enforcement officers and, most importantly, young people themselves – in shaping the life and direction of the community. This is the kind of innovative transplanting of the youth development approach that will have to be done if we are to see changes at the scale needed to change the landscape for young people, especially older adolescents and young adults.

CHAPTER TEN

ON THE HORIZON: AMERICA'S YOUTH FACE THE NEW CENTURY

Harold Howe II

Like it or not, today's children and youth will be our leaders, followers, believers and doubters well into the next century. Their knowledge, feelings and viewpoints will fashion not only their world but that of the generation after them. Are we as a nation doing what needs to be done for and with our young people in order to look ahead with confidence? As former Chair of the William T. Grant Foundation Commission, educator and advocate for children and families, I offer this closing chapter of personal perspectives on The Forgotten Half and its future.

REACHING UPSTREAM TO PREVENT DAMAGED LIVES

In 1986, our Commission began its study of American youth and the factors that help them succeed in school, at work, in their families and as members of their communities. Almost as though we were facing a great river, our attention was drawn quickly downstream. There we saw large numbers of older youth struggling in surprisingly deep and turbulent waters. We knew that without immediate help, many would be lost. The real problems of teenagers and young adults cried out for attention. We responded as best we could and with a sense of urgency.

At the same time, the Commission wasn't fooled by more shallow waters upstream filled with younger children seemingly well afloat. We understood that the most troubled teenagers were young children not long ago and that eventually they would become parents of children themselves — often way too soon. Our November 1988 Final Report addressed some of the economic and social issues facing very young families and called for a series of recommendations to support them, including expansion of Head Start, the nation's preeminent preschool program for low-income children. We pointed to the early years as critical, but they were not the major focus of our study.

Ten years later, I am convinced that we must increase our attention to this upstream section of the river. The concept of prevention offers new and powerful possibilities as we learn more from the behavioral and social sciences about human development, particularly in early childhood. We know that academic success is critical. But unless we do much more to improve the broad conditions of children's lives that allow academic achievement to occur — and the many other indicators of lives well lived — we will not have done our job as caretakers of the river and stewards of the future.

Failure to make use of what we know about prevention in the early years is the parent of failure in the later years. Indeed, the first of America's eight National Education Goals, announced by the President and Governors in 1989 states that: *By the year 2000 all children in America will start school ready to learn.* So what has been accomplished since then? According to a 1997 report of the National Education Goals Panel:

> *Current conditions are far from ideal. Too many begin life with health risks. Too few are regularly engaged in supportive activities at home with their families. And far too many do not have the opportunity to participate in high quality care and education programs in safe, caring environments that support their continual development.*

One can't help wondering whether the dignitaries on the National Goals Panel and the rest of this country's leadership take seriously what they say we know about the lives of children — that the least expensive strategy for their healthy intellectual and emotional growth is support in their early years, for all children, not just those whose families can financially provide it. We may know this is true, but most European countries, along with Japan, Australia and other modern countries around the Pacific Ocean have more comprehensive and often higher quality preschool programs, health services and community activities for young children from poor families than does the United States.

Head Start is America's major and most visible and admired enterprise to help the children of poverty prepare for school. But its original purposes have been eroded by thin, rather than generous, financial support and by increasing demands that it serve as a primary source of day care as well as child development.

Head Start was launched — as was Job Corps, a largely successful second-chance program for older youth — in the Lyndon Johnson administration. Its purpose was to help children build confidence in their first steps toward formal learning; to address problems and develop good habits in health and nutrition; to build social skills for dealing with peers and adults; and to actively engage parents in all facets of their children's education. It was also designed to ready children for "the three R's" in imaginative, age-appropriate ways, not by replicating elementary school practices that even older children too often find frustrating and deadly dull.

Head Start's long overdue attention to young children was quickly embraced, especially by the poor and working families it served. Although originally designed as a half-day summer program, parents who needed day care to allow them to finish their own education or to work were anxious to have program hours expanded. Using child care funds, many Head Start centers extended their program hours to meet the needs of working parents. In recent years, funding to increase the number of children served has gained ground — in large measure due to organized parent advocacy. But financial support has been inadequate to attract the most qualified teachers or to provide the training and staff development necessary to stay focused on its original and most innovative developmental purposes. And with current funding, Head Start serves only about 40 percent of the children eligible for its services.

Without new money and hard work, Head Start risks moving from a powerful instrument to launch children and families of poverty into a world of opportunity and learning into a child care custodial program, far short of its original promise. It would also be particularly disastrous if well meant but misguided efforts to strengthen Head Start were allowed to introduce into its curriculum the excessive emphasis on standards and test scores that dominates much of K-12 "school reform" efforts.

Clearly, at our current levels of effort, all children in America will *not* start school in year 2000 ready to learn. As prisons in our society grow many times faster than the growth of adequate early learning and child care, or much needed improvements in teacher skills and knowledge or health services for the poor, don't we have to ask ourselves whether we have forgotten that venerable truism: "an ounce of prevention is worth a pound of cure?" If we intend to keep alive the concept of "The Forgotten Half" as a call to both conscience and action, we must broaden its scope to include the entire river of experience that lies before maturity. In doing so we must reawaken our commitment to education broadly viewed and our investment in our youngest citizens. As we quarrel about what to do with America's first federal budget surplus in many years, we seldom mention Head Start as the best investment for the future, which it surely is.

ACADEMIC EXCELLENCE VS. DECENT LIVES FOR CHILDREN AND YOUTH

In recent years, much of our national attention concerning the preparation of America's youth for future roles as workers, parents and members of their communities has focused on school achievement measures. Without doubt the most powerful document shaping America's views on public education in recent memory was the 1983 report of the National Commission on Excellence in Education, entitled *A Nation at Risk*. On its first page, this remarkable document charged public schools with committing an act of "unthinking, unilateral educational disarmament" and pointed to "a rising tide of mediocrity" among our nation's students. Proving that bad news sells, the report's negative analysis spread like wild fire on editorial pages and talk shows across the country. Its main effect was to focus education reform not on the conditions of young people's lives that lay the foundation for school success, but on standards and assessments as vehicles to improve academic achievement — as though tests alone could help children learn!

Between birth and age 18, young people spend about ten percent of their time in school and 90 percent elsewhere. The quality of experience in the latter sector is a robust determinant of success in the former. It should come as no surprise that standardized test results consistently show higher scores for students from well-to-do-families. This is partly because more affluent students often attend better schools, but mostly it is because their families have the resources to protect them from the hazards of poverty and the multiple risks associated with it. We must bolster our children's in-school hours with a broad range of out-of-school learning experiences.

Average test scores are profoundly affected by the economic status of test takers. The main cause of the SAT score decline in the 1960s and early 1970s was not due to a sudden failure of the schools. Instead, it reflected rapid change in *who* was taking the test. With the opening of new opportunities for college brought on by increased student aid money and the effects of the civil rights movement, large numbers of very low income students, often with less than adequate preparation, began taking the SAT. Their participation increased the number of low-end test scores.

Heavy reliance on test scores to measure school success is equally problematic today. As schools make important efforts to reduce dropout rates and keep lower achieving students in school, state and district-wide assessment measures can show discouragingly low levels of improvement even in committed and effective schools — simply because more young people who otherwise might have dropped out are taking the tests. This perceived lack of progress puts at risk the real accomplishments of these schools: keeping the doors of opportunity open to more children. Lower test scores may result initially, but we can get to work on raising them without getting rid of the children who most need our help.

As Samuel Halperin has explained in Chapter One, many of the young families that schools look to as partners in child and youth development are themselves facing the most serious difficulties. Is it any wonder that families struggling against the economic undertow of poverty do not always have the resources to support their children's schooling as fully as they would like? While the largest number of poor families are white, a disproportionately large percentage come from African American, Latino and other minority groups. As Americans, we are rightfully proud of a Constitution which protects our most cherished freedoms, prohibits discrimination, and ensures fairness. But there are no constitutional rights that protect children from poverty and no legal right that says all children must have a decent life.

Despite constitutional fairness and the vigor of this century's civil rights movement, we are at risk of creating a second class citizenship for our least fortunate young people — damaged primarily because they happened to be born in a poor family. As members of the wealthiest and most powerful country in the world, do we really want to allow this disparity to gain ground? This century's civil rights movement forced a complacent nation to advance it's commitment to fairness and human decency. From where I sit, we have a moral imperative to finish that fight — by doing whatever we can to undo the discrimination caused by the repercussions of a financially unlucky birth.

The education reform movement in the United States over the last 20 years has been dominated by efforts to fix our schools far more than by broader initiatives to improve children's lives. School reform, a long running ball game, is currently being played on two separate fields. One is pitching a narrow emphasis on higher standards and tests to measure their attainment, top down dealing with teachers, and fear of failure as the central motivation for student improvement. Jack Jennings and Diane Rentner speak to some of these issues in Chapter Five. But the real action is on the second field. The game there has concentrated on building change, at least partly, from the bottom up. Its major strategy has been to focus on individual schools and to engage teachers — as professionals

— in the long hard task of making classrooms and schools more effective and interesting places for students and teachers. It stresses more flexible designs created by local schools based on the needs and nature of their students and community. This is exactly what happens in numerous, excellent private schools with no help from government, and we can learn a good deal from their example. Freedom on what to teach and how to teach it in a school's plans for its students constitutes the foundation of academic freedom and of professional status for teachers.

I have been heartened by this later approach to school reform and by the significant and growing involvement of the philanthropic foundation community since the 1980s in helping schools understand their needs and supporting their efforts to try out new ideas. Even though few clear, test score-based results are yet present to verify progress in learning, there is evidence of both improved school attendance and changes in the operation and ethos of schools vigorously seeking change. We need to keep focused on raising young people's school achievement. But the strongman style of Hercules isn't likely to help us untangle the Gordian Knot of school reform. A combination of patience, mutual respect and human relationships that work in each school must join with higher expectations and attention to measuring academic progress.

At the same time, though to a lesser extent, steps have also been taken within a broad education reform movement to improve the conditions of children's lives. A number of these are directly linked to schools by bringing services or activities to complement learning in schools, or by otherwise involving school staff and resources in providing supports that recognize the totality of children's developmental needs. Other initiatives, not formally connected to the schools, are based in the community and available to children and families of school-age children. Wherever they are located, these approaches positively affect the "experiences, values, and ideas they acquire from the environment in which they live," factors which scholars like Professor Mihaly Csikszentmihaly at the University of Chicago remind us profoundly affect the quality of young people's learning. It is for lack of these opportunities to develop "social capital," based on well-developed personal talents, purposeful and trusting relationships with adults and connections to the broader community that both young people and school reform efforts too often fail.

The Grant Foundation Commission contributed to both thought and action in the area of community-based efforts to improve the conditions of young people's lives. The Commission especially called attention to the power of mutual responsibility between young people and their communities' adults; the need to improve the access of children and families to high quality health and social services; and the importance of providing many more vehicles for positive youth development, including mentoring, service-learning and other forms of volunteerism. Martin Blank and Carol Steinbach's Chapter Four describes some of the encouraging actions that communities have taken over the past decade to create better lives for children and youth in the schools they attend and in the neighborhoods where they live. In Chapter Eight, Shirley Sagawa looks at the evolution of youth service during that same period. The Commission's 1988 recommendation for federal funding for youth service programs has become a reality, and the concept of service-learning has taken root in many schools, communities and college campuses.

School reform and efforts to improve the condition of children's lives have moved forward on separate tracks. Each has been wedded to its own strategy and both have been loathe to undertake joint efforts. The Commission viewed this rigid compartmentalization, even animosity, as seriously mistaken. In its Final Report, it underlined the necessity of bringing together these perspectives, noting that "Efforts to produce success in school — without complementary efforts in families and communities — are unlikely to make a substantial difference for young people." Such misguided efforts are shoveling sand against a rising tide.

Today this dichotomy still exists, but there are encouraging signs that the breach is narrowing. A soon-to-be-released study of school-community initiatives suggests that school reform efforts and other school-based, community-involved initiatives focused on service delivery, youth development and community development are increasingly borrowing strategies from each other and blurring the boundaries that have in the past kept them too narrowly focused. It finds that: "The school-community terrain is characterized not so much by separate and conflicting approaches as by an evolution toward blended and complementary purposes and strategies that together constitute an emerging field of knowledge and practice."[1]

Schools and community institutions should both be applauded for opening their doors, expanding their boundaries and putting their arms around our children. But much more needs to be done to sustain and expand these efforts. How should this be done? Daniel Yankelovich argues in Chapter Two, and I largely agree, that major efforts in local communities, corporations, religious institutions, and above all families, have to be at the forefront of building new processes to guide our young people to maturity. He also says that young people themselves must take considerable responsibility for overcoming the public's deep feeling of disenchantment toward them. The current degree of aggravation felt among adults toward youth *is* unusual, though I daresay that adults' negative views about adolescents go back at least to Socrates.

Where I part company is with Dan's view that most new efforts to support young people should not be originated or supported by national or state governmental initiatives and in the extent to which he thinks self-help solutions alone are equal to the immense task. Initiatives like work-study, service-learning and more comprehensive efforts to provide after-school enrichment, access to health and social services or job development and school-to-work opportunities, require a sound institutional base or organizational support. Sponsorship of such efforts in the past has come successfully from the public as well as the private sector. There have, of course, been cases where a government program — and even an occasional privately-funded initiative — has deservedly been faulted for "throwing money at a problem" they didn't know how to solve. But I see the current suspicion of government sponsorship of initiatives for the young as overdone and sometimes merely an excuse to avoid providing much-needed services. In a country that has benefited as mightily as ours has from ideas like the GI Bill, Social Security, Head Start and Title I, we ought to be more willing to consider the possibility of measured, carefully conceived, nationwide initiatives for the young.

From where I sit, the view of the 1991 National Commission on Children, quoted in Carol Emig's Chapter Three makes good sense. That group declared that solutions for children and families "will require creative public policies and private sector practices, thoughtful investments of public and private resources and significant commitment of individual time and attention to the needs of children and their families."

Were we as a nation to meld an emphasis on self-help, with strong support by organized public and private initiatives, the prospects for young people in the next century would be a better bet than they are now. Even so, uncertainties abound. The effects of new welfare reform legislation on children and families are as yet unknown. As Emig asserts, "Welfare was more of a response to public distaste for the system (AFDC) than an effort to alleviate child poverty." Only time will tell whether poor families will be able to survive the impact of tough work requirements when the economy slows down and produces fewer jobs than is now the case.

RACE, ETHNICITY AND SCHOOLING

We are in Hartford, Connecticut. Ninety-three percent of the school children in the public schools are either Latino or African American. More than two thirds of the city's students live in poverty. Six minutes away on the highway are affluent, nearly all-white, suburban, high-achieving school districts that seem a world away.[2]

Halperin's presentation in Chapter One of the stark facts of young families' economic standing speaks volumes about the realities of race, ethnicity and schooling in America. Whether in Hartford or in most other American cities, the continuing effects of poverty have kept low-income youth and their families from riding the current wave of economic growth and prosperity that the rest of the country has enjoyed. But the effects are much greater among some racial and ethnic groups than others.

The gap between the haves and the have-nots warned against in *The Forgotten Half* reports has continued to grow over the last decade. Some gains have been made, as Chapter One shows. But these don't change a central message of *TFH*: In America, poor and minority young people are more forgotten than most. Too many will march into the next century with the firm belief that their country has failed them. It is not surprising that some turn sour in their relationship to this country, our government or to white people generally.

I make no claim to understanding fully the interrelated effects of race and ethnicity on schooling. But we need to begin sorting out these matters more deeply than we have. Two areas of concern offer useful starting points.

#1: What should our policy be toward language learning in American schools by students who don't speak English?

This question goes to the heart of the current intense controversy about bilingual education. Some want to abandon it; some want to change it; and some want to keep and improve it. In my view, informed by competent recent research, bilingual education continues to be our best bet for dealing with students who speak little or no English. When taught by capable teachers, it is way ahead of English-only instruction. This is because young people easily learn the fundamentals of how to read, write and spell in their own language. Then, equipped with strong basic skills, they are able to use them to learn a second language — English. I am concerned that a great deal of the support for English-only instruction has its origin in political and pseudo-patriotic enthusiasm without valid research backing. At its worse, there is an element of discrimination among those who ask "Who do these foreigners think they are, intruding their languages into the purity of our English?"

Far from diluting the purity of English, good bilingual education offers a start in helping American children develop real fluency in more than one language — an enviable skill that is much more widely developed in other countries than in the United States. The recent decision in California to dump bilingual education will come at the expense of young non-English speaking students. In the long run, the provincial attitude it creates will sorely limit our mobility in an increasingly global economy that gains from improved communication.

#2: What school-based activities are needed to help students understand our country's diverse population and their own rights and obligations within it?

Helping students to understand and appreciate America's growing diversity in a country that uses family income as a guide to deciding who goes to school with whom promises to be one of the longest innings in the school reform game. Consider the brief statement about Hartford, Connecticut that begins this discussion. It offers a prime example of how race and ethnic groups are kept separate — and unequal — by economic divisions.

Ours is a country in transition between two points of view toward newcomers. The older "melting pot" approach, dominant in the first decades of this century, said: "Your language and your culture are un-American and unacceptable here. Leave them and become one of us." But today we are moving toward pluralism as a more desirable approach. It says: "We recognize that you bring with you your music, your religions and your customs. Tell us about them and ask us about ours. We ask you to learn about and use democracy's fundamental rights and to share your ideas about what you find here."

In the spirit of these declarations, Americans must begin planning now how their schools will fashion the experiences of children and youth in 2050, when the present minorities will be majorities in many schools. California, at the cutting edge of demographic shifts in minority enrollment, has led all others in developing educational activities to promote successful pluralistic relationships in schools. California Tomorrow, a small but highly capable outfit, for example, has developed truly imaginative ideas using schools as proving grounds for building mutual respect in the midst of the state's growing diversity. But there has also been strong resistance to the changes inherent in pluralism. State legislators have essentially wiped out bilingual learning; they are attacking the eligibility of immigrants for supports that help the poverty-stricken; and they have put such a close lid on school spending that a once admirable school system is in serious danger of becoming a model to avoid.

If the current trend in the Golden State is any predictor of the future, we could find ourselves facing social unrest far worse than the devastating Watts upheaval. Indeed, perhaps a new book about California by Peter Schrag, entitled *Paradise Lost*,[3] describes our fortunes in the next century. If there is a chance to avoid that disaster, it will occur in part because the public schools have been enlisted as places in which Americans can learn about each other. Henry Louis Gates, Jr., a Harvard professor, eloquently outlines such understanding as our last, best option:

> *Ours is a society that simply won't survive without the values of tolerance; and cultural tolerance comes to nothing without cultural understanding. In short, the challenge facing America in the next century will be the shaping, at long last, of a truly common public culture, one responsive to the long silenced cultures of color. For if we relinquish the ideal of America as a plural nation, we abandon the very experiment that America represents. And that, surely, is too great a price to pay.*[4]

In the light of these observations, it is daunting that this country's National Education Goals proclaimed in 1989 make no mention at all of the challenges inherent in our increasingly diverse society. There are reasons for this reticence. Politicians wish to be reelected while diversity issues are often divisive. The most important national questions often are. But Americans have faced worse challenges and prevailed. Helping young people and our society reach for intercultural understanding is by no means a lost cause as long as we, as average citizens, clearly decide that it is the right thing to do.

CONCLUSION

My sense of the effects of *TFH* reports in the last ten years is, first of all, that they helped extensively to change the idea of school reform to a broader concept of *educational* reform. A youngster's schooling occupies about ten percent of his or her time from birth through age 18; but education includes schooling along with all the learning that occurs from birth to maturity. It takes place in families, in communities and in all the environments that shape a youngster's life on the road to responsible adulthood. *TFH*, more than any other recent study I am aware of, put into the equation of growing up all the realities that make it a complex process — particularly so in a society with rapid changes in its economy, family structure, political balance and forms of communication.

TFH has helped to change thinking in a number of areas. Among them are: 1) The connection of work and learning into a viable route to employment with a future; 2) the development of service-learning as part of schooling, as well as in other settings, to gain both better lives for those served and better understanding of human needs among the servers; 3) the opening of doors for youth to participate in public affairs; 4) the difficult task of reorganizing agencies serving the young so that duplication is avoided, accessibility is improved and budgets are coordinated. In addition, the continuing follow-up work of the Commission staff after *TFH* 1988 publication ensured that the report would do more than raise some useful ideas and then be retired to a bookshelf. This book proves that assertion.

TFH avoided preaching about the "sins" of American youth and young families. Instead, it chose to lay out the realities of their lives, to point to the shared responsibility of young people and adults to make changes and to suggest ways to help with their problems. In health, housing, family income and other areas of necessity for a decent life, it painted a picture of conditions for which Americans should feel ashamed, but it never made that last judgement.

Today, the statistical picture remains discomforting — and in many ways worse than in 1988. Our knowledge about children and youth, based upon both experience and good research, tells us to treat problems sooner rather than later. Such efforts cost less and are more successful than expensive initiatives in later years. Repairing troubled lives of older youth is now a growth stock in American society; too often it fails, as our rapid increase in the population of prisons demonstrates. Since the release of *TFH* there has been some action on this front, but it is best described as slow, often grudging and inadequate. In the meantime, our society suffers from their unemployment and undeveloped potential.

Perhaps what America needs in order to move forward is to see more clearly the enormous possibility for young people's success that lies within our reach — a new moral vision to give us strength against the often disheartening realities of daily life. A well balanced and accurate description of its children and youth based on data gathering and interpretation is essential. But our country also needs to be reminded that young people do grow up and, with our guidance and support, will take responsibility for our country, our world and a new century. Their success in life is by far the best investment our country could make. We even have the money!

Throughout its report and recommendations, the Commission attempted to capture the qualities of hope, fortitude and the essential importance of working at improving human relationships across the boundaries of economic status and other barriers. The recommendations speak of caring adult-youth relationships, the demands of family life, community-based activities, service opportunities and other such concepts. All these elements demand a quality of caring for each other that cannot be measured. Neither can it be legislated. Its presence among us is the business of all of us. The fact that *The Forgotten Half* has put these elusive concepts on the table for planning the future may well turn out to be its most valuable contribution.

NOTES

[1] Melaville, Atelia. *Learning Together: The Developing Field of School-Community Initiatives.* Flint, MI: Charles S. Mott Foundation, 1998.

[2] Orfield, Gary and Susan E. Eaton. *Dismantling Desegregation: The Quiet Reversal of Brown v. Board of Education.* New York, NY: The New Press, 1996.

[3] Schrag, Peter. *Paradise Lost: California's Experience, America's Future.* New York, NY: The New Press, 1998.

[4] Gates, Henry Louis, Jr. "Rethinking Schools." (Milwaukee, WI), October, November 1991, p. 1.

YOUTH

They will sit where we are sitting

And when we are gone, attend to

Those things we think are important.

We may adopt all the policies we

Please, but how they will be carried

Out depends on them. They will

Assume control of our cities, states

And nations. They are going to build

Our homes and take over our churches,

Schools and corporations.

All our work is going to be judged,

Praised or condemned by them.

The fate of humanity is in their hands

So it might be well to pay them

Some attention.

—*Author Unknown*

ABOUT THE AUTHORS

THOMAS BAILEY is Director of the Institute on Education and the Economy, Director of the Community College Research Center and an Associate Professor in the Department of International and Transcultural studies at Teachers College, Columbia University. An expert on the educational and training implications of changes in the workplace, he earned his Ph.D. in labor economics from MIT. He has served as a consultant to many public agencies and foundations, including the U.S. Departments of Labor and Education, Alfred P. Sloan Foundation, William T. Grant Foundation and several state and local economic development and educational agencies. *The Double Helix of Education and the Economy,* written with Sue Berryman, examines the poorly understood link between the needs of the workplace and contemporary understanding of effective learning. *Learning to Work: Employer Involvement in School-to-Work Transition Programs* analyzes the roles of employers in the education system and *School to Work for the College Bound* argues that the school-to-work model is effective in teaching high-level academic skills and preparing students for college.
Contact: Institute on Education and the Economy, Teachers College, Columbia University, Thorndike Hall, Room 439, 535 West 120th Street, Box 174, New York, NY 10027.

MARTIN J. BLANK is Director for Community Collaboration at the Institute for Educational Leadership. He supports communities and states pursuing collaborative strategies to enhance the well-being of children, youth and families; staffs the Emerging Coalition for Community Schools; manages the Together We Can Initiative to build the capacity of community collaboratives and, in partnership with the United Way of America, promotes Community Schools within the United Way system. His publications include *Together We Can: A Guide for Crafting a Profamily System of Education and Human Services* and *What It Takes: Structuring Interagency Partnerships to Connect Children and Families with Comprehensive Services.* He earned a B.A. from Columbia University, a J.D. from Georgetown University Law Center and served as a VISTA volunteer in the Missouri "Boot Heel."
Contact: Institute for Educational Leadership, 1001 Connecticut Avenue, NW, Suite 310, Washington, DC 20036.

CAROL EMIG is Director of Public Information and Policy at Child Trends, a nonprofit, nonpartisan research center that studies children and families. Previously, she was a senior associate at the Center for the Study of Social Policy; Deputy Director of the bipartisan National Commission on Children, a Congressional-Presidential body chaired by U.S. Senator John D. Rockefeller IV; director of a Chicago-based children's advocacy organization; and research assistant to First Lady Rosalynn Carter. Carol has an undergraduate degree from Georgetown University and a master's in public policy from the Kennedy School of Government at Harvard University, where she was a Kennedy Fellow and recipient of the Littauer Prize for Distinguished Writing in Public Policy.
Contact: Child Trends, 4301 Connecticut Avenue, NW, Suite 100, Washington, DC 20008.

LAWRENCE E. GLADIEUX is Executive Director for Policy Analysis of The College Board, a national association of 3,400 schools and colleges that provides testing, financial aid, guidance, training and other services to the education community. Through his leadership, The College Board's Washington DC office has gained a reputation for reliable, independent policy analysis on issues of the high school-to-college transition, college affordability and equal opportunity for higher education. A graduate of Oberlin and Princeton, he has authored or edited four major volumes on student financial aid and the politics of higher education.
Contact: The College Board, Washington Office, 1233 20th Street, NW, Suite 600, Washington, DC 20036.

SAMUEL HALPERIN is founder and Co-Director of the American Youth Policy Forum and a former president of the Institute for Educational Leadership. From 1986-1993, he was Study Director of the William T. Grant Foundation Commission on Work, Family and Citizenship, where he directed the publication of the two 1998 reports on *The Forgotten Half*

and over 35 working papers and policy reports. After earning his undergraduate, master's and doctoral degrees in Political Science at Washington University, St. Louis, he served on the U.S. House of Representatives and U.S. Senate education committees and as Assistant Commissioner for Legislation in the U.S. Office of Education and Deputy Assistant Secretary for Legislation in the former U.S. Department of Health, Education and Welfare.
Contact: American Youth Policy Forum, 1836 Jefferson Place, NW, Washington, DC 20036.

HAROLD HOWE II chaired the William T. Grant Foundation Commission on Work, Family and Citizenship. After 17 years in three states as history teacher, junior high and high school principal and superintendent of schools in both private and public schools, he moved to wider horizons helping Governor Terry Sanford of North Carolina plan educational change. In 1965, President Lyndon B. Johnson called him to Washington as the U.S. Commissioner of Education. He worked for The Ford Foundation in India for two years and then became its Vice President for Education and Public Policy. He retired from Ford in 1981 to join the education faculty at Harvard until 1994. His articles and books and numerous education projects, ranging from launching The Children's TV Workshop to advising the mayor of New York on the finances of CUNY, have made his voice familiar in education circles. A graduate of Yale, he served four years on minesweepers in World War II.
Contact: Kendal at Hanover, 80 Lyme Road #145, Hanover, NH 03755-0218.

MERITA IRBY is Manager of Learning and Issues Development at the International Youth Foundation (IYF). Her responsibilities include designing and implementing IYF's long-term plan for developing useful information on youth development, youth conditions and what works to increase the effectiveness, scale and sustainability of programs serving children and youth in the United States and internationally. She is working to strengthen YouthNet International, a global network of effective programs and is assisting in the development of IYF's evaluation. She received her Master in Public Policy from the John F. Kennedy School of Government, Harvard University and has published extensively and produced videofilms on youth development and education.
Contact: International Youth Foundation, 34 Market Place, Suite 800, Baltimore, MD 21202.

JOHN F. JENNINGS is Director of the Center on Education Policy, an independent national, nonpartisan advocate for improved public schools. From 1967 to 1994, as the senior education staff aide on the U.S. House of Representatives Committee on Education and Labor, he was deeply involved in nearly every major education debate of the past quarter century. A lawyer by training and a graduate of Loyola and Northwestern University Law School, he has written and edited numerous books and articles on education policy and been honored by over 25 education and civic associations for his knowledge of and leadership in education policy.
Contact: Center on Education Policy, 1001 Connecticut Avenue, NW, Suite 619, Washington, DC 20036.

VANESSA SMITH MOREST is a doctoral candidate in the Sociology and Education Department at Teachers College, Columbia University. Her research focuses on urban education and educational reform. She earned an M.A. from Teachers College and a B.A. in English from the College of William and Mary. While at Teachers College, she studied New York City's magnet schools with the Institute on Education and the Economy and was a research assistant with the University of Minnesota's Institute on Race and Poverty.
Contact: Institute on Education and the Economy, Teachers College, Columbia University, Thorndike Hall, Room 439, 535 West 120th Street, Box 174, New York, NY 10027.

KAREN PITTMAN is the Senior Vice President at the International Youth Foundation. A sociologist and recognized leader in the youth development field, Karen started her career at the Urban Institute, conducting studies on social services for children and families. At the Children's Defense Fund, she promoted an adolescent policy agenda through a bi-monthly report series linking pregnancy prevention to broader youth development strategies. In 1990, she founded the Center for Youth Development and Policy Research which she directed until January 1995, when she joined the Clinton Administration as Director of the President's Crime Prevention Council. Widely published, Karen has written three books, many articles on youth issues and is a regular columnist and public speaker. She has served on boards of the

Carnegie Council on Adolescent Development, Search Institute, Family Resource Coalition, E.M. Kauffman Foundation, Educational Testing Service, American Youth Work Center and is a member of the National Research Council's Forum on Adolescence.
Contact: International Youth Foundation, 34 Market Place, Suite 800, Baltimore, MD 21202.

DIANE STARK RENTNER is Associate Director of the Center on Education Policy. She has served as a legislative associate with the U.S. House of Representatives Committee on Education and Labor, where she worked on the reauthorization of major education programs including Elementary and Secondary Education, Higher Education, Carl D. Perkins Vocational and Applied Technology Education, National School Lunch and Child Nutrition and Goals 2000: Educate America Acts. After graduating from the University of Utah, she worked for the National PTA and the Council of Chief State School Officers in their government relations offices.
Contact: Center on Education Policy, 1001 Connecticut Avenue, NW, Suite 619, Washington, DC 20036.

SHIRLEY S. SAGAWA recently rejoined the White House as Deputy Assistant to the President in the Office of the First Lady. A graduate of Smith College, London School of Economics and Harvard Law School, she served in several senior leadership positions particularly associated with the national service movement: Chief Counsel for Youth Policy, Senate Committee on Labor and Human Resources; Vice Chair, Commission on National and Community Service; and, most recently, Executive Vice President, Corporation for National Service. She has also served as Special Assistant to President Clinton and on the White House Domestic Policy Council.
Contact: The White House, Office of the First Lady.

CAROL STEINBACH is a journalist specializing in reporting about community development. An operating partner of The Citistates Group, a network of journalists focusing on metropolitan issues, she has served as managing director at the Hamilton Securities Group, an investment bank specializing in housing and community economic development; contributing editor at *National Journal;* and founder and editor of *State Legislatures* magazine. Carol holds a master's in Journalism from The American University and a B.A. in Political Science from Duke University. With Neal Peirce, she coauthored the Ford Foundation's landmark 1987 study of community development corporations, *Corrective Capitalism.*
Contact: 2816 McKinley Place, NW, Washington, DC 20015.

WATSON S. SWAIL is Associate Director for Policy Analysis of The College Board, where he produces the Board's annual *Trends in Student Aid,* providing detailed financial data on federal, state and institutional student aid programs. Other research projects focus on issues relating to the educational opportunity of low-income, disadvantaged students. A former classroom teacher, he taught in his native Canada and earned degrees from the University of Manitoba, Old Dominion University and a doctorate from The George Washington University.
Contact: The College Board, Washington Office, 1233 20th Street, NW, Suite 600, Washington, DC 20036.

DANIEL YANKELOVICH is a leading interpreter of trends shaping American society and the global economy. He is President of the nonprofit Public Agenda, Chairman of DYG, Inc. and Visiting Professor at the University of California at San Diego. He is the author of ten books, including *Coming to Public Judgment, New Rules* and *The Magic of Dialogue* (forthcoming). In 1995, he won the prestigious Helen Dinerman award of the World Association of Public Opinion Researchers; this year, he won an award for Outstanding Achievement by the American Association for Public Opinion Research. He was educated at Harvard College, the Graduate School of Arts and Sciences at Harvard and the Sorbonne, and holds honorary degrees from The George Washington University and St. Bonaventure University.
Contact: 424 West End Avenue, #7-F, New York, NY 10024.

WILLIAM T. GRANT FOUNDATION COMMISSION ON WORK, FAMILY AND CITIZENSHIP (1986-88)

COMMISSION MEMBERS

(professional affiliations as of 1986)

HAROLD HOWE II, *Chairperson*
Senior Lecturer, Graduate School of Education, Harvard University, Cambridge, MA

BYLLYE Y. AVERY
Executive Director, National Black Women's Health Project, Atlanta, GA

MARY JO BANE
Professor of Public Policy, John F. Kennedy School of Government, Harvard University, Cambridge, MA

LEWIS H. BUTLER
President, California Tomorrow, San Francisco, CA

FLETCHER L. BYROM
Chairman and CEO (retired), Koppers Company, Carefree, AZ

HILLARY RODHAM CLINTON
The Governor's Mansion; Partner, The Rose Law Firm, Little Rock, AR

BARBARA J. EASTERLING
Executive Vice President, Communications Workers of America, Washington, DC

JOSUE M. GONZALEZ
President of the Board, Latino Institute; Director, Bureau of Resource Development, Chicago Public Schools, Chicago, IL

ALBERT H. HASTORF
Professor of Psychology, Stanford University, Stanford, CA

REV. THEODORE M. HESBURGH, C.S.C.
President (Emeritus), University of Notre Dame, Notre Dame, IN

DAVID W. HORNBECK
Former Maryland State Superintendent of Schools, Baltimore, MD

DOUGLAS X. PATINO
President and CEO, Marin Commmunity Foundation, Larkspur, CA

MICHAEL V. REAGEN
Director, Missouri Department of Social Services, Jefferson City, MO

HENRY W. RIECKEN
Professor of Behavioral Sciences (Emeritus), School of Medicine, University of Pennsylvania, Philadelphia, PA

KENNETH S. ROLLAND
Managing Director, Chemical Bank, New York, NY

BERNARD C. WATSON
President and CEO, William Penn Foundation, Philadelphia, PA

WILLIAM JULIUS WILSON
Professor of Sociology and Public Policy, University of Chicago, Chicago, IL

DANIEL YANKELOVICH
Chairman, Daniel Yankelovich Group, New York, NY

ROBERT H. HAGGERTY, M.D. (ex-officio)
President, William T. Grant Foundation, New York, NY

AMERICAN YOUTH POLICY FORUM
RESOURCES THAT WILL WORK FOR YOU!

The Forgotten Half Revisited: 200+ pages. $15 prepaid.
American Youth and Young Families, 1988-2008   Summary $2 prepaid.

A ten-year update of the 1988 reports of the William T. Grant Foundation Commission on Work, Family and Citizenship. Includes essays and the latest data on a range of topics — employment, youth and community development, school reform, higher education, service — by a number of the nation's leading scholars and youth policy advocates. Essayists include Thomas Bailey (Teachers College, Columbia University), Martin Blank (Institute for Educational Leadership), Carol Emig (Child Trends), Lawrence Gladieux and Watson Scott Swail (The College Board), Samuel Halperin (American Youth Policy Forum), Harold Howe II (former U.S. Commissioner of Education), John F. Jennings and Diane Stark Rentner (Center on Education Policy), Karen Pittman (International Youth Foundation), Shirley Sagawa (The White House) and Daniel Yankelovich (Public Agenda). (Available November 1998)

Employers Talk About Building a School-to-Work   104 pages. $10 prepaid.
System: Voices From the Field

Joan Wills, editor

Representatives of 13 employers and seven intermediary organizations offer their perspectives and lessons learned from their school-to-work experiences. Provides insight into employer motivation, activities and support for participation in STW across the country.

Exploring Systems for Comprehensive Youth   64 pages. $6 prepaid.
Employment Preparation in Switzerland, Austria and Germany

Glenda Partee, editor

Observations of a group of Congressional policy aides and senior U.S. civil servants in the field of education and training for employment as they examined systems of youth employment preparation in the three countries.

A Young Person's Guide to Earning and Learning: 28 pages. $2 prepaid.
Preparing for College, Preparing for Careers

by John F. Jennings and Diane Stark Rentner

Practical, easy-to-use information for young people trying to make sense of a complex education, training and employment system. Offers facts and figures about the costs and benefits of a college degree, the benefits of pursuing other types of postsecondary training and the education required and salaries offered in a broad range of careers not requiring a BA degree.
(Co-published with Center on Education Policy)

A Young Person's Guide to Managing Money   36 pages. $2 prepaid.

by Harriet Tyson

Quick, easy-to-read reference on pressing issues of money management. Key areas covered include savings and checking accounts, credit cards and borrowing, health insurance, budgeting, paying bills, paying taxes and living independently. The Guide also provides valuable contact information for youth trying to make the most of their hard-earned money.

Some Things DO Make a Difference for Youth: 196 pages. $10 prepaid.
A Compendium of Evaluations of Youth Programs and Practices

Donna Walker James, editor

This user-friendly guide summarizes 69 evaluations of youth interventions involving mentoring, employment and training, education and youth development for policymakers and program practitioners as they craft strategies affecting services and support for our nation's youth, particularly disadvantaged young people.

MORE Things That DO Make a Difference for Youth $10 prepaid.

Donna Walker James, editor

Volume II of a compendium of evaluations of youth programs. Summarizes more than 50 additional initiatives on school-to-work, vocational education, Tech Prep, school reform, juvenile justice and other areas of youth policy.
(Available January 1999)

Youth Work, Youth Development and the Transition   72 pages. $5 prepaid.
from Schooling to Employment in England

by Glenda Partee

Summarizes the observations of an 18-member U.S. delegation of federal and state policy aides, researchers, program practitioners and representatives of non-profit and youth serving national organizations about policies and practices in England to reform the education system, support youth work and the delivery of services and prepare youth for the workplace.

Preparing Youth for the Information Age: 64 pages. $5 prepaid.
A Federal Role for the 21st Century

by Patricia W. McNeil

The author argues for high expectations for all students, offers a compelling vision of a high school "redesigned for success" and outlines strategies to support youth in their learning. Offers insights into issues such as developing state and local consensus on results, improving accountability at the state and local level, improving school quality, linkages to careers.

Revitalizing High Schools: 38 pages. $5 prepaid.
What the School-to-Career Movement Can Contribute

by Susan Goldberger and Richard Kazis

The authors believe that school-to-career must be an integral part of a high school reform strategy if it is to achieve scale and be of maximum benefit to young people, employers and educators.
(Co-published with Jobs for the Future and National Association of Secondary School Principals)

Opening Career Paths for Youth: 16 pages. $2 prepaid.
What Can Be Done? Who Can Do It?

by Stephen F. and Mary Agnes Hamilton

The directors of Cornell University's acclaimed Youth Apprenticeship Demonstration Project share practical lessons in implementing essential components of school-to-career programs.

Prevention or Pork? A Hard-Headed Look at   48 pages. $5 prepaid.
Youth-Oriented Anti-Crime Programs
     by Richard A. Mendel
     Surveys what is known about the effectiveness of youth crime prevention programs. What works and what does not?

The American School-to-Career Movement: 28 pages. $5 prepaid.
A Background Paper for Policymakers
     by Richard A. Mendel
     Interviews and analysis of current efforts to link schooling and the world of employment; essential tasks to be addressed by each of the social partners in the community.

Dollars and Sense: Diverse Perspectives   80 pages. $5 prepaid.
on Block Grants and the Personal Responsibility Act
     Eleven authors offer a wide spectrum of opinion on improving efforts to promote support for children and families.
     (Co-published with The Finance Project and the Institute for Educational Leadership)

Contract With America's Youth: Toward a National   64 pages. $5 prepaid.
Youth Development Agenda
     Twenty-five authors ask what must be done to promote youth development, supportive communities and effective youth services.
     (Co-published with Center for Youth Development and the National Assembly)

Improving the Transition from School to Work   40 pages. $5 prepaid.
in the United States
     by Richard Kazis, with a memorandum on the Youth Transition by Paul Barton
     A detailed analysis of the transition of American youth from school to employment. Offers strategies for improving career preparation and recommendations for more workable federal policy.
     (Co-published with Jobs for the Future)

Youth Apprenticeship in America: 90 pages. $5 prepaid.
Guidelines for Building an Effective System
     Discussion of educational theory and practical application by six experts at the forefront of research *and* on the front lines in implementing youth apprenticeship. Outlines approaches and important lessons learned from experience in the U.S. and abroad.

Children, Families and Communities: 48 pages. $5 prepaid.
Early Lessons From a New Approach to Social Services
     by Joan Wynn, Sheila M. Merry and Patricia G. Berg
     Offers both a big-picture analysis of comprehensive, community-based initiatives and a more focused look through the lens of one such initiative in eight different Chicago neighborhoods.

What It Takes: Structuring Interagency Partnerships   56 pages. $3 prepaid.
to Connect Children and Families with Comprehensive Services
     by Atelia Melaville with Martin Blank
     Guidance for schools, social welfare agencies and CBOs on how to advance the well-being of children and families.

ORDER FORM (Cut Out or Photocopy)

Name _____

Address _____
_____

City _____ State _____ Zip _____

QUANTITY		PRICE	AMOUNT
____	The Forgotten Half Revisited	$15.00	_____
____	Summary of The Forgotten Half Revisited	$2.00	_____
____	Employers Talk About School to Work	$10.00	_____
____	Youth Employment Preparation in Europe	$6.00	_____
____	A Young Person's Guide to Earning and Learning	$2.00	_____
____	A Young Person's Guide to Managing Money	$3.00	_____
____	Some Things DO Make a Difference for Youth	$10.00	_____
____	MORE Things That DO Make a Difference for Youth	$10.00	_____
____	Set of both Make a Difference Volumes	$17.50	_____
____	Youth Work, Youth Development in England	$5.00	_____
____	Preparing Youth for the Information Age	$5.00	_____
____	Revitalizing High Schools	$5.00	_____
____	Opening Career Paths for Youth	$2.00	_____
____	Prevention or Pork? Youth-Oriented Anti-Crime Programs	$5.00	_____
____	American School-to-Career Movement	$5.00	_____
____	Dollars and Sense	$5.00	_____
____	Contract with America's Youth	$5.00	_____
____	Improving the Transition from School to Work	$5.00	_____
____	Youth Apprenticeship in America	$5.00	_____
____	Children, Families and Communities	$5.00	_____
____	What It Takes	$3.00	_____

TOTAL $_____

PREPAID ORDERS ONLY, PLEASE. Send all orders to: **AMERICAN YOUTH POLICY FORUM, 1836 Jefferson Place, NW, Washington, DC 20036-2505** (Federal ID 31-1576455). Call (202) 775-9731 for rates on bulk orders.

AMERICAN YOUTH POLICY FORUM
RESOURCES THAT WILL WORK FOR YOU!

The Forgotten Half Revisited: 200+ pages. $15 prepaid.
American Youth and Young Families, 1988-2008   Summary $2 prepaid.
     A ten-year update of the 1988 reports of the William T. Grant Foundation Commission on Work, Family and Citizenship. Includes essays and the latest data on a range of topics — employment, youth and community development, school reform, higher education, service — by a number of the nation's leading scholars and youth policy advocates. Essayists include Thomas Bailey (Teachers College, Columbia University), Martin Blank (Institute for Educational Leadership), Carol Emig (Child Trends), Lawrence Gladieux and Watson Scott Swail (The College Board), Samuel Halperin (American Youth Policy Forum), Harold Howe II (former U.S. Commissioner of Education), John F. Jennings and Diane Stark Rentner (Center on Education Policy), Karen Pittman (International Youth Foundation), Shirley Sagawa (The White House) and Daniel Yankelovich (Public Agenda). (Available November 1998)

Employers Talk About Building a School-to-Work   104 pages. $10 prepaid.
System: Voices From the Field
     Joan Wills, editor
     Representatives of 13 employers and seven intermediary organizations offer their perspectives and lessons learned from their school-to-work experiences. Provides insight into employer motivation, activities and support for participation in STW across the country.

Exploring Systems for Comprehensive Youth   64 pages. $6 prepaid.
Employment Preparation in Switzerland, Austria
and Germany
     Glenda Partee, editor
     Observations of a group of Congressional policy aides and senior U.S. civil servants in the field of education and training for employment as they examined systems of youth employment preparation in the three countries.

A Young Person's Guide to Earning and Learning: 28 pages. $2 prepaid.
Preparing for College, Preparing for Careers
     by John F. Jennings and Diane Stark Rentner
     Practical, easy-to-use information for young people trying to make sense of a complex education, training and employment system. Offers facts and figures about the costs and benefits of a college degree, the benefits of pursuing other types of postsecondary training and the education required and salaries offered in a broad range of careers not requiring a BA degree.
     (Co-published with Center on Education Policy)

A Young Person's Guide to Managing Money   36 pages. $2 prepaid.
     by Harriet Tyson
     Quick, easy-to-read reference on pressing issues of money management. Key areas covered include savings and checking accounts, credit cards and borrowing, health insurance, budgeting, paying bills, paying taxes and living independently. The Guide also provides valuable contact information for youth trying to make the most of their hard-earned money.

Some Things DO Make a Difference for Youth: 196 pages. $10 prepaid.
A Compendium of Evaluations of Youth Programs and Practices
     Donna Walker James, editor
     This user-friendly guide summarizes 69 evaluations of youth interventions involving mentoring, employment and training, education and youth development for policymakers and program practitioners as they craft strategies affecting services and support for our nation's youth, particularly disadvantaged young people.

MORE Things That DO Make a Difference for Youth $10 prepaid.
     Donna Walker James, editor
     Volume II of a compendium of evaluations of youth programs. Summarizes more than 50 additional initiatives on school-to-work, vocational education, Tech Prep, school reform, juvenile justice and other areas of youth policy. (Available January 1999)

Youth Work, Youth Development and the Transition   72 pages. $5 prepaid.
from Schooling to Employment in England
     by Glenda Partee
     Summarizes the observations of an 18-member U.S. delegation of federal and state policy aides, researchers, program practitioners and representatives of non-profit and youth serving national organizations about policies and practices in England to reform the education system, support youth work and the delivery of services and prepare youth for the workplace.

Preparing Youth for the Information Age: 64 pages. $5 prepaid.
A Federal Role for the 21st Century
     by Patricia W. McNeil
     The author argues for high expectations for all students, offers a compelling vision of a high school "redesigned for success" and outlines strategies to support youth in their learning. Offers insights into issues such as developing state and local consensus on results, improving accountability at the state and local level, improving school quality, linkages to careers.

Revitalizing High Schools: 38 pages. $5 prepaid.
What the School-to-Career Movement Can Contribute
     by Susan Goldberger and Richard Kazis
     The authors believe that school-to-career must be an integral part of a high school reform strategy if it is to achieve scale and be of maximum benefit to young people, employers and educators.
     (Co-published with Jobs for the Future and National Association of Secondary School Principals)

Opening Career Paths for Youth: 16 pages. $2 prepaid.
What Can Be Done? Who Can Do It?
     by Stephen F. and Mary Agnes Hamilton
     The directors of Cornell University's acclaimed Youth Apprenticeship Demonstration Project share practical lessons in implementing essential components of school-to-career programs.

Prevention or Pork? A Hard-Headed Look at   48 pages. $5 prepaid.
Youth-Oriented Anti-Crime Programs
      by Richard A. Mendel
      Surveys what is known about the effectiveness of youth crime prevention programs. What works and what does not?

The American School-to-Career Movement: 28 pages. $5 prepaid.
A Background Paper for Policymakers
      by Richard A. Mendel
      Interviews and analysis of current efforts to link schooling and the world of employment; essential tasks to be addressed by each of the social partners in the community.

Dollars and Sense: Diverse Perspectives   80 pages. $5 prepaid.
on Block Grants and the Personal Responsibility Act
      Eleven authors offer a wide spectrum of opinion on improving efforts to promote support for children and families.
      (Co-published with The Finance Project and the Institute for Educational Leadership)

Contract With America's Youth: Toward a National   64 pages. $5 prepaid.
Youth Development Agenda
      Twenty-five authors ask what must be done to promote youth development, supportive communities and effective youth services.
      (Co-published with Center for Youth Development and the National Assembly)

Improving the Transition from School to Work   40 pages. $5 prepaid.
in the United States
      by Richard Kazis, with a memorandum on the Youth Transition by Paul Barton
      A detailed analysis of the transition of American youth from school to employment. Offers strategies for improving career preparation and recommendations for more workable federal policy.
      (Co-published with Jobs for the Future)

Youth Apprenticeship in America: 90 pages. $5 prepaid.
Guidelines for Building an Effective System
      Discussion of educational theory and practical application by six experts at the forefront of research and on the front lines in implementing youth apprenticeship. Outlines approaches and important lessons learned from experience in the U.S. and abroad.

Children, Families and Communities: 48 pages. $5 prepaid.
Early Lessons From a New Approach to Social Services
      by Joan Wynn, Sheila M. Merry and Patricia G. Berg
      Offers both a big-picture analysis of comprehensive, community-based initiatives and a more focused look through the lens of one such initiative in eight different Chicago neighborhoods.

What It Takes: Structuring Interagency Partnerships   56 pages. $3 prepaid.
to Connect Children and Families with Comprehensive Services
      by Atelia Melaville with Martin Blank
      Guidance for schools, social welfare agencies and CBOs on how to advance the well-being of children and families.

ORDER FORM (Cut Out or Photocopy)

Name _____

Address _____
_____

City _____ State _____ Zip _____

QUANTITY		PRICE	AMOUNT
____	The Forgotten Half Revisited	$15.00	____
____	Summary of The Forgotten Half Revisited	$2.00	____
____	Employers Talk About School to Work	$10.00	____
____	Youth Employment Preparation in Europe	$6.00	____
____	A Young Person's Guide to Earning and Learning	$2.00	____
____	A Young Person's Guide to Managing Money	$3.00	____
____	Some Things DO Make a Difference for Youth	$10.00	____
____	MORE Things That DO Make a Difference for Youth	$10.00	____
____	Set of both Make a Difference Volumes	$17.50	____
____	Youth Work, Youth Development in England	$5.00	____
____	Preparing Youth for the Information Age	$5.00	____
____	Revitalizing High Schools	$5.00	____
____	Opening Career Paths for Youth	$2.00	____
____	Prevention or Pork? Youth-Oriented Anti-Crime Programs	$5.00	____
____	American School-to-Career Movement	$5.00	____
____	Dollars and Sense	$5.00	____
____	Contract with America's Youth	$5.00	____
____	Improving the Transition from School to Work	$5.00	____
____	Youth Apprenticeship in America	$5.00	____
____	Children, Families and Communities	$5.00	____
____	What It Takes	$3.00	____

TOTAL $_____

PREPAID ORDERS ONLY, PLEASE. Send all orders to: AMERICAN YOUTH POLICY FORUM, 1836 Jefferson Place, NW, Washington, DC 20036-2505 (Federal ID 31-1576455). Call (202) 775-9731 for rates on bulk orders.

AMERICAN YOUTH POLICY FORUM
RESOURCES THAT WILL WORK FOR YOU!

The Forgotten Half Revisited: 200+ pages. $15 prepaid.
American Youth and Young Families, 1988-2008   Summary $2 prepaid.

A ten-year update of the 1988 reports of the William T. Grant Foundation Commission on Work, Family and Citizenship. Includes essays and the latest data on a range of topics — employment, youth and community development, school reform, higher education, service — by a number of the nation's leading scholars and youth policy advocates. Essayists include Thomas Bailey (Teachers College, Columbia University), Martin Blank (Institute for Educational Leadership), Carol Emig (Child Trends), Lawrence Gladieux and Watson Scott Swail (The College Board), Samuel Halperin (American Youth Policy Forum), Harold Howe II (former U.S. Commissioner of Education), John F. Jennings and Diane Stark Rentner (Center on Education Policy), Karen Pittman (International Youth Foundation), Shirley Sagawa (The White House) and Daniel Yankelovich (Public Agenda). (Available November 1998)

Employers Talk About Building a School-to-Work   104 pages. $10 prepaid.
System: Voices From the Field

Joan Wills, editor

Representatives of 13 employers and seven intermediary organizations offer their perspectives and lessons learned from their school-to-work experiences. Provides insight into employer motivation, activities and support for participation in STW across the country.

Exploring Systems for Comprehensive Youth   64 pages. $6 prepaid.
**Employment Preparation in Switzerland, Austria
and Germany**

Glenda Partee, editor

Observations of a group of Congressional policy aides and senior U.S. civil servants in the field of education and training for employment as they examined systems of youth employment preparation in the three countries.

A Young Person's Guide to Earning and Learning: 28 pages. $2 prepaid.
Preparing for College, Preparing for Careers

by John F. Jennings and Diane Stark Rentner

Practical, easy-to-use information for young people trying to make sense of a complex education, training and employment system. Offers facts and figures about the costs and benefits of a college degree, the benefits of pursuing other types of postsecondary training and the education required and salaries offered in a broad range of careers not requiring a BA degree.
(Co-published with Center on Education Policy)

A Young Person's Guide to Managing Money   36 pages. $2 prepaid.

by Harriet Tyson

Quick, easy-to-read reference on pressing issues of money management. Key areas covered include savings and checking accounts, credit cards and borrowing, health insurance, budgeting, paying bills, paying taxes and living independently. The Guide also provides valuable contact information for youth trying to make the most of their hard-earned money.

Some Things DO Make a Difference for Youth: 196 pages. $10 prepaid.
A Compendium of Evaluations of Youth Programs and Practices

Donna Walker James, editor

This user-friendly guide summarizes 69 evaluations of youth interventions involving mentoring, employment and training, education and youth development for policymakers and program practitioners as they craft strategies affecting services and support for our nation's youth, particularly disadvantaged young people.

MORE Things That DO Make a Difference for Youth $10 prepaid.

Donna Walker James, editor

Volume II of a compendium of evaluations of youth programs. Summarizes more than 50 additional initiatives on school-to-work, vocational education, Tech Prep, school reform, juvenile justice and other areas of youth policy.
(Available January 1999)

Youth Work, Youth Development and the Transition   72 pages. $5 prepaid.
from Schooling to Employment in England

by Glenda Partee

Summarizes the observations of an 18-member U.S. delegation of federal and state policy aides, researchers, program practitioners and representatives of non-profit and youth serving national organizations about policies and practices in England to reform the education system, support youth work and the delivery of services and prepare youth for the workplace.

Preparing Youth for the Information Age: 64 pages. $5 prepaid.
A Federal Role for the 21st Century

by Patricia W. McNeil

The author argues for high expectations for all students, offers a compelling vision of a high school "redesigned for success" and outlines strategies to support youth in their learning. Offers insights into issues such as developing state and local consensus on results, improving accountability at the state and local level, improving school quality, linkages to careers.

Revitalizing High Schools: 38 pages. $5 prepaid.
What the School-to-Career Movement Can Contribute

by Susan Goldberger and Richard Kazis

The authors believe that school-to-career must be an integral part of a high school reform strategy if it is to achieve scale and be of maximum benefit to young people, employers and educators.
(Co-published with Jobs for the Future and National Association of Secondary School Principals)

Opening Career Paths for Youth: 16 pages. $2 prepaid.
What Can Be Done? Who Can Do It?

by Stephen F. and Mary Agnes Hamilton

The directors of Cornell University's acclaimed Youth Apprenticeship Demonstration Project share practical lessons in implementing essential components of school-to-career programs.

Prevention or Pork? A Hard-Headed Look at   48 pages. $5 prepaid.
Youth-Oriented Anti-Crime Programs
    by Richard A. Mendel
    Surveys what is known about the effectiveness of youth crime prevention programs. What works and what does not?

The American School-to-Career Movement: 28 pages. $5 prepaid.
A Background Paper for Policymakers
    by Richard A. Mendel
    Interviews and analysis of current efforts to link schooling and the world of employment; essential tasks to be addressed by each of the social partners in the community.

Dollars and Sense: Diverse Perspectives   80 pages. $5 prepaid.
on Block Grants and the Personal Responsibility Act
    Eleven authors offer a wide spectrum of opinion on improving efforts to promote support for children and families.
    (Co-published with The Finance Project and the Institute for Educational Leadership)

Contract With America's Youth: Toward a National   64 pages. $5 prepaid.
Youth Development Agenda
    Twenty-five authors ask what must be done to promote youth development, supportive communities and effective youth services.
    (Co-published with Center for Youth Development and the National Assembly)

Improving the Transition from School to Work   40 pages. $5 prepaid.
in the United States
    by Richard Kazis, with a memorandum on the Youth Transition by Paul Barton
    A detailed analysis of the transition of American youth from school to employment. Offers strategies for improving career preparation and recommendations for more workable federal policy.
    (Co-published with Jobs for the Future)

Youth Apprenticeship in America: 90 pages. $5 prepaid.
Guidelines for Building an Effective System
    Discussion of educational theory and practical application by six experts at the forefront of research and on the front lines in implementing youth apprenticeship. Outlines approaches and important lessons learned from experience in the U.S. and abroad.

Children, Families and Communities: 48 pages. $5 prepaid.
Early Lessons From a New Approach to Social Services
    by Joan Wynn, Sheila M. Merry and Patricia G. Berg
    Offers both a big-picture analysis of comprehensive, community-based initiatives and a more focused look through the lens of one such initiative in eight different Chicago neighborhoods.

What It Takes: Structuring Interagency Partnerships   56 pages. $3 prepaid.
to Connect Children and Families with Comprehensive Services
    by Atelia Melaville with Martin Blank
    Guidance for schools, social welfare agencies and CBOs on how to advance the well-being of children and families.

ORDER FORM (Cut Out or Photocopy)

Name _____

Address _____
_____

City _____ State _____ Zip _____

QUANTITY		PRICE	AMOUNT
____	The Forgotten Half Revisited	$15.00	_____
____	Summary of The Forgotten Half Revisited	$2.00	_____
____	Employers Talk About School to Work	$10.00	_____
____	Youth Employment Preparation in Europe	$6.00	_____
____	A Young Person's Guide to Earning and Learning	$2.00	_____
____	A Young Person's Guide to Managing Money	$3.00	_____
____	Some Things DO Make a Difference for Youth	$10.00	_____
____	MORE Things That DO Make a Difference for Youth	$10.00	_____
____	Set of both Make a Difference Volumes	$17.50	_____
____	Youth Work, Youth Development in England	$5.00	_____
____	Preparing Youth for the Information Age	$5.00	_____
____	Revitalizing High Schools	$5.00	_____
____	Opening Career Paths for Youth	$2.00	_____
____	Prevention or Pork? Youth-Oriented Anti-Crime Programs	$5.00	_____
____	American School-to-Career Movement	$5.00	_____
____	Dollars and Sense	$5.00	_____
____	Contract with America's Youth	$5.00	_____
____	Improving the Transition from School to Work	$5.00	_____
____	Youth Apprenticeship in America	$5.00	_____
____	Children, Families and Communities	$5.00	_____
____	What It Takes	$3.00	_____
		TOTAL $	_____

PREPAID ORDERS ONLY, PLEASE. Send all orders to: AMERICAN YOUTH POLICY FORUM, 1836 Jefferson Place, NW, Washington, DC 20036-2505 (Federal ID 31-1576455). Call (202) 775-9731 for rates on bulk orders.